CHASING SHADOWS

SHADOWS

CYBER ESPIONAGE, SUBVERSION, AND THE GLOBAL FIGHT FOR DEMOCRACY

Ronald J. Deibert

Published by Simon & Schuster

NEW YORK   AMSTERDAM/ANTWERP   LONDON
TORONTO   SYDNEY   NEW DELHI

SIMON &
SCHUSTER
CANADA

A Division of Simon & Schuster, LLC
166 King Street East, Suite 300
Toronto, Ontario M5A 1J3

This Simon & Schuster Canada edition February 2025

SIMON & SCHUSTER CANADA and colophon are registered trademarks
of Simon & Schuster, LLC

For information about special discounts for bulk purchases,
please contact Simon & Schuster Special Sales at 1-800-268-3216
or CustomerService@simonandschuster.ca.

Manufactured in the United States of America

1   3   5   7   9   10   8   6   4   2

Library and Archives Canada Cataloguing in Publication

Title: Chasing shadows : cyber espionage, subversion, and the
global fight for democracy / Ronald J. Deibert.
Names: Deibert, Ronald, author.
Description: Simon & Schuster Canada edition. | Includes bibliographical
references and index.
Identifiers: Canadiana (print) 20240327594 |
Canadiana (ebook) 20240327675 | ISBN 9781668014042
(hardcover) | ISBN 9781668014066 (EPUB)
Subjects: LCSH: Munk Centre for International Studies.
Citizen Lab. | LCSH: Computer crimes. | LCSH: Espionage. |
LCSH: Electronic surveillance. | LCSH: Disinformation. | LCSH: Computer security. |
LCSH: Intelligence service. Classification: LCC HV6773 .D45 2025 |
DDC 364.16/8—dc23

ISBN 978-1-6680-1404-2
ISBN 978-1-6680-1406-6 (ebook)

To the many victims and survivors of
digital transnational repression.

Without their courage in the face of
enormous personal risks, none of the stories
in this book would be possible.

We're a complete ghost. We're totally transparent
to the target, and we leave no traces.

—SHALEV HULIO, FORMER CEO OF NSO GROUP

Never interrupt your enemy when he is making a mistake.

—NAPOLÉON BONAPARTE

Contents

The White House

DECEMBER 8, 2022
WASHINGTON, DC

On a cold, crisp December morning I stand outside the black wrought-iron fence and take it all in. *The White House.* Nothing symbolizes the epicenter of political power more than this one building. Countless coups, targeted assassinations, and even cruel and inhumane experiments with psychedelic drugs on unwitting victims have been discussed, planned, and approved behind these walls. But so have momentous policy decisions that have furthered the cause of human rights and freedom worldwide. I've stopped here on Pennsylvania Avenue many times over the years, along with the usual ensemble of tourists, school groups, camped-out protestors, TV crews, and US Secret Service agents with their bomb-sniffing dogs. But today is the first time I am going inside.

There has been a flurry of regulatory activity around mercenary spyware, a core focus of our work at the Citizen Lab—the research group based at the University of Toronto, Canada, that I founded in 2001 and still direct. A massive, largely unregulated industry has emerged and proliferated globally that gives government spies the ability to snoop on digital devices anywhere in the world. The latest versions can do so silently, vacuuming up unsuspecting targets' entire private life, following them around, reading their emails and texts, and turning on their camera and microphone. Autocrats, despots, police, and intelligence agencies have gobbled up this technology and used it for all sorts of nefarious purposes, from harassment and extortion to targeted murder. We were well ahead of others in being able to track this industry using precise forensic and network scanning methods, and we have been raising alarms for more than a decade that it is unregulated and prone to abuse. Now, finally, the powers that be—some of them, anyway—are waking up to its risks.

In November 2021, the US Commerce Department added several mercenary spyware companies whose malfeasance we helped expose to a special "designated entity" list—including the notorious Israel-based mercenary spyware vendor NSO Group.[1] While the designation is mostly symbolic—it restricts the export of a narrow class of US goods and services to firms on the deny list—it's also a kind of scarlet letter signaling to all concerned that doing business with these firms is now taboo. NSO Group's valuation dropped by about a billion dollars after being red-carded by the Commerce Department's designation. That must have hurt.

A few weeks after that designation, Senator Ron Wyden, Congressman Adam Schiff, and several other prominent lawmakers sent a letter to the Biden administration advocating that the government go further and "punish" firms like NSO Group and their executives with Global Magnitsky Act sanctions—sanctions aimed at foreign autocrats and their oligarch benefactors involved in human rights abuses.[2] The work of the Citizen Lab was mentioned explicitly in their letter too.

Then, in the summer of 2022, the influential House Permanent Select Committee on Intelligence convened hearings on mercenary spyware and invited one of our senior researchers, John Scott-Railton (JSR), who leads our targeted threats team, to testify alongside a prominent victim of mercenary spyware, Carine Kanimba, and Google's head of threat intelligence, Shane Huntley.[3] The hearing was powerful. Kanimba, the daughter of Paul Rusesabagina, whose bravery in the Rwandan genocide was portrayed in the Hollywood movie *Hotel Rwanda*, relayed personal experiences that were riveting, scary, and emotional. "It is horrifying to me that they knew everything I was doing, precisely where I was, who I was speaking with, my private thoughts and actions, at any moment they desired," Kanimba told the committee.[4] Forensic analysis from both the Citizen Lab and Amnesty International determined that her phones had been hacked with NSO Group's spyware multiple times, once around the time her father was kidnapped and later when she was meeting with senior US government officials and members of Congress to plead for their help with his release. That revelation was bad news for NSO Group. Nothing like helping an autocrat to eavesdrop on meetings with US policymakers to get you on the receiving end of congressional investigations.

Late in 2022 we received the invitation to the White House to brief members of the powerful National Security Council. And so it was that JSR and I arrived to describe our research and to give our opinion on what we saw looming on the horizon.

As we settle into a paneled boardroom with a portrait of George Washington flanked by statues of bald eagles presiding over our discussions, the small talk soon gives way to introductions. "Before we begin," says the most senior intelligence official in the room, "I want you to know what respect and admiration there is around here [in the White House] for the work of the Citizen Lab. None of this," he continues, waving a hand at the stack of papers in front of him, "would be possible without your group."

I have a tough time concentrating for the next few minutes after those remarks. While we deserve to be there because of our well-earned reputation, it is still profoundly strange to hear it from a high-ranking official in this storied building. The irony of the meeting is not lost on me either. When I founded the Citizen Lab, I had a dream of building a university-based group that would use the skills and techniques of evidence-based research to lift the lid on the internet and expose wrongdoing in the digital realm. My aim was to have a group of top-notch sleuths undertake "counter-intelligence for civil society." At the time, it was all aspirational. Now, here I was sitting with senior officials who oversaw the most sophisticated intelligence operations on behalf of the most powerful government in human history—and they were telling *me* how much they respected *our* work.

As the meeting ends, we are escorted out of the Eisenhower Executive Office Building to the covered causeway leading to the

West Wing. A busy day, judging by the armored black Chevrolet Suburbans with tinted windows and crowned with antennas lining the inner driveway. I scan the rooftops and take in the CCTV cameras and other sensors planted along the roof of the White House. I imagine how fully and completely this particular space is under intense electronic surveillance. Biometric scanners, cellphone interception gear, explosives sensors, and who knows what else. No doubt about it: we are at the apex of the intelligence-industrial complex—in more ways than we imagine, I am sure.

Later that day, as I walk through the airport on my way back to Toronto, I lean down to scan the headlines of the *Financial Times* and one pops out: "Israel's NSO Bets Its Future on Netanyahu's Comeback."[5]

Former Israeli prime minister Benjamin Netanyahu, a convicted criminal, stands at the precipice of a remarkable political revival. He is about to forge the most right-wing and extremist political coalition in Israel's history, which will return him to power. It was Netanyahu who personally spearheaded the commercialization of cybersecurity and Israel's formidable signals intelligence resources into a mercenary surveillance marketplace. And now he's back—on the verge of reclaiming power and authority and aligning himself with ultraconservative and militaristic allies. Not a good omen.

I imagine the industry's high-paid lobbyists running circles around our visit to the White House, pushing falsehoods about the Citizen Lab and our investigations. There is always the prospect of something more insidious too. We have already experienced several underhanded covert attempts to undermine our work. What could be next? As I stare at the article, I think about the behind-the-scenes maneuvering to obstruct our progress and impede our ability to carry out investigations that might be on the way—with our funders, the University of Toronto, Canadian authorities, or others.

"Don't worry," Shalev Hulio, one of the founders and then CEO of NSO Group, is quoted in the *Financial Times* article. "Netanyahu is coming back."

"Oh, you better believe I'm worried," I mutter as I toss the paper down and head to the boarding gate.

– PART ONE –

THE CHASE

– 1 –

A Near-Perfect Hack

There are roughly 7.64 billion people on the planet, and nearly three-quarters of them own at least one mobile phone.[1] No matter the brand, those pocket devices are electronic portals to the world outside—to the good, the bad, and the ugly. Every night, while you sleep, the microprocessors in your device keep on working: applications digest and process data; data get sent and instructions are received. It's all very safe and normal—most of the time.

On one particular night, something very different happened to the personal phones of several dozen specially chosen people spread around the world—something dangerous and without their knowledge or permission. As these targets slept, their lives crossed paths with certain unsavory individuals thanks, in part, to those ubiquitous phones.

From across the internet and over radio waves and ethernet cables, moving at nearly the speed of light but in complete silence, a special message containing elaborate instructions was delivered to each of the targets' devices. Masquerading as a video call on the popular communications application WhatsApp, the instructions took advantage of an error in the app's code that even WhatsApp's highly trained engineers were not aware of. The instructions executed a "buffer overflow"—the digital equivalent of a short circuit. This overflow confuses the application's memory processing system, sends it momentarily off-balance, and leaves it vulnerable to further exploitation. Its one purpose is to unlock the door and leave it ajar for a more elaborate program to slip in undetected.

This spyware, as the program is called, provided complete and unfettered access to each of the unwitting targets' devices. The people operating the spyware could now read every email and text message sent and received, even if encrypted. They could scan the camera roll for incriminating private photos to be used as potential blackmail. They could track the phone's movements by reading its GPS system. They could silently activate the camera and microphone, converting that personal device into a real-time wiretap. Most important, they could initialize the spyware's self-destruct feature and remove all traces of the fake WhatsApp call itself, as if sweeping back over a crime scene to eliminate fingerprints. It was as though an invisible spy had now slipped undetected into the targets' pockets and was looking at the world through their eyes—and they had no clue. It was a near-perfect hack.

But the engineers who constructed this powerful spyware were also human and fallible in important ways. While the counterfeit WhatsApp call was well crafted to trigger a buffer overflow, it couldn't be coded to anticipate every possible setting it would encounter on a target's device, and some instructions would fail. Those failures left a telltale sign that couldn't be erased: a missed video call in the phones' logs from an unknown caller coming from an unexpected area code. Most targets who received these dropped calls wouldn't even notice or would shrug them off as some kind of spam.

Not Ahmed Aziz (a pseudonym), however, who treated anything remotely "off" with his phone with utmost suspicion. Aziz, at thirty-seven, is a Palestinian by birth and a professor at a prominent law school in Great Britain. As a practicing attorney, he has worked for a range of high-profile targets, including the Palestine Liberation Organization. He had signed on as part of the legal team representing journalists, exiled opposition figures, and human rights defenders from Mexico and Saudi Arabia, all of whom had their phones hacked by mysterious government security agencies using a surveillance program called Pegasus, sold by the Israel-based "cyberwarfare" firm NSO Group.

Although not an engineer himself, Aziz was well informed about Pegasus and the type of hacking his clients experienced. As part of the team of attorneys representing victims suing NSO Group, the world's most notorious mercenary hacking firm, in Israeli courts, Aziz had good reason to suspect that a well-resourced adversary might attempt to hack his phone too. He knew the defendants were world leaders in espionage and veterans of Israel's elite signals intelligence agency, Unit 8200.[2]

More worrisome, NSO Group's principals had demonstrated a complete disregard for ethics, laws, and other conventions of appropriate behavior. The thin protections around attorney-client privilege meant nothing to the soldiers of fortune behind these types of targeted operations. In fact, some of Aziz's Mexican clients, lawyers like him, had been hacked by government operatives who also used Pegasus, presumably to tap into any confidential information their clients in turn might have to incriminate them. Some of those lawyers represented families of government critics whose members had disappeared, possibly assassinated by Mexican paramilitary forces or one of the country's drug cartels.

Many other powerful groups would have wanted the privileged information Aziz held about clients—Israel's own spies, the Mossad, perhaps, or one of NSO Group's government clients such as Saudi Arabia, the United Arab Emirates, or Mexico.[3] Only a few months earlier, Associated Press journalists had discovered that Aziz and one of his colleagues had been tracked by operatives connected to the Israel-based spies-for-hire firm Black Cube.[4] Who hired them? Hard to say, as the list of Aziz's antagonists would be a long and dark one. Aziz was, in short, justifiably paranoid.

On the night of the fake WhatsApp call, just before retiring for the night, Aziz noticed that his phone's screen glowed softly in short intervals, signaling an incoming call on silent mode. Too tired to answer after a long day, he placed his phone on the bedside table and drifted off to sleep. The next morning he checked to see who it was. Oddly, there was no record in the phone's logs. He rubbed his eyes and scrolled through again. Nothing. "I swear I saw it," he mumbled to himself. "Was I hallucinating?" He knew

he couldn't leave anything to chance. He went into his device's settings, scrolled through a few options, and settled on "factory reset."
If he clicked, he would delete all his phone's contents—a huge inconvenience. He lingered for a moment and then pressed "OK"—
which was likely the last thing the spies observed before all went
dark at their end of the line.

But Aziz was a valuable target, and the spies were persistent.
For the next couple of months, they tried—repeatedly—to re-
commandeer his phone via the WhatsApp exploit. Again and again
it failed to initiate a buffer overflow, though it left a mess of evidence in Aziz's call logs. Totally mystified by all these calls from
strange area codes, Aziz dropped everything and reached out to us
at the Citizen Lab.

———

Our devices contain tens of millions of lines of computer code—
brackets, colons, dashes, and other bits of programming language
that get compiled into an application. Each line of code instructs
the computer to do something: adjust the screen size; play some
music; send and receive instructions from other computers. This
code has all been written by someone, somewhere, and humans
make mistakes. Most of these defects are inconsequential and unlikely to cause headaches, but sometimes they do, as when email
addresses and passwords, social security numbers, and other identifiers are improperly secured and end up circulating on the dark
web. The internet's open secret is that it is riddled with software
flaws.

Thousands of individuals around the world routinely scrutinize
those millions of lines of code, spot the errors, and act on them.
Some do it in the public interest, to find vulnerabilities and disclose
them so the relevant companies can patch the flaws. Others do it
for mischief. But some do it for criminal purposes or more sinister
reasons. Mercenary firms like NSO Group and the spies they serve
exploit these insecurities in the digital ecosystem to "find, fix, and
finish" their adversaries. Many of these targets are innocent victims

of the thugs, sociopaths, and tyrants who have grabbed hold of the reins of power in governments around the world.

At the Citizen Lab, we do the opposite. Drawing on the skills of some of the most dogged and talented investigators, we specialize in using careful tools, methods, and open-source investigative techniques—network scanning, field research, forensics, reverse engineering, access to information requests, and corporate document analysis—to gather the incriminating evidence that bad actors inevitably leave behind them. We then write it up in our reports, publish widely, and try to disrupt their machinations. And when we discover insecurities and software flaws, we report them to the appropriate entities to get them fixed. Our mission is to serve the public interest, not subvert it.

Our reports have made world news—the front pages of the *New York Times*, the *Washington Post*, the *Globe and Mail*, *El País*, the *Guardian*, and others worldwide. This exposure has irritated the people behind the operations we bust. They thrive in the shadows and recoil at the sunlight our research brings with it. As our successes have accumulated, we have become targets ourselves—of governments, private security firms, and the dubious lawyers and public relations companies they employ to try to intimidate, discredit, or ultimately silence groups like us. Academics in my field are used to studying the world as if it were a distant object; we find ourselves in the rather unique position of having the world we study push back.

We had crossed paths with Aziz before. The Lab had investigated the computer hacking of many of the clients he represented, and our public reports became the evidentiary basis for their lawsuits. Our digital detectives had been closely monitoring and carefully documenting widespread abuses associated with NSO Group for years: collecting logs from devices and examining suspicious emails or text messages received by unwitting targets; outing the names of NSO Group's autocratic clients on the basis of incriminating digital bread crumbs left behind through some operational security mistake they made; and scanning the entire internet with the digital equivalent of a microscope to uncover their constantly evolving network infrastructure.

We live in the era of privatization, and the Israeli state openly encourages security firms like NSO Group.[5] That explains why many of the world's leading surveillance, facial recognition, and cellphone-cracking companies happen to be headquartered in or originate from Israel.[6] The implications of this type of privatized surveillance are enormous. Over the last several decades, the Israeli state security apparatus and its extremely well-trained spies and hackers have burst into the global commercial marketplace with few restrictions or redlines. Thanks to companies like NSO Group, autocrats and dictators who lack in-house clandestine capabilities can simply buy them, as if purchasing a sophisticated global intelligence apparatus directly from eBay or Amazon. This commercialization of state intelligence practices is a profound development for world politics: it's nothing short of despotism as a service.

Mercenary spyware is extremely lucrative. NSO Group has been valued at various times at over $1 billion.[7] A company already unprincipled enough to sell its surveillance tools to dictators and corrupt security agencies is going to attract a lot of unscrupulous investors, lawyers, consultants, and PR firms while constantly scouring every possible loophole in tax laws and regulations to obfuscate its operations. Studying NSO Group's corporate structure is to enter a labyrinth of shell companies, tax-free havens, and offshore law firms. There's a retinue of reprobate investors, advisors, and sister companies too.

A sampling of NSO Group's past investors and associates reveals a rogues' gallery of some of the best-known scoundrels of our times. There's Michael Flynn, the disgraced former national security advisor to first-term President Donald Trump, indicted by US Special Counsel Robert Mueller for making false statements to the FBI and later pardoned by the president.[8] Flynn was once an advisory board member and consultant for OSY Technologies, one of NSO Group's parent companies, as well as a previous ownership group, US-based private equity firm Francisco Partners.[9] One degree of separation away is Erik Prince, ex–US Navy SEAL officer, founder of the notorious private military contractor Blackwater, and another ally of Trump's investigated by the Mueller inquiry for suspicious meetings in the Seychelles with known Russian intelligence agents.[10] Prince was once a director of a company registered in Cyprus called Eitanium Ltd. that included on its board an Israeli named Eric Banoun, who once worked as a distributor of NSO Group products and was one of the founders of Circles Technologies, a telecommunications surveillance vendor and previously a sister company to NSO Group.[11]

And then there are NSO Group's government clients: Rwanda's autocratic president, Paul Kagame, known for his dispatch of death squads; Saudi Arabia's Mohammed bin Salman, or MBS as he's called, a ruler who approved the brutal execution of journalist Jamal Khashoggi in broad daylight; and Sheikh Mohammed bin Rashid al-Maktoum of the United Arab Emirates, who has used Pegasus to hunt human rights activists and oversee their torture and electrocution in UAE prisons.[12] (The sheikh once used other forms of commercial surveillance technology to locate a private yacht chartered by his daughter Princess Latifa, who was desperate to escape his tyrannical rule.)[13]

Sadly, NSO Group is like a microcosm of the world in which we now live: unprincipled billionaires dodging taxes and regulatory oversight, looking to cash in on the national security moneymaking machine; mercenary companies employing highly trained software vulnerability hunters to exploit fissures in the always-on, invasive-by-design digital ecosystem and package instant access to a victim's most intimate details; authoritarians and kleptocrats ruthlessly maneuvering to undermine anything or anyone who might get in their way; and assassins who will slip a nerve agent into your tea at your London hotel—the coup de grâce. Yet NSO Group is only one among scores of such companies selling to government clients. There are Russian, Chinese, French, German, Swiss, Spanish, Italian, and other cyber mercenaries too.[14] The market is exploding. What's worse is that the industry is now expanding its client base beyond governments to other private businesses, oligarchs, and organized criminal groups. It's not uncommon for hacker-for-hire operations run out of storefront walk-ups in New Delhi or Manila to be contracted by private security firms that are working for Big Oil conglomerates or pharmaceutical companies looking to thwart some kind of pesky litigation or public relations problem.

There were only a handful of other groups in the world doing anything like what we were doing—NGOs including Access Now, Amnesty International, and Human Rights Watch and a small number of reporters and investigative journalists' consortia such as Forbidden Stories and Bellingcat (the latter responsible for exposing the Russian agents who poisoned opposition politician Alexei Navalny).[15] Our collective efforts in the public interest were noble but nerve-racking in light of the risks. Warnings from state authorities or others about an entity that doesn't like what we are doing and may have nefarious plans afoot have become fairly routine. After I gave a presentation in a private meeting in Zurich, a sharply dressed man in his thirties approached me and asked, in a clipped German accent, whether I was concerned for my personal safety: "Someone could pass some toxin into your blood by shaking your hand," he said . . . a moment after shaking my hand.

———

When Aziz reported the dropped calls to the Lab, we were as mystified as everyone else. At this time, spyware of the sort that NSO Group uses to hack into a device required some kind of interaction on the part of the target. Victims are tricked into clicking on a link in a text message to their phone or opening an attachment in an email that is embedded with malicious spyware, which is then silently activated and installed. In the most well crafted of these attacks, links are included in provocative messages designed to play on targets' fears or emotions. The objective is to get a target to click.

Those links were also NSO Group's Achilles' heel—like strands of hair left at a crime scene with incriminating DNA. When clicked on, they would trigger a connection over the internet to a series of "anonymized" computers NSO Group controlled, so-called command and control servers that relayed the pilfered information through a complicated circuit meant to disguise the company's and its clients' operations. Although NSO Group went to great lengths to cover the tracks, our sleuths, led by the brilliant computer scientist on our team, Bill Marczak, discovered, over years of dogged research, that those communications followed a distinct pattern. Computers NSO Group used as anonymous relays responded to queries sent over the internet in a particular way. Using this pattern as a "fingerprint," we could send probes to every one of the billions of internet-connected devices in the world and then triage them down to those we suspected were part of NSO Group's system. We would then zero in on those computers and subject them to more fine-grained analysis.

Meanwhile, firms that specialize in cybersecurity and were sympathetic to our mission provided our researchers with access to specialized databases and network feeds that are typically reserved for high-paying clients. This information enabled us to further scope activities by NSO Group and its government clients. In public presentations, I often described this bundle of methods metaphorically as an "X-ray of the internet," but what we were really doing was a sophisticated, concerted effort of continuous countersurveillance against some of the world's worst violators of human rights and their corporate enablers. We were turning the interrogation spotlight on the interrogators themselves, spying on the spies.

In the same way we were aware of NSO Group's tools, techniques, and procedures, it was aware of ours. Each time we exposed its operations in a report, NSO Group engineers would mix things up and find ways to better hide their tracks. We had heard rumors they had devised a new version of their spyware that required no interaction on the part of the target, so, when Aziz reached out, our spidey senses began to tingle.

———————

Citizen Lab senior researcher John Scott-Railton, known informally as JSR, is one of our most resourceful investigators, a human Swiss Army knife of open-source investigation techniques. He's as fluent ferreting through corporate tax filings as he is scouring through network traffic dumps, and he's got the nose of a blood-hound when it comes to tracking down "digital badness" in the cyber world.

After Aziz reported to us the suspicious behavior on his phone, we set up a system to monitor his network traffic with his consent and observed several failed WhatsApp calls as they occurred. JSR reached out to the security team at WhatsApp to see if it had any clues to the mystery. It turned out its engineers were already inde-pendently zeroing in on the problem. Teams in London and San Francisco had been working around the clock, and they had just pushed out a security patch for their billion-plus users worldwide to close the loophole. It was likely the latter that foiled the last few infection attempts on Aziz's device we had observed. WhatsApp's investigation also surfaced evidence on who was responsible. "This attack has all the hallmarks of a private company known to work with governments to deliver spyware that reportedly takes over the functions of mobile phone operating systems," the company said to the *Financial Times*, announcing its findings.

We discovered WhatsApp was not only determined to fix the vulnerability, but it wanted to alert innocent people who had been victimized. "We have briefed a number of human rights organisa-tions to share the information we can, and to work with them to notify civil society," the firm said. We jumped at the chance to vol-unteer, knowing the urgency of the matter. Scores of victims were walking around completely unaware they were being watched by someone out to cause them harm. Our aim was to identify those people fast and, before it was too late, alert them that they were victims of a high-tech hack job and that their lives were at extreme risk. As investigators we were also excited at the opportunity to dis-cover more victims of NSO Group's latest attack technique. If one victim had been targeted, chances were high that others in their circle had been targeted too.

Once we got down to business, however, it was a surprise to learn just how little data WhatsApp was able to recover about the victims' identities and share with us. WhatsApp is owned by Meta (at this time, Facebook), and no other company vacuums up as much personal data from its customers as Facebook does. However, WhatsApp's code had originally been developed by the engineering equivalent of privacy vegans. After Facebook acquired WhatsApp, the former CEO Brian Acton donated $50 million to support Signal, an end-to-end, open-source encrypted messaging app that preserves "zero data" on its customers—or as little as possible.[16] While many of the original engineers departed alongside him, they left a privacy-by-design legacy at WhatsApp that was preserved for a while after the Facebook acquisition.

Although WhatsApp engineers could identify that Pegasus had successfully breached their systems, all they could observe was that it happened to about a thousand of their customers over a two-week period in the spring of 2019. The only information they retained about those customers was a phone number for the account—no name, no address, no occupation, no context, just ten digits. With those phone numbers as our only starting point, we got down to work.

———

You'd be surprised how much a person with skills and access to data can find out about you based on your phone number. Like any other bit of personally identifiable information, over the course of a life a phone number can be scattered all over the internet, connected to other fragments of your life, and stored in thousands of other devices. It ends up in the hands of a multitude of third parties: location tracking companies, data brokers, peddlers of spam, low-rent fraud artists who send robocalls in the middle of the night. Some of these outfits make big dollars selling information to companies like NSO Group or NSO Group's shadowy government customers, who use it to undertake reconnaissance on a potential target.

Before you fire Pegasus at a device, you need the number and a verification that the person behind that number is your actual target. We were aware of the irony: that starting with only a phone number and working from there to identify a person's identity involves many of the same investigative techniques and data sources as those used by the spies whose operations we sought to disrupt.

We were undertaking a kind of online surveillance of our own, but with a twist. All these sources and techniques were for us a means to an end, but those means were carefully controlled to meet the highest ethical standards. We were trying to save lives, not destroy them.

As the actual identities behind the numbers gradually materialized and were confirmed, our pulse quickened. It was like peeling back the plastic drapes on one active crime scene after another. We were getting an insider's view before anyone else knew about it, except the agents who had undertaken the spying. They had become accustomed to spying on unsuspecting others. Now we were the ones watching them.

Among the victims we could identify, we were focused on the cases targeting innocent people. NSO Group markets its spyware as something to assist governments to investigate serious matters of crime, terrorism, and national security. But what constitutes "crime," "terrorism," or a "serious national security issue" is in the eye of the beholder. Once acquired, secret services in places like Kazakhstan, Azerbaijan, or Bahrain are going to use Pegasus to hack the devices of journalists, lawyers, human rights defenders, and anyone else they consider irritants to their illegitimate rule or who have valuable information that can further some despotic aim—people like Aziz.[17] It's those people we were most concerned about identifying and notifying—and there were plenty. Their stories were nightmares of harassment, abuse, blackmail, and even murder.

In the end, we were able to identify more than 140 such people based on the phone numbers we were given—victims from countries spread around the world, each a national story of abuse of power. More than thirty were in India alone, including a woman who had accused a member of the Indian government of rape. Others were Rwandans who had been hunted by Paul Kagame's regime and had fled to South Africa or Belgium for fear of their lives. Among them was David Batenga, nephew of the former head of Rwanda's intelligence service, Patrick Karegeya, whose body had been discovered on New Year's Day 2014 at the Michelangelo Hotel in Johannesburg, strangled to death presumably by Kagame's paid assassins.[18] Had the hacking of his nephew's phone been used to determine his location?

We discovered that the mobiles of the Catholic bishop of Togo and several priests, and also of an imam, were hacked using Pegasus, almost certainly by the Togolese dictatorship, whose history is littered with numerous cases of arbitrary detentions, torture, inhumane prison conditions, and random killings by security forces.[19] Others were members of the Catalan independence movement, including Anna Gabriel, a former MP for the far-left, anti-capitalist Popular Unity Candidacy (CUP), who fled Spain for Switzerland after helping to organize what Spain declared was the illegal Catalan referendum.[20] Aziz's number was of course there, but also that of his colleague, also a lawyer who represented victims of surveillance.

With a list of more than 140 civil society victims, our next step was to reach out and alert each of these people to what we had discovered. But how? How do you ring someone up on their personal phone and warn them they are under surveillance when the very device itself is likely under surveillance? Our goal was to get them off their phones and using an alternative means of secure communications.

Easier said than done. What would you do if someone called you, claiming to work for some academic research lab you've never heard of and saying your phone had been hacked by the regime you fled from in fear of your life? We had a lot of instant hang-ups and justifiably paranoid people who said, "Please leave me alone." Among those we convinced to find an alternative means of secure communication, only a few dozen agreed to go public. Most of them were too frightened. We empathized with and respected those decisions. Almost all the victims we encounter in our research live with an omnipresent cloud of fear over every aspect of their lives.

JSR, who has excellent interpersonal skills and is adept at putting anxious people at ease, did the bulk of the notifications, with other Citizen Lab staff covering those that required special language capabilities. At this point I stepped back and surveyed the landscape before us. A two-week window—a snapshot in time—into a monster of despotism spreading its stealthy digital tentacles through the ether, across the planet, and into the devices of scores of unwitting victims. At the center of it all, a single unprincipled company. It was mind-boggling to think these individuals were the casualties of just one firm in just fourteen days.

And then there was the sophistication of it all. No need to trick anyone with a clever text message. One minute your phone is fine, the next it's compromised, and you're none the wiser. Shalev Hulio, the CEO of NSO Group at the time, had the ambition, foresight, and networking skills to outfit his company with some of the most talented cyber warriors in the world—people like Almog Benin, an ex–Israel Defense Forces soldier, said to be one of the best vulnerability hunters in Herzliya—the Silicon Valley of Tel Aviv. NSO Group is staffed by dozens of graduates of the Israeli military, and particularly the extremely secretive Unit 8200, the country's illustrious signals intelligence agency, sister organization to the Mossad and Shin Bet. These agencies are responsible for some of the twentieth and twenty-first centuries' most well-executed covert operations. To think that the tradecraft involved in those operations was now being deployed as a private service in a poorly regulated global marketplace gave me chills.

By October 2019, we felt we had exhausted the notification process. It was time to go public with the victims who were willing to do so. The schedule was contingent on WhatsApp, which intended to make an announcement that would be co-timed with the publication of a short summary of our research findings.

To our surprise, WhatsApp dropped a legal hammer on NSO Group on October 29, 2019, when it filed a lawsuit in the US District Court for the Northern District of California.[21] The suit alleged that NSO Group violated WhatsApp's terms of service, illegally accessed its servers, and violated the Computer Fraud and Abuse Act, among other US laws. It was an astonishing turn of events.

For years, NSO Group and companies like it had been able to

flagrantly assist governments to execute horrible acts of despotism without any consequence. Their flippant responses to our research reports of these abuses were arrogant and dismissive. Finally, it seemed, there would be serious pushback from a massive tech platform with the deep pockets necessary to sustain a prolonged legal battle. If WhatsApp's suit was successful, NSO Group and its investors would be facing serious financial consequences. It would also send a loud shot across the bow of the entire mercenary spyware market warning that the rules of the game were changing.

In an opinion piece in the *Washington Post* published alongside the lawsuit, Will Cathcart, WhatsApp's CEO, said that the firm "was grateful to experts at the Citizen Lab at the University of Toronto for their work."[22] He continued: "They volunteered to help us understand who was affected by the attack and engaged with journalists and human rights defenders to help them better protect themselves in the face of these threats." The fact that more than a hundred civilians had been targeted "should serve as a wake-up call for technology companies, governments and all Internet users. Tools that enable surveillance into our private lives are being abused, and the proliferation of this technology into the hands of irresponsible companies and governments puts us all at risk."

As I reflected on the epidemic of surveillance abuses revealed in this one limited snapshot, I realized that the dark forces that were once contained in the shadows had come to dominate the world. The ancient arts of espionage, sabotage, assassination, and subversion—typically exceptions to the normal practice of international politics—were not only normalizing but becoming professionalized and commercialized. The world was now being run by Russian and Chinese oligarchs, petroleum-enriched Gulf monarchies, Central Asian and Middle Eastern strongmen, African kleptocrats, Manhattan-based billionaires, and British private equity firms. It was as if the villains in James Bond movies were stepping out of the screens and were now to take charge of world affairs.

And that's not a world my team and I intend to just sit back and welcome.

Hunting a Stealth Falcon

AUGUST 10, 2016

Citizen Lab senior researcher Bill Marczak was about to fall asleep when he checked his phone one last time. As soon as he saw the message, he knew it was significant. Ahmed Mansoor, an outspoken human rights defender in the United Arab Emirates, had just received an unsolicited text message on his Apple iPhone. The message contained a link purporting to show evidence of torture in Emirati prisons, something Mansoor might be tempted to explore further. And that was precisely what it was designed to do.

Mansoor was a member of the infamous UAE Five, a group of outspoken critics of the Emirati regime who had been imprisoned for insults to the royal family—their "insults" being mere calls for greater accountability.[1] As a human rights defender in a state with many sophisticated tools of repression, he had been a target of phishing attacks many times before. He was always vigilant, cautious about anything that came over the internet or the cellular network. When the notification arrived on the morning of August 10, 2016, Mansoor's instincts immediately kicked in. Instead of clicking on the link, he forwarded it to Marczak.

The Lab's research brings us into regular contact with dissidents, journalists, activists, and others worldwide who are targets of real-time espionage. These interactions can be exhilarating, with an adrenaline rush that comes from an unexpected hot tip. Sometimes it feels like defusing a bomb before the timer runs out. Hunting down powerful, self-entitled, despotic bullies is invigorating and even addictive. These are the moments when the team is most energized, dropping everything and entering overdrive mode.

Marczak knew anything coming from Mansoor was likely a strong lead. He was a target who got harassed and hacked so often that he served as a feeder for the latest spyware samples. This new development was no exception: a shortened link to a website domain contained in that text message immediately caught Marczak's eye. It was like a calling card for what, up until that moment, had been a mysterious, highly secretive, mercenary spyware firm. NSO Group was truly a "ghost," as its founders then bragged, its spyware advertised as being "untraceable." A few hours later, with Marczak now hunched over his laptop in the middle of the night, Mansoor received a second message from the same group of attackers, and he promptly forwarded it along too. It had the same shortened link. Once again we found ourselves in the midst of an espionage operation unfolding in real time.

Like many victims of cyber espionage, Mansoor knew he was being watched and understood the enormous risk of communicating with a group like ours. The safe thing would have been to delete the messages and carry on, but he chose to fight back, and his courage paid off. His decision had a profound impact on the practical security of billions of people worldwide. His actions would alter his world, our world, and the world of mercenary spyware forever.

––––––––

The Arab Spring reshaped the geopolitical landscape of the Middle East and Gulf region, and it also reshaped the Citizen Lab. Before 2011, our cyber espionage research was mostly focused on China, thanks primarily to our trusted relationships with exiled Tibetans who were the frequent targets of that country's voluminous spying operations and China's notoriously sloppy handiwork. Although we continued to track China-based espionage for years to come, after the Arab Spring we pivoted to examine offensive operations in other parts of the world and to zero in on the opaque commercial market for surveillance technology—a much more challenging prey.

In part, this shift was due to changes in personnel among the Citizen Lab's researchers. Some key contributors to our research during the Lab's first decade moved on, and a new group arrived. Marczak and John Scott-Railton (JSR) brought with them special experiences in the Middle East and Gulf region. Marczak, who was pursuing a graduate degree in computer science at the University of California, Berkeley, had spent part of his youth in Bahrain and aligned himself with pro-democracy activists after leaving the country. He was looking for a way to put his computer science and engineering skills to use on political issues he cared about, and he had heard reports in the activist community of strange things happening on computers, of eavesdropping and spying.

For his part, JSR was pursuing graduate studies in a discipline unrelated to digital rights and security issues, with fieldwork in West Africa, when the Arab Spring broke out. Always resourceful and driven by a powerful commitment to justice and rights, he organized one of the most widely used and publicized means of getting messages out in spite of internet blackouts throughout the Middle East: the #Jan25 and #Feb17 Voices projects.[2] Situated squarely at the fulcrum of civil society, activist, and journalist networks, he was well positioned to field reports about targeted espionage attacks. Before long, Marczak and JSR found each other, and reached out to me and the Citizen Lab.

The team was rounded out by several other dedicated researchers with a variety of complementary skills: Masashi Crete-Nishihata, a methodological polymath who developed a bond with victim groups and NGOs, especially the perennially targeted Tibetans; Jakub Dalek, whose previous training in system administration made him an expert in navigating the deep recesses of the internet's plumbing; Irene Poetranto, an Indonesian by background and an expert in Southeast Asian culture and politics, who helped manage a growing team of collaborators based in the Global South; Adam Senft, a meticulous researcher and operations manager—the "chief mate" of the Citizen Lab ship; Jeffrey Knockel, a brilliant computer scientist who earned his PhD studying censorship and surveillance on popular China-based apps; Sarah McKune and then later Siena Anstis, both exceptionally well-trained lawyers with a passion for ethics and an intolerance for corruption and despotism of any kind; Christopher Parsons, a policy analyst with an encyclopedic understanding of signals intelligence and telecommunications networks; and Bahr Abdul Razzak and Noura Aljizawi, Syrians by birth who fled the country for their safety in the midst of the civil war after experiencing detentions and torture. Others with their own special skills would soon follow. A digital fire brigade was taking shape at the Lab.

Little did pro-democracy activists know at the time, but by using cellphones and the internet to organize and mobilize, they were inadvertently creating conditions for their own undoing. Simultaneously, rulers in that part of the world had actively been acquiring spy tools to counter potential threats to their regimes.[3] Even before the eruption of the Arab Spring, tensions were escalating, prompting security services not only in the Middle East but also in other regions to eagerly seek advanced surveillance technology capable of monitoring protest organizers and potential dissenters.[4] "Best practices," tradecraft, and technology were quietly being shared, particularly among security agencies and police forces in closed-door regional security venues, with assistance from European and North American law enforcement and intelligence, all under the conveniently broad umbrella of "countering terrorism."[5] To sweeten it all, everyone made oodles of money in the exchanges.[6] Waves of digital securitization started to sweep over Central Asia, South and Southeast Asia, the Middle East, the Gulf, Africa, and Latin America, almost entirely outside public scrutiny and without legal restraints. A movement was slowly consolidating, using the inherent insecurities of the internet, cellphone networks, and social media to track, disrupt, and neutralize challenges to regime stability.

A significant breakthrough in shedding light on this industry occurred in March 2011, when Egyptian activists occupied Egypt's state security offices and rifled through cabinets and files.[7] Within the pilfered documents were what appeared to be proposals for work between Egypt's intelligence agencies and a little-known Europe-based company called Gamma Group, the manufacturer of a spyware tool called FinFisher.[8] The documents showed product names for spy tools with an invoice adding up to €333,607, but it was unclear whether the contracts were finalized and the equipment ever installed. (Gamma Group later denied it.)[9] What the Egyptian activists unearthed was the first concrete evidence of something that would dominate the sector for years: there is a market for sophisticated hacking tools developed by companies based in technologically advanced industrialized regions, and these companies have no qualms about pitching their gear to authoritarian regimes where there's a high likelihood they'll be used for repression.

Shortly afterward, WikiLeaks published a Gamma Group sales brochure and promotional video boasting about its technology that were distributed at trade shows where such wares are marketed. But the spyware itself remained elusive.[10] Finnish threat intelligence researcher Mikko Hyppönen said, "We know it exists, but we've never seen it," even as Martin Muench, the German entrepreneur behind Gamma Group, was pitching his surveillance technology to potential government clients at closed-door military and intelligence trade fairs.[11] The spyware itself appeared to be so closely guarded that it seemed unlikely that anyone outside the intelligence world would get their hands on it.

Before long, however, the mystery around Gamma Group's spyware was punctured by a hot tip that came our way. Marczak, who had not yet formally joined the Citizen Lab, was alerted around this time to several suspicious emails received by Bahraini activists based in London, Washington, DC, and Manama (the capital of Bahrain). After some preliminary analysis, he passed them on to *Bloomberg News* journalist Vernon Silver, who in turn shared them with Morgan Marquis-Boire, then a threat intelligence analyst at Google and later a Citizen Lab fellow for a few years. Once Marczak and Marquis-Boire began sleuthing, they soon busted Gamma Group. Contained in the code of a computer infected with the malware were multiple references to "FinSpy"—a mobile variant of Gamma's FinFisher product. Marczak followed the network traffic and discovered demonstration versions of the spyware that connected to two websites with "ff-demo" and "gamma-international" in the names of each one—an obvious lead.

The FinSpy/Bahrain report we published subsequently, in July 2012, was the first time anyone had been able to forensically dissect a live spyware attack and attribute it to a particular firm.[12] It had all the elements of what we'd be consumed with over the next decade: an authoritarian regime misusing a lawful intercept tool to target democratic activists both at home and abroad; a window into a highly invasive exploit that is designed to surreptitiously commandeer a target's device and scoop up all the private information, read emails, intercept text messages, turn on the camera, and capture audio from the device's microphone; a glimpse into an unaccountable sector featuring irresponsible entrepreneurs who enrich themselves by empowering autocrats and dictators to carry out their dirty deeds.

On a more personal level, the attack brought Bill Marczak into the Citizen Lab's fold. At the time he was working on a conventional "big data" analysis topic for his PhD, and he switched his focus to mercenary spyware. I was asked to serve on his PhD committee at Berkeley. I hired Marczak first as a part-time fellow and then full time as the Lab's lead technical investigator around our targeted espionage investigations. He went on to engineer some of our most important discoveries over the next ten years and built our technical methodology for hunting spyware. He and JSR formed a tight partnership with complementary skills that drove our espionage investigations from that point forward.

———

Investigations typically start with tips from the field: activists or others who are targeted, recognizing something suspicious, pass leads along to us or to a trusted journalist who does the same. If necessary, we seek help from experts in the threat intelligence space outside the Citizen Lab who can provide expertise we may be lacking. Over time, partner organizations have gravitated to the cause and have been enlisted in joint investigations too. Together we form a kind of collective immune system to fight off viral infections that threaten civil society.

The next case on mercenary spyware abuse came almost di-

rectly after our FinSpy report and led us to our first interactions
with Ahmed Mansoor. Around the time of our report's publication
in the summer of 2012, a Moroccan-focused website based outside
of the country called Mamfakinch received an unsolicited message
directing recipients to a remote web page that, translated roughly
from French, said, "Please don't mention my name and don't say
anything at all [about me]. I don't want to get mixed up in this."
Analysis of the message showed it was sent from Morocco-based
3G networks serving the region of Morocco's capital, Rabat. Further analysis revealed that visits to the website contained in the
message would execute an exploit employed by another mysterious
hacking firm based in Milan, Italy, called Hacking Team.

At roughly the same time as Mamfakinch staffers received this
message, Mansoor received one from a sender claiming to be "Arabic WikiLeaks." It asked him to look at an "urgent message" in
an attached Word document with the file name "veryimportant
.doc." Not yet fully conditioned to be suspicious of unsolicited
attachments, Mansoor opened the document and noticed some
garbled information passing across his screen. Looking for outside help, he recalled reading about the Citizen Lab's FinSpy report, so he reached out to Marczak to see if he'd be willing to
look. "He didn't know me," Marczak told me, "but he had seen
the Bahrain Watch statement we put out about the FinFisher case
and contacted me saying he was a UAE activist who had received
something similar."

Marczak's analysis of the document showed that it contained
an exploit for Microsoft vulnerabilities that would insert spyware
onto the target's computer. Once implanted inside Mansoor's computer, it made connections to server addresses based in the UAE
and matching the address for the corporate headquarters of a conglomerate of Emirati companies called the Royal Group. Our analysis determined that this spyware was manufactured by Hacking
Team and that the first-stage exploit—the tool used to crack open
the operating system to allow the spyware to be implanted—was
concocted by a French exploit broker called Vupen.

We published our findings in October 2012 in a second mercenary spyware report, *Backdoors Are Forever: Hacking Team and the Targeting of Dissent?*[13] Hacking Team's spokesperson, Eric Rabe, immediately responded dismissively, saying, "Frankly, the evidence that the Citizen Lab report presents in this case doesn't suggest anything inappropriately done by us."[14] That translates as: "We just sell spyware. What governments do with it is their business."

Ironically, this new notoriety may have even helped the mercenary spyware industry—at least initially. The same week that we published our findings, Muench of Gamma Group presented "Government I.T. Intrusion: Applied Hacking Techniques Used by Governments" at yet another military and intelligence trade show, ISS World Americas.[15] Presumably the media coverage of our investigations helped fill the room with curious potential clients. I wonder, though, if any of the officials who signed deals with Muench that day realized just how exposed their espionage operations would soon become.

In our line of work, cases often overlap and intertwine. The 2016 investigation into Mansoor's targeting is a prime example. The groundwork for our revelations around his unsolicited text messages had already been laid long before he was targeted. It all began with a different target in another country, someone else who had also incurred the wrath of the autocratic sheikhs of the UAE.

In November 2015, Rori Donaghy, a UK-based journalist, received an unsolicited email containing what appeared to be a link to an Al Jazeera article. His reporting posed a threat to the royal families of the UAE as he exposed their corruption, human rights abuses, and ruthless suppression of dissent. Inevitably, they wanted to silence him, and they had plenty of resources to do so, especially in the cyber realm.

The email Donaghy received took the form of an invitation to join a human rights panel. The operators who sent the message were banking on his moral and political sensibilities, his eagerness to promote human rights, to get him to click on the link. "We would like to formally invite you to apply to be a member of the panel by responding to this email," the invitation began. "You should include your thoughts and opinions in response to the following article about what more David Cameron can be doing to help aid the Middle East." A link to a website promised to provide more details.

The link was created using a URL shortener—a free, web-based service that condenses a lengthy link into something easier to copy, paste, and share and redirects the request to the desired destination. Unfortunately, it's also a service that is often abused by malicious actors. Those who lack training in network traffic analysis or are too busy or lazy to double-check don't see the multiple split-second transactions between servers occurring behind the scenes. It's another deceptive ruse of the cybercriminal world adopted by the purveyors of espionage tools.

At the time of this attack, spyware required some form of user interaction to initiate an exploit on a device. The attacker had to convince the victim to do something that would trigger a web request, such as clicking on a link. That is where URL shorteners come in handy. By combining a message crafted to entice the recipient into clicking with a deceptive ruse (the "social engineering" part of the operation), the attacker could disguise the real destination of the web request thanks to the shortener, to further obfuscate what was really going on. A lengthy website address is more likely to raise eyebrows and produce caution. Using a fixed address may also inadvertently risk exposure of a command and control server used by the spyware's operators. The URL shortener, though imperfect, helps mask those intentions while obscuring the attacker's infrastructure.

While shortened link services can be a useful tool for attackers, they can also become their Achilles' heel. Some of the shortening services are open source and free, and therefore can be tracked and searched, allowing an investigator to unravel the ultimate destination of a particular shortened link that was used months or even years ago. By searching for instances of the same variation of the shortened link, investigators can uncover other targets or contexts where the same operator was hunting for unsuspecting victims.

Social media platforms, mailing lists, and archives of individuals' inboxes and message histories can all be searched for the presence of a distinct shortened URL—another example of the way cyber espionage operators leave digital traces in the online ecosystem.

Like Mansoor, Donaghy had been targeted numerous times before and had grown suspicious of anything unsolicited that came his way. He was also aware of the Lab's previous reporting on UAE cyber espionage, so he forwarded the email to Marczak for analysis. Marczak clicked on the link in a controlled environment that collected detailed network traffic information, effectively capturing the instructions going back and forth between the target and the operators. Clicking on the shortened link revealed that it retrieved information from Al Jazeera's website as advertised, but it also surreptitiously sought to undertake reconnaissance on the target computer. This type of profiling is common in cyber espionage, where a scan is used to identify the operating system, locate antivirus software to be disabled, and obtain other features and settings that might be useful for future precision exploits. It's the equivalent of mapping the layout and security cameras in an art gallery before a heist.

When we're actively investigating a live operation, we sometimes try to engage with the operators, either directly ourselves or with the cooperation of targets. The operators may inadvertently reveal details about themselves or their government clients in such exchanges. Typically, we create our own ruse to encourage them to send more information, playing a game of *Spy vs. Spy*. Sometimes these schemes pay off. Other times, the operators become wary or annoyed: one of JSR's exchanges with a South American hack-for-hire operation in 2015 ended with a death threat to him and his family sent by the attackers to his research machine, which he had just infected with their spyware. "You keep analyzing processes," they typed in a pop-up message on JSR's screen. "We are going to analyze your brain with a bullet—and your family too."

Marczak asked Donaghy, "Can you respond to them and ask for another link? Say it's not working." To our surprise, the operators sent a further email, this time with another shortened link to a password-protected web portal where Donaghy could supposedly download a document securely.

On opening the document, it revealed a fake version of Microsoft's legitimate security portal, Proofpoint. The operators had labeled it in English and Arabic: "This Document Is Secured." The portal directed the user to "enable macros"—ironic because macros are executable code snippets within a Word document that can be used to implement malicious code.

The Word document was designed specifically for Donaghy. Whoever was behind the ruse had constructed an entire fictitious organization in hopes of getting him to click on the link. However, they took a lazy shortcut and had appropriated a banner graphic from a previously existing and much older antislavery campaign, which we easily identified through a basic reverse image search.

Marczak then searched through Donaghy's inbox looking for any other messages he might have received in the past that contained the same shortened link. Bingo! An email surfaced from two years before, from someone presenting themselves as "Andrew Dwight" who was engaged in research on authoritarian regimes in the Middle East. Back in 2013, Donaghy, unprompted and none the wiser, had responded to a message asking for more details about his work in the Middle East. "Andrew Dwight" replied:

> Hello Rori, Happy New Year! I apologize for the delay in getting back to you. I was on a ski holiday in upstate New York for the New Year and just returned to my current accommodations in the city.

In this way, "Dwight" constructed a persona of someone based on the East Coast (as opposed to the Gulf, presumably), a person with a real life and genuine interests (as opposed to a trained operative working for a despotic regime).

> I am currently situated in the US while I complete my book to be closer to my publisher and editor. The book focuses on the various guises used by Middle Eastern

countries to demonstrate that they are providing equal and fair treatment with concern to human rights. I am working with several organizations in identifying cases that reveal their true lack of concern for liberty and personal freedoms.

I'm using these cases as testimony about this under reported issue. Have you heard of a Swedish organization named Al Karama?

There [*sic*] website: http://en.alkarama.org/index.php?option=com_content&view=article&id=1005&Itemid=74&slid=102

I have spoken to one of their junior editors and I am hoping to obtain input from some of their sources as well.

This issue never gets any smaller does it? I hope that a few loud voices (and a well received book) can make a difference.

Cheers,

Andrew

As our searches continued, we uncovered new information that led us to more layers of the mystery, clues to additional victims, and, gradually, a picture of who might be behind it all. A Twitter search for the same shortened link service showed that the operators who targeted Donaghy had also targeted at least twenty-seven other Twitter handles. Of those, the owners of twenty-four of them had been arrested by UAE authorities, indicating Emirati involvement in the operation. We also found that the Twitter account of one of the arrested individuals had been taken over by the operators, who used it to send out further malicious messages while posing as the owner (another common tactic in the cyber espionage tool kit). We discovered more than four hundred shortened URLs that the operators had created, all containing bait content related to UAE political and human rights issues.

At this point, we were confident that the operator was connected to the Emirati security services. Drawing from the UAE's long history of the falcon as a symbol of pride and cultural heritage, Marczak coined a name for the operator group: Stealth Falcon.

The "Stealth" part of the label referred to the group's clandestine nature. We were impressed with the operators' knowledge of targets and their own operational security. In the report we eventually published in May 2016, we wrote:

> Stealth Falcon demonstrates some familiarity with the patterns of behavior, interests, and activities of its targets, suggesting that the operators may have been working with other sources of information about their targets' behaviors. In addition, Stealth Falcon displayed above-average operational security throughout the campaign . . . [and] familiarity with creating and maintaining a range of fictitious personas, and registering and managing a significant amount of attack and C2 [command and control] infrastructure with concern for operational security.[16]

No doubt about it: Stealth Falcon was a professional operation.

I would soon learn the people we called Stealth Falcon read the report with a mixture of amusement, admiration, and anxiety.

———

Three months later, in August 2016, Mansoor's tips arrived in Marczak's inbox. The shortened link embedded in the text message made Marczak gasp with excitement. Among the various artifacts we had collected as part of the Stealth Falcon investigation were a few registered domains that seemed to point toward a then largely secretive mercenary spyware firm, NSO Group.

We had little visibility into this firm, although the lead from the Stealth Falcon investigation prompted Marczak to start mapping out what he could of its command and control infrastructure. We had seen mention of NSO Group on Israeli government licensing websites, in leaked data from other mercenary spyware firms that was posted online, and in the intelligence gossip portal *Intelligence Online*. Now we were beginning to trace the outlines of the "ghost" itself.

Marczak raced to set up a simulated iPhone environment on his laptop and clicked on the links embedded in the SMS messages. After a few minutes of code scrolling by, the system crashed and the exploit failed to initiate. He needed something less artificial and more like Mansoor's iPhone 6 that the attackers were targeting.

At the time, Marczak was affiliated with the International Computer Science Institute, an organization set up by faculty connected to the engineering school at the University of California, Berkeley. He asked his colleagues if anyone had an old iPhone 6 that we could use for our investigation. When he got one, he reset it to its factory settings. He connected the phone to a laptop that was running a program to intercept the network traffic between the phone and whatever exploit server might be on the other end. He clicked on the link and waited anxiously for something to happen. The built-in browser on the iPhone opened and closed, which was highly unusual. And then internet traffic started flowing between the phone and the exploit server. Marczak's laptop was recording it all. When the phone downloaded the exploit and spyware, we had all the instructions captured and preserved.

While Marczak was working in his Berkeley office, JSR was busy tracking down some additional expertise on the mobile security front. Seth Hardy, who had previously been a threat analyst at the Citizen Lab, was now working for a company called Lookout. JSR reached out to him to see if we could collaborate. Hardy, in turn, introduced us to several of Lookout's experts. We entered a twenty-four-hour cycle of frenetic work: Marczak and Lookout's analysts scouring through the exploit chain, and JSR and the rest of us focusing on the coordination around our teams' respective publications.

The significance of what we found cannot be overstated. We obtained the blueprints for NSO Group's Pegasus spyware and the exploits used to deliver it—the world's most sophisticated, stealthy, and enigmatic hacking technology at that time. It had been designed to be undetectable by some of the world's most elite computer scientists, trained by Israel's most advanced signals intelligence agency. When Hardy was interviewed by *Vanity Fair* magazine, he compared the exploit chain used to implant Pegasus on a victim's device to a "stealth bomber."[17] NSO Group had a series of exploits to take advantage of flaws in Apple's highly engineered operating system and take over the device without the user being any the wiser. As Hardy put it, "It's one thing to know they exist. It's an entirely different thing to have one crash into your backyard."

Had Mansoor clicked on the link, his phone's Safari browser would have opened and closed in a blink of an eye. A vulnerability in Safari would have then allowed the planting of more sophisticated spyware to gather information. The operators would have then been able to read every message he sent or received, even those that were encrypted. They would have been able to turn on the camera and microphone, follow him around, spoof messages, and more. His device would have become an unwitting spy in his pocket.

Exploits like the ones we found are incredibly rare and valuable. To put it into perspective, consider the highly exclusive market for "zero-day" vulnerabilities—exploits that take advantage of flaws in software unknown to the software's manufacturer. When we made our discovery, a single Apple zero day could fetch up to a million dollars. But the exploit chain we uncovered contained not one but three separate Apple zero days, making it worth three times as much. The weapon the UAE used to hack into Mansoor's device, and which we now possessed the blueprints for, was extremely valuable—at the time, a street value worth around $3 million.

We all knew what needed to happen next: share the details of our discovery with Apple so that it could patch its system and prevent NSO Group's clients from further exploitation. JSR handled outreach to Apple's notoriously insulated security team and acted as the liaison between the Lab and Lookout. Needless to say, no one on the team slept much for several days while working around the clock.

We were amazed at how swiftly Apple responded to our findings.

Just two weeks after we received the second of Mansoor's SMS messages and made our disclosure, the company had issued emergency security patches for its more than one billion users around the world. It was by far the most significant practical outcome of the Citizen Lab's research on user security up to that point. We disarmed a cyber mercenary and made billions of people safer, at least temporarily. It would be the first such disclosure of many more to come.

The report was published August 25, 2016, coordinated with Apple's announcement and a technical post on Lookout's website.[18] It was yet another report for the Citizen Lab that made world news, including prominent coverage in the *New York Times* written by cybersecurity reporter Nicole Perlroth.[19] In her interview with Mansoor, Perlroth described how "the discoveries were a sad reminder that no matter what he does to protect his devices and digital security, he will continue to be a target for companies that provide this sort of spying technology." This attack was one of at least three separate attempts to hack into his devices using three different spyware tools sold by separate mercenary firms—products that would have been very expensive for UAE authorities to procure. He was for that reason the "Million Dollar Dissident."

"I guess I am their regular customer," Mansoor said. "I am the guinea pig." He was also our canary in a coal mine.

Attribution is always difficult. We had the blueprints of the weapon, but who pulled the trigger? A lot of leads pointed back to the UAE: NSO Group sold only to government clients, and Mansoor was a UAE-based dissident who had a long track record of having his devices targeted by operators presumably in the Emirati security services. There was also the overlap with what we called "Stealth Falcon," which itself we attributed with high confidence to the UAE. The whole process is like assembling a puzzle with missing pieces, where all we can do is make educated guesses based on fragments of data and secondary reporting. Fortunately, we soon received a rare window into what was really going on behind the scenes, thanks to some persistent investigative journalism and an unexpected email from Hawaii.

Aloha from Hawaii

AUGUST 2018

When the unsolicited email arrived, I gave it only slight consideration before forwarding it to Bill Marczak. He, in turn, recalls replying but not hearing back. Or maybe it just got lost in the shuffle.

> **From:** Lori Stroud
> **Date:** August 5, 2018, at 8:20:26 AM EDT
> **To:** r.deibert@utoronto.ca
> **Subject:** STEALTH FALCON—Working for an APT [advanced persistent threat, a cyber espionage operator]
>
> aloha Mr. Deibert,
>
> I would like to offer information and perspective re: the STEALTH FALCON APT as I was an offensive operator on that program. Regarding "insider threat" i think it would be cool to share a story illustrating when it is ethically the right thing to do to become an insider threat (as I was). I did the right thing ethically, despite an APT targeting my [*sic*] after. I hope I hear back from your team, thank you!
>
> Lori Stroud

We receive floods of inquiries every day much like this one, the vast majority of which are not appropriate for us to engage with or difficult to decipher. Some are long, others loaded with conspiracy theories or stories of loved ones lured into online cults, and many include attachments of blurry photographs, diagrams, geocoordinates of cell towers, or inexplicable screenshots of incoming calls or text messages. After Edward Snowden appeared as a guest on the Joe Rogan podcast singing our praises and urging Rogan's millions of fans to send us anything suspicious that arrived over the internet, we were totally inundated.[1] We receive packages of paraphernalia via the mail or FedEx. A few individuals have traveled long distances to visit us in person—most are benign, but some are unpredictable, accusing us of being pawns of some imagined government agency.

Little did we know the relevance of Lori Stroud to our work on Stealth Falcon. A few months later, after reading the reports when she told her story, we recalled her name and outreach, and began to appreciate just how significant her experiences were for us.[2]

———————

The United Arab Emirates, like many other modern sovereign states in the Gulf region, is a by-product of British colonialism, with artificial boundaries drawn in the sand. The discovery of massive oil reserves in the late 1950s catapulted the country within a few short years from a collection of Bedouin tribes into a supercharged, plutocratic monarchy. Today, it is a curious blend of authoritarianism, sharia law, flamboyant consumerism, and migrant worker exploitation.[3]

Money defines everything in the UAE, from the giant buildings that seem to sprout out of the inhospitable desert to the rampant impunity and corruption. Artificial ski slopes defy the climate crisis, vending machines dispense high-end vehicles, and a replica of the Louvre competes with a Ferrari World theme park. But behind all this extravagant indulgence is barely concealed brute-force repression. The UAE is the epitome of late-modern authoritarian capitalism, where dissent is treated swiftly and harshly by torture and execution. As the International Consortium of Investigative Journalists noted, "the UAE has two faces: an open economy and a police state."[4]

The UAE's vast sovereign wealth funds are increasingly directed toward military and intelligence ventures. The country has an impressive defense budget, currently estimated at about $22 billion a year, up from $6 billion only twenty years ago.[5] Each major global security event that has affected the Gulf—the First Gulf War, the 9/11 attacks, the invasion and occupation of Iraq, the Arab Spring, the October 7 Hamas attacks and the wars in Gaza and Lebanon that followed—has triggered increases in spending on the latest warmaking and intelligence-gathering technology. They include F-35s, THAAD missile defense systems, troop carriers, drones, CCTV cameras, data analytics platforms, social media monitoring, and spyware. UAE public relations consultants like to trumpet the regime as "Little Sparta," but the military buildup is equally driven by conspicuous consumption and graft.[6] It's another way to grease the wheels, curry favor, and give everyone involved—lawyers, hotels, accountants, airlines, security consultants, PR firms—a slice of the pie.

For years, scores of Israeli and American veterans of intelligence and military agencies have worked as contractors in the UAE, some as mercenaries and others as consultants to the state or state-owned enterprises.[7] They protect oil fields, undertake counterterror operations, help build foreign espionage and domestic surveillance capabilities, and advise on strategy against threats to the regime.

Along with retired CIA officers, Pentagon officials, and National Security Agency directors, a long list of dubious characters, amoral grifters, and opportunists have fed from the Emirati trough. The venture fund run by Jared Kushner, Donald Trump's son-in-law and former special advisor on Middle East affairs, has received $2.5 billion in investments from Gulf countries, including the UAE, since he exited the White House.[8] Erik Prince, founder of the private mercenary firm Blackwater, contracted with the crown prince of Abu Dhabi, Mohamed bin Zayed, to create an elite counterterrorism unit.[9] Tom Barrack, a longtime friend and ally of Trump's, was indicted in 2021 for illegally lobbying on behalf of the UAE.[10] Lebanese American businessman George Nader acted as a liaison between Trump's political campaign and the UAE and is currently serving a ten-year prison sentence for child pornography charges.[11] Shady governments attract shady people.

A key player in the UAE's defense and intelligence buildup is Sheikh Tahnoon bin Zayed al-Nahyan, the regime's top spook and a peer among a new cohort of "millennial authoritarians" that includes Mohammed bin Salman (MBS) of Saudi Arabia and Nayib Bukele of El Salvador. The House of Nahyan is extremely wealthy, worth about $300 billion by some estimates, and the sheikh has used that capital to acquire the latest spying platforms and to finance companies in the defense and intelligence sector.[12] He manages a portfolio that straddles national security and the corporate sector, including chairing several major conglomerates such as the Royal Group, the International Holding Company, the cybersecurity subsidiaries of the G42 holding company, and the warfare technologies firm Edge Group and its cyber offensive subsidiary Beacon Red.[13] As his influence has grown, so have his responsibilities over national security. Sheikh Tahnoon facilitated covert cooperation between Israel and the UAE before the normalization of relations, and he also helped lure elite security contractors from Israel, the United States, and Europe with the promise of high salaries and luxurious accommodation.[14]

Although Israel and the UAE did not establish formal diplomatic relations until September 15, 2020, with the signing of the Abraham Accords in Washington, DC, the covert trade in defense and intelligence products and services has been thriving for years. In the 2000s, scores of Israeli entrepreneurs, including nearly all the most prominent surveillance and spyware companies, landed big contracts with the Emiratis.[15] These companies include NSO Group and its onetime sister firm Circles, which specializes in exploiting insecurities in global mobile cellular systems to offer mobile device tracking services. It has been reported that NSO Group and Circles demonstrated their products to prospective Emirati clients on the UAE's national security council by intercepting the communications of the UAE's rivals in Qatar, including the editor of a prominent newspaper.[16] Leaked emails from a lawsuit connected to the company show that NSO Group licensed its surveillance software to the UAE beginning in August 2013.[17]

Sales in the Gulf have always been more lucrative than in other parts of the world. "A product that you sell in Europe for $10 million, you can sell in the Gulf for 10 times that," said one person familiar with NSO's financial activity.[18] Mati Kochavi, who had companies registered in Israel and Switzerland and employed dozens of former Israeli security and intelligence operatives, including a former chief of Israeli military intelligence, was a key interlocutor between Gulf-based companies and Israeli defense and intelligence vendors.[19] He reportedly sent "two flights a week to Abu Dhabi [to sell] all the best of Israeli products."[20]

It's conventional to divide the world into regime types—authoritarian versus democratic, for example—but the extensive involvement of US and Israeli personnel in the UAE demonstrates how questionable those divisions can be. US and Israeli national security expertise has penetrated so deeply into the security apparatuses of numerous Gulf countries that it is fair to ask whether the distinction makes a difference, especially for those profiting from the engagement.

US intelligence contractors began making their way to the UAE in large numbers in the 2010s, primarily through a company called CyberPoint. Founded in Baltimore in 2009 by Karl Gumtow, former vice president of the defense contractor SRA International, CyberPoint was one of many ventures capitalizing on the cybersecurity boom in the post-9/11 world.[21] With the help of several American citizens who had held senior positions in the US defense or intelligence community and who now acted as highly paid consultants or advisors to Emirati sheikhs, CyberPoint made inroads with the UAE.[22] For example, Richard Clarke, George W. Bush's former advisor for counterterrorism and cybersecurity, is now a high-paid advisor to Abu Dhabi and helped secure CyberPoint's contract with the Emirati regime.[23] Paul Kurtz, a veteran of the Office of Cybersecurity at the National Security Council who also works for Clarke's Good Harbor consulting practice, was in charge of CyberPoint's contract with the UAE at the time.[24]

CyberPoint's principals have asserted that their business with the UAE focused solely on defensive measures to safeguard networks against outside attacks. In fact, the company's operations also included "hacking back" and taking offensive actions against Emirati targets. Similar to other companies in this field, CyberPoint's personnel were experienced cyber operatives who had worked for government agencies with three-letter acronyms, such as the CIA or NSA. When they moved to the UAE, they were given significant salary increases, sumptuous accommodation in a tax-free zone, and access to state-of-the-art surveillance equipment that conferred godlike abilities—all purportedly justified by the fight against extremism and the war on terror.

Among this group of high-priced cyber operatives were former NSA contractors Lori Stroud and her husband, Jonathan Cole. Although we didn't make the connection in August 2018, a few months later Stroud gave an interview about her work in the UAE to Reuters reporters Christopher Bing and Joel Schectman. After reading their article on Stroud, I retrieved her email and made contact. Both she and her husband agreed to talk. I also spoke to Bing and Schectman. Through these interviews, a detailed picture emerged of the contractors' day-to-day work, which previously was a closely guarded secret. Stroud and Cole helped provide the missing pieces for our attribution puzzle around the Stealth Falcon case.

Stroud and Cole began working on contract for the Emiratis in May 2014. Stroud had previously been an intelligence contractor for the NSA in Hawaii and was part of the team at Booz Allen Hamilton that hired Edward Snowden. She had even vouched for him to her colleagues. After Snowden leaked his massive cache of classified documents, Stroud felt she was ostracized, her reputation damaged. She and Cole decided to seek new opportunities. They began working in the UAE to help develop the capacity of the Emirati's signals intelligence agency, the National Electronic Security Authority (NESA).

Stroud and Cole worked in a complex in Abu Dhabi called the Villa. There they focused on a highly sensitive cyber espionage project, Project Raven. On arrival, they and other employees were given two briefs: a "defensive" one, the notes of which were contained in a purple folder, and an "offensive" one, with notes organized in a black folder, code-named Dread. Project Raven contractors were told that the Dread folder was a full "denial" operation: as the text on the outside explained, it contained details about "the offensive, operational division of NESA and will never be acknowledged to the general public." The first rule of Dread was "You do not talk about Dread."

Stroud and Cole had drawn a diagram of the building for Bing and Schectman, which was featured in their exclusive report. Thanks to Stroud's description, we went from having a vague idea of attribution to a detailed description of the layout of the building in which the hacking operation was mounted and the room that housed their servers. According to Stroud, most of the work was done by outside contractors like her who handled everything from reconnaissance and open-source information gathering on targets to developing exploitation methods specific to each victim. In the "management room," UAE agents selected individuals whose devices would be hacked or who would be placed under surveillance, while the "infrastructure room" housed servers paid for with Bitcoin and fake identities to prevent tracing.

The former NSA operators worked in the "targeting room," scouring all they could find from the open web and other sources on the victims and also their relatives and friends, practicing what we called "relational targeting." That involved selecting not just the primary target but also their spouses, children, and others in order to gather information on a principal target through collateral means, putting innocent individuals in the crosshairs in the process. We've seen this pattern so many times now that checking the devices of close friends and relatives of principal subjects is now standard practice in Lab investigations.

Hacking tools were assembled in the "initial access development" room. On the second floor, the actual hacking took place in the "operations center." All the collected data was funneled into the "data processing room," where it was archived, sorted, and analyzed to be used later for criminal proceedings or perhaps blackmail and extortion. Stroud and Cole, as US contractors with NSA-trained skills, helped identify vulnerabilities in the devices of selected individuals and then developed or acquired spyware and other tools for the actual targeted attacks. At the final stage, young and privileged members of what Stroud assumed was the extended royal family would arrive and, after being prompted, carry out the actual hacking. Stroud told me she felt they regarded it as some kind of live-action role-playing game. It was "hip" to hack using the world's most expensive spyware.

Stroud found the work exhilarating and liberating at first. "It was incredible because there weren't these limitations like there was at the NSA. There wasn't that bullshit red tape," she told Bing and Schectman.

Project Raven targeted numerous individuals who were subjects of our investigations, including Donaghy and Mansoor. Both men were tracked obsessively. Internally, Donaghy was given the code name Gyro, while Mansoor was referred to as Egret. Interviews with Raven operatives and analysis of documents by Bing and Schectman closely mirrored what we observed in the emails, tweets, and malware sent to Donaghy. To get close to Donaghy, a Raven operative was instructed to "ingratiate himself to the target by espousing similar beliefs." Donaghy was "unable to resist an overture of this nature." As our investigation revealed, the operatives succeeded in their effort.

Mansoor was also under constant surveillance, and the operators had gathered incriminating information on him, including photographs he had taken at a prison in violation of prison policy that he had later tried to expunge from his personal computer. Targeting instructions would come down from senior Emirati officials in NESA, but not always. Stroud recalled that one US contractor, an ex-intelligence officer with the NSA, had become obsessed with Donaghy and was showing the fruits of his compromises to impress his superiors. Unwittingly, we were essentially reverse engineering the work Stroud and her colleagues had done at Project Raven. The Twitter accounts were theirs, along with the socially engineered bait content from "Andrew Dwight," the URL shorteners, and the infrastructure of servers we tracked.

As time passed, Stroud and Cole's initial excitement turned into apprehension. Things began to change when UAE officials became nervous about their overreliance on Americans and American firms such as CyberPoint. Emirati elites likely also wanted a larger share of the profits for themselves. Why funnel huge appropriations to an American company when a homegrown one could do just as well? In 2016, CyberPoint was replaced by a UAE firm called DarkMatter, founded by Faisal al-Bannai, whose father was a senior member of the UAE police and a well-connected person in private intelligence and security circles. Without doubt, Sheikh Tahnoon had his tentacles in it as well.

The US contractors were given the option of transferring their employment to DarkMatter or going home. Once DarkMatter took charge of Project Raven, whatever slim restraints existed around hacking operations were loosened. That led to a surge of targeted espionage against civil society both within the UAE and abroad. Anyone whose behavior even remotely threatened the regime was suspect.

DarkMatter pulled numerous other companies into its cyber operations orbit, including Canada's BlackBerry.[25] Going back to the late 2000s, rumors circulated that the popular mobile provider's much-heralded security was not so secure after all and that the company had made secret deals for backdoor access to its customers' data with several governments, including the Emiratis. In August 2010, I wrote a lengthy exposé in Canada's national newspaper, the *Globe and Mail*, on some of the questions raised by BlackBerry's operations in the region, including the ultimatums it received from governments there to cooperate and facilitate state surveillance of its users or face expulsion.[26] Shortly afterward, a person working for BlackBerry's lawful intercept compliance office—the office charged with liaising with government security agencies—contacted me and asked for a private meeting. Clearly, this person was taking considerable risks to reach out to me, so we arranged to meet at a discreet location.

"I just want you to know that you're not only right—it's much worse than you imagine," he began, grim-faced. He told me extensive details of the firm's secret deals with Emirati officials and how senior company executives were well aware that the regime's surveillance of their customers led to the arrest of human rights defenders. As we spoke, he pulled a contract from his briefcase and placed it on the table between us. To my astonishment, it detailed an agreement with compensation between the firm and UAE authorities about targeted surveillance of BlackBerry customers. There was even a provision for technicians to travel to Waterloo, Ontario—the BlackBerry headquarters—for training on interception of the BlackBerry network.

Coincidentally, immediately afterward I had an interview with BBC's *Click* on the Citizen Lab's research. After the interview, the journalist mentioned to me that his next interview was with Black-Berry cofounder Mike Lazaridis. "Do you have any suggestions for questions I could ask him?" he inquired. "I do indeed," I said, still reeling from my meeting: "Ask him whether BlackBerry helps governments undertake surveillance of their users." When the journalist did just that, Lazaridis abruptly ended the interview and walked off the set, pleading, "Come on, guys—this is national security you're talking about." To this day, you can watch an excerpt of that interview on YouTube.[27]

Several years later, a Canadian government official told me that on a visit to DarkMatter's offices in the UAE, he noticed Bell Canada phone bills lying around the Villa. When he asked about them, he was told they were all from BlackBerry contractors on staff with DarkMatter who were assisting with the UAE's surveillance operations. Suddenly, my conversation with the nervous BlackBerry employee made sense. Later I learned that DarkMatter established a local R&D shop in Toronto, headed by a person who had worked for BlackBerry.[28]

Even all these years later, BlackBerry's collusion with authoritarian regimes has received scant attention and no reckoning by its former principals. The company is seen as a national innovation success story by most Canadians, and a recent major film focused only on its achievements.[29] Jim Balsillie, a co-CEO of BlackBerry, is a revered multimillionaire who has founded public interest charities and think tanks, including the Balsillie School of International Affairs in Waterloo, Ontario.[30] But how much of that money was earned enabling dirty work for dictators abroad?

————

When the Citizen Lab reports were released, Cole and Stroud remember them as "all hands on deck" emergencies. They were called into the office to scour the reports and see what assets and tools had been burned and what would be needed to reconstitute the Villa's attack methodologies. It was surreal to hear how our reports sent off alarm bells once they were published, a reaction we can usually only imagine.

Reporting by the *New York Times* claims that the Citizen Lab itself was targeted at some point by Project Raven.[31] When I asked Stroud about it, she replied, "I don't recall if we ever actually went after your organization, but almost certainly the Citizen Lab and its senior staff would have been profiled and mapped for counterintelligence purposes." The relevant agencies would also have been filtering email traffic based on outbound domains to the Citizen Lab and other human rights organizations. "Active operations would collect it up and pursue the people in the country," she said. "They were dedicated to domestic repression." That revelation sent shivers down my spine, thinking about possible risks arising from any operational security lapses that might occur as we communicated with victims in a particular country.

These discussions offered unprecedented insights into the inner workings of the operations we were investigating. Attribution in our type of detective work is almost always a challenging and mysterious task. With the UAE, my previous assumptions were limited to imagining officers in fatigues stationed in desert bunkers, along with a few consultants and imported equipment. It was uncanny to learn from Stroud and Cole about the layout of the very building where the targeting was taking place and the processes going on within it. If someone had told me in 2017 that the Stealth Falcon operation was being carried out by dozens of US contractors who were veterans of the NSA's elite Tailored Access Operations, I would have dismissed it as implausible.

The power dynamics at work here were revealing: a small team of investigators versus a handful of former NSA contractors being paid hundreds of thousands of dollars and given access to a plethora of hacking tools, all while acting in what they perceived to be legal operations. We were definitely outgunned. And yet, somehow, we managed to peel the story back and expose it.

————

Stroud and Cole were fed up with the targeting of Americans and the duplicity behind some of their bosses saying otherwise. A final straw came when Stroud discovered a long list of dossiers on American citizens. After she reported these findings, her contract was canceled. Paranoia set in, and she began to fear she might be targeted as well.

In previous trips back to the United States, FBI agents—concerned about the work of American DarkMatter contractors—had stopped her at the border and asked detailed questions, which she refused to answer. There is a story that DarkMatter contractors had eavesdropped on Michelle Obama's communications during one of her trips to Qatar—a frequent target of UAE cyber espionage.[32] Had the rumor made its way back to US law enforcement, it would have triggered an official FBI investigation.

Previously uncooperative, Stroud now faced a different calculation after her dismissal from Project Raven. She had kept the card of one of the FBI agents and made contact, now as a whistleblower for the work she did while employed by the UAE. The information she provided led to criminal indictments against three Americans who also worked for DarkMatter. According to the US Department of Justice, "U.S. citizens, Marc Baier, 49, and Ryan Adams, 34, and a former U.S. citizen, Daniel Gericke, 40, all former employees of the U.S. Intelligence Community (USIC) or the U.S. military, entered into a deferred prosecution agreement (DPA) that restricts their future activities and employment and requires the payment of $1,685,000 in penalties to resolve a Department of Justice investigation regarding violations of U.S. export control, computer fraud and access device fraud laws."[33] Unlike Israel, which implicitly condones veterans of military intelligence units taking their learned skills with them for profit, the United States deems such work as unlawful.

While Stroud's cooperation with a law enforcement investigation was commendable, I am troubled that the tipping point for her was the targeting of Americans, rather than other members of civil society who were neither criminals nor terrorists. I could never justify the type of surveillance that these contractors were engaging in. The "last straw" for me would have been the moment I discovered they were targeting people like Donaghy or Mansoor.

———————

After relentless harassment, trolling, hacking, and other forms of intimidation, eventually the sheikhs had had enough with Mansoor. In 2017, he was arrested and sentenced to ten years in prison for "publicly insulting" the regime.[34] Mansoor's conditions in prison are sadistic.[35] He has gone on several hunger strikes to protest his solitary confinement, and he is allowed only infrequent visits from his legal team. It's a brutal epilogue to one of the most consequential of the Lab's investigations and a potent reminder of the human part of what can often be regarded as abstract technical detective work.

The UAE's offensive surveillance and espionage operations continued to expand and grow more sophisticated and refined. DarkMatter's offensive activities were eventually spun out into a complicated and opaque web of other firms associated with Sheikh Tahnoon's various conglomerates.[36] Since 2016, we have uncovered numerous other targets of the UAE's hacking, both inside the country and beyond—many of them people advocating for greater public accountability and democracy. The despots who run the regime face few obstacles buying up the most advanced war-fighting and repression technologies from a slew of companies and unleashing them on anyone they suspect. At the time of writing, leaked US intelligence documents reveal that American intelligence officials are concerned the UAE has plans to cooperate more closely with China on defense and intelligence matters; reporting by *Intelligence Online* has described Russian cyber operatives now working for Beacon Red (one of the successor companies to DarkMatter).[37] Both these revelations are a dark harbinger for the future.

The investigations into Donaghy and Mansoor led to another major series of case studies for the Citizen Lab. In August 2016, while searching for any mention of domains linked to NSO Group's attack infrastructure, we discovered a tweet by Mexican journalist Rafael Cabrera. He was part of a group of journalists investigating alleged corruption surrounding Mexican president Enrique Peña Nieto and the construction of a luxurious official residence funded by China. In August 2015, Cabrera received an unsolicited text from a purported Mexican news organization claiming that he and others involved in the investigation would soon face a defamation lawsuit. The real Mexican news organization then tweeted a reply to Cabrera saying it had nothing to do with the message he received. Our analysis showed the domain in the shortened link sent to Cabrera was one of those associated with NSO Group's infrastructure. Our network scanning of NSO-related domains revealed a plethora of seemingly Mexican-themed ones, some impersonating news organizations. We decided Mexico was worthy of further investigation. These leads would produce a series of jaw-dropping discoveries in Mexico and an ensuing scandal that would soon rock the country (chapter 11).

Sometimes seemingly small choices can end up having major unexpected consequences. Mansoor's decision to share his experiences with us is a case in point. While he has paid a steep personal price for his bravery in the face of injustice, the leads he sent our way opened a door into the corridors of a shadow world of covert operations.

– 4 –

Breakfast in Uzbekistan

MARCH 3, 2016

The engineers from the sales department arrived late at night and checked into the Radisson Blu in downtown Tashkent, Uzbekistan, the hotel favored by visiting foreigners and trade delegations. When they got to their room, they opened their demonstration laptop, which was infected with the latest version of Cyberbit's spyware, PC Surveillance System (PSS).

Cyberbit is a subsidiary of the massive Israeli defense giant Elbit Systems and was at the time one of many firms in the growing mercenary spyware marketplace.[1] Elbit acquired another Israeli surveillance contractor in 2015, NICE Systems, and carved out its offensive repertoire and called it Cyberbit Solutions: same hacking technology, different brand.[2] (A few years later, Elbit would reorganize Cyberbit and reorient its services to focus on purely "defensive" cybersecurity missions, but in 2016 it was eking out a niche in the offensive game.)[3] Like many surveillance companies, Cyberbit tried to keep a low profile: government clients don't want anyone to know they have spyware up their sleeves, let alone what they might do with it.

Trips like this one were part of the job. The salespeople did a dry run through their pitch that showed off how the spyware could scan through an infected laptop without the owner being aware, sift through the files, open encrypted emails, and scour through the photographs contained in the image directory. Satisfied, they shut the computer down and relaxed.

The next morning, the engineers checked their equipment one last time before they headed to their destination: the headquarters of the Uzbek National Security Service. In a world that is filled with acts of cruelty and repression, few can match the excesses of the autocratic Uzbekistan government and its secret services.[4] There is no tolerance for independent political opposition or criticism of the government. It's as though the country transitioned from the old Stalinist system into a kind of brutalist neo-medievalism where dictators build colossal statues glorifying their rule and boil dissidents to death (both of which in Uzbekistan are true). But the spyware vendors weren't concerned with that: they were here for one thing only—a sale.

The meeting with the Uzbek National Security Service was highly sensitive, and details about it are closely guarded secrets to all those who were in the room. But it's not hard to imagine what happened next.

The salespeople would have brought with them their demo laptop, to demonstrate how their covert spyware could take it over remotely. They showed off their slick control panel—an all-in-one interface through which commands could be sent to the infected device to gather information on the owner, including emails, photographs, and any other files of interest.

They likely fielded questions about whether their spyware was stealthy and avoided outside detection. I imagine them sliding over to their potential clients Cyberbit's glossy brochure that boasts how PSS "eliminates the possibility that the operation will be traced back to the origin."

But they were wrong about being undetectable—and they would soon find out why.

————

The entire time the Cyberbit salespeople were demonstrating their product, *we* were the ghosts peering over *their* shoulders. Despite the claims featured in their brochures, there is no invisibility cloak in the digital ecosystem. Everyone leaves a trace, even the most sophisticated purveyors of surveillance technology, provided one knows where to look. And we knew where to look.

Cyberbit's engineers had made a sloppy and easily preventable mistake, and an operational security error laid their highly sensitive operations bare. A directory on one of their command and control servers was not password protected. In that directory was a log file, regularly updated, that itemized the details of all the machines infected with their spyware: the who, what, and where of all their government clients' unsuspecting victims. Not even the log file was encrypted.

As with so many Citizen Lab investigations, this one had its roots in the experiences of its victims. In this case, it all began with Ethiopian journalists working for the Oromia Media Network—a diaspora media organization advocating for the rights of the oppressed Oromo ethnic minority in Ethiopia. The Oromo people, the largest ethnic group in the country, have endured a history of persecutions including land displacement, cultural marginalization, political oppression, human rights abuses, and even extrajudicial killings.[5] Oromo journalists had long suspected that the Ethiopian government was spying on them.[6] Spies seemed to lurk everywhere. Mysterious people often showed up taking photographs at demonstrations or meetings, and there were fears of undercover operatives penetrating their communities.

As the digital world became part of their daily routine, Oromo journalists received unsolicited emails that looked dubious. Some of them suspected their machines were hacked. The targeted Oromos reached out to us at the Lab for help in their investigations. Our analysis showed that their computers had indeed been hacked with at least two separate spyware products: FinFisher, marketed by UK-based Gamma Group, and the Remote Control System from Hacking Team, based in Milan, Italy.[7] A second wave of targeted digital attacks against the Oromia Media Network, shared again with the Citizen Lab for analysis, unveiled yet another mercenary spyware vendor employed by the Ethiopian intelligence agencies, Cyberbit, and provided us with a glimpse into its worldwide operations.[8]

Someone was likely watching those exchanges because, not long after the Oromo journalists shared their emails, our lead technical investigator, Bill Marczak, was targeted with the same spyware via an unsolicited email with an attachment sent his way. The spyware was disguised as an Adobe Flash update and communicated back to a series of command and control servers with distinct features. As soon as we scanned the internet looking for servers whose behavior matched these features, we rolled in positive finds.

The log file we accessed turned out to be a trove of information. We were able to meticulously analyze over a year's worth of Cyberbit's recorded activity. The logs provided minute details, down to the second, of every interaction involving each infected device compromised by Cyberbit's technology worldwide—the sales trip to Uzbekistan with the demo laptop included. Each entry in the file contained a unique identifier, known as a GUID, which was associated with a particular infection. It also indicated whether the entry recorded victim or operator activity, the IP address from which the infected device or operator connected to the spyware's server, and a time stamp indicating the time of communication. We regularly downloaded and analyzed this file for over a year, obtaining a total of 388 samples from the servers we detected during our scanning efforts. Overall, the log file consisted of more than thirty-two million entries, with twenty-eight million corresponding to operator interactions and the remainder representing victims. To verify its accuracy, we intentionally infected one of our own devices in a controlled environment with Cyberbit's PSS spyware and observed as our machine checked in, with the details recorded in the log file.

We had clear evidence from the log file that Cyberbit was aware of what its clients were doing with its hacking technology. When spyware firms are confronted with allegations that their government clients have been misusing their technology, most respond, like weapons dealers and firearms manufacturers, that they merely sell their products and have no idea or responsibility for how they are used. Some, like NSO Group, contradict this assertion when they claim they can also investigate allegations of their clients' abuses. With Cyberbit, we had proof that it not only knew precisely whom its clients were targeting but was carefully documenting and archiving the information too.

Thanks to Cyberbit's recordkeeping, we were able to track the movements of victims by correlating their IP addresses with other available information, such as universities or other institutions in which they were resident for long periods of time. This additional information was relatively easy to search for and obtain from the open net. For instance, we identified a hacked device that had traveled with its owner from Eritrea to the United Nations Office at Geneva, passing through Germany along the way. It appeared to belong to someone in the diplomatic corps. One device frequently connected from the University of Tsukuba in Japan and then appeared in Eritrea, while another that connected from York University in Canada also checked in from an IP address in Eritrea—likely two academics conducting field research. Based on these bits of information, it became relatively straightforward to conduct further open-source investigations and narrow down the victims' identities, allowing us to notify some of them. Understandably, most chose not to go public because of concerns for their safety.

Another sloppy mistake that allowed us to attribute the spyware in question, PSS, to Cyberbit was the use of "PSS" in a URL string of one of its own command and control servers. We also found some components of its spyware that contained a digital signature that pointed to an address in Tel Aviv and contained a reference to something called "C4 security." Elbit Systems, the parent company of Cyberbit, had acquired C4 Security in June 2011 for $10.9 million.[9] At the time, C4 described itself as "specializ[ing] in information warfare, SCADA and military C&C systems security."[10] According to one employee's LinkedIn page, C4 also developed a product called "PSS Surveillance System," billed as a "solution for intelligence and law enforcement agencies." That same PSS Surveillance System was now marketed by Cyberbit. More clues emerged: one of the servers had a domain name registered to a particular person—a certain Yevgeniy Gavrikov—who on his LinkedIn profile said he worked for Cyberbit as an "integration specialist."

The true treasure lay in the details recorded in the log file pertaining to the demonstration laptop infected with PSS—the one Cyberbit employees carried when traversing the globe to promote their products. Once we comprehended the significance of these data points, it became a straightforward task to pinpoint their travel destinations and, in some instances, identify their meetings with potential clients down to the minute. Regular activity during business hours originated from IP addresses that seemed to correspond with government clients. Off–business hours activity often coincided with connections to Wi-Fi networks in hotels or airports. Although some data provided limited information, in other cases we could use a lead, such as an IP address from the log file, to cross-reference public or leaked information, ultimately revealing the identity of the prospective client. LinkedIn has proven to be a gold mine for threat analysts because it often showcases job experiences, résumés, and endorsements shared by engineers and others on their profiles. Over the years, we have used such data, along with corresponding information, to identify specific vendors.

The data stolen from another mercenary spyware vendor, Italy's Hacking Team, and published on WikiLeaks in 2015 proved to be exceptionally valuable too.[11] It provided insights into potential customers who overlapped with those of other mercenary spyware firms that were Hacking Team's competitors. That duplication enabled us to cross-reference IP addresses found in the leaks with those in the log files to determine specific government agencies to which Cyberbit might be pitching. This level of visibility was extraordinary; it was as though we were traveling along with the salespeople as they hopscotched around the globe to meet with clients.

Sometimes we felt we were piecing together all the clues in an exhilarating puzzle, until we remembered the harsh reality behind it all—the specific spy agencies to which the vendors were peddling their invasive surveillance technology. Most of these prospective clients were masters of deceit, serial violators of human rights, and ruthless intelligence agencies. As the pieces came together and we realized what we were observing in near real time, I felt as though we had wandered into the pages of a spy novel, except this investigation wasn't a work of fiction. It was the real deal: a kind of geopolitical voyeurism.

The Uzbek hotel information was relatively simple for us to sort out, based on a subdomain associated with it—rdhotel.uz—which was registered to an individual listed on LinkedIn as the manager of the Radisson Blu hotel in Tashkent. We were able to connect other IPs accessed during daytime hours to the Uzbekistan National Security Service, thanks to leaked data from the Hacking Team breach.

There were many more countries on the sales tour. The Cyberbit salespeople gave a demonstration in Zambia, a country with a track record of systematic media suppression, police brutality, violence and intimidation against political opposition, and criminalization of same-sex relations. The demonstration we tracked was for the Zambia Financial Intelligence Centre. Information published a year later by *Intelligence Online* would corroborate that Cyberbit had done business with Zambia: Elbit "took some major orders from the country a year ago."[12] Zambia reportedly ordered $240 million worth of spyware services, backed up by a loan from Bank Hapoalim, an Israeli financial institution. Two years later, and as testimony to the type of unscrupulous institutions that get involved in private intelligence deals, Bank Hapoalim would find itself in the crosshairs of a US Department of Justice tax evasion and money laundering investigation.[13] The bank was eventually charged with stashing billions of dollars in thousands of secret Swiss and Israeli bank accounts and helping to launder money used for bribes and kickbacks to soccer officials as part of yet another FIFA World Cup corruption scandal.[14]

The traveling Cyberbit demo laptop made a stop at the Manila New World Makati Hotel in the Philippines, followed closely thereafter by a demonstration at the Malacañang Palace, then the primary residence and official office of Rodrigo Duterte, the president of the Philippines. Duterte was notorious for encouraging extrajudicial killings as part of his "war on drugs" and issuing threats against media organizations and their staff, including Nobel Prize–winning journalist Maria Ressa, a friend and colleague of mine.[15] With companies willing to sell highly sophisticated eavesdropping technology to people like him, it's clear why the term "mercenary" is so appropriate.

We observed a demonstration for the Royal Thai Army in Thailand, an agency accused of extrajudicial killings, torture, forced disappearances, and involvement in human smuggling.[16] There were also demonstrations to clients we could not specifically identify in Vietnam, Kazakhstan, Rwanda, Serbia, and Nigeria. Vietnam routinely arrests dissidents and bloggers for expressing their views online.[17] Kazakhstan has a history of using violence to disperse peaceful protests and has arrested journalists investigating high-level corruption.[18] Rwanda has been linked to the harassment and even murder of political opposition figures and regime critics, many of whom fled abroad for safety.[19] In Serbia, another potential customer, there are numerous reports of bribery, abuse of power, and collusion between criminal elements and individuals within the police and intelligence agencies.[20] Nigeria has been dogged by extensive documented instances of police brutality, harassment of political opposition, corruption, and unchecked surveillance of civil society.[21] It's almost as though Cyberbit was specifically targeting the dregs of governments worldwide as potential clients.

The sales force gave several demonstrations at military and surveillance trade shows: one in Prague at the infamous ISS World and another in Milipol in France. These kinds of trade shows, closed to the public, exhibit the latest surveillance and military gear to government agents: modified AR-15 air-powered GPS trackers, mobile cell-site simulators, and radar jamming equipment. All in all, it was quite the world tour for these Cyberbit staffers—and highly revealing for us as we went along for the ride.

————

The Cyberbit story, though the most dramatic and revealing, was not the first global sales profile we were able to exploit through unintentional leaks or digital traces. We had done the same with several other vendors over the years, using slightly different leads or starting points. Sometimes the command and control servers for a particular brand of spyware would behave in a distinct fashion, which we could then use as a "fingerprint" for internet-wide scanning. Basically, an analyst can automate the process of sending short queries to computers connected to the internet and then analyze the responses that match elements of the fingerprint. Network measurement tools can be run twenty-four hours a day, seven days a week for every single one of the billions of internet-connected devices on the planet. As batches of results come in and partial fingerprints are obtained, an analyst can zero in on the interesting results and subject them to further manual analysis.

There are even third-party databases, such as Censys or Shodan, that have developed automated systems to do this type of internet-wide scanning every day and then archive the results for later interrogation.[22] These systems allow an investigator to "go back in time" and analyze matches for fingerprints that may have been operational years ago.

Scanning for potential government clients and other significant details using these methods was one of the first tasks we set ourselves when we became aware of the mercenary spyware industry. As early as 2012, our team analyzed samples of the mobile malware tool kit called FinSpy, marketed by Gamma Group.[23] When we reverse engineered malware we had received from targets who reached out to us, we found a reference to the product "FinSpy" in the code, a developer's certificate listing the name Martin Muench, the CEO of the firm, and references to a person named Johnny Debs, who we discovered represented Gamma Group at the 2011 Milipol trade show in France. We then scanned the internet looking for servers that performed the "handshake" distinctive to the FinSpy command and control protocol, allowing us to identify FinFisher servers in several countries.

Ultimately, we successfully pinpointed Gamma Group's clients to Australia, Bahrain, Bangladesh, Brunei, Canada, the Czech Republic, Estonia, Ethiopia, Germany, India, Indonesia, Japan, Latvia, Malaysia, Mexico, Mongolia, the Netherlands, Qatar, Serbia, Singapore, Turkmenistan, the United Arab Emirates, the United Kingdom, the United States, and Vietnam. Although we couldn't identify the exact agency operating the spyware, just the country in which the spyware was being operated from, I can only imagine the shock among those customers when they read our report and recognized that their espionage tradecraft had now been at least partially compromised. Undoubtedly, Martin Muench received a deluge of complaints in response to our publication. Our exposure of the highly sensitive tradecraft used for espionage by more than two dozen state intelligence agencies in one single publication was truly unprecedented.

We also observed in this first case something that would become common later: firms would alter their infrastructure after reading our reports—introducing a kind of cat and mouse game to our investigations. When we published a preliminary set of findings on FinSpy listing what we believed were potential government clients, we observed Gamma Group changing its protocol, possibly to evade our analysis. But further interrogation of command and control servers would usually give us another distinctive signature to work from and we'd be back in business.

After the FinSpy work, we went on to perform a similar set of scans for government clients of the Italian mercenary spyware vendor Hacking Team, which marketed its spyware as being "stealthy and untraceable."[24] Hacking Team employed various techniques, including the use of proxy servers, to try to obscure its activities and make it more challenging to trace its operations. These proxies acted as intermediaries between Hacking Team's servers and the targeted devices, adding several layers of masking and making it difficult to track the ultimate operator of the spyware. Mexico's Hacking Team connections were laundered through servers in as many as four different countries. But these precautions proved to be futile. After we were done, we observed Azerbaijan, Colombia, Egypt, Ethiopia, Hungary, Italy, Kazakhstan, Malaysia, Mexico, Morocco, Nigeria, Oman, Panama, Poland, Saudi Arabia, South Korea, Sudan, Thailand, Turkey, the UAE, and Uzbekistan as all likely government customers of Hacking Team. It was another curtain-parting exposure of global spying in one fell swoop.

Hacking Team's principals responded to the press about our reports with what would become a familiar public refrain from mercenary spyware vendors: the Citizen Lab's methodologies were flawed, and Hacking Team's technology was strictly controlled to allow governments to investigate only serious matters of crime and terrorism.[25] In fact, no spyware vendor has ever produced any evidence of flaws with our methods. Later, when Hacking Team's data were hacked and its internal corporate communications were splayed all over WikiLeaks for the world to see, the UK-based NGO Privacy International analyzed the breached data and pronounced: "Citizen Lab was right."[26] Email after email from managers to sales officers showed Hacking Team had secured contracts in all the countries we had listed and had pitched to others as well.

There were some other nuggets of information in the roughly four hundred gigabytes of Hacking Team's proprietary corporate files.[27] Citizen Lab's senior legal researcher at the time, Sarah McKune, prudently advocated that we should send letters to firms before we published our reports about them. The letters would provide a high-level summary of our findings and then list a set of questions about the company's human rights policies and due diligence procedures—indeed, whether the company had any at all. We didn't expect a reply, but the process was a useful exercise to highlight the obvious lack of international regulation and corporate social responsibility practices in the sector.

Hacking Team's internal correspondence shows that my questions really annoyed the company's principals: "Prof. Deibert seems to think he is running a regulatory organization that has some authority over worldwide business," one complained. After publication of our reports, their emails would exhibit greater levels of frustration, such as the subject line in one series: "URGENT: Yet another Citizen Labs' [sic] attack."[28] We were ruining their claims about being "untraceable," and their clients were not happy about it. Business would evaporate unless they did something drastic. "I am wondering if there is a way to hit CL hard," wrote CEO David Vincenzetti, adding, "I would love having a few options."[29] They might well have pursued such an option had they not been subjected to the hack, which effectively killed their business. In 2020, Vincenzetti announced on LinkedIn that Hacking Team had folded, its principal assets sold to another vendor and eventually rebranded as Memento Labs.[30] Subsequently in 2023, Vincenzetti was arrested for attempted murder after a stabbing incident involving a cousin, which certainly provided, in hindsight, a new spin on his musings about whether it was possible to "hit CL hard."[31]

As an aside, the perpetrator of both the Hacking Team breach and an earlier hack of Gamma Group used the name Phineas Fisher. In an episode of the *Vice* series *Cyberwar*, called "Cyber Mercenaries," where the hacker appeared as a puppet, they were asked why they did it. "Well," they replied, "I just read the Citizen Lab reports on FinFisher and Hacking Team and thought that's fucked up. And I hacked them."[32]

———

Not all the internet scanning we did focused on spyware vendors. A Canadian internet filtering company called Netsweeper was often the focus of our work because we found its technology was being used by internet service providers (ISPs) in authoritarian or other dodgy country contexts to block web access to human rights and political opposition content that we believed was protected under international human rights conventions.[33] We also felt that citizens in those countries deserved to know what was being withheld from them. At one point, for example, we determined that Netsweeper offered a filtering category called "Alternative Lifestyles," in which it appeared that mostly legitimate LGBTQ+ content was targeted for blocking.[34] This category was selected in the UAE and was preventing internet users from accessing the websites of the Gay & Lesbian Alliance against Defamation and the International Foundation for Gender Education. Netsweeper eventually discontinued the "Alternative Lifestyles" category after one of our publications outed it.

In January 2016, after we published a report on the company's censorship system being used in Yemen in the midst of an armed conflict and in service of an ISP controlled by the Houthi rebels, Netsweeper filed a $3.5 million defamation lawsuit against both the University of Toronto and me.[35] We viewed it as a baseless charge, an attempt to intimidate us, but it meant hours of consultation with lawyers and preservation of relevant records. As we awaited litigation, we used the signatures we had developed to track down every instance of Netsweeper's installations we could find worldwide and prepared a report for eventual publication. Through a combination of internet scanning methods that searched for responses indicative of a Netsweeper installation and in-country tests to verify our findings, the team confirmed that Netsweeper's internet filtering systems were present in thirty countries worldwide. Among those, at least ten—Afghanistan, Bahrain, India, Kuwait, Pakistan, Qatar, Somalia, Sudan, the UAE, and Yemen—were countries with troublesome human rights and other problems. We couldn't publish anything until the lawsuit was resolved, so we bided our time and filled in as many details as possible.

Timing didn't work out well for Netsweeper. Shortly before it filed the lawsuit, on November 3, 2015, the Ontario government passed a new law called the Protection of Public Participation Act.[36] It was designed to mitigate against "strategic litigation against public participation," or SLAPP suits, of the precise sort that Netsweeper launched against us. When Netsweeper subsequently withdrew its lawsuit, we published our latest findings, *Planet Netsweeper*.

We also conducted various scanning projects to monitor the activities of an American company known as Blue Coat.[37] It specializes in deep packet inspection (DPI) technology, which enables filtering, monitoring, and tracking of network traffic by examining data packets. DPI is a network device that operates like a tap placed strategically at crucial network choke points—typically on the premises of a major ISP or internet exchange point—where it gathers substantial actionable intelligence about communication patterns, machine addresses, and protocols used as data traverses across the network. This information allows for the identification and restriction of specific applications, effectively controlling their usage by slowing them down or turning them off completely. While DPI is a standard practice for telecommunications, it can also be employed to subject users within a country to extensive surveillance and information control measures.

We first identified Blue Coat devices in Syria and some in Myanmar, which caused some regulatory blowback to the firm because Syria was under US sanctions at the time, and Myanmar was in the midst of political turmoil and domestic repression.[38] Once we had identified the signatures for Blue Coat devices, we undertook internet scanning and other network measurement techniques to identify countries in which these products were operational. As in other case studies, we came up with a long list of problematic countries with poor human rights records or other political problems that had access to Blue Coat's systems.

Another DPI vendor whose technology we identified being abused in government surveillance was Sandvine (which ultimately merged with a US-based company known as Procera Networks), based in Waterloo, Canada.[39] Through internet scanning, we located Sandvine's "PacketLogic" middleboxes on Türk Telekom's network. The middleboxes—network appliances that are located between the source and destination in a network infrastructure— were being used to inject malware onto the computers of unwitting users in Turkey and Syria when those users attempted to download certain legitimate Windows applications. Bizarrely, we also discovered that the same PacketLogic devices were configured by ISP operators in Egypt to commandeer unwitting internet users' traffic there but not to spy on them. Instead, user requests were being manipulated to covertly raise money through online ads and cryptocurrency mining scams. Both took place through a technique known as "network injection," in which Sandvine's middleboxes were used to intercept unencrypted requests for web content and then redirect that traffic elsewhere or covertly return malicious software instead.

In this case, our network scanning was aided by having access to a secondhand Sandvine-Procera middlebox that we purchased from eBay. The PacketLogic box even had the default credentials still taped to the top, allowing us to interrogate how it functioned and develop signatures we could use to scan for and identify the middleboxes at key internet chokepoints. On February 12, 2018, before we published our findings, we sent letters to Sandvine and its owner, Francisco Partners (which also owned NSO Group at the time), summarizing our report and asking detailed questions about their corporate social responsibility practices. A few days later, Sandvine's legal counsel replied, characterizing the statements in our letter as "false, misleading, and wrong," demanding that we return the secondhand device we used to confirm attribution of our fingerprint, and threatening litigation if we did not. The University of Toronto responded to the demands with a letter from legal counsel saying that the firm's "recent correspondence impugns the integrity and conduct of Citizen Lab, Mr. Deibert, and the University of Toronto, without any factual foundation whatsoever."[40] We went ahead with our publication and kept the secondhand device.

In 2023, we discovered the same type of Sandvine-Procera middlebox still being used in Egypt, this time as part of a scheme to try to inject a type of spyware called Predator, manufactured by another mercenary vendor, Cytrox, into the phone of then presidential candidate and opposition politician Ahmed Eltantawy.[41] Sandvine's equipment was used to isolate Eltantawy's internet traffic and redirect his website requests to one that was loaded with Predator spyware. Working with Google's Threat Analysis Group and with Eltantawy's consent, we monitored his network traffic and captured copies of Predator's exploit chain and the first stage of its spyware, which we determined included three separate Apple zero days. Our responsible disclosure to Apple about those zero days resulted in yet another emergency security patch issued to Apple's billions of customers and another mercenary spyware vendor momentarily disarmed.[42] Following the publication of our report, the US Department of Commerce sanctioned Sandvine for "enabling human rights abuses."[43]

One of the most interesting scanning projects focused on the surveillance vendor Circles, which was acquired in 2014 by private equity firm Francisco Partners, which merged it with NSO Group for a time.[44] Circles is known for selling services to government security agencies to exploit Signaling System Number 7 (SS7)—a protocol developed in 1975 to handle interoperability among telecommunications firms. In the '70s, before the deregulation and privatization measures that swept through the global industry, the telecommunications marketplace was very different—more like an old boys' club (although in many respects it still is).[45] There were far fewer firms, and most of them were state-owned, crown corporations, or utility-like monopolies. The UK industry, for example, was entirely state-run and was called, quaintly, Post Office Communications.

Ironically, SS7 was rolled out to solve a preexisting flaw in telecommunications protocols that was being exploited by "phone phreaks" using "blue boxes" (instructions for which were shared in hobbyist magazines) to hack their way into free long-distance phone calls.[46] A young Steve Wozniak, cofounder of Apple, infamously used one to phone the Vatican and, posing as Henry Kissinger, asked to speak to the pope.[47]

To solve this problem (and protect revenue), the SS7 protocol was developed and has remained in place ever since, principally because a lot of older equipment and systems are still in use and require some means to function properly. SS7 is predominantly used in 2G and 3G mobile networks, and even later-generation 4G and 5G networks are susceptible to security issues because they need to interconnect with SS7 networks to work for everyone.[48] One of its central functions today is to handle billing and other services as subscribers roam from one network to another when they travel internationally.[49] When travelers land in another country, they receive an SMS notice on their mobile phone informing them of the foreign network on which they are now roaming and the charges they'll be billed. That's SS7 at work.

The SS7 protocol's "authentication" has relied mostly on trust among a small group of insiders. But as the global telecommunications market rapidly diversified and numerous companies entered the arena, SS7 has become ripe for exploitation. Access to the SS7 network can allow a malicious actor to track virtually any target's location and even intercept voice calls and text messages.

Although high-end state intelligence agencies have been quietly benefiting from SS7's weaknesses for a long time, privatization and deregulation have opened the door to a whole new array of entrants into the club, including criminals and cyber-surveillance firms—one of which is Circles.

Circles's operations are difficult to investigate and track. Unlike some other types of targeted surveillance, exploiting SS7 does not leave traces on a target's device for investigators like us to discover. Before our search, the little that was known about Circles came from leaked documents or investigative reporting on a few country clients, such as Nigeria.[50] Marczak discovered, however, that Circles's installations on customers' premises left a distinguishing fingerprint associated with the Check Point firewall that it employs. With that fingerprint as our starting point, we used internet scanning methods and gathered data from various sources and feeds to identify specific country clients. In total, we were able to determine that twenty-five governments and seventeen specific government agencies were likely Circles's customers.

Among those clients was the Internal Security Operations Command of the Royal Thai Army—a unit that has been found to be involved in torture.[51] Another client was the Investigations Police (PDI) of Chile, which has a checkered history around extralegal surveillance against journalists and political opposition. We identified a single Circles system in Guatemala that appeared to be operated by the General Directorate of Civil Intelligence (DIGICI). It has used surveillance equipment to conduct illegal shadowing of journalists, businesspeople, and political opponents of the government.

We identified ten Circles deployments in Mexico—a major concern because the Citizen Lab's research had shown that Mexico's government serially abuses NSO Group's Pegasus spyware to target reporters, human rights defenders, and the families of individuals who had been killed and disappeared by cartels.[52] We also identified a Circles installation in Nigeria that was likely operated by the country's Defence Intelligence Agency. A recent report by Front Line Defenders concluded that Nigeria's government "has conducted mass surveillance of citizens' telecommunications."[53] Our scanning identified what appear to be three active clients in the UAE: the UAE Supreme Council on National Security, the Dubai Government, and a client who may be linked to both Sheikh Tahnoon bin Zayed al-Nahyan's Royal Group and former Fatah strongman Mohammed Dahlan.

Circles's technology, just like NSO Group's Pegasus spyware or other mercenary spyware, can be deployed against targets both domestic and abroad. In other words, the international reach afforded by Circles's services allows despots and autocrats to silently target political opponents who may have gone into exile in foreign jurisdictions. Some of the government clients we identified have been suspected of organizing extraterritorial targeted killings of dissidents and political opposition figures.

Our worldwide mapping exercises produced evidence of what most of us in the arena already long suspected: a burgeoning industry of internet censorship, surveillance, and targeted espionage service providers was putting powerful tools in the hands of government officials or telecommunications companies operating in their jurisdictions that were used to monitor customers, citizens, and foreigners alike. Countries that lack in-house math, science, and engineering expertise can now simply purchase sophisticated information control systems off the shelf. As our investigation showed, in Ethiopia, one of the poorest countries in the world with less than 15 percent internet connectivity, buyers can, with Cyberbit, mount a global cyber espionage campaign targeting individuals in at least twenty countries worldwide.[54]

The other, more frightening takeaway from this scanning was the prospect for uncontrolled proliferation. By our reckoning, over the period that we had visibility, Cyberbit had demonstrated its spyware to at least a dozen countries and at two major military trade shows in nearly every region of the world. Our research exposed numerous other firms selling to a wide cross-section of dictators and illiberal regimes. What was being revealed here was a highly disturbing nexus: a lucrative industry with almost no regulatory limits, operating in the shadows and blanketed with layers of official secrecy involving highly dubious and, in some cases, morally depraved human beings. We started to get a sense of the scope and scale of the industry's excesses, but also its obvious lack of regard for any human rights considerations. It became crystal clear that this was a serious problem, that it was spreading fast, and that the number of unsuspecting innocent victims would likely be astronomical.

———

Typically, the Lab's workflow would begin with a tip from a victim suspicious of some kind of unsolicited email or SMS message they received. Our analysis of any malware sent their way might allow us to map out a surveillance company's wider infrastructure of command and control servers. In other situations, we might be able to capitalize on an operational mistake made by the vendors or their clients to map their operations and, occasionally, identify unsuspecting victims whose devices had been infected in real time. Marczak's use of an obscure network measurement method called "DNS cache probing" to analyze NSO Group's operations is but one example. For years, security researchers and practitioners in the field of network analysis and cybersecurity have used DNS cache probing. Marczak recognized he could use this technique to help identify who might be hacked in real time with Pegasus spyware anywhere in the world.

To understand how Marczak made this ingenious discovery, we first must understand the domain name system (DNS). Whenever you visit a website, either by clicking on a link or by entering a domain into your browser, your computer needs to find out where that website is located on the internet. DNS is like the internet's phone book. It translates human-friendly website addresses (www.nytimes.com, for example) into machine-friendly IP addresses (such as 151.101.193.164). To speed up future requests, DNS servers store recently accessed translations in their memory.

DNS cache probing checks the contents of a DNS server by sending specific requests to the DNS server for the IP addresses of various websites. A researcher can then analyze the responses and determine which websites are cached in the DNS server's memory. Marczak developed an ethically responsible variation of the method to search for IP addresses of Pegasus victims in different countries. When Pegasus infects a device, it needs to communicate with its command and control servers to receive instructions and transmit the collected data. By analyzing the responses from the DNS servers, Marczak could determine if the servers had cached the IP addresses associated with the suspected Pegasus server domain names. Using this technique meant we could map potential Pegasus infections globally—an extraordinary discovery.

Over the course of two years of scanning using these methods, we identified forty-five countries where NSO Group's government clients were conducting ongoing surveillance operations. We then organized those ongoing Pegasus hacking operations into thirty-six different operator groups—the government agencies or clients that were responsible for the hacking. Marczak gave each operator a code name drawn from national symbols or geographic features of the country, such as "Kingdom" for Saudi Arabia or "Atlas" for Morocco. Of those thirty-six, we found that most were engaged in domestic surveillance operations, with ten conducting cross-border surveillance.

For the first time ever, we identified operator groups in Europe, such as Operator Orzelbialy (Polish for "white eagle"), which we attributed primarily to Poland. That finding foreshadowed a series of major Pegasus scandals in that country a few years later (chapter 17).[55]

We identified five operators focusing on Africa, including one that was hacking devices primarily in the West African country of Togo, an authoritarian regime that routinely employed torture and excessive force against peaceful opposition and was also a long-standing ally of Israel. The mapping also showed a significant increase in Pegasus activity in the Gulf region, with operations in Bahrain, the United Arab Emirates, and Saudi Arabia, ten of which were engaged in cross-border surveillance.

Finally, in 2018, we published our report, *Hide and Seek*, which included a world map showing the forty-five countries in which government spies using NSO Group's technology were engaged in ongoing hacking activities.[56] It marked a breakthrough achievement for the Lab.

As we prepared the report for publication, I couldn't help but notice that the Saudi operator, code-named Kingdom, was spying on an unwitting victim in Canada—our own backyard. It was a lead we were not going to pass up.

"Trust Me, I Am the One"

JUNE 2018

Omar Abdulaziz had just put the final touches on his latest You-Tube show heaping scorn on the Saudi regime and its ruler-in-waiting, Crown Prince Mohammed bin Salman (MBS, as he's widely known).[1] As he prepared to leave for the athletic facility at Bishop's University in Sherbrooke, Quebec, where he was enrolled, he realized his protein powder supply was running low. A fitness enthusiast, he followed a meticulous workout routine. He reopened his laptop, placed an order, and departed.

Abdulaziz had arrived in Canada in 2009 to study English and later made the choice to pursue a bachelor's degree at McGill University in Montreal.[2] Canada presented a stark contrast to Saudi Arabia. The winter weather was cold, with snowfall unlike anything Abdulaziz had ever encountered. However, in Quebec he felt a sense of safety: it offered a refuge from tyrants, or so he believed.

Like many individuals of his generation and background, 2011 marked a significant turning point in Abdulaziz's life as he witnessed the eruption of the Arab Spring in the Middle East and North Africa. Inspired by these events, he took to social media and specifically Twitter to engage in political discussions and advocate for democracy and accountability. Connecting with a community online, he swiftly gained a substantial following. Over time, his posts grew progressively bolder and more outspoken.

Saudi authorities soon took notice. In 2013, they pulled his scholarship as punishment for what they saw as insubordination.[3]

"I was vocal. I started to criticise the regime, the royal family . . . they weren't happy with my activities," he said. "They left me with no option."[4]

As the likelihood of safely returning to Saudi Arabia diminished, Abdulaziz made the decision to seek political asylum in Canada, which was granted in February 2014. Armed with Canadian permanent residency status, he launched a YouTube program that showcased his sarcastic wit and unapologetic critiques of the Saudi royal family—a DIY version of *The Colbert Report* for the Arab world—sometimes referring to MBS as "a dangerous guy."

By the summer of 2018, Abdulaziz's sense of security was gradually unraveling. Earlier that year, he received a phone call from someone who claimed to work for MBS in Saudi Arabia, urging him to return home with promises of favorable treatment.[5] Abdulaziz declined the offer. A few weeks later, in May, Saudi agents traveled to Canada to persuade him to come back.[6] To taunt him with their power to inflict arbitrary harm, they brought his brother Ahmed along. They said they worked for Saud al-Qahtani, one of the crown prince's key national security henchmen, who would later gain notoriety as a principal architect behind the October 2018 execution of *Washington Post* columnist Jamal Khashoggi.[7] "He's our mentor," Abdulaziz recalls them saying. The men told Abdulaziz that MBS liked him and wanted him back in Saudi Arabia. They promised they would support a new online show there and help him become "the voice of youth." They told him to go to the Saudi embassy in Ottawa to renew his passport. Abdulaziz refused.

Abdulaziz was aware that, under MBS's rising power, Saudi intelligence operatives were organizing harassment and kidnappings of dissidents abroad.[8] Although he had no way of knowing it at the time, in July 2018 MBS had issued a "bring him back" order to his operatives in the Rapid Intervention Force about Khashoggi. Similar orders were given regarding other prominent Saudi dissidents, and some were forcibly returned to Saudi Arabia, where they were held captive, questioned, and tortured in palaces in the desert. It is safe to assume that Abdulaziz was on that list too.

Not long after Abdulaziz ordered the protein powder, a text

message arrived on his cellphone. It was a DHL notification for a link to track a package. "I clicked on it," he says, "and didn't think much more about it."

At the instant he clicked on the link, a sequence of instructions traversed back and forth across the internet. Custom exploits pried their way into his iPhone's operating system. Acting as a wedge, they opened a door that allowed NSO Group's Pegasus spyware to be instantly loaded onto his device, leaving no visible trace of tampering. Unaware, Abdulaziz slipped the iPhone into his jacket pocket and headed to the gym. As he settled into his weight routine, his data seamlessly streamed back across the internet, traveling through a series of server relays until it ultimately landed with Saudi intelligence. He was then subjected to the ultimate form of electronic surveillance: all his photos, emails, and texts; the ambient sound picked up by his device's microphone; and his precise location were all being vacuumed up by Saudi security agents. Only later that fall would the gruesome consequences of the hack become apparent for Abdulaziz and the world to witness.

———

Around the same time, Citizen Lab's senior researcher Bill Marczak was running a series of ingenious tests to track the infrastructure of NSO Group's customers and the hacking operations undertaken with its spyware. His DNS (domain name system) cache probes allowed us to map the IP (internet protocol) addresses of infected devices as they "checked in" with Pegasus command and control servers, and another method allowed us to group the government operators into clusters.

Our visibility into NSO Group's client base that summer was stunning but incomplete. We could observe devices being hacked with Pegasus by dozens of security agencies all over the world but had no idea who the victims were. All we had was an IP address and a time stamp, and without further contextual information, they would lead nowhere.

The Saudi operator group, which we code-named Kingdom, stood out in the cluster of clients. We noticed that among the devices hacked by the Saudi regime was one located in Quebec connecting from two different ISPs (internet service providers) at relatively consistent intervals: a consumer ISP called Vidéotron and an academic ISP used by universities across Quebec called RISQ (Réseau d'informations scientifiques du Québec).

This lead was intriguing, especially at this time. Throughout the summer of 2018, Canada and Saudi Arabia were embroiled in a full-blown diplomatic dispute.[9] In August, Chrystia Freeland, Canada's foreign affairs minister, criticized the Saudi regime's civil rights record following the arrest of Samar Badawi, sister of Raif Badawi, a Saudi activist and writer whose family lives in Canada.[10] Raif had been imprisoned and subjected multiple times since 2012 to torture and lashings in Saudi Arabia for "insulting Islam through electronic channels." The official Twitter (now X) account of Canada's foreign ministry also weighed in on social media, calling on Saudi Arabia "to immediately release them [Samar and Raif Badawi] and all other peaceful #humanrights activists."[11]

In retaliation, the Saudis expelled the Canadian ambassador, reduced the number of student scholarships to Canada, and posted a series of hostile tweets lambasting Canada.[12] Saudi Arabia's minister of foreign affairs issued a number of tweets of his own, saying Canada's charges were "utterly incorrect" and constituted "interfer[ence] in the internal affairs of the Kingdom."[13] Canada's actions, he said, meant that "we are allowed to interfere in Canada's internal affairs"— a sinister threat, considering what we would uncover later.[14]

Another tweet, posted by a pro-Saudi account, depicted a passenger jet diving into the CN Tower and captioned, "He who interferes with what doesn't concern him finds what doesn't please him."[15] It was shocking to see a Saudi-aligned entity using such a meme, given allegations that the Saudis may have provided material support to al-Qaeda operatives who carried out the 9/11 terror attacks on the United States.[16]

"What can we say about whoever the Saudis are spying on in Canada?" I asked Marczak.

"Not much," he replied. "We have an IP address and some time stamps, and it's coming from two ISPs in the Sherbrooke region."

"How about doing a field trip to try and track this person down?" I asked Marczak. I didn't have to ask twice.

This mission was unprecedented for us. Never had we attempted to identify an individual based on such limited information and to cross-check whether their phone had been hacked. An IP address can be linked to general information about the geographic location and ISP associated with the address, but connecting it to a specific individual is much more challenging. Law enforcement agencies with a court order or subpoena can acquire additional information about a user behind an IP address, but this process requires collaboration between authorities and ISPs and is subject to legal procedures and privacy protections that are beyond our mandate.

Given the ISPs we knew the infected device was connected to, we hypothesized that this person was either a faculty member or a student living in the Montreal area. We assumed the target would be of interest to the Saudi regime and speculated it was likely a dissident. Thousands of Saudis have chosen Canada as a destination for school, work, or resettlement, and some of them are outspoken about the regime, including the exiled Saad al-Jabri, the former chief of Saudi intelligence who, after falling out with MBS, now lives in Toronto.[17] We checked through our network of contacts and drew up a short list before Marczak flew to Montreal to start knocking on doors.

When Marczak met these potential subjects, he inquired about their pattern of life and then, with their explicit consent, searched through their SMS history to see if they had received any texts that matched known Pegasus domains. After a few negative results, he got to Abdulaziz, who had never heard of the Citizen Lab. Fortunately, we had an overlapping point of contact in Yahya Assiri, a Saudi activist based in the United Kingdom who had previously been targeted with an SMS message laden with a Pegasus exploit link.[18] We had recently copublished a report with Amnesty International about this incident. Assiri and Abdulaziz were in regular contact, and Assiri assured Abdulaziz he could trust us.

When Marczak met Abdulaziz, he explained that we believed someone in Quebec had been hacked by the Saudis and were searching for the victim. Abdulaziz replied without any hesitation,

"I am the one." Marczak laughed at Abdulaziz's self-confidence: "Okay, but things don't work like that. We have to check first."

Marczak's outreach seemed to answer a puzzle for Abdulaziz. The Saudis had arrested several of his friends and his brothers in Saudi Arabia, and, he said, "they seemed to know everything that was going on with me." He had no idea that the Saudis might have access to his phone. When Marczak explained his mission, everything suddenly came into focus for Abdulaziz. *Of course*, he thought, *my phone has been hacked!*

Marczak asked Abdulaziz to explain his daily routine. He worked from home during the day and went to Bishop's University's athletic facility in the evening. These details matched our DNS cache probing results perfectly. "Can I search your SMS messages?" Marczak asked. Abdulaziz handed over his phone. Boom, we had another match: a fake DHL courier notification that included a domain, sunday-deals.com, which we attributed to NSO Group's infrastructure and the Kingdom operator. It was rock-solid confirmation Abdulaziz had received an SMS with an exploit link earlier that summer. We had found our needle in the haystack.

———

Citizen Lab reports follow a typical trajectory, starting from initial discoveries and culminating in a published report on our website. Multiple team members contribute to different sections of the report, which then undergoes various types of peer review. As it nears completion, we usually provide embargoed copies to carefully selected and trusted journalists, in the hope they will write more detailed stories about the cases, ask questions of stakeholders in ways we cannot or won't, and help raise awareness with the general public. In this instance, we anticipated that journalists would reach out to NSO Group as well as the Saudi and the Canadian governments for comments.

At this point, knowledge of our investigation is out of our hands, and all sorts of unexpected outreach may follow. Sometimes this interlude can be stressful, as opposing parties may try to engage with us in unwelcome ways, intervene to alter what we publish, or even neutralize the publication. The days leading up to the publication of our Kingdom report were especially pressured.

As a courtesy, when we gave journalists embargoed copies of the report, I also alerted two individuals in the Canadian government: one at the Privy Council Office and the other at Global Affairs Canada (our foreign affairs department). I told them only that a major report was forthcoming and that it pertained to espionage we had uncovered by a foreign government, likely Saudi Arabia, on a victim residing in Canada.

As the publication date drew near, I left for a prearranged conference on cybersecurity in The Hague, where I was scheduled to speak about the Lab's investigations into targeted threats against civil society. The Dutch Ministry of Justice and Security, the top law enforcement body in the Netherlands, had sponsored this event, and among the attendees were law enforcement and intelligence agency officials from numerous countries, including from the Gulf and the Middle East. I knew that many of these agencies might already have heard rumors of our forthcoming publication. Our *Hide and Seek* report, published only a few months earlier, had outed the Netherlands itself as a likely government operator of Pegasus spyware. Perhaps the individuals responsible for that procurement were at this conference and resented what we were doing—or at least wanted to find out how much more we knew about their intelligence operations. Because my participation was widely advertised in the program, I felt very conspicuous and kept a low profile until I delivered my talk. I then left The Hague as soon as possible for the University of St. Gallen in Switzerland, where I was invited to lead a research seminar.

Almost immediately, my phone started ringing and filling up with voicemails. It was the Royal Canadian Mounted Police (RCMP). Tipped off by journalists that we had a report coming out that detailed a Saudi espionage operation in Canada, the RCMP was apparently eager to find out more. I returned the call of an officer working in a Quebec detachment.

"Hello, Dr. *Diebert*," he said in strong French-Canadianaccented English, mispronouncing my last name. "I am looking at a very interesting report," he began, reading the title slowly. *"Hide and Seek: Tracking NSO Group's Pegasus Spyware to—"*

"Yes, I'm well aware of that report," I interrupted. "I am the director of the Lab that published it and one of the authors."

"Ah, yes," he replied. "We are aware you have some further information about Saudi espionage in Canada. Can you please tell me the name of the person that is being spied on?"

"I'm sorry, I cannot tell you that."

"Why not?"

"Because our research ethics protocols forbid us from naming the subjects of our research to anyone without their explicit consent."

"Where are you? Are you in Toronto?"

That question made me pause and took the conversation in a more serious direction. I am guarded when speaking to government officials about anything related to our work, but this query made me especially so.

"That's none of your business," I replied. I got the distinct feeling he already knew I was out of the country, possibly because of my talk at the conference. I told him he could read the report when it was published just like everyone else.

My intransigence really frustrated him. Over the next few days, he and other RCMP officers left several voicemails asking more questions about the victim and the forthcoming report, but I didn't believe it was necessary to respond any further.

On September 28, 2018, four days before our report was due to be published, Canada's Centre for Cyber Security and its Computer Incident Response Team also reached out by email, asking for information on the victim. I replied in writing:

Under the Research Ethics protocol for this study, we are not permitted to disclose the identity of research subjects without their permission. We will be publishing a report on this topic early next week, and the subject may choose at that time to speak to relevant authorities.

A few years later, an access to information request I filed with the Canadian government revealed the scramble in government circles over the forthcoming report once journalists reached out for comment. "RCMP will have comms lines ready saying that they are investigating," read an email circulated across several departments. Another exchange explains that "RCMP is having an investigator contact the Citizen Lab . . . that will allow them to say they are investigating when the story breaks on Monday."

One document noted that Canadian officials would "inform Saudi officials of the publication of the report," followed by a set of talking points to be used, including that "Citizen's Report [*sic*] has an excellent reputation with both Canadian and international media and its allegations are likely to generate significant media attention." A large section of this exchange is redacted, suggesting that some particularly sensitive information was being relayed to the Saudi government related to our report that the Canadian government didn't want to share with the public.

I was struck by how many of the emails were about talking points and crisis communications, and none whatsoever about the spying itself. Not one of the exchanges I received in my access to information request expressed alarm or indignation that Saudi Arabia was spying on a Canadian permanent resident. It was as if that part was ignored altogether.

On October 1, 2018, the report went live on our website, and the news stories followed all over the world. Then, suddenly, everything changed. "Jamal has gone missing, and I'm very afraid," Abdulaziz wrote to me in a WhatsApp text that day. I turned on CNN and watched the mystery that was unfolding at the Saudi consulate in Turkey.

––––––––––

At the very moment I received Abdulaziz's text, nearly three thousand kilometers away in Istanbul, Jamal Khashoggi was being sedated, strangled to death, and dismembered by his executioners.[19] The story has been so well documented now that the gruesome details are imprinted on the mind of everyone who paid attention.

But few had such a real-time, one-degree-of-separation experience of the episode as we did.

Earlier that day, Khashoggi had arranged to visit the consulate to collect documents he needed for his upcoming marriage to his fiancée, Hatice Cengiz. Closed-circuit television footage shows him entering the consulate—the last images of him alive. Waiting for him behind those doors were fifteen Saudi intelligence agents—a kill squad—who had been assembled and flown into Turkey from Saudi Arabia on private jets for the premeditated murder. Turkish intelligence had managed to wiretap the Saudi consulate, and portions of recordings of the macabre scene were shared with UN investigators and other government officials. They revealed that Khashoggi was confused by the ambush, struggled with the assailants as they grabbed hold of him, and pleaded for his life. "I can't breathe," he gasped repeatedly—his final words.[20]

One of the Saudi agents—Salah Muhammed al-Tubaigy, the "head of forensic evidence in the Saudi general security department"—then put on a pair of headphones and advised others around him to do the same. "When I do this job, I listen to music. You should do [that] too," he said with ghoulish nonchalance, before systematically dismembering Khashoggi's body with a bone saw.[21]

According to the timelines published by the UN's special investigation, at the precise moment I received Abdulaziz's text, Khashoggi's body parts were likely being secretly transported in plastic bags and suitcases to the Saudi consul general's Istanbul residence to be disposed of. Images from security cameras show that one of the Saudi operatives left through the back door of the consulate dressed in Khashoggi's clothes, possibly as some kind of deception. The ruse didn't work because the man's face was clearly visible on numerous security cameras.[22] I don't think MBS really cared whether the operation was exposed. Part of the rationale may have been to advertise the lengths the kingdom would go to silence critics. MBS rightly calculated there would be no real consequences: only a few weeks later, he was photographed high-fiving Putin and shaking hands with other world leaders at the G20 summit.[23]

Outside the front of the consulate stood Khashoggi's fiancée, Cengiz, holding his phones for safekeeping and looking increasingly desperate. Abdulaziz texted us a picture of her at this time and circled her hands holding the devices. "You guys should check these too!" We wish. Unfortunately, she turned Khashoggi's devices over to Turkish authorities, where presumably they remain to this day.

All this information was coming in fast, and I was trying to piece together one event (Abdulaziz's hacking, as we had just announced) and Khashoggi's disappearance (the top story in world news). I didn't realize until October 2 that Abdulaziz and Khashoggi had been close confidants. They communicated regularly in the months and days leading up to his execution and had developed a close bond: "He was missing his kids and I was missing my parents, so that's why we built this kind of relationship, like between a son and father," Abdulaziz said later.[24] Only after Khashoggi went missing did I and the rest of the world get the full picture.

––––––––

Khashoggi and Abdulaziz shared a common cause regarding their home country. Both were concerned about the bold steps the regime was taking to silence Saudi activists and journalists as MBS gained power. They took note of the scores of trolls and others who would harass and overwhelm online discussions related to Saudi Arabia, including when one of Khashoggi's columns was published.

A key figure behind these operations was Saudi Arabia's chief of digital repression, Saud al-Qahtani. According to the *New York Times*'s Ben Hubbard, MBS "deputized him to build an arsenal of new electronic weapons."[25] Archives of obscure cybercrime forums show that al-Qahtani, writing under pseudonyms and sometimes admitting to being intoxicated, had been acquiring the latest spyware, hacking tools, and credential-stealing techniques for years. It's a fair assumption that he was also involved in some way with the Pegasus deal in Saudi Arabia, given his prominent role as MBS's special wizard of digital darkness.

Al-Qahtani was also behind Saudi Arabia's sophisticated and aggressive counter–social media campaign. In authoritarian jurisdictions like Saudi Arabia, access to websites and social media is routinely censored by authorities. But these measures are easily circumvented and do little to affect access to information among the Saudi diaspora abroad, for whom Twitter (now X) and other platforms have become a kind of "public sphere." Rather than relying exclusively on internet censorship, al-Qahtani went on the offensive, choosing to flood social media with artificial accounts and paid trolls. Influential Saudi account holders were bribed or extorted to push hashtags and narratives favorable to the regime while bombarding opposing views with intimidating threats and insults. Saudi dissidents and opposition figures referred to these pro-regime tweeters as "flies," while al-Qahtani was given the nickname the "Lord of the Flies."[26]

Al-Qahtani enlisted the consulting firm McKinsey & Company to prepare an internal brief aimed at identifying key social media "influencers."[27] The underlying purpose was likely to assist in prioritizing targets for his cyberwar against the opposition. He covertly infiltrated Twitter by employing several Saudi-born, Silicon Valley–based engineers to acquire confidential user data, including real names, private direct messages, geolocations, and IP addresses. Among the individuals targeted in the Twitter infiltration operation was Abdulaziz.[28]

Al-Qahtani subsequently engaged the services of a Saudi public relations company, Smaat, which has close ties to Saudi security services.[29] Smaat's objective was to inundate Twitter and other social media platforms with pro-regime narratives. In December 2019, Twitter suspended eighty-eight thousand accounts associated with Smaat for engaging in "platform manipulation" to support Saudi-backed information operations.[30] The contextual information from McKinsey, combined with the data illicitly acquired from Twitter, enabled al-Qahtani and his associates to target their spyware to silently monitor the activities of Abdulaziz and Khashoggi as they devised plans to mobilize opposition against MBS and the Saudi regime.

Khashoggi and Abdulaziz wanted to enlist a large number of Saudi activists to counter al-Qahtani's flies, whom they referred to as their swarm of "bees." They planned to distribute untraceable US and Canadian SIM cards to collaborators around the world who would combat the Saudi propagandists online. Khashoggi financed the cards, reimbursing Abdulaziz for his expenses. That act may have been his ultimate undoing, however—crossing the line from journalist to activist and political opposition organizer. In the eyes of the Saudi despots, such plans amounted to treason punishable by death.

Abdulaziz and Khashoggi communicated using WhatsApp, assuming the app's end-to-end encryption would provide a degree of security for their exchanges. Throughout the summer of 2018, they chatted with each other, unaware that Saudi operatives were eavesdropping. Saudi spies, and quite likely al-Qahtani himself, observed the exchanges as they heaped disdain on the Saudi regime and on MBS personally. "The more victims he eats, the more he wants," Khashoggi said in one message, describing MBS as a "beast."

When Abdulaziz learned from us that his phone had been hacked with Pegasus, he immediately let Khashoggi know. "God help us," Khashoggi replied. "He was very scared," Abdulaziz told me. He assumed his phone might be hacked too. "I'm really worried about my privacy," he wrote to Abdulaziz. "They will have so many private pictures with my family members." Abdulaziz recommended that Khashoggi get another phone for their communications.

It is not clear why Khashoggi, after receiving this information, still chose to visit the consulate in Turkey. Only a few months earlier, when Saudi agents visited Abdulaziz in Canada and invited him to the Saudi embassy in Ottawa, Khashoggi advised him not to go. "I wouldn't trust them," he said. Why didn't he take his own advice? A CIA report alleged that MBS's brother Khalid bin Salman, the Saudi ambassador to the United States, told Khashoggi to pick up his papers from the Saudi consulate in Turkey and assured him that his visit there would be safe.[31] This reassurance was part of a ruse designed to lure Khashoggi to a third country, outside the United States, to dispose of him more easily.

In the aftermath of Khashoggi's murder, as TV crews were fixated on the Saudi consulate, we were concerned with Abdulaziz's safety. He was afraid he might be next on the Saudi hit list. He was certain his schemes with Khashoggi were the precipitating factor in the execution.

———

Now that the story was public, the RCMP contacted Abdulaziz and requested he come to the station for questioning. We wanted him to have proper legal representation and hurriedly helped search for suitable counsel to recommend to him. When he went for the interview, the RCMP took possession of his devices and gave him a temporary phone. Several days later, they returned his phones, but it remains unclear what they did with them.

Subsequently, several RCMP investigators requested a visit to the Citizen Lab, where we detailed the nature of our investigation, but by then everything of interest had already been disclosed. The RCMP told journalists they were on the case, but I never heard back from them, and nothing materialized. Nor did Abdulaziz feel the investigation went anywhere. In the end, there wasn't much Canadian law enforcement could do, considering that the parties responsible for the hacking were outside Canada and protected in Saudi Arabia.

I heard a more cynical theory from a well-placed Canadian government official during a private chat a few months later. He felt there was a lot of concern among Canadian authorities about offending other governments, especially Saudi Arabia and Israel, and that explained the stalled investigation. After all the hullabaloo earlier that summer about the Saudi human rights record, there was barely a peep from the Trudeau government when it came to a Canadian permanent resident being spied on in our own country, a man possibly linked to the kidnapping and execution of a journalist in broad daylight. I was disappointed not to hear even a mild protest.

———

In a world full of breaking news, Khashoggi's execution was among the biggest stories for the next few weeks. The connection between what happened to this renowned journalist and the spying we uncovered became a key part of the narrative.

CBS's *60 Minutes*, one of the world's most respected television news programs, decided to feature the story and invited the Lab to participate.[32] I had watched this show since I was a child and was excited to get the invitation. I grew somewhat leery, however, when I heard that NSO Group would be featured prominently and that Abdulaziz had decided not to participate, possibly because of the emotional trauma he was experiencing at the time. He was flooded with media requests, some of them funneled through me to him, and I knew they were beginning to take a toll. Still, the show went ahead, and the crew filmed Marczak and me in the Citizen Lab's headquarters. I even did the *60 Minutes* stroll with lead journalist Lesley Stahl.

Shalev Hulio, one of the founders and CEO of NSO Group, was given more airtime than I had hoped, but he came across as an untrustworthy con artist, sweating and smiling awkwardly. When asked about Khashoggi's execution and the connection to Pegasus, he emphatically denied that NSO Group's technology was in any way implicated. "Khashoggi murder is horrible. Really horrible," he said. "And therefore, when I first heard there are accusations that our technology been [*sic*] used on Jamal Khashoggi or on his relatives, I started an immediate check about it. And I can tell you very clear [*sic*], we had nothing to do with this horrible murder."

Hulio did not provide any details on how he conducted the check or how Abdulaziz's device got hacked with NSO Group's spyware. He also refused to answer whether NSO Group sold Pegasus to Saudi Arabia, saying he could not speak about a "specific customer."

Lesley Stahl: "It begs the question, did you shut down the Saudis?"

Shalev Hulio: "I'm not going to talk about customers and I'm not gonna go into specific [*sic*]. We do what we need to do. We help create a safer world."

Of course he didn't want to talk about that specific customer because NSO Group was continuing to earn revenue supplying hacking technology to Saudi Arabia at that very moment. Repeatedly, in the months and years to come, we would discover more victims of hacking perpetrated by Saudi operators using NSO Group's flagship spyware. It's easy to deny that Khashoggi's devices were hacked with Pegasus when they are not available to be examined. Only Turkish intelligence, which obtained them from his fiancée, Cengiz, can say for sure.

What we do know is damning enough. We know for certain that Abdulaziz's phone was hacked using Pegasus, meaning that every message and phone call Khashoggi had with Abdulaziz was under surveillance by the Saudis.

But that's not all. Two years later, in December 2021, we discovered that Pegasus had also been implanted onto the phone of Khashoggi's wife, Hanan Elatr, in the summer of 2018, just before his execution.[33] Elatr, a flight attendant, flew to the United Arab Emirates from Toronto in April that year. When she arrived at Dubai International Airport, she was met by seven security officials. They handcuffed her and took her to a prison outside the city, where they seized her devices and questioned her over several days.

Later, journalist Dana Priest of the *Washington Post*, who was investigating Pegasus cases, connected us with Elatr. She, in turn, gave us her devices for forensic analysis. Marczak's investigation revealed that, at precisely 10:18 a.m. on April 18, 2018, an individual manually opened the Chrome browser on her device and typed in the website address for an active NSO Group command and control spyware implant server. We could determine that the entry was made manually because the examined logs indicated that the person initially made a typo and then corrected it by retyping the address accurately. The time of this entry corresponds exactly to the period during which Elatr was in custody and being questioned, after surrendering her device to Emirati authorities. The logs we examined also reveal subsequent communications traffic between her device and that server as the spyware was implanted. Thanks to intelligence gathered by the Saudi regime's close allies the Emiratis, in addition to Abdulaziz's conversations and communications with Khashoggi, the Saudis were also likely privy to those Khashoggi had with his wife in the weeks before his execution.

We also determined that the device of *New York Times* Middle East correspondent Ben Hubbard had been hacked by Saudi operatives using Pegasus numerous times, contrary to NSO Group's explicit denials.[34] Immediately after our Abdulaziz report was published, Hubbard reached out to me and said he had recognized one of the Saudi-linked domains we had published in our Kingdom report from an SMS he had received in June 2018 promising details about "Ben Hubbard and the story of the Saudi Royal Family." That text message was proof he too had been targeted at roughly the same time as Abdulaziz by the same government operatives. After considerable delays related to the concerns of *New York Times* management about going public with the story, we eventually published our report in January 2020. Hubbard was the first case we found of an American journalist being targeted with Pegasus.

NSO Group vehemently denied that Pegasus was used to target Hubbard but offered no proof. "Off the record," Hubbard wrote in the *New York Times*, "a company official told me that its software had not been used to target my phone. I gave NSO Group multiple opportunities to say on the record how it had come to this conclusion and to state publicly whether its technology had been used on me. It did not, nor did it address this issue in its most recent statement."[35]

Later, armed with much more refined forensic methods, we more closely examined Hubbard's device and found unassailable proof in his device's logs that it was targeted and then hacked with Pegasus multiple times, including around the time frame he was in communication with Khashoggi. "I was definitely in touch with Jamal after he moved to DC," Hubbard told me. We discovered that Hubbard's phone received an unsolicited Kingdom-related Pegasus WhatsApp message on June 2, 2018. The message was largely identical to a Pegasus message targeted at an Amnesty International staffer in 2018 and coincided with the targeting of Abdulaziz too. There was also evidence of Pegasus infections in July 2020 and June 2021, after Hubbard complained to NSO Group that he was targeted in June 2018 and the firm swore it was not true. This time, the version of Pegasus used against Hubbard was of the "zero-click" variety, meaning that no interaction with a target is required for exploitation, such as clicking on a malware-laden link. "It's like being robbed by a ghost," Hubbard explained.[36]

Finally, there's Khashoggi's fiancée, Hatice Cengiz. Amnesty International did forensic analysis on her devices in 2021, as part of its involvement in the Pegasus Project investigation.[37] Investigators discovered that her phone had been hacked several times shortly after Khashoggi's murder: on October 6 and then again on October 9 and 12. It seems that someone in Saudi Arabia was keenly interested in finding out what Cengiz knew or with whom she was speaking. In addition to Abdulaziz, Elatr, Hubbard, and Cengiz, several other Saudi activists who had been in communication with Khashoggi at various times before his death also had their phones targeted or hacked with Pegasus spyware.[38]

While we may never know what happened to Khashoggi's devices, we do know that a surveillance web was cast around his entire inner circle, thanks to NSO Group's technology. We know that al-Qahtani was not only the principal manager of Khashoggi's execution but also the main person responsible for spyware procurement for the regime's security services.[39] It is disingenuous for NSO Group to claim that its technology had no role in Khashoggi's murder when it is evident that the assassins had prepared the ground for his execution by bugging the devices of multiple people around him—and quite likely his devices too. Moreover, it's morally reprehensible that NSO Group would continue to serve a regime despite this horrific execution.

———

After the international outrage around Khashoggi's execution, the Saudi regime made a showy pretense of an investigation.[40] Several people, including al-Qahtani, were relieved of their positions, while others involved in the assassination were sentenced to token jail terms. But the ultimate perpetrator went scot-free.

In February 2021, the Biden administration declassified an intelligence report that said Crown Prince Mohammed bin Salman of Saudi Arabia had personally directed the assassination of

Washington Post journalist Jamal Khashoggi.[41] According to a *Wall Street Journal* report, the CIA assessment determined that MBS had sent at least eleven messages to his digital enforcer, al-Qahtani, who "supervised the 15-man team that killed Mr. Khashoggi and, during the same period, was also in direct communication with the team's leader in Istanbul."[42]

But the administration stopped short of punishing MBS directly, saying that the strategic relationship with Saudi Arabia was too important to disrupt.[43] At least it was frank about it. In May 2023, Canada restored full diplomatic relations with Saudi Arabia.[44] Despite the government's well-trumpeted concern for human rights, Saudi Arabia is one of Canada's most important customers for military equipment, representing "about 54 per cent of the value of total military exports from Canada to non-U.S. destinations."[45] In short, the criminal hacking of Abdulaziz's device and Khashoggi's subsequent murder were simply swept under the rug as minor disruptions to what were determined to be larger and more important realpolitik calculations.

Some of the victims around Khashoggi have tried to seek justice through available legal means, with mixed results. Abdulaziz filed a lawsuit against Twitter alleging negligence in allowing Saudi agents employed by the company to access his Twitter account's private details. But the court dismissed the suit because it failed to connect the Twitter infiltrators to the harms that Abdulaziz experienced.[46] Abdulaziz has also filed a lawsuit against NSO Group in Israeli courts that is still underway at the time of writing.[47] In 2022, Yahya Assiri filed a lawsuit against NSO Group and Saudi Arabia in UK courts, and in 2023, Hanan Elatr, Jamal Khashoggi's widow, filed a lawsuit in the Eastern District of Virginia against NSO Group, but the latter was dismissed in October 2023.[48]

Suits like these can be important for victims' morale but may be drawn out over years and are legally complicated, as the dismissals of Elatr's case against NSO Group and Abdulaziz's case against Twitter show. The damage that will be most difficult to repair concerns the emotional and psychological trauma and the ongoing climate of fear and paranoia that surrounds victims like Abdulaziz.

Although he puts up a brave face, the toll has been enormous. "It really hurts every morning waking up and knowing that so many people get arrested because of you," he said.[49]

Abdulaziz remains understandably anxious about his personal safety. In 2020, Canadian officials warned him that specific, credible threats had been made against his life. "[The Canadian authorities] received some information . . . that I might be a potential target," he told the *Guardian*. "MBS and his group . . . want to harm me. They want to do something, but I don't know whether it's assassination, kidnapping . . . something not OK for sure." Abdulaziz's lawyer, Alaa Mahajna, said, "The warning about serious threats to his life was different this time. It was formal and conveyed with a clear sense of urgency and advice to take precautions. It felt more credible and more concrete."[50]

A few months later, those risks were again dramatically illustrated after a Saudi PhD student, Ahmed Alharby, who, like Abdulaziz, had been vocal in his criticism of the Saudi regime and sought political asylum in Canada, suddenly in 2021 returned to Saudi Arabia.[51] A new Twitter account mysteriously appeared in his name showering praise on MBS. Abdulaziz was among his Canadian friends who were taken aback by his departure, which seemed to involve yet more Saudi agents traveling to Canada to persuade him to visit the Saudi embassy in Ottawa.[52] After that, he disappeared into Saudi Arabia.

"I'm not really scared," Abdulaziz says, "but I'm really worried about the people of my country. . . . I'm protected here, but it's about . . . my friends, my family members."[53]

– 6 –

"How Often Do You Pray?"

DECEMBER 18, 2018

"Can I speak to you?" he asked as he made his way into my office. "I just had a very strange meeting . . ."

Bahr Abdul Razzak is one of those highly versatile researchers we covet at the Citizen Lab. A Syrian by birth, he is adept at unraveling complicated digital threads and hunting online mysteries. He has that DIY ingenuity often found in people who had to make things work in a zone of conflict where basic equipment and supplies are in short supply. His advice on digital security, especially precautions to take while traveling, has been invaluable to me and the rest of the Lab staff ever since he joined.

We met Abdul Razzak along with his wife, Noura Aljizawi, also a Syrian, as part of the Lab's investigations into Syria-related targeted threats. Before they knew each other, they had both participated in anti-Assad activism in 2011 and been arrested and horribly tortured before they were incarcerated, at different times, coincidentally in the same prison cell in Damascus.[1] They then met in person when they each made their way separately to Turkey, where they were helping to support camps for activists and civic journalists. They soon learned of their shared experiences in Damascus. Being incarcerated at different times in the very same prison cell helped forge a close bond. Eventually they married.

While fighting for justice in Syria, Aljizawi became a prominent senior member of the Syrian National Coalition. In October 2015, she received a suspicious email purporting to come from a human rights documentation organization she had never heard of called "Assad Crimes." The sender, using the email address office@assad crimes[.]info, was promising information about "Iranian crimes." Concerned, she and Abdul Razzak contacted the Lab, and together we analyzed what turned out to be a persistent hacking campaign we attributed to an Iran-aligned network, possibly Iranian intelligence operatives working on behalf of the Assad regime.[2]

After I hired Abdul Razzak as a security researcher, I encouraged Aljizawi to enroll as a scholar at risk at the University of Toronto's Massey College, where I'm a senior fellow. When she completed her master of global affairs degree, I hired her to help lead our research on digital transnational repression—attempts by governments, using digital means, to suppress dissent outside their borders. Her experiences as a victim of this type of repression provided the Lab with someone who not only understands what the experience entails but has extraordinary empathy for the victims we engage with in our research.

I knew that anything Abdul Razzak wanted to speak about was usually important. "Of course, come in," I said. "What's up?" He proceeded to tell me about an unsolicited outreach he received on LinkedIn from a person named Gary Bowman who presented himself as working for FlameTech, a financial start-up based in Madrid, Spain.

Bowman claimed to be interested in providing financial solutions around banking for Syrian refugees, an important cause for people like Abdul Razzak. Refugees and asylum seekers fleeing their home countries are often unable to access their bank accounts and other important documents, so the idea of some kind of financial app that eases these challenges seemed to make sense—at least enough for Abdul Razzak to want to hear more.

Always willing to help a good cause, Abdul Razzak agreed to talk to Bowman, who just happened to be in Toronto. But the unsolicited outreach gave him pause, and out of an abundance of caution he did not take any electronic devices with him. Bowman suggested they meet at 10:00 a.m. on December 18, 2018, at the swanky Shangri-La hotel in downtown Toronto. Abdul Razzak recognized Bowman from his LinkedIn profile and sat down across the table from him.

Almost immediately, Abdul Razzak sensed something was fishy. Bowman had a folder of papers in front of him, some of which he passed over and asked Abdul Razzak to review and fill out. When he asked what they were, Bowman replied they were the job application for a position he hoped Abdul Razzak would apply for. Abdul Razzak said he already had a job at the Lab but was interested in hearing more about how he could help as a volunteer.

Abdul Razzak noted that Bowman had an old Samsung phone, which he laid on the table between them with the microphone pointed in his direction. Although the conversation started out focused on Syrian refugees and banking, it very quickly detoured into personal topics. "How often do you pray?" Bowman asked out of the blue. "Do you eat halal food?"

What really took Abdul Razzak aback were questions about the Citizen Lab and specifically its work on NSO Group, which seemed completely unrelated to the topic of financial support for Syrian refugees.

"Who are the Citizen Lab's donors? Are you getting paid well by the Citizen Lab?" Bowman probed. "Why do you focus on NSO Group? Is it because it is an Israeli company? Are you against Israel? What do you know about Omar's lawsuit?" he asked, referring to Omar Abdulaziz, the exiled Saudi student based in Canada whose phone we determined was hacked with Pegasus spyware and who had just filed a lawsuit against NSO Group in Israel.[3] "Does the Citizen Lab provide details to Omar or anyone else involved in the lawsuit?" After some more odd questions about Abdul Razzak's travels to Europe and Turkey, the meeting wrapped up with Bowman promising to be back in touch.

"It was weird," Abdul Razzak said, relaying the conversation. "I think I was the target of some kind of op."

I had heard enough. Time to raise the alarm. Abdul Razzak had already briefed our senior researcher John Scott-Railton (JSR), and together we brought in a few other Lab staff to start our investigation. Who was this guy who reached out to Abdul Razzak? Was he who he said he was? What was going on?

Bowman had given Abdul Razzak some documents and a business card, which showed the name of a company, FlameTech, and a business address in Madrid. We also looked carefully at the LinkedIn profile of FlameTech. On closer inspection, it began to look suspicious. Some of the senior employees listed as working for the company had stock photos as profile pictures. Whoever met Abdul Razzak, his name almost certainly was not Gary Bowman.

We asked Abdul Razzak to sit down in a quiet room and memorialize the conversation in writing as best he could. When we reviewed the details, it seemed that the person claiming to be Bowman was mostly interested in the Lab, its work on NSO Group, and, in particular, information related to our funding and our role in the lawsuit that Omar Abdulaziz had launched. The detail about the Samsung phone on the table definitely seemed suspicious. We were leaning toward this meeting being a covert operation.

We alerted close associates in the digital rights community that something fishy was up and they should be mindful of any unsolicited outreach. I also reached out to Omar Abdulaziz and gave him a rundown, assuming he might also be targeted. I called up the lead RCMP investigator working on Abdulaziz's case too, although there had been no tangible developments in that investigation.

JSR contacted Raphael Satter, then a journalist with the Associated Press who had covered several of the Lab's previous research reports, to say we had a potentially interesting story: a mystery man who had reached out to one of our staff in what we thought might be some kind of covert operation designed to gather incriminating or embarrassing information to discredit us. Satter, in turn, enlisted the help of a European colleague at the Associated Press, who visited the address listed for FlameTech in Madrid. He found no such business. FlameTech, it seemed, was made up, just like Gary Bowman. Without doubt, we had been targeted in an underhanded operation against Abdul Razzak and the Citizen Lab.

Everything stops on a dime when something like this happens.

You have no idea why it started or how it will end, or who is involved and what they might do. You start second-guessing everyone and everything around you. It's nerve-racking and deeply unsettling.

After more research, Satter and the Associated Press felt they had enough of a story to publish. But then JSR received a surprise. "Ron!" he exclaimed over a secure call. "I just received an unsolicited outreach from someone claiming to work for a company asking questions about the aerial kite photography I was working on in Senegal as part of my graduate work."

We asked Satter to stop the presses. A much bigger story was unfolding. We were not going to sit idly by and let it all unfold at the scoundrel's discretion. We were determined to take charge.

———

Whoever was targeting us made a huge tactical error in targeting JSR. He is a bloodhound of open-source investigations. When he received the unsolicited outreach from Michel Lambert claiming to be working for something called CPW Consulting and interested in his long-obsolete aerial kite photography experiments, JSR went into an overdrive of digital sleuthing.

In his first phone call, Lambert immediately engaged JSR in French. Although he's fluent in the language, it is not widely known, suggesting there was already a dossier on him. They had numerous conversations over the next several days, which JSR duly recorded and archived.

JSR also developed a ruse to make it appear as though he were living in the New York City area. He tweeted a short video clip of skaters in Rockefeller Plaza and posted about searching for an apartment in the city. His purpose was deliberate: he's an American by birth, and the clandestine operation targeting him on US soil would be reportable to the US authorities. Lambert suggested they meet at Clement, a restaurant attached to the swank Peninsula hotel. Private operatives, it seems, prefer to dine out at five-star restaurants when they're on someone else's tab.

On our end, we made a plan to covertly record the operative. Satter and two of his colleagues would be positioned at the restaurant during the meeting and, on a signal from JSR, would swoop in and ask Lambert questions. The night before, JSR prepared surreptitious audio and video recording devices, including a necktie camera that he tried to rig up himself but which ultimately failed to work. He decided against the hidden pen camera, assuming Lambert would likely bring one of his own—and the prospect of two pens pointing at each other seemed too bizarre to contemplate. But he was still well outfitted for the task at hand.

While making his way to the restaurant, JSR was caught in a traffic jam, so he exited the taxi and made his way on foot through a massive rainstorm to get to the meeting on time. His adrenaline was pumping as he rushed into the restaurant, and so was mine, even though I was hundreds of miles away in Toronto. As director of the Lab, I felt responsible for his well-being, but there was little I could do other than stay posted.

Satter and a colleague had arrived early to avoid drawing attention to themselves. Their Associated Press budget was capped, and the restaurant was pricey. They ended up sharing a single shrimp cocktail and glasses of water while they waited for the signal.

Lambert had also brought company of his own. Two private intelligence subcontractors, Roman Khaykin and Igor Ostrovskiy, were assigned to watch his back for any countersurveillance, take discreet photos of JSR without showing Lambert's face, and provide backup should anything go wrong. As we learned later, Ostrovskiy was already growing uncomfortable with some of his assignments. Most of his clients were involved in divorce cases or insurance scams, but some of the recent jobs for that day's client, the Israeli firm Black Cube, seemed dodgy. He had been asked, for example, to do covert surveillance of Ronan Farrow, an investigative journalist covering sexual assault allegations against Hollywood mogul Harvey Weinstein, soon to be convicted of rape.[4] Typically, agents providing backup support are given little information about the targets. Their job is to observe and shepherd their client, not pay attention to who specifically is under surveillance.

When JSR arrived, Lambert got up from his table and escorted him to a different table beside a window. That immediately raised red flags, and the reason, we realized later, was to allow Ostrovskiy, stationed outside the restaurant, to take covert photographs of JSR's face.

As the meeting got underway, Lambert ordered a martini and encouraged JSR to do the same. JSR doesn't drink alcohol, so he ordered tea instead, but Lambert still tried to entice him to accept a drink throughout the lunch. The discussion proceeded with a mixture of small talk sprinkled with questions from Lambert about the Citizen Lab and our work on NSO Group.[5] He also used racial slurs repeatedly, seemingly to goad JSR into saying something that could be recorded and used to discredit him. JSR noted that Lambert's black pen was pointed directly at him throughout the conversation.

Strangely, Lambert seemed to be using color-coded cue cards. The green cards corresponded to innocuous biographical questions, the yellow cards to more prying questions about the Citizen Lab, and the red cards to the really juicy stuff.

"You support the people who go to court?" Lambert asked.

"So you're asking me if I get paid to work on court cases?"

Lambert was keen to dig up dirt on the Lab's internal affairs.

"Work drama? Tell me! I like drama! Is there a big competition between the people at the Citizen Lab?"

Lambert steered the conversation to what he hoped would be evidence of anti-Semitism in the Lab's work, or at least an errant comment that could be misconstrued that way after the fact. "There is not also a racist connection, no?"

As the conversation plodded along, JSR received a text message from Satter that his battery was running low and to wrap it up. JSR steered the conversation back to kites, pointing outside to explain that it is possible to use such a kite in a dense urban environment such as Manhattan. This maneuver was intended to distract Lambert so that Satter and his cameraperson could sidle up to the table.

"Hi, nice to meet you," said Satter, suddenly appearing next to Lambert, who was clearly puzzled by the new guest at the table.

"Bonjour," Lambert replied.

"My name is Raphael Satter, and I'm with the Associated Press in London. I'd like to talk to you about your company, CPW Consulting."

"I don't have to speak to you," Lambert retorted, waving his hand in front of the phone camera that JSR had just pulled out.

Thrown entirely off guard, Lambert stood abruptly and tried to get away from the table, knocking over a chair in the process. Satter, his colleague, and JSR followed and filmed him while peppering him with more questions about who he really was and whom he was working for. Increasingly rattled, Lambert moved to an open door to a private dining room and asked for help from a restaurant staffer. That was the last they saw of Lambert.

By this point, one of the subcontractors, Khaykin, had departed for another mission, leaving Ostrovskiy alone to act as support for Lambert. Moving inside the hotel, he had positioned himself at a bar near the restaurant but out of sight of the meeting. Until his phone rang, he was oblivious to the melee taking place. Lambert had alerted Khaykin that the operation had been exposed and he desperately needed help, so Khaykin phoned Ostrovskiy. "The agent is in trouble," Khaykin screamed over the phone. "We need to help get him out of there."

Ostrovskiy found Lambert hiding in the private dining room and escorted him to a vehicle outside. Still flustered, Lambert instructed him to take him to the Marriott hotel, where his luggage was being held at reception. On the way over, Ostrovskiy overheard him speaking in Hebrew, desperately trying to book a flight out of New York. When he went into the hotel to retrieve Lambert's luggage, he noticed a tag with the name Aharon Almog-Assouline on it and an address in Israel. He took a photo for posterity.

"How'd it go?" I asked anxiously, as soon as JSR and I were able to connect on the phone.

"Unbelievable," he said, and recounted the entire story.

It was a gamble, but it paid off. We turned the tables on the operatives and exposed them for what they were. But even as we celebrated, we knew it was just one battle in a much larger war.

———

Although the incident came as a shock, we had realized that someday we would be targeted. We angered a lot of people—people who had the means and motivation to do something about it.

A sea change has been unfolding in the clandestine realms where covert operations are undertaken. A new type of globalized elite has emerged: a transnational class of oligarchs and superwealthy magnates benefiting from waves of privatization and deregulation. Some are autocrats in power; others are part of the upper power structure of governments—heads of ministries and agencies and those around them—using corruption and access to the machinery of government to advance their own interests. This superrich class of gangsters is serviced by a retinue of lawyers, investment managers, strategists, accountants, real estate professionals, and, on the darker side, "fixers," "solution providers," and private investigators. Their vast support networks run through global cities such as New York, London, Zurich, Toronto, Doha, and Dubai; "offshore" jurisdictions including the Cayman Islands, Panama, Jersey, and Delaware; and seamier sides of the supply chain in Manila, New Delhi, Cyprus, and Nairobi. This shadow globalization cuts through "democratic" and "authoritarian" jurisdictions alike. Arguably, it's the defining feature of today's world order.

For this ultrarich elite, undertaking illicit activities is normalized—acts of espionage, sabotage, subversion, and even assassination now mere commodities in a growing dark bazaar. Most people are aware of the worldwide market for mercenary armies, but only a few know about the market for mercenary CIAs, Mossads, and KGBs. It's common to see retired veterans of spy agencies building lucrative start-ups offering risk analysis, litigation support, PR strategy, and other "solutions" for thorny problems. Veterans of state intelligence have real-life experience in source management, extortion, blackmail, and psychological manipulation. A professional veneer provided by a glossy website, LinkedIn profile, or marketing materials combined with generic-sounding services ("reputation management," "deep background checks") can help obscure highly duplicitous and harmful operations done on behalf of despots, oligarchs, and billionaire sociopaths.

The digital communications ecosystem we inhabit provides an ideal breeding ground for the flourishing of privatized covert operations. Take, as one example, the algorithms used by social media to engage attention by promoting sensational, extreme, and conspiratorial content. Many people around us now live in a never-ending tsunami of conspiracies, fake news, and half-truths that leave them cynical and disengaged from civic life. New techniques of disinformation, such as the use of deepfakes and AI-enabled content, are cheap, accessible, and spreading quickly, effectively "democratizing" the tradecraft of dark PR. With location tracking, social media scraping, data analytics, hacking, and facial recognition services now readily available to any paying client, details about people's movements, habits, and other private details can be acquired to create a multidimensional dossier on a target with the mere click of a purchase order.

"Social media allows you to reach virtually anyone and to play with their minds," Uzi Shaya, a former senior Israeli intelligence officer, said. "You can do whatever you want. You can be whoever you want. It's a place where wars are fought, elections are won, and terror is promoted. There are no regulations. It is a no man's land."[6] He should know: for years, Israeli intelligence perfected psychological warfare against its enemies to undercut their narratives and covertly influence their populations.[7] Now these skills are available to any client—for a price.

Among the biggest risks for civil society today are disinformation campaigns that can hardly be distinguished from genuine expressions of personal opinions and other innocent communications. They use natural language processing (NLP) capabilities and AI-generated content to create videos of realistic news anchors, plausible-looking copies of mainstream media websites, fabricated news stories, and reams of comments to promote any cause they wish or to attack any target. Who needs to surreptitiously record incriminating conversations when you can simply make them up with the help of a deepfake?

The combination of NLP and AI-generated photorealistic images and videos will transform influence operations, overwhelm fact-checkers, and demoralize targeted people who are unable to muster the energy or the money to fight back against the tidal waves of disinformation. Among the most effective may be "slow burning"—seemingly ridiculous but persistent campaigns against an individual's integrity, seeded in various forums and spread like whispers.

While platforms have occasionally made efforts to rein in this toxic content, such efforts work at cross-purposes to their own profits. After purchasing Twitter, for example, Elon Musk laid off the entire trust and safety team and restored the accounts of neo-Nazis and misogynists who had been deplatformed. Musk himself—the world's richest man—started spewing out a litany of harmful, inaccurate, and racist content. In 2021, Meta removed hundreds of accounts that it discovered were being misused as part of covert operations by Black Cube (the private intelligence agency for which "Lambert" was working) and another Israeli surveillance vendor, Cognyte (formerly WebintPro). It said Black Cube "operated fictitious personas tailored for its targets: some of them posed as graduate students, NGO and human rights workers, and film and TV producers."[8] In 2023, however, Meta dismissed tens of thousands of its staff, including entire teams fighting disinformation and targeted threats.[9]

Social media, a technology designed and once widely heralded for providing citizens with freedom of speech and liberty, has now become a major source of insecurity and division. Our mission at the Lab has always been to uncover risks to human rights in the digital sphere, and this exploitation of the digital communications ecosystem will make our task ever more challenging. I sometimes think of our efforts as similar to those of firefighters: futilely pointing a hose at apocalyptic blazes fueled by the climate crisis.

————

We got our first real glimpse into this growing private intelligence underworld during a long investigation we called Dark Basin.[10] In July 2017, a *Financial Times* journalist sent us phishing emails he and his sources had received. The journalist's beat was in the energy and financial sector in eastern Europe and the former Soviet Union, and the emails appeared to come from a typical Russian hack-and-leak operation. Led by JSR and Citizen Lab research fellow Adam Hulcoop, we had just completed a major investigation called Tainted Leaks, in which hacked emails of the prominent writer David Satter (father of the journalist Raphael Satter) and one of our funders, Open Society Foundations, were doctored and then published on pro-Russian social media and state television.[11] There they were made to appear as though Satter were a CIA agent and both he and OSF were funding Russian opposition figure Alexei Navalny (both demonstrably false).

Using a similar methodology to the one we used in the Tainted Leaks investigation, in which we were able to unravel the shortened links in engineered emails to identify tens of thousands of other unwitting victims, we started to disentangle a network of operations targeting a bewildering array of seemingly unrelated people: lawyers, financial short sellers, US-based advocates for net neutrality, and climate change activists. Among the victims were organizations and individuals working on the ExxonKnew campaign, which alleged that Exxon management was aware of the impact of fossil fuels on climate change but hid the science from the public and its shareholders for years.

A big breakthrough occurred when we capitalized on sloppy errors made by the culprits. There were already indications of an India nexus to the hacking operation. Time stamps of the phishing emails sent corresponded to business hours in New Delhi. There were also references to Hindi slang in the code used by the attackers. But the real payoff came when we discovered that hackers responsible for the campaign had used personal documents as bait content when testing URL shorteners. Once we started digging into social media and LinkedIn, we found that behind this sprawling hack-for-hire operation was a single India-based company called BellTroX. Staff members there had even boasted on LinkedIn about their various skills, including email penetration and corporate espionage. Some had their profiles endorsed by high-profile shadowy clients, including government officials and retired FBI and other law enforcement personnel.

Our Dark Basin report, published in June 2020, detailed how this one hack-for-hire group had hacked the email accounts of "thousands of individuals and hundreds of institutions on six continents." Among the victims we discovered were advocacy groups and journalists, elected and senior government officials, hedge funds, multiple industries, and organizations working on the ExxonKnew campaign. We received a taste of disinformation payback shortly after the report's publication. When the *New York Times* covered the hacking of the environmental groups we uncovered, a spokesperson for Exxon tried to discredit our work with guilt by association, saying that "the Citizen Lab receives financial support from 'anti-fossil fuel groups,'" an aspersion that was echoed by a front group called Energy in Depth, which wrote on its blog that "Citizen Lab is funded by many of the same groups funding the 'Exxon Knew' campaign, including the Hewlett Foundation, Oak Foundation, and Open Society Foundation."[12] Obviously, our report touched a raw nerve with the dirty energy giant and its minions.

Among the many victims we uncovered of BellTroX's phishing operations, one rivaled any Netflix series on white-collar crime and international espionage. The case centered on a Munich-based payment processing company called Wirecard—once a darling of the German fintech scene. In February 2016, a short seller named Matthew Earl copublished a detailed exposé online called the Zatarra Report, casting doubts on Wirecard's earnings and alleging widespread fraud by its executives.[13] The next day, Wirecard's shares fell by 21 percent.

Earl soon found himself followed by individuals working for the private investigation company Kroll, threatened with lawsuits by Wirecard, and the focus of criminal investigations launched by German police for market manipulation (thanks to a complaint lodged against him by Wirecard). In December 2016, documents appeared online claiming to come from a whistleblower working for Earl (he had no employees), including verbatim extracts from email and Skype conversations Earl had with journalists. In fact,

Earl was among BellTroX's victims, and the emails had been stolen from him by the Indian hackers and were being used to discredit him. It was a classic mercenary hack-and-leak operation.

Although Wirecard and its private investigators tried to paint Earl as a criminal, it was Wirecard itself that was the one undertaking criminal activities. *Financial Times* journalist Dan McCrum, who had been digging for years into Wirecard's dubious financial practices, had been subjected to harassment and legal threats from the firm too.[14] On June 2, 2020, we published our Dark Basin report, which included details on the hacking operations against Wirecard's critics and journalists covering the firm. A few days later, a fraud investigation began, and former Wirecard COO Markus Braun was arrested.[15] Wirecard soon went insolvent, but the criminal investigations of the principals are ongoing.

What made the story truly bizarre, however, concerned Wirecard's former CEO Jan Marsalek, who fled Germany after Wirecard was exposed in 2020.[16] According to the *Financial Times*:

> The 40-year-old Austrian has led multiple lives, with complicated and overlapping commercial and political interests. Sometimes those interests cleaved to Wirecard's aggressive expansion plans in frontier markets. Sometimes they coincided with Mr Marsalek's own sprawling and unusual range of personal investments. And sometimes they seemed to fit neatly with the work of Russia's intelligence agencies.[17]

In addition to his fintech work with Wirecard, Marsalek had an ongoing interest in mercenary work in Libya, a lawless country racked for years by a bloody civil war. In 2019, the *Financial Times* discovered that Rami el-Obeidi, the former head of foreign intelligence in Libya's Transitional National Council and a shareholder of Wirecard, had contracted out surveillance operations targeting short sellers and investors whom he suspected of market manipulation.[18] The firms he hired to undertake the clandestine operations are leaders in the world of privatized subversion: "Sloane Risk Group in London, run by a former British counter-terrorism operative Hayley Elvins, and APG Protection, a Manchester-based firm run by a former special forces soldier Greg Raynor." The operation they launched employed "the services of 28 individual private investigators" and apparently cellphone site simulators, known as IMSI catchers, to intercept mobile phone identifiers and "suck the blood out of suspicious people."[19]

Colleagues reported that Marsalek boasted of trips to Syria at the invitation of senior Russian officials. He also traveled dozens of times over a few short years to Moscow from Austria.[20] While in Munich working for Wirecard, he lived at Prinzregentenstraße 61, a palatial home conveniently located next to the Russian consulate. Marsalek belonged to the Austrian-Russian Friendship Society, an organization reportedly backed by Russian spies.[21] He used this membership to cultivate Austrian investment in his Libyan business ventures, which included the involvement of Russian mercenaries such as the notorious Wagner Group.

At one point Marsalek turned up in London on Wirecard business and showed investors and others a dossier seemingly stolen from the Organisation for the Prohibition of Chemical Weapons. It included highly sensitive details on the precise formula for the toxic agent Novichok, which had been recently used in the botched assassination attempt in the United Kingdom of Russian defector Sergei Skripal. What was not clear was how Marsalek had obtained the documents or why he was recklessly showing them around London at a time when British investigators were on high alert in the wake of the Skripal poisoning.[22] That raised questions about his network of contacts and his motives.

On June 19, 2020, shortly after our Dark Basin report was published, Marsalek took off for Minsk, Belarus, then made his way to Russia under an assumed name: Max Mauer. Investigators have tracked Mauer to a swank gated community in Moscow called Meiendorf Gardens, presumably under the protection of the FSB or the GRU.[23] An Interpol red notice is out for his arrest, but there's no chance he'll be extradited as long as he's under the protection of the Russian state.[24] The combination of high-stakes white-collar crime, Indian hack-for-hire firms, Kroll private investigators, Libyan intelligence, Russian mercenaries, and fugitives from the law seemingly protected by Russian spies makes the Wirecard case a bonanza of twenty-first-century privatized subversion.

At the request of some of the American victims of the Dark Basin phishing scheme, we turned the information we had gathered in our investigation over to the US Department of Justice, which proceeded to launch a criminal investigation. Eventually, two Israeli private investigators connected to the case were arrested, Aviram Azari and Amit Forlit. Azari pleaded guilty in a New York court to charges of wire fraud, conspiracy to commit hacking and aggravated identity theft, and working as a middleman between Wirecard and BellTroX.[25] According to *Intelligence Online*, our report and the subsequent indictment of Azari "caused panic in Western corporate intelligence circles" because a "large number of firms have used the Indian company to hack emails for their clients, either directly or for brokers such as Azari, to provide evidence for court cases and or documentation for press campaigns."[26] US authorities say he made about $4.8 million running his schemes, and he's now being required to turn it over to the US government. In 2023, he was sentenced to eighty months in US prison.[27]

Meanwhile, in May 2024, Forlit was detained in the United Kingdom on an Interpol red notice as he was attempting to board a flight at Heathrow Airport bound for Israel.[28] He was released on a minor technicality and then rearrested by UK authorities shortly afterward. Legal proceedings around his extradition case are ongoing at the time of writing. Whether the ultimate perpetrators of the many hacks we uncovered in the Dark Basin investigation will ever be held to account remains to be seen. Given his stiff sentence, it is likely Azari kept his mouth shut. For Forlit's part, follow-up investigations by Reuters showed that he had business dealings with the PR company DCI Group, based in Washington, DC, and that he had told friends that the FBI had questioned him about the firm—an indication that DOJ investigators were busy working their way up the chain of entities involved in the Dark Basin scheme.[29]

———

The unbelievable web of clandestine operations we exposed in the Dark Basin investigation is but one example of the exploding market for mercenary intelligence services. Numerous other cases have been unearthed by other teams of investigative journalists and organizations, almost all characterized by the same combination of former intelligence operatives, deep-pocketed clients (typically oligarchs or autocrats), and a hubris that comes from operating in the shadows with seeming impunity.

During Julian Assange's refuge at the Ecuadorian embassy in London, for instance, a security firm contracted by the embassy discreetly installed audio and video recording equipment to spy on him, his visitors, and even his privileged conversations with his lawyers.[30] This sensitive information was shared with the CIA, which sought evidence to support the case for Assange's extradition to the United States. UC Global, the firm responsible, was founded by David Morales, a former member of the special operations unit of Spain's marines. Though its advertised services included high-risk protection, risk mitigation, and evacuation and rescue missions in conflict zones, UC Global's whistleblowers revealed that Morales, while attending a security conference in 2017, boasted of acquiring new clients he described as "American friends" involved in the "dark side."[31]

The whistleblowers disclosed that the firm not only eavesdropped on Assange but also copied visitors' mobile phones and shared the data, including passwords and other private information, with the CIA. These revelations prompted a Spanish judge to launch a criminal investigation, leading to Morales's arrest and the shuttering of UC Global.[32]

Professional sporting events, and especially football, have always been cesspools of global corruption. Qatar reportedly paid ex-CIA officers working as part of a firm called Global Risk Advisors, founded by ex-CIA operative Kevin Chalker, hundreds of millions of dollars to help Qatar in its bid to host the 2022 World Cup.[33] Part of the espionage operation included secretly bugging a meeting between a Swiss prosecutor investigating football-related wrongdoing and the head of FIFA when they met in a hotel owned by Qatar.[34]

The Associated Press also notes that Global Risk Advisors developed a plan to install a surveillance system in Qatar that "could track mobile phones in the country 'with extreme accuracy' and allow analysts to 'isolate individual conversations and listen in real-time.'"[35] One component of the operation reportedly involved sixty or more undercover operatives across five continents. Investigative journalists obtained slides revealing that Global Risk Advisors presented a proposal for achieving "worldwide penetration," aiming to provide Qatar with comprehensive information awareness to prevent or effectively counter future attacks.

In one of those "small world" details, Qatar, or its private investigation intermediaries, hired an Indian hack-for-hire firm called Appin, a predecessor to BellTroX.[36] Sumit Gupta worked at Appin before helping to found BellTroX and become its director. The links are not surprising: India is home to a bonanza of private espionage firms, sheltered, most knowledgeable people suspect, by the Indian government's own intelligence agencies. As JSR told the *New Yorker*'s David Kirkpatrick, "You know how in some industries, everybody 'knows a guy' who can do a certain thing? Well, in hacking for hire, India is 'the guy.'"[37]

A June 2022 Reuters investigation undertaken by Raphael Satter and Christopher Bing identified "35 legal cases since 2013 in which Indian hackers attempted to obtain documents from one side or another of a courtroom battle by sending them password-stealing emails."[38] The investigation was based on tens of thousands of emails that were shared with the Reuters journalists on condition of anonymity by email providers used by Indian hackers. Reuters found that "at least 75 U.S. and European companies, three dozen advocacy and media groups and numerous Western business executives were the subjects of these hacking attempts."

In 2023, Bing and Satter published a detailed follow-up on Appin and the Indian hack-for-hire industry.[39] Shortly after their story was published, Reuters took it down when it received notice of an Indian defamation court ruling. That court ruling was triggered by a lawsuit filed by Indian tech mogul Rajat Khare, a cofounder of Appin. Khare had retained a prominent law firm, UK-based Clare Locke, which was described by the *Daily Beast* as a "powerhouse 'media assassin'" firm.[40] The law firm boasts on its website of "killing stories" and was previously retained by such moral luminaries as disgraced NBC news anchor Matt Lauer and the *National Enquirer*'s David Pecker.[41] Shortly afterward, I too received a takedown demand from something called the Association of Appin Training Centers, which took issue with a blog post I had published referencing Bing and Satter's report.[42] I ignored the request.

––––––––––

The aftermath of our counter-sting against the Black Cube operation was enormous. The story was covered widely in the Associated Press and the *New York Times*. A big picture of Almog-Assouline trying in vain to cover his face was splashed all over the world, instantly ruining his employment as an undercover operative.[43]

A major weakness of undercover operations is that once they're exposed, all the operatives' previous missions are exposed as well. Immediately after our story appeared, people came forward who recognized Almog-Assouline and described similar covert operations in which they had been ensnared. One of them included a major financial litigation battle in Ontario, Canada, between two private equity firms, Catalyst Capital and West Face Capital. An individual engaged in the litigation, lawyer Darryl Levitt, said in court documents he filed that he recognized Almog-Assouline as the same operative who had approached him under a different identity years earlier—a person describing himself as Victor Petrov.[44] "I recognized the individual, down to the accent and the anecdotes," he said. Three lawyers involved in lawsuits against NSO Group in Israel reported similar encounters, as did a London-based journalist reporting on NSO Group.[45] As we had experienced, the victims told the Associated Press that "the covert agents tried to goad them into making racist and anti-Israel remarks or revealing sensitive information about their work in connection with the lawsuits."

Another interesting intersection was between our counter-sting and another Black Cube operation involving Ronan Farrow and the private investigator with a conscience, Igor Ostrovskiy. Farrow featured the details of our experience in his bestselling book and podcast series, *Catch and Kill*, which outlined how Harvey Weinstein had contracted Black Cube to try to discredit Farrow and victims who made rape and sexual assault allegations against Weinstein via surreptitious surveillance recordings.[46] After we crossed paths, Farrow started to cover the Lab's work into mercenary spyware, and in one of his visits to Israel to interview NSO Group, he got Shalev Hulio to acknowledge that the firm contracted Black Cube, contrary to NSO Group's previous on-the-record adamant denials.[47]

Our suspicious interactions with dishonest entities reaching out to us didn't end with the Black Cube operation. In February 2019, I received an email from a former research assistant and student, Vivek Krishnamurthy. Years earlier, I had written him a reference letter for a successful Rhodes Scholarship and had occasionally kept in touch as he rose through the ranks of various digital rights initiatives adjacent to the Lab's work.

Reading his email, I was shocked to find that despite the publicity around the abuses we and others had uncovered about NSO Group and the Black Cube operation against my staff, Krishnamurthy had been employed by his law firm, Foley Hoag, to act as a special advisor to Novalpina Capital, then owners of NSO Group, and was hoping to meet. I declined the invitation.

A few months later, Krishnamurthy sent another message asking to meet, this time outside his official responsibilities as an advisor to NSO Group: "You'd be having a drink with me in my capacity as your former student, and not as anything else!" Again, I declined.

I wouldn't have given the outreach much further thought had I not decided to send in a formal right of access to personal data to Novalpina in the hopes of discovering any details about the Black Cube targeting. I was not expecting to receive anything back.

But eventually I did: 473 emails that contained my personal data. (JSR did the same and received a large tranche too.) They, as well as subsequent investigations undertaken by *Guardian* journalist Stephanie Kirchgaessner, showed that Krishnamurthy was hired specifically because of his previous relationship with me: he was in a "unique position to conduct outreach to Citizen Lab should the NSO Group find it desirable to do so."[48]

In one of the exchanges, Novalpina's cofounder Stephen Peel emailed Krishnamurthy—shortly after a journalist reached out to Peel about Pegasus abuses—instructing him that it was time to "reach out to Deibert to find out what is going on." Krishnamurthy promptly replied that he would, adding, "He can be prickly, and he's clearly worked up about NSO." Krishnamurthy's initial outreach to me followed. A few months later, Peel encouraged Krishnamurthy to try again with a new approach: inviting me for a casual beer.[49] This time Krishnamurthy used his Harvard email address, not his law firm's, and blatantly lied about his intentions. A source told Kirchgaessner that NSO Group paid Foley Hoag about $220,000 for its work.

Meanwhile, Kirchgaessner managed to find out from at least two separate sources that Peel had tried, unsuccessfully, to put pressure on George Soros, founder of one of the Citizen Lab's funders, the Open Society Foundations, to kill the philanthropy's support for the Lab. Peel reportedly said to Soros that the Lab's motives and approach were "a little less pure than we might of [*sic*] hoped."[50]

A few months after the Black Cube operation was exposed, one of our researchers had a strange encounter with two agents working for Canada's domestic intelligence agency, CSIS. Before joining the Lab, he had worked for a Canadian intelligence agency and knew one of the operatives. Over coffee, the operatives suggested they place all their cellphones in a Faraday bag. Then they explained they were interested in the type of work the Citizen Lab was doing but realized it would be impossible to work together formally, given trust issues and the impression such collaboration would have with targeted communities. Instead, they asked whether the researcher would be interested in opportunities "to work together indirectly."

They also inquired what protocols the Lab had put in place to ensure its security in the face of new threats such as NSO Group and the increased attention around our Black Cube investigation. Our researcher indicated we did have protocols but wouldn't provide details. He said the Canadian government's silence about the Black Cube targeting "left a bad taste" with me. He could have added that this surreptitious recruitment of one of my staff behind my back made it even worse. A few months later, the same operatives reached out again to the researcher, this time saying they had some evidence that the Black Cube operation against the Lab was still ongoing, but they never followed up with specifics.

Not long after those encounters, I received a request from an individual working for Global Affairs Canada asking for a phone conversation. The caller explained that the Canadian embassy in Hong Kong had received a mysterious package from a group called the Committee to End American Interference in Internal Chinese Affairs, and my name was prominently included on the list of enemies. "I suspect you no longer travel to mainland China," he said, "but I'd advise you not to go to Hong Kong now either." The list of countries to which I could safely travel was diminishing rapidly.

———

Our Black Cube sting was so successful that many people came away from the story of the "bumbling spy" with the impression that the private intelligence agency's operations were amateur and sloppy. On the face of it, our interactions with Almog-Assouline looked amusing, but it feels different when you're on the receiving end. Although we managed to clue in, how many other victims go along with such a scam unwittingly?

The impact of this encounter on our collective psyche was substantial, and not necessarily for the better. We were often anxiously undertaking due diligence, spending hours analyzing whether we had received a genuine inquiry from a well-intentioned person or something malicious and professionally organized. After the Black Cube operation, it seemed that our risks were amplified in every possible way: physical, digital, travel-related, and more. Having to be constantly on guard, second-guessing every interaction, and always worried about my own and my staff's safety was challenging. Even Canadian agencies in our own backyard seemed to be orbiting around us suspiciously.

In a way, though, it was also a mark of our success. We wouldn't be targeted in this manner if we weren't making a difference. The key was to manage it all without locking ourselves into a straitjacket of risk mitigation measures. We still had a job to do. Being victimized ourselves made us feel closer to the targets we studied. We felt a common cause. All the malfeasances coming at us from seemingly every quarter only emboldened us. It was a reminder of how the mission we had envisaged for the Citizen Lab years ago, to serve as "counterintelligence for civil society," had now become a very serious reality.

Or, as that old adage goes, "Be careful what you wish for."

– PART TWO –

THE LAB

"Trust No One"

"In this figure, we can clearly see a seismic signal from a 0.25 kiloton explosion at the Soviet test site near Semipalatinsk, which we recorded at our NORESS seismic array station about four thousand kilometers from the blast site." The Norwegian scientist's face was haloed in the light of the overhead projector as he leaned in to pull one transparency from the glass on the top of the machine and replace it with another. "Okay. Now the signal-to-noise ratio is around thirty, which shows that a much smaller explosion could be detected even at this great distance."

I should be taking notes, I thought, desperate not to be unmasked for the neophyte I was in this group of about forty international experts. I resigned myself to absorbing what I could: the details of the scientific presentation, the collection of oddballs in the room.

"Next, let us turn to the seismic signatures involved in differentiating between a nuclear explosion and a standard earthquake."

The next slide was difficult to make out at first, a photograph of some kind of crater.

"When a nuclear device explodes underground, it sends uniform pressure to the walls of the cavity it creates. Explosions are thus observed through our seismic measurements as highly concentrated sources of compressional waves, moving out with approximately the same strength in all directions from the point of the detonated device," the seismologist explained. "An earthquake, by comparison, which is the result of two blocks of the Earth's crust slipping past each other along a fault line, produces shear waves—like *these*," he said, underlining for emphasis.

"Now what of the hypothetical scenario, of a test that is 'hidden' in the signature of an earthquake?" he asked, showing a slide with two blocks of squiggly black lines that looked to me like some kind of EKG readout. "Well, the answer is not so hypothetical after all," he said triumphantly. "Here you can see two seismogram recordings: one of a large earthquake that occurred in the eastern part of the Soviet Union, and the second one at one hundred seconds, a very small half-kiloton underground nuclear explosion undertaken by the Soviets at their Kazakhstan test site. Using a passband filter for higher-frequency seismic waves, we can verify the signal is for an explosion."

Well, that was very convincing, I thought, looking around the room for affirmation. But then the round of questions began, and the atmosphere in the room changed palpably to a slightly hostile one.

"I am still skeptical," said a middle-aged American. "What about decoupling? How could you detect the detonation of a nuclear device in a large underground cavity designed to muffle the seismic signal?"

"Exactly. Like in deep salt domes," piped in an Australian. "There's no definitive proof that we could distinguish one from the other in such a scenario."

Some of the other scientists began casting sidelong glances and rolling their eyes at each other, as if signaling "here we go again."

What the hell is going on? The presentation seemed rock solid to me. I'm no seismologist, but I got the gist. Any country that thinks it's going to secretly test a nuclear weapon and get away with it in the face of the monitoring systems this expert just presented to us is, well, either fooling itself or does not care about getting caught.

A similar scene then played itself out repeatedly. Some of the content concerned sensitive programs and advanced technology I had never heard about before—developments in hydroacoustic sensors, infrasound stations, and radionuclide detectors (equipment that measures radioactive particles and gases in the air).[1] And then there were the space-based remote sensing systems—the rationale for my participation in this event. Since the late 1950s, the United States, the Soviet Union, and a few other major powers had secretly developed fleets of extraordinarily sophisticated orbiting spy satellites.[2] Some were used for optical reconnaissance and included advanced lenses that could resolve details on Earth to the level of centimeters, allowing operators to read license plates on cars or even identify a person. There were also signals intelligence satellites positioned at much higher altitudes that sucked up and analyzed radio traffic and other telecommunications signals emanating from terrestrial communications.[3] Other satellites used synthetic aperture radar technology, which could resolve images at night or through cloud cover in all weather conditions.[4]

The Canadians were about to launch their own version of this type of satellite, called Radarsat, which was pitched to the public as a resource and Arctic management platform but undoubtedly was connected to and derived from classified programs.[5] Whenever data from satellites came up during the conference, everyone carefully tiptoed around the topic, cautious not to inadvertently expose some top secret factoid to others in the room.

The big development around this time was the growing sophistication and availability of commercially available space-based imagery. Previously constrained by national security regulations that limited their ground resolution, the end of the Cold War brought about a relaxation of these rules, and gradually more and more sophisticated imagery became available to the public for purchase. Decades later, a group of investigative journalists called Bellingcat would capitalize on these and other "open-source" data to undertake investigations into Syrian chemical weapons attacks and Russian clandestine operations.[6] What was being described in this conference was thus truly ahead of its time.

All these presentations were part of a proposed network of hundreds of applications outfitted with state-of-the-art technological systems that would encircle the planet in a web of sensors. They all had the goal of monitoring governments to verify they were keeping their pledge not to test a nuclear bomb—assuming a nuclear test ban would be ratified. This planetary sensor network was called the International Monitoring System, and at this time it was transitioning from design to material reality.[7] Hundreds of the proposed systems were already operational or were under construction, deployed in undersea sensors in the Pacific and Atlantic Oceans or on seismic measuring stations sprinkled around northern Sweden and Norway. Hundreds more were being designed and developed in research labs.

Although I was not a specialist in any of these areas, I did appreciate the big picture, and what I was observing felt truly spectacular: a planetary grid of inward-focused monitoring systems; the latest data collection instruments and analytical techniques used as a means of political constraint; science holding governments accountable. It was as though the entire planet was under not just one but several thousand distributed platforms each resolving on a different data point to monitor government actions in the public interest.

But there was something confusing at the core of these discussions. Why was it that the governments I imagined would be most supportive of the International Monitoring System were placing obstacles in the process?

I leaned over to ask the person responsible for my invitation to this meeting, retired Canadian air force colonel F. Ron Cleminson: "What's going on?"

"Well, looks like some people are finding other ways to communicate what they can't say out loud," he said.

What the hell does that mean? Cleminson, speaking in riddles, again.

———

I actually had two Canadians to thank for my presence at this conference: Cleminson and Dr. George Lindsey, a boffin who toiled for decades in the obscurity of Canada's top secret defense and intelligence establishment and was then transitioning from behind the curtains of the classified world. Although it was not publicly disclosed at the time, Lindsey was among those responsible for Canada's decision to abandon its nuclear weapon program in the 1960s.[8] He would go on to specialize in exploring technical systems for arms control verification, such as those being discussed at the conference.

Like so much else in my professional life, fortune played a role propelling me into Lindsey's orbit. As a graduate student at the University of British Columbia, I had decided to focus my doctoral work on information technology and international security. The internet was marginal to most people's lives at this time, yet the writing was on the wall: the "implications of the telecommunications revolution are going to be huge," my thesis advisor, Professor Mark Zacher, said when I enrolled in the program. "You should study the impact of the information revolution on global security."

I dove headlong into a broad swath of material on technology, politics, and information controls. The classics: Harold Innis, Marshall McLuhan, John Dewey, Norbert Wiener, Lewis Mumford. The science fiction: Mary Shelley and H. G. Wells through to William Gibson. Digital postmodernists: Paul Virilio, Donna Haraway, and Jean Baudrillard. Futurists and forecasters: Buckminster Fuller, Carl Sagan, Arthur C. Clarke, and Alvin Toffler.

I became fascinated with the material infrastructure of communication technologies—the overlooked elements of cables, transmission lines, broadcast towers, integrated circuits, and satellites. Every aspect of this world was undergoing profound transformation: speed, processing power, miniaturization of computer chips, semiconductors, packet switching. There was incredible hype too. It was difficult not to be enthralled by it all and to see only the benign implications: more personal communications; fewer monopolies of information; the collapse of distance. Those who speculated on how it might all go wrong were in the minority.

My interests in international security drew me to classified programs. I absorbed what little there was in the public domain. I learned about top secret wiretapping systems in the United Kingdom and the United States that had evolved alongside and even shaped the development of telecommunications going back to the first days of the telegraph. I explored the role of military research and development behind advances in computerization, especially in ballistic missile guidance systems and the space program. The most fascinating to me were the space-based reconnaissance systems, about which the general public knew little. These systems could not be contained in classified silos forever, I decided. It was only a matter of time before the type of overhead transparency available to a few spy agencies would be more widely available, and then what?

One day in the early 1990s, a professor circulated to us doctoral students a scholarship opportunity from the Canadian Department of National Defence. I decided to apply, proposing I would research the implications of the growing market for satellite reconnaissance systems for global security and arms control. It was a decidedly subversive topic. If I was awarded the scholarship, I would be receiving funding to research how the technology developed by states in secret might be turned around and focused on them to hold them in restraints.

Dr. George Lindsey was a member of the selection committee. Fortuitously, he was passionate about the theme I proposed and was actively promoting it in government circles. I was awarded one of the scholarships.

The scholarship winners were invited to a conference in Ottawa organized by the Department of National Defence. I felt out of place: I had no previous military experience, and I bristled against the culture of conformity and deference to authority. I came of age in the 1970s and 1980s, an era when military and intelligence abuses were being exposed by investigative journalists who were my heroes: Vietnam, Cambodia, El Salvador, Watergate, COINTELPRO, Iran-Contra. As a working-class street kid from a hardscrabble East Vancouver neighborhood (across the lane from our house when I was growing up was the local Hells Angels headquarters), I witnessed bullying and organized coercion that instilled an intimate appreciation of the dark side of human nature. Influenced by historian Charles Tilly, I saw states, especially autocratic ones, as merely larger and legitimized versions of those types of organized "protection rackets."[9] My project was about exploring how technological restraints might be applied to check those dark tendencies on a global scale. Everyone else's research was on more traditional topics, such as arms races and first-strike capabilities—as though mirroring the needs of the machine they wanted to ultimately serve. They all seemed dismissive of my unconventional topic too—except Lindsey. He introduced himself to me at the conference, and we spoke excitedly about the topic at length.

"You should connect with the Verification Research Unit at the Department of Foreign Affairs," he advised. "There's a person there named Ron Cleminson who commissions research projects, and I am sure there would be a welcome reception there for this topic."

A brilliant, unconventional thinker, Cleminson served for decades in the Royal Canadian Air Force, including stints flying aerial reconnaissance missions in modified twin-engine Lancaster bombers over the Canadian Arctic Archipelago and North Polar Basin taking photographs with tri-camera installations for evidence of the possible encroachment of Canadian territory by the Soviet Union. The Russians had even employed ice drifts as floating spy stations, which meandered into Canadian sovereign territory with the movement of the currents and ice. Cleminson kept tabs on these incursions, photographing the installations and equipment from the belly of a bomber.

After Cleminson's retirement from the air force, he was seconded to Canada's Department of Foreign Affairs and International Trade, where he established the Verification Research Unit. His experiences with overhead reconnaissance opened his eyes to the broader possibilities of preventing war. Like few others at the time, he foresaw the implications of a coming transparency revolution thanks to new information and communication technologies. He wanted to harness those means to build mutual confidence and prevent misunderstandings that lead to arms races and wars.

Cleminson commissioned me to undertake two separate studies on satellite reconnaissance and arms control: one evaluating a French-led proposal for an international satellite monitoring program, and the other a detailed analysis of the potential use of the then emerging market for commercial satellite imagery as a tool for arms control verification for nuclear, chemical, and ballistic missile weapons agreements.

"Take a look at synthetic aperture radar systems," Cleminson suggested. "Go speak to this person," referring to experts in other departments and agencies. I began to realize he was using my inexperience as a pawn, as part of his agenda to open uncomfortable questions for others and perhaps produce a body of work that could be used to push back against skeptics and conservatives who preferred the status quo.

I did not have any sort of security clearance at the time, but people got used to me being around. I saw extraordinary high-resolution images taken during the First Gulf War of Iraqis in the desert burying drums of something prohibited or suspicious and of vessels being used for clandestine weapons trafficking off the coast of Angola. I sat in rooms with contractors working for private corporations like SRI International and Raytheon, Rand, or Los Alamos National Laboratory—straight out of Eisenhower's military-industrial complex. I lingered around groups at conferences, eavesdropping on snippets of conversations. I was getting glimpses of a hidden geopolitics that almost no one in the academic world seemed to be describing or aware of. Canada is part of a close alliance, the Five Eyes, that dates back to World War II.[10] Relations within this community were tight, but not without tensions and internal machinations. I got the sense that we were not always "on the same team."

Cleminson and Lindsey were quietly pushing what I know now was a multilateral, planetary-wide arms control regime. This type of regime made strategic sense for a "middle power" country like Canada: embed other states in a system of interlocking controls, and there will likely be less of the type of chaos that could overwhelm us. But there were competing interests to manage as well. The Americans were emerging triumphant from the end of the Cold War and the collapse of the Soviet Union. The First Gulf War demonstrated their awesome military power, embedded in high-altitude stealth bombers strung together electronically through space-based systems that had no parallels. It was their unilateral moment, and a lot of people in the United States wanted to keep it that way.

Lindsey and Cleminson were attempting to push a global arms control agenda that would rely on digital technologies and space-based systems to help protect against the apocalyptic destructiveness of nuclear weapons. I was fascinated by the image they put forward, and the subversion of the establishment that went along with it. They spoke in aphorisms and made curious allusions that seemed to suggest some kind of hidden intrigue to which I was not privy, but which I might discover if I kept digging.

At times, it felt as though the people I was meeting and the shadowy worlds into which I was given partial access were mirroring a new cult sci-fi television series I was fascinated with: *The X-Files*. The show followed the travails of Fox Mulder, a maverick FBI investigator who was tailed by his skeptical partner, scientist-agent Dana Scully, as they chased unsolved cases and mysterious government conspiracies. The series tracked a world of clandestine operations and was a blend of alien technology, top secret government agencies, and sinister covert operations. Even when the plot lines were absurd, they were always thrilling and moody. What really grabbed my attention was the idea of a deep state manipulating people and institutions from behind the scenes—a parallel to some of my experiences working at the Verification Research Unit. There I encountered trenchcoated spooks who always seemed a bit severe and to have an ulterior agenda—much like those featured in *The X-Files*.

The show was filmed mostly in North Vancouver, Canada, and the old shipyard neighborhood near which I then resided.[11] I would routinely walk past film crews as they were in production. One episode, "Ghost in the Machine," was about an artificial intelligence system run amok that starts selectively murdering people to protect itself. The season finale was about a secret government program involving genetic experiments on fetuses using DNA nucleotides of extraterrestrial origin. The tagline for the series was "The Truth Is Out There," except for the first season's thrilling finale, where it changed to "Trust No One"—the phrase uttered by a dying Deep

Throat character who was encouraging Mulder and Scully from behind the scenes to keep up their investigations.

Only with the benefit of hindsight can I see how much the show inspired me at the time. A dogged young antiestablishment researcher; the search for truth amid a world of intrigue and treachery; a healthy degree of paranoia. I am not ashamed to say there is a bit of Fox Mulder still inside me today.

————

The conference on disarmament ended without agreement. The International Monitoring System continued to develop and deploy in the absence of a nuclear test ban agreement it was ostensibly meant to serve. I came to learn that the skeptical questions being asked were not genuine questions at all. They were tools of an ulterior agenda, using doubts about the accuracy of verification systems to prolong the discussions and forestall a nuclear test ban from ever coming to fruition. Plainly, the United States and its allies wanted to continue to test their nuclear arsenal to stay ahead of their rivals—an unpopular decision they did not want to admit out loud. The challenges around the implementation of the International Monitoring System were not technological but political, and for that reason they seemed so illogical to me at the time. With the Cold War over and liberal internationalism on the rise, I thought everyone would be on the same page. The time was right to develop a worldwide web of sensors monitoring the planet, locking down governments in legal agreements backed up with advanced technologies and scientific methodologies.

How wrong I was: we were, instead, putting roadblocks in the way, paralyzed by backroom maneuvering and deceptions motivated by power politics. "Trust No One" indeed. But I now knew what I wanted to do professionally: to help develop an evidence-based system, using the latest scientific instruments, to monitor governments' covert and other operations that presented threats to democracy and to hold them all to account. All I needed was a professional home to get on my way.

– 8 –

Surveillance Specialists

God, I love New York, I thought as I shuffled through Manhattan in the early-morning sidewalk rush, coffee in hand. There really is no other place like it on Earth. I walked along First Avenue, passed the United Nations, and then strolled up Forty-Third Street to the main entrance of the Ford Foundation building.

I had been summoned here unexpectedly by a young program officer named Anthony Romero, who would later go on to become the executive director of the American Civil Liberties Union. After earning my doctorate, I'd landed a tenure-track position at the University of Toronto in 1996 and begun building a research portfolio around information technology and global security. Romero wanted to learn more about it, and I wasn't about to pass up an opportunity at one of the world's largest foundations with an endowment of over $16 billion.

Romero began by explaining how the Ford Foundation occasionally gets involved in "field building"—supporting research on over-the-horizon topics it believes are not receiving the attention they deserve. "There's obviously so much happening with the internet right now," he said, "but so few people are studying the implications for international security, for human rights."

When he asked me to describe my research, I explained I was concerned about the design and security of global communications networks—the architecture—particularly as they relate to civil society, human rights, and privacy. "Everyone is really excited right now about everything digital," I said, "but I do not think enough people appreciate the underlying vulnerabilities in the internet's infrastructure—from the code in operating systems to the telecommunications networks and right up to satellites orbiting in space— and how they could be exploited by governments and the private sector to put civil society at risk."

I showed him a pilot study a student of mine, Nart Villeneuve, had written that used technical means to undertake reconnaissance of filtering installations on China's national backbone. I explained that these methodologies might provide a basis for a much larger project: a worldwide sensor network that would gather evidence of government attempts to control information—to "lift the lid" on the internet.

"Would you consider moving to New York and working with me as a program officer to help spur on research in this area?" Romero asked.

Briefly I contemplated managing a pool of funds, supporting cutting-edge research, maybe helping to build something along the lines of the elusive International Monitoring System but oriented toward documenting infringements on civil liberties, human rights, and privacy online. But no, I had four small children in Toronto and a not yet tenured position at the university. "I don't think I can do it," I said, with a pit in my stomach.

Romero was disappointed but understood my reasoning, thanked me, and said he'd be in touch. I took the elevator down and walked out into the busy Manhattan street wondering if I had just passed on the biggest opportunity in my life.

———

Around the time I was dreaming of an international monitoring system to hold governments in check, Jacob "Kobi" Alexander was scheming to get rich using surveillance technology for a much narrower and more conventional national security purpose: helping governments to snoop. An Israeli by birth, he had moved to the United States to pursue business opportunities. He had done his military service in an Israeli intelligence unit and applied the skills he learned there to develop profitable private ventures—value-added services for the exploding telecommunications market.[1]

By the late 1980s and early 1990s, the world of telecommunications and computer-based networking was on the cusp of a massive transformation that would alter every aspect of human life. This change was driven by a combination of technological advancements and the active involvement of the US government. Recognizing the potential of integrated circuits for missile guidance systems, for example, the Pentagon procured massive volumes of computer chips for its ballistic missile programs, which helped drive development and production and lowered costs, to the benefit of the consumers.[2] There were also important regulatory initiatives, including separating AT&T from local telecommunications companies following an antitrust suit in 1982, which brought competition to the telecommunications sector.[3]

Around the same time, the internet was gradually emerging from university labs and military research and development centers into the consumer marketplace. Government decisions played a crucial role in boosting the internet market too. In 1991, the National Science Foundation lifted restrictions on the commercial use of the internet, paving the way for its widespread adoption.[4] The National Information Infrastructure Act of 1993 and the subsequent Telecommunications Act of 1996 incentivized investment in broadband infrastructure and computerization.[5] A tornado of change swept across the country and spread around the world.

During this period, the concept of the "information superhighway" emerged as an odd, backward-sounding metaphor for the convergence of traditional telecommunications and computer-based networks. A multitude of new technologies flooded the marketplace as a result of digitization, fiber optics, exponential growth in computing power, the widespread adoption of the World Wide Web, and advancements in wireless communications. These developments, fueled by both government initiatives and technological advancements, laid the foundation for the rapid expansion and integration of digital technologies into society, ultimately transforming the way people communicate, access information, and interact with the world. This ecosystem of information and communications had no precedent in human history. Government security agencies took notice.

In 1993, *Fortune* magazine called Alexander's company, Comverse Technology, a "company to watch."[6] In fact, it was also a company that would be watching. The storefront business seemed innocuous enough: a computer-operated voice messaging service called Trilogue. At the time, voice messaging was performed mostly at the customer end, using a recording device on each telephone receiver. Trilogue moved the recording functions to "the cloud," as we call it today. The product was particularly appealing to clients in developing country markets, where telecommunications infrastructure was often poor and unreliable. Thanks to Comverse, businesses could rent a virtual mailbox that recorded voice messages, with no risk of interruption or loss of service.

But Comverse had another even more profitable product: "AudioDisk Multi-Channel Fax and Modem Monitoring."[7] *Fortune* said it was "used by police and intelligence agencies to record and store wiretap data" and "now accounts for just over half Comverse's sales."[8] Comverse's "aboveground" business, in other words, had a doppelgänger commercial line involving the same core technology but for a different clientele: government eavesdroppers.

This other business could monitor hundreds of telephone and fax machine lines simultaneously and make them available for concurrent searches by analysts at remote locations.[9] Government law enforcement and intelligence agencies were increasingly eager to get their hands on precisely this sort of capability. They feared "going dark"—meaning that new information technologies were effectively nullifying their time-tested eavesdropping methods. Speaking to the American Law Institute in 1994, and employing tropes that would be repeated by his successors up to the present, FBI director Louis Freeh warned that the agency's inability to eavesdrop on digital technologies would lead to "increased loss of life" and the "increased availability of much cheaper illegal drugs."[10]

What was not brought up, and is still rarely emphasized, is

how many opportunities were created for state surveillance by the emerging personal data ecosystem.[11] The digital nature of technology, where everything could be reduced to quantifiable ones and zeros, made the recording, storage, and parsing of communications traffic much easier. All that was needed was the right equipment and software placed at key choke points in telecommunications networks. The advent of retrieval and storage systems even made it possible to observe historical traffic patterns retrospectively. Everything passing through the network could be monitored and analyzed more readily, thanks to digital technologies.

To be sure, there were some challenges. Old-school wiretaps that involved manually attaching alligator clips to telephone poles or rerouting individual phone calls to law enforcement offices would not be so simple with packet-switched networks that blended thousands of streams of communication in the same fiber-optic lines. With the breakup of AT&T, the US government also had to negotiate with more than one giant firm.[12] There were now numerous "Baby Bells," each with its own legal team, equipment specifications, and other idiosyncrasies, that would need to be coerced or persuaded into cooperating with lawful interception requests—unless some standardization could be enforced.

The FBI wish was fulfilled, at least in part, with the passage of the Communications Assistance for Law Enforcement Act (CALEA) in 1994.[13] Similar measures would be implemented shortly thereafter in Europe by the newly created European Telecommunications Standards Institute. Both required telecommunications carriers to install equipment that would enable the government to intercept all communications traveling through their networks in real time and to interrogate what had been recorded in the past. There was also a provision for the storage and sharing of envelope information: the who, what, and where of each communication.[14] Forget "going dark"—this was more like putting on X-ray glasses. The US Department of Justice wanted to go much further, including being able to geolocate any cellphone within seconds, but that requirement was initially put off amid outcry from industry and privacy groups.[15] The changes wrought by these legislative initiatives were fundamental.

As one analysis put it: "Before CALEA, the needs of policing and crime control were incidental to the regular workings of the telephone system. After CALEA, telephone networks were designed to facilitate court-ordered surveillance from start to finish."[16]

The technology was moving too fast for government agencies and telecommunications companies to handle the engineering in-house. The race to outsource "wiretapping" and "communications surveillance" was about to explode, and firms like Comverse had a head start. Comverse's AudioDisk, which evolved into a product suite called T2S2, was a perfect fit for the lawful intercept specifications: plugged into telecommunications switches, it created a bifurcated line—one mirrored and delivered to a recording room for the government eavesdroppers; the other continuing on its way to its destination without interruption or the slowing down of the stream of data.[17] CALEA would penalize firms $10,000 a day for noncompliance with the requirements.[18] The telecommunications and industry groups complained, quite rightly, that these requirements would cost them a lot of money, so the government included provisions in CALEA for $500 million for reimbursement of those expenses.[19] For firms like Comverse, that was a bonanza.

Over time, as a major revenue stream, Comverse's lawful intercept line would grow more elaborate and sophisticated. An *Intelligence Online* article from 1995 said Comverse's next generation system "can intercept fax and modem communications but also process and store radio transmission and microwave telephone calls and retrieve images from surveillance cameras," information from which is stored in a central database and is "instantly accessible."[20] This line of business was renamed Comverse Infosys and spun out as an entirely separate subsidiary, Verint Systems, around 1994.[21] Although registered in Delaware and servicing government clients all over the world, it was in essence an Israeli firm. It would go on to become one of the world's most profitable surveillance vendors. By 1995, Alexander was boasting he had sales of his AudioDisk system in twenty-five countries.[22] Within a few years, that number would jump into the hundreds, including many with a checkered history of human rights abuses that Verint's technology would facilitate.[23]

Verint had few competitors, and those that did exist—NICE Systems (1986) and Narus (1997)—were strikingly similar.[24] Both were founded by veterans of Israeli military and intelligence and had significant American presence. Narus would be bought out by the US giant Boeing in 2010, but almost all its R&D and engineering took place in Israel.[25] Its core business lines were adaptations of Israeli signals intelligence systems, modified for the commercial marketplace and developed with extensive Israeli government R&D incentives. Like Verint, NICE and Narus also took advantage of the dual-use nature of their commercial product lines.[26] They all began by developing suites of value-added telecommunications services, particularly at the intersection of digital and mobile technologies (both of which were then taking off): call center recordings, voicemail, and SMS texting. Obviously, for law enforcement and intelligence clients, it would be useful for national security purposes to have systems that were positioned on top of telecommunications networks and designed to monitor, archive, and analyze the data as it flowed through.

There were revolving doors too. David Worthley, once the head of the FBI's liaison office with the telecommunications industry, went on to head the Verint unit that peddled its surveillance gear to the FBI, the National Security Agency, and other US federal agencies.[27] Verint even set up an office in Chantilly, Virginia, right next to the FBI's CALEA Implementation Unit. As investigative journalist James Bamford put it, "The company that secretly taps much of the country's telecommunications is now very closely tied to the agency constantly seeking greater access to the switches."[28]

The clients for these firms spread internationally, principally because the companies had no competition. "Israel is the Harvard of antiterrorism," one US police chief remarked.[29] It had the products, the on-the-ground experience, and the discharged soldiers and intelligence personnel that everyone in the world wanted. According to Bamford, "Never before in history have so few people wiretapped so many. From China to America and from Europe to Southeast

Asia and Australia, countries use Verint and Narus equipment to eavesdrop on—and in many cases repress—their citizens."[30]

It is striking just how much Israeli companies have dominated the surveillance landscape from the beginning of the digital age. And within each of those companies, the number of individuals with experience in Israeli intelligence or the military is striking too. Consider Verint. Although it is located in the United States, its roots were planted back in Israel. "Comverse does nearly all its manufacturing in Israel, where it can take advantage of government subsidies and tax credits for high-tech industries," the *Fortune* profile stated.[31] Almost all the key people involved in Comverse and Verint were Israelis with a background in intelligence or the Israel Defense Forces. It helps that military service is mandatory in Israel. Comverse senior employees all served in elite intelligence units in the IDF. Dan Bodner, who was employed as Verint's president and CEO since its founding, was a former Israeli army engineer.[32] The chief operating officer of Comverse and Verint, Carmel Vernia, was Israel's top government scientist and oversaw the government R&D tax credit and grant program for Israeli start-ups from which Comverse received numerous financial benefits.[33] He would later join the board of a Verint spinoff called PerSay, whose business specialized in biometric voice recognition—the type used to authenticate holders of financial accounts or to sift through oceans of data to look for suspects uttering specific key words.[34] "We just need two seconds of audio to be able to recognize a speaker," said PerSay's CEO.[35]

What explains the huge shadow cast by Israel over the global surveillance industry? As is often the case, the explanation is not found in some farsighted design or secret conspiracy (as some might conjure up), but rather in the by-products of that country's unique history, politics, and culture—in contingencies, in other words.

The Israeli state was founded in 1948 amid hostile nations bent on its destruction.[36] A roster of enemies, from neighboring Arab states and later Iran to Hezbollah, Hamas, Islamic Jihad, and other terrorist organizations, has organized violent attacks over decades on Israelis and Jewish sites not only in Israel but all over the world.

This omnipresent existential risk placed a premium on homegrown defense and intelligence gathering. The Israeli military established specialized units dedicated to reconnaissance and espionage, including telephone and telecommunications interception, to try to anticipate and neutralize what its adversaries were planning.[37] Surveillance technology enabled the Mossad and Israeli authorities to undertake covert operations without always putting human personnel at risk, and that technology has evolved and grown more sophisticated over time.

While numerous elite intelligence units operated within the Israeli military, the signals intelligence group Unit 8200, founded in 1952, stood out. Highly secretive for most of its history until recently, Unit 8200 has garnered widespread admiration within intelligence circles as Israel's homegrown counterpart to the much better resourced US National Security Agency, serving as a training ground for the nation's most skilled hackers and computer engineers. In the words of the *Financial Times*, "If there is a beating heart to Israel's high-tech security state—the spot on the Venn diagram where 'cool' meets 'creepy'—it is Unit 8200."[38]

Early on, a strategic decision was made to invest heavily in high-tech industries, positioning Israel's computer sector well ahead of most other countries. One of the world's first large-scale, stored-program computers, WEIZAC, was developed in Israel at the Weizmann Institute of Science in the mid-1950s.[39] Then an influx of Russian immigrants brought with them expertise in mathematics, computer science, and engineering, fueling technological research and development. Institutions were gradually established to train the youth in computer engineering and channel the talents of the best into the intelligence services. A feeder system called "Magshimim" was developed—a three-year after-school program targeting sixteen- to eighteen-year-old students with exceptional computer coding and hacking skills.[40] To this day, programs like these act as a pipeline for potential recruits to Unit 8200. Moreover, Israel is one of the few countries in the world that offers the option in high school to take matriculation exams in "cybersecurity," and many Israeli universities have long provided specialized advanced graduate degrees in that same field.[41] From its founding, in other words, Israel was seated near the front of the information revolution train, positioning Israeli companies as world leaders.

Several key unexpected events also played a significant catalyzing role. Following the Six-Day War in 1967, a French arms embargo prompted the Israeli government to double down on homegrown weapons and on research and development in information technology.[42] Similarly, the initial shock of the 1973 Yom Kippur War, akin to the impact of the events of 9/11 on the US intelligence community, led to an important reassessment of intelligence organization. In response to Israel's unpreparedness, the Agranat Commission was established to investigate, and its report speeded efforts to streamline and modernize intelligence gathering.[43] They included a new special forces reconnaissance unit, known as Sayeret Matkal, and investments in indigenous surveillance systems for unmanned aerial vehicles, telecommunications interception, signals intelligence, and other reconnaissance methods—what we now refer to as "cyber."[44]

Within the intelligence agencies, a culture of entrepreneurship, internal competition, and flexible ingenuity permeated the entire system, and especially Unit 8200. Soldiers in this group operated in small teams, often under resource constraints, tackling time-sensitive matters where disruption and challenging authority were actively encouraged. They were taught to think creatively and "outside the box."[45] They were hackers before the term was invented. They carried this culture of experimentation with them into the private sector, contributing to Israel's reputation as the "Start-up Nation."[46] Having Unit 8200 as part of your résumé came to be seen as a major calling card.

The Israeli government had a direct hand in promoting the commercial surveillance industry too. It encouraged the privatization and commercialization of military and intelligence innovations. It offered tax credits and provided support for research and development from the Israel Office of Science and Technology, but always without controls on intellectual property or any strict nondisclosure requirements that were typical among other governments' clandestine services.[47] The message was simply: "After your service is complete, take what you've learned and go forth and profit."[48] Retired brigadier general Hanan Gefen, a former commander of Unit 8200, told *Forbes* in 2007 that "Nice, Comverse and Check Point . . . three of the largest high-tech companies . . . were all directly influenced by 8200 technology."[49] A 2018 study cited by the Israeli newspaper *Haaretz* estimated that "80% of the 2,300 people who founded Israel's 700 cybersecurity companies had come through IDF intelligence."[50]

The Israeli government also used its diplomatic channels to facilitate sales negotiations for Israel-based companies with government and other clients abroad. As with the trade in conventional weapons systems, trade in surveillance products and intelligence-gathering services was used as a lever in Israel's strategic foreign policy—a way to curry favor with allies and loosen the country's diplomatic isolation. The overall approach was driven by realpolitik considerations and Israel's self-interest, particularly with respect to votes in the UN General Assembly. Documents made available through leaks or access to information requests show that Israeli officials were pushing sales of arms and surveillance technology and providing counterinsurgency training to government clients they knew were among the world's worst dictatorships—apartheid-era South Africa, Morocco, Saudi Arabia, and genocidal regimes in Rwanda and Central America.[51] Israeli human rights activist and lawyer Eitay Mack noted that unlike the United States, where Congress imposes all sorts of restrictions on US arms sales to controversial regimes or to war zones, there has been no comparable oversight regime in Israel: "There is nothing like that here."[52]

There is also the uncomfortable question of the Palestinian occupation.[53] According to author Antony Loewenstein, Israel has treated Palestine as a "laboratory," with successive waves of technological experimentation being conducted on an unwitting population and then exported around the world as commercial products—similar in a way to China's experimentation with the latest surveillance and information control measures in Xinjiang or Tibet.[54] But others I have spoken to say the reality is more complex. Although there is no doubt that Israel's control over the telecommunications system in the occupied territories has been instrumental in everything from population control to targeted as-sassinations, and closed-circuit TV cameras and drones dominate checkpoints and settler territories, the reality of the occupation is that it has relied mostly on (sometimes flawed) human intelligence and the raw application of military force.

Surveillance technologies have been used as part of counter-insurgency and terrorist operations, but mostly as an adjunct to more physical, often brutal means of population control—some of it highly controversial even among those on the implementation side. In 2014, for example, a group of forty-three former Unit 8200 reservists published an open letter revealing the use of coercive surveillance tactics on Palestinians, including collecting incrimi-nating or embarrassing details on their sexual lives or gathering personal details on innocent family members for extortionary pur-poses.[55] The alarms raised by the reservists highlighted the same type of tactics that we later discovered were being used routinely by government clients of Israel-based mercenary spyware compa-nies abroad.

The high degree of specialization and proficiency in surveil-lance, both human and technological, would become a major selling point for Israeli technical exports. Israeli surveillance and private intelligence firms would routinely score huge contracts supplying crowd control and other population monitoring services for major world sporting events, including the Olympic Games and the World Cup.[56] These major events were used to experiment with and refine the latest video surveillance, biometric, cellphone-scanning, and other high-tech systems. After the event was over, the technology would become a permanent feature of the social and political landscape, with renewable contracts for ongoing ser-vice provision. As Loewenstein put it, "Alongside protecting nu-clear plants, airport security, and law enforcement, among many other areas where surveillance and tight security were viewed as essential, Israeli expertise or equipment were routinely the answers to almost any security question."[57] To this day, while there are many firms in the surveillance sector based in other jurisdictions, Israeli firms have an unmistakable allure. Their surveillance specialists dominate the global marketplace.

———————

In 2006, Kobi Alexander became a fugitive from the law.[58] Charged in the United States with money laundering and securities fraud, he fled to Namibia.[59] For years he remained outside the reach of justice, protected from extradition thanks to his generosity to certain well-placed government officials.[60] In 2016, however, he reached a settlement and eventually paid a fine of $53 million to the US government. Comverse's general counsel, William F. Sorin, pleaded guilty and was sentenced to a year and a day in prison.[61]

The scandal around Alexander and several other top Comverse officials took a toll on the business and its subsidiaries. Both Comverse and Verint were briefly delisted from the NASDAQ.[62] Eventually, Verint split off entirely from Comverse, buying out its ownership shares, and settled into the government surveillance market.[63] Its technology would continue to spread, as would those of its competitors Narus and NICE, to some of the world's worst human rights abusers in Central Asia, Africa, South America, and Southeast Asia.

Alexander's entrepreneurialism paved the way for many surveillance firms that followed. But in a sense, so did his corruption. Businesses operating in the shadows, evading public scrutiny, lacking transparency, and servicing government clients who themselves operate in a kind of extralegal terrain tend to attract individuals of questionable morals. Before long a new generation of Israel-based surveillance vendors stepped into the mix, following the same playbook to success—and eventual ill repute—as Comverse. The invention of smartphones, with their store of highly revealing personal data, would present yet another technological challenge and an irresistible opportunity for the next wave of surveillance entrepreneurs.

2001

TORONTO

"Hi, Professor Deibert," the voicemail began from a program officer at the Ford Foundation. "Please give Anthony Romero a call back. He has some news he'd like to share with you."

After I passed up the offer to join the Ford Foundation, Romero had generously offered to evaluate a project proposal from me that it might sponsor: "It should be focused on some aspect of what we spoke about—information security and global civil society— and ideally something that is collaborative and interdisciplinary." The proposal was fairly simple for me to write because I had been thinking about the idea for some time. I wanted to pull together a team of researchers who would use a variety of skills and methods to "lift the lid on the internet" and document patterns and practices of information control: internet censorship, surveillance, information warfare, whatever we could empirically observe. I also thought the initiative could help to design tools and applications that could better protect users' communications, bypass internet censorship, and enable activists and others to communicate without the fear of snooping. I framed the project as helping to fill a gap in the existing landscape by spurring on a kind of "counterintelligence for global civil society." I called the project the Citizen Lab.

"Congratulations," Romero said when I called back. "We are excited to support your project."

Although I had received some grants in the past, this one was on a different scale. *I'm going to have my own research lab!* I would need a home for the staff I intended to hire, a place where we could brainstorm and collaborate as a team.

Ask any professor, and they will tell you the most contentious issues on any campus typically revolve around space allocation. I knew it wasn't going to be easy. I was still a junior professor and had no bargaining power. I needed something workable but inconspicuous, so as not to draw attention.

I recalled that a new center for international studies had recently been announced, and an old heritage building, Devonshire

House, was in the process of being renovated to accommodate the new facility. My colleague and mentor Janice Stein was the inaugural director, so I went over to have a look. Pulling on some protective gear and a vest that was near the entrance to the site, I squeezed through the fencing and made my way to the basement. There I located a large space that was being framed in. *Perfect!* I pulled out my mobile phone and called Janice.

"Hi, Janice," I said, looking around the dusty construction site. "I've got some good news. I've just received a grant from the Ford Foundation to start a research lab on digital security."

"That's great!" she replied. "Congratulations!"

"One issue is that I need some space for it. I'll be hiring a team of interdisciplinary researchers."

"Oh? Where do you think you'll do that?"

"I'm hoping to convince you that I can use the space I'm standing in right now."

To her credit, she took a big risk and agreed.

A few months later, as the finishing touches were coming together for the Citizen Lab's headquarters, I woke to a spectacularly beautiful September morning in Toronto, grabbed a coffee, and turned on CNN.

"This just in. You are looking at obviously a very disturbing live shot there. That is the World Trade Center, and we have unconfirmed reports this morning that a plane has crashed into one of the towers."

I sat and stared at the television, gobsmacked. As my mind raced at the many implications of this horrific event, one thing became clear: a major reckoning would be coming from the US defense and intelligence community and its allies that would change the landscape worldwide for years to come. The Lab's mission suddenly took on a whole new urgency.

Close Calls in Guatemala City

JUNE 2003

GUATEMALA CITY

The large room was lit by sunlight peeking through half-shut curtains. The windows were open, it was hot and humid, and flies were buzzing. Several long rows of tables lined the interior. On each were human skeletal remains—some partial, others more complete.

A small group of forensic investigators from the Fundación de Antropología Forense de Guatemala (FAFG) were working there, equipped with scientific instruments, cameras, and notepads. Since its founding in 1992, the foundation had carried out 191 exhumations of more than two thousand victims of the Guatemalan Civil War, which ravaged the country from 1960 to 1996.[1]

"Here we have the bones of the children which have been processed and cleaned," explained Mario Alberto Vásquez Gómez, a member of the team as he led me through the room. "This corresponds to a child that is two years old, and this to one approximately three months old." He gestured at the remains on the next table. "These belong to two adults who died through violent causes. According to the testimonies of this event, they were fleeing their communities. The army reached them and assassinated them. We discovered sixteen very sharp blows that were inflicted on this person."

I asked him how he feels about his profession. "It's very difficult work," he says in a somber tone. "We don't see these as cold pieces of bone but as an individual that had a life."

I paced slowly alongside the tables, taking in what he was describing. A feeling of nausea crept over me. How could there be such unfathomable cruelty?

I had founded the Citizen Lab as a kind of "counterintelligence for civil society" two years earlier, and we were just finding our feet—exploring where and how we could make a mark. There was, at the time, an almost universal excitement about the internet and digital technologies. They were widely seen as unequivocal forces for democratization and people power, but even then I was doubtful.

The initial proposal for the Lab included a combination of missions. One was focused on the investigatory side: we wanted to document "the exercise of power in cyberspace," as I articulated it, which meant using a combination of evidence-based, digital research methods and techniques to uncover what governments and companies might be doing to control the internet and undermine human rights. I regarded the planetary-wide verification system, which I had observed in my work for the Verification Research Unit, as the model for this set of activities. This part of the mission is still our major occupation.

At this early stage, we also had a second vision for what the Lab could do, one that was more proactive. We wanted to try to build better security for civil society, in part through the development and provision of new technical systems or equipment. We thought a lot of good NGOs had no idea how vulnerable they were and could use our help. We imagined auditing their systems, doing penetration testing, and working with others to develop tools to communicate better without interception or to store data on secure servers to prevent theft and inadvertent data exposure. That was how I defined "hacktivism" at the time: as a John Dewey–type practical art with the political purpose of developing technologies and helping organizations adopt them to better secure their rights and freedoms. Today, that term has morphed into something pejorative. A hacktivist is someone who engages in criminal offenses online for a political purpose.

Over time, it became clear that the more proactive part of the mission would be unsustainable for a small group such as ours. Although many other organizations would eventually emerge to do security training, the reality was that security risks are highly dependent on their context. Getting security right requires local organizations to buy in and build their own internal capacity. Having outsiders parachute in to fix and advise, and then leave, is not a viable solution. Our visit to Guatemala was an early lesson in that respect.

We had come to Guatemala City to undertake security audits of the generally unreliable internet setups then used by human rights NGOs and war crimes investigators. We also brought a few computers and Wi-Fi routers to give to those in need. To help finance our visit and to promote awareness of the issues, I had helped conceive of a documentary project that was picked up by a Canadian public television broadcaster. Called *Hacktivista*, and directed and coproduced by filmmaker and close friend Mike Downie, the documentary followed myself and three Citizen Lab researchers—Graeme Bunton, Michelle Levesque, and Nart Villeneuve—as we traveled to Guatemala and then on to Chiapas, Mexico. Accompanying us on the trip was Robert Guerra, a former student of mine, who was then with an organization called Privaterra, which was one of the few NGOs focused on practical digital security at the time.

Since 1960, Guatemala had been devastated by successive dictatorships and a long period of civil war in which hundreds of thousands of innocent people had disappeared or been murdered. The human rights situation was so bad in the period leading up to our visit that the US government decided to cut off military aid.[2] There was an omnipresent risk of random violence. Almost all the offices we visited were situated in the crime-infested zones of Guatemala City. The annual murder rate had risen 14 percent the year we arrived, to an average of 35 per 100,000 inhabitants—the fourth highest in the world that year and the worst in Central America.[3] Everyone seemed to be carrying a weapon. Pickup trucks driving along the main streets with several rifle-toting men in the bed were a common sight. Banks and other stores typically had several armed private security guards who appeared at least as dangerous as anyone who might rob the bank. Muggings and assaults were common. The human rights NGOs and war crimes investigators we were meeting had a heightened level of risk, and during our interactions with them, we joined this amplified category too.

One NGO we visited over several days, the Rigoberta Menchú Tum Foundation, was continually harassed and its members targeted for assassination because it defended the rights of Indigenous people and combated human rights abuses. A few years before our trip, the foundation had initiated a legal case alleging torture, genocide, and terrorism against several high-profile Guatemalan army officers, senior congressional figures, and former president Efraín Ríos Montt.[4] Guatemala was one of those countries that had a real "deep state" of landowning elites who dealt severely with any efforts to hold them accountable for their crimes. Staff pointed out how several armed men took shifts across the street watching the building's entrance from 7:00 a.m. to 7:00 p.m. every day. The men were clearly visible in the closed-circuit TV camera the foundation had set up and made no effort to disguise their presence or conceal their assault weapons. I stared at the black-and-white image on the CCTV monitor every time I passed it: the men standing in plain view, weapons clearly visible, the halo of the streetlight giving them a sinister glow. This type of harassment drained the staff and caused palpable anxiety for everyone. In addition to the CCTV camera, a "mantrap" was installed in the entrance to the office to vet visitors, and the staff had developed secret escape routes in case of an assault on the facility. But there are only so many precautions an organization like this can take to keep its employees safe—especially because they have to leave the building eventually.

In the period around our site visits, Rigoberta Menchú, the president of the foundation, was followed by a white pickup truck that attempted to run her off the road. A few days later, the head of security was assaulted at gunpoint by men who forced him into a taxi and beat him with the butts of their guns, all the while issuing threats against the foundation. The same day, another death threat was received over the phone: "Stop causing trouble, because we know who you are, where you live, and we'll soon be joining you." I was wracked with anxiety every time I visited their office, worried about the safety of my researchers.

The investigators at Fundación de Antropología Forense de Guatemala were also routinely singled out for harassment and death threats. Amnesty International reported that FAFG members had their homes watched, were followed in cars, or had weapons discharged at them at least sixteen times in the previous year.[5] A few months before our visit, a letter delivered anonymously to staffers working on the exhumations threatened that their families would "soon be burying their bones and those of their children." While we met in the office over several visits, I overheard several phone calls in which anonymous men issued similar threats. I had the impression that while the staffers tried to treat them nonchalantly and carry on with their work, the constant threats were taking a large emotional and psychological toll.

Our support for the organizations also triggered attention. We were initially booked into a large chain hotel in a relatively safe zone in the city, but our local contacts told us it wasn't safe and we had to move. We later learned that only a few weeks earlier a different group of visitors working for another NGO had been assaulted by armed men who broke into their rooms at that same hotel.

The Guatemala trip demolished our expectations. We arrived thinking that our audits and scans of their internet connections, and the installation of a few firewalls, would protect them. While the ideas were noble, the practical implications were far off the mark. We were worrying about hypothetical problems that wouldn't materialize for years in this country. The bad actors who terrorized the organizations we worked with were largely oblivious of the internet, which was either inaccessible or slow and unreliable. The real threats were mostly physical: drive-by assassinations on motorcycles; random assaults in alleyways; death threats over the phone or dropped off in manila envelopes; guns fired at windows and doorways. Who needs sophisticated spyware when you can simply break into an office, beat up the staff, and take the computers?

That's not to say there was no electronic surveillance. Everyone assumed all the landline phones were bugged. We heard vague rumors of Israeli agents, but it all seemed conspiratorial and impossible to verify. Little did we know how deeply Israeli expertise,

weaponry, and high-tech reconnaissance gear had already penetrated this country.

———

Around the late 1960s and early 1970s, Israel began a diplomatic
outreach effort to Central and South America, in part to develop
markets for exports of weapons and other Israeli products and services and in part to court allies and try to end the country's international isolation. According to a 1982 *New York Times* report,
"The Israelis are not there, as are most of the others, as participants
in a form of East-West confrontation or to engage in revolution-
ary or counterrevolutionary intrigue. Israel, the officials explain,
is there . . . for its own reasons: to build markets essential to the
economic strength of its large military industries and to cushion its
diplomatic isolation caused by Arab diplomacy."[6]

Starting in the 1970s, Israel began exporting large amounts
of military and intelligence technology to Guatemala, including
Israeli-made Arava aircraft, artillery, and small arms such as Uzi
submachine guns and Galil assault rifles.[7] Israeli technicians and
military advisors gave training and advice on counterinsurgency
operations, such as those that led to the massacre and the skeletal
remains we had just observed.

The imports and training were highly prized by Guatemala's
ruling elite because they arrived without the "condescending" restrictions that US weapons exports and advice carried with them.
The Israelis asked no questions and offered advice on how best to
handle local insurgencies—a job they knew well from their own
experience in the occupied territories.

The Israelis also exported high-tech equipment. In the late
1970s, Israel Aerospace Industries, controlled by the Israeli Ministry of Defense, installed an ELTA radar air defense and traffic
control system at Guatemala City's airport.[8] And in 1980, Tadiran
Israel Electronics Industries' technical teams built a computer monitoring center, the Centro Regional de Telecomunicaciones, which
was reportedly used for domestic surveillance. It was located in
Guatemala City in a block-long data center within the presidential

guard complex situated behind the National Palace that houses the regime's intelligence and law enforcement operations.[9] One Israeli journalist claimed the system was used to "follow up the guerrilla movements in the capital."[10] A 1981 Amnesty International report described the data center as the operational hub for Guatemala's "extensive secret and extra-legal security operations."[11] It was also reportedly used to store dossiers used by "death squads" in Guatemala's program of "pacification." We walked by that building on several occasions, oblivious to what lay inside.

In the early 1980s, the Guatemalan army opened a school for computer networking and electronics that was reportedly "built, funded, and staffed by Israelis."[12] Then president Fernando Romeo Lucas García claimed the school would be used to train specialists in counterinsurgency technologies and methods, including electronic interception and radio jamming.[13] The colonel who headed the school was quoted as saying that the "teaching methods, the teaching teams, the technical instruments, books, and even the custom furniture were designed and built by the Israeli company DEGEM Systems."[14] Well before we "hacktivists" were moving from NGO to NGO in a relatively primitive attempt to secure their internet communications, Israeli technicians were being paid huge sums to advise the Guatemalan regime on how to monitor the entire electromagnetic spectrum. We were outmatched, and we didn't even realize it.

Israeli technical advisors and counterinsurgency specialists played an undeniable role in Guatemalan repression and the mass violence committed against the Indigenous Mayan population. We met some of these victims, and they gave us firsthand accounts of brutal massacres against entire villages. A 1983 *Washington Post* article described how "Israeli advisers—some official, others private—helped Guatemalan internal security agents hunt underground rebel groups."[15] When Guatemalan president Ríos Montt carried out a coup in 1982, he did so with the assistance of Israeli military advisors. He even bragged to reporters that the coup was successful "because many of our soldiers were trained by the Israelis."[16]

According to the Commission for Historical Clarification

(CEH), which was established through the Accord of Oslo on June 23, 1994, as many as two hundred thousand people were killed or disappeared during Guatemala's civil war between 1960 and 1996.[17] Israeli weapons and know-how, served up by private military firms staffed by reserve and retired Israeli army and intelligence personnel, were indispensably linked to it all. Similar deals were made throughout the region, in Chile, Colombia, Argentina, and other Latin American countries wherever a dictator engaged in domestic repression. A 1986 study assessed that "Latin America was undisputedly Israel's largest market for arms, accounting for approximately 50 to 60 percent of its total military exports."[18]

Israeli human rights lawyer Eitay Mack told me that "the Israeli officials who approved the defense export and were involved in it knew very well about the atrocities taking place in Guatemala and why Guatemala purchases weapons from Israel." Israel supplied the cylinder guns to the military forces and the Arava planes, armed with machine guns and rockets, that were used to suppress Indigenous communities living in mountainous areas. Moreover, Mack continued, the Israeli government approved the training of Guatemalan military and intelligence officials in Israel and sent Israeli instructors and technicians "to teach Guatemalan military personnel radio communication, surveillance techniques, and information interception."

————

After Guatemala City, we made our way by car along the highway to Chiapas, Mexico—home of the infamous Zapatista hacktivists. As we drove through rural Guatemala and into southern Mexico, we were stopped by a small group of armed men. Fortunately, after some lengthy negotiations, we were allowed to pass without further incident. We were lucky. We could have very easily been just another random murder in the backwoods of southern Mexico.

We drove in relative silence the rest of the way to our destination in Chiapas, the beautiful San Cristóbal de las Casas. The Zapatistas, an insurgency connected to a social movement for independence and spearheaded by a charismatic leader calling himself

Subcommandante Marcos, had been percolating over several years, occasionally erupting in violence or mass protests. The movement was widely publicized in hipster leftist circles worldwide, in part because of the anti-capitalist, anti-globalization ideology and rhetoric of Marcos and his allies but also because the group used novel electronic civil disobedience tactics to further its cause, including denial-of-service attacks against the Mexican government and other websites. We spent our time meeting organizers of the Zapatistas' digital rebellion. San Cristóbal had become a magnet for anti-globalization activists, and the city felt like a "place to be" for northerners making anti-authority pilgrimages. After the trauma and dread of Guatemala City, it felt to us like a spa retreat.

We made it out of Guatemala just in time. Within days of our leaving, a political riot initiated by former president Ríos Montt engulfed Guatemala City. On that "Black Thursday," thousands of government supporters from the countryside were trucked into the capital.[19] According to an Amnesty International report, on arrival they were issued "guns, machetes, clubs, gasoline, and tires to burn."[20] In a move echoed later by Donald Trump before the January 6, 2021, insurrection in Washington, DC, Ríos Montt, who had been denied a ticket in the upcoming presidential campaign, issued veiled threats about violence, announcing "that he and his party would be unable to control the anger of his followers."[21]

Armed thugs proceeded to attack various targets, including the Supreme Court of Justice, the Constitutional Court of Guatemala, and major media outlets. Human rights organizations were singled out, including those we had visited many times on-site. Fearing for their lives, staffers fled their offices and sought shelter in the headquarters of the Myrna Mack Foundation, the NGO with the best physical security protections. According to Amnesty International's account, "The events were so threatening that all schools sent their students home, and the judicial branch closed down all of its buildings after receiving several bomb threats. Foreign embassies also shut down, but many of their personnel were unable to reach their homes because the area of the city where many live had been blocked by the mob."[22] It wasn't until the Constitutional

Court reversed its decision on Ríos Montt, allowing him to mount a presidential campaign, that the crowds eventually dispersed.

————

We went into our Guatemala trip prepped to check internet security risks that had not yet materialized. Our "threat model" was off by a decade, but it soon synched up. At the time of our visit in the early 2000s, Israeli technicians and consultants were already preparing the ground for what would become a selling spree to equip Guatemalan security agencies with the latest internet and mobile phone surveillance equipment. Among them was Israeli operative turned weapons dealer Ori Zoller, whose business ventures included selling AK-47s to Colombian rebels and brokering deals for Israeli consultants and arms dealers throughout Central and South America.[23] Leaked emails from the Italian spyware vendor Hacking Team show that by 2013 Zoller had helped broker a deal to deliver Hacking Team's phone-hacking technology to Guatemala—technology that was used against the human rights NGOs we had visited.[24]

The Guatemala trip completely reshaped my understanding of digital security issues and, on a much broader scale, the Lab's entire mission moving forward. Previously, my perspective had been predominantly technical in nature. I envisioned our role as part of a global observation network dedicated to documenting threats to a free and secure internet. We had already begun using network scanning tools and remote probes to investigate censorship and surveillance in distant jurisdictions, making significant progress in refining these techniques. However, our Guatemala experience illuminated the essential human aspect that had been missing from our work. It vividly exposed the risks inherent in conducting human rights activities within a hostile and oppressive environment. Above all, it emphasized the significance of local context, highlighting the need to immerse ourselves in the situation, engage directly with affected individuals, and adopt a victim-centric approach to our work. Before long we would broaden our collaborations with partners in dozens of countries in nearly every region of the world—

brave individuals who would take enormous risks serving as our ears and eyes on the ground.

Beyond recalibrating our approach, I emerged from the experience inspired as never before. Witnessing firsthand the harassment and intimidation, hearing the chilling stories of murder and genocide, and walking past the haunting skeletal remains of those who fell victim to the Guatemalan dictatorships fueled my determination to alleviate the suffering that often accompanies despotic rule. I was acutely aware of the privilege I had by living in Canada and holding a tenured professorship. I felt a deep sense of obligation to go beyond merely "speaking truth to power"; I wanted to pursue and expose clandestine operations that undermine human rights and public accountability, no matter where they are found or however powerful those behind them may be. The more powerful the better, in fact.

"So, You Are Paid by the Aga Khan?"

APRIL 29, 2010
PRIVY COUNCIL OFFICE, OTTAWA

Professor Janice Stein and I arrive at the Privy Council Office in downtown Ottawa—the nerve center of the Canadian government. It provides the prime minister and the cabinet with assessments of intelligence, national security, and other key public policy issues. Stein, as director of the Munk School of Global Affairs at the University of Toronto, was well connected in government circles. She offered to arrange this meeting to help smooth things over for me.

The Citizen Lab was part of the research team that published two pathbreaking reports on cyber espionage in back-to-back years: the *Tracking GhostNet* report (March 2009) and *Shadows in the Cloud* (April 2010).[1] Both were blockbusters widely covered in global media, including the *New York Times*.[2] They were the first public reports to effectively expose and disrupt massive spying campaigns in real time. Both were unprecedented in their raw detail, and they put the Lab on the map, for better or for worse.

I heard rumors that some people in the Canadian government were suspicious about these reports—and about us too. One high-level source told me that a classified briefing on our investigations went all the way to Prime Minister Stephen Harper's desk, and "it was not very flattering at all." A second source from Canada's Public Safety agency told us cryptically that had we disclosed our *GhostNet* report to them before publication, "they would have shut us down."

Shut us down? My mind drifted to trenchcoated agents with a retinue of RCMP officers in tow, forcing their way into the Lab with a warrant and seizing our computers, like a scene out of *The X-Files*. The mere threat was enough to give me pause. We had always conceived of our work as independent of governments, but we were open to constructive dialogue and appropriate information sharing. Hearing that vague threat made me wonder whether such constructive engagements were even possible.

When Stein and I arrived at the Privy Council Office, we proceeded through an airport-style security checkpoint before being guided into a crypt-like room where we waited . . . and waited. Finally, two government officials entered the room, one clad in bureaucratic attire and the other with two mobile phones holstered to her waist. Given our reports on cyber espionage and her demeanor, I inferred the woman was probably from our ultra-secretive signals intelligence agency, the Communications Security Establishment. They took their seats across the table, opened a folder of papers, and immediately delved into the business at hand.

"So, you are paid by the Aga Khan?" the man asked assertively.

"Excuse me? I have no idea what you're talking about."

He checked his notes. "Not the Aga Khan. I mean the Dalai Lama. How much did he pay you?"

"We weren't paid by him or anyone else to do this research." *This is starting to feel like an interrogation.*

"What you have done is illegal. You guys are hacking," the woman chimed in, simmering with apparent irritation.

Aha. So that's what was in the classified briefing! "That's not true at all—" Before I could begin to explain our methods, she interrupted with more misrepresentations of what we do and how we do it.

I don't respond well to bullies. Stein intervened as the discussion became heated and tried to calm the situation by appealing to the public value of a group like ours. "This is a world-leading organization doing cutting-edge public interest research. The Canadian government should be celebrating and protecting them." They didn't seem convinced. After some back and forth between Stein and the two officials, we packed up without exchanging the usual perfunctory pleasantries. The meeting ended on a sour note.

"What was that?" we asked each other, once back on the street.

"I'm shocked," she said. "I have never experienced anything like it."

Clearly, we had rubbed some people in high places the wrong way.

———

The 2000s were a time of enormous turbulence around the digital domain. There was extensive experimentation and innovation, investment was booming, and endless new applications were being rolled out with excitement. It was a time of great promise, and of peril too.

The rapid pace of technical development outstripped the meager efforts to keep things secure. Cybercrime—perennially the most dynamic sector of internet innovation—took off and flourished. Operating out of newly connected internet cafés in the slums of Lagos, Bangalore, and Rio de Janeiro, or via tech start-ups in Saint Petersburg, Prague, and Bucharest, cyber criminals could prey on insecure networks in advanced economies worldwide with little risk of consequences.

There were contradictory social movements at play. Thanks to the internet, mobile phones, and early social media, citizens were mobilizing in ways that caught dictators and autocratic regimes off guard—at least initially. The "color revolutions" of the former Soviet republics and eastern Europe that percolated throughout the 2000s were among the first. Email lists, bulletin boards, blog posts, and text messages were used to organize massive street demonstrations in Georgia, Ukraine, Kyrgyzstan, and Russia.[3] They were followed by similar popular uprisings in Africa and Asia, eventually culminating in the 2011 Arab Spring.[4] Waves of optimism spread far for the future of liberal democracy. The internet was perceived, as the American political sociologist Larry Diamond described it, as a "liberation technology."[5] Few, unfortunately, realized how exposed their communications really were, relying as they did on an infrastructure that was invasive by design, poorly regulated, and prone to abuse.

At that same time, a different type of digitally enabled mobilization was in progress: the global war on terror. It's impossible to overstate the impact of the September 11 terrorist attacks on state power, information controls, and clandestine digital surveillance. Sweeping legislative changes were initiated in the United States right after the attacks to rectify what was widely perceived to be an intelligence failure to "connect the dots." Section 215 of the Patriot Act and Section 702 of the Foreign Intelligence Surveillance Act (FISA) Amendments Act of 2008, as well as several other directives, authorized the secret collection of vast swathes of digital communications, both domestically and abroad.[6] Though Congress imposed some limits on the government's right to search and collect data, the technical ability to snoop simply migrated to the "black budget" underworld, where it expanded under cover and outside normal laws.

Because most of the dominant tech platforms were domiciled in the United States, American law enforcement and intelligence agencies enjoyed a massive advantage. The FBI quickly allowed the expanded use of secret administrative subpoenas, called "national security letters," to obtain customer records and communications data from internet service providers, financial institutions, and telephone companies.[7] Through top secret programs like PRISM and Stellar Wind, US agencies accessed huge volumes of data in real time, reaching directly into companies like Facebook, Microsoft, Verizon, and AT&T.[8] Government-backed hacking operations were soon normalized, led by the elite Tailored Access Operations group.[9] Almost all these programs were hidden from the public, though the occasional whistleblower provided a glimpse, as when Mark Klein, an AT&T technician, discovered in 2006 that the National Security Agency had set up a secret room at an AT&T facility in San Francisco where it installed Narus surveillance equipment to capture internet and phone communications.[10] Most dramatic of all were the revelations of Edward Snowden in 2013.[11]

The US-led global war on terror had major international repercussions as well. The United States sought to build a planetwide information collection apparatus that was used to hunt terrorists, target drone assassinations, undertake forced renditions and enhanced interrogations at black sites, and infiltrate foreign telecommunications networks. Other governments were enlisted or strong-armed into that effort. Police and intelligence cooperation spread "best practices" on counterterrorism, including with unsavory regimes whose checkered behavior was overlooked out of national security expediency. In places like Nigeria, Egypt, Indonesia, and the states of the former Soviet Union, sweeping emergency laws were passed that justified draconian measures, including the arrest and frequent torture of political opposition, journalists, and broad cross-sections of civil society. Violations of international law became routine. Norms of appropriate conduct around the rule of law, free and fair elections, and general civility evaporated as violence and cruelty spread. "Combating terrorism" became a convenient umbrella justification for extending domestic surveillance and foreign espionage operations, monitoring and clamping down on dissent and political opposition, and keeping tabs on NGOs. Simultaneously, the proliferation of digital communication platforms, social media networks, and online services was portrayed as a kind of murky underworld within which terrorists, criminals, and other shadowy forces thrived—a "Wild West" that needed to be tamed.

Within a few short years, a vast market for sophisticated data analytics tools and surveillance equipment took off. The epicenter was in the United States, with its pool of gigantic private subcontractors such as SAIC, Boeing, and Northrop Grumman, while Israel's surveillance specialists followed closely behind. The market expanded alongside the war on terror. Autocrats went on a shopping spree for the latest surveillance gear and began to build information control systems on top of already poorly regulated telecommunications and internet infrastructure. American, European, and Israeli firms were well positioned to capitalize on this expanding market—and they had little incentive to withhold lucrative contracts out of concerns for human rights.

It wasn't just technology that was sold: human intelligence (HUMINT) was also being outsourced. Retired veterans of MI6, Mossad, and the CIA built lucrative private intelligence firms to serve oligarchs, multinational corporations, and dictators. The privatization of covert operations began to spread. Where resources were scarce, cybercriminals and patriotic hackers were enlisted to hack into the laptops and phones of democratic activists to neutralize civil society before it could mount credible challenges to authority. Filters were quietly erected at critical choke points and internet border gateways, snuffing out access to content that was critical of incumbents or that violated social and religious norms. The internet's free-flowing environment was in the process of being gradually carved up and militarized.

The Citizen Lab thrived in this turbulent environment. Threats to civil society were plentiful and growing, and NGOs and activists were sitting ducks, yet the public was hardly aware of the danger. Fortunately for us, the rapid procurement and deployment of censorship and surveillance systems on existing infrastructure left a lot of "open doors" for experts who knew where and how to look. Our trusted relationships with individuals and organizations in countries of concern were growing too as we developed a chain of ears and eyes on the ground.

In 2003, the Citizen Lab cofounded a project called the OpenNet Initiative, and I was one of the four principal investigators. The others were Professors John Palfrey and Jonathan Zittrain of Harvard University's Berkman Klein Center, whose team, like ours, was experimenting with the technical means to document internet censorship worldwide, and Rafal Rohozinski, who was affiliated with the security group at the University of Cambridge and had extensive networks of contacts in the former Soviet republics and the Middle East. Funded by the Open Society and MacArthur Foundations, we gathered a large network of analysts, hackers, and field researchers. For my part, I strove to have the OpenNet Initiative mirror the gold standard of intelligence gathering, combining our technical interrogation efforts with in-country information gathering (TECHINT and HUMINT). Partners living under some of the world's most dangerous regimes conducted network reconnaissance tests, often at great personal risk, feeding data back to the Lab for analysis. They also spoke to sources inside industry and government, whose witness accounts of equipment purchases or technological installations provided us with leads. We combined those ground-level data-gathering missions with what could be gathered via network reconnaissance and remote probes of the internet's underbelly from afar. The Citizen Lab was the technical hub for it all—a digital Bletchley Park for the OpenNet Initiative.

Even though our methodologies then were sometimes primitive or poorly conceived, our reports were truly pathbreaking. We produced the first evidence-based investigations into website censorship in China, Saudi Arabia, Iran, India, and dozens of other countries. We uncovered hidden censorship and surveillance on widely used applications such as the Chinese version of Skype.[12] Led by Rohozinski's group, we documented politically motivated denial-of-service attacks on civil society networks in Belarus, Kyrgyzstan, Georgia, and elsewhere in the former Soviet republics.[13] We fingerprinted filtering and "deep-packet" (network traffic) inspection equipment made by Western vendors operating as part of information control regimes in the Middle East, South Asia, and the Gulf region, including Canada's Netsweeper and US-based Cisco Systems, Blue Coat, and Websense.[14] The OpenNet Initiative was evolving into a variation on the International Monitoring System I had envisaged years before. We were becoming an early warning system and independent verification mechanism for civil society and digital security.

It was during this period that I first began to appreciate the significance of targeted malware as a tool of surveillance. We had heard accounts of malware spreading within activist communities. While there were suspicions that certain instances could be attributed to covert government agencies, concrete evidence was lacking: viruses and trojan horses were rampant throughout the internet, and it was difficult to establish whether the intrusion was common cybercrime or something more organized and targeted.

In the early 2000s, Oxblood Ruffin, a member of the hacktivist network Cult of the Dead Cow who was living in Toronto, introduced me to Greg Walton, an independent security researcher. I was impressed by Walton's comprehensive examination of China's

Great Firewall plans, published in 2001 as *China's Golden Shield*, which relied on meticulous analysis of primary documents and site visits to security exhibitions in mainland China (thanks to a Team Canada mission to Beijing led by Prime Minister Jean Chrétien).[15] Walton identified several Western vendors involved in China's Great Firewall, including Canada's Nortel Networks and the US-based Cisco Systems. The Citizen Lab's research interrogating China's firewall would shortly afterward confirm, with technical data, Walton's claims about Cisco routers.

Although we'd exchanged correspondence for years, Walton and I had our first in-person meeting at a conference organized by the World Association of News Publishers (WAN) in Paris in 2008. That year was a heady time to be studying information operations. All eyes were focused on China, with the Beijing Olympics nearing in August. Like all authoritarian regimes that have hosted major world events, China was using every available means to stifle dissent and neutralize criticism of its abuse of human rights.[16] For their part, activists were gearing up for a series of high-profile campaigns to shed light on China's dismal record. Walton and I had mutual friends at the dynamic NGO Students for a Free Tibet, whose members had recently been arrested briefly in mainland China for unfurling a banner on the Great Wall to raise awareness of Tibetan issues. At our first in-person meeting, Walton described the malware samples Tibetan activists had shared with him and how they could be windows into a new type of covert cyber espionage.

At that time, Walton was pursuing a master's degree in software development at the University of Sunderland in the United Kingdom. The surge in malware samples he received from pro-democracy activists and exiled diaspora networks—from two in 2006 to almost two hundred in the first three months of 2008 from just one organization alone—led him to focus his dissertation on targeted malware attacks. But the University of Sunderland's computer science department had concerns about engaging in such work because it risked displeasing the Chinese government, whose nationals paid a premium in tuition fees to attend the university.

I invited Walton to present a paper, "Year of the Gh0stRAT," at a meeting we were having later that year in Chiang Mai, Thailand, with activists from Southeast Asian countries. I was intrigued by his preliminary accounts of targeted malware operations that complemented discoveries by individuals working in the threat intelligence space such as Mikko Hyppönen of the Finnish computer security company F-Secure and security researcher Maarten Van Horenbeeck. Both Hyppönen and Van Horenbeeck had samples of documents loaded with cybercrime exploits and remote access trojans targeting Tibetan communities and others, but they were unable to trace the origin of these attacks.[17] Van Horenbeeck reached out to Walton and taught him how to do basic dynamic analysis on malware and how to capture network traffic from malware samples in a virtual machine environment—a software-based emulation of a physical computer system.

As I listened to Walton's presentation, I had a major epiphany: first, there were likely many malware operations targeting civil society via unwitting victims; and second, there was a viable research path to documenting internet surveillance using careful, structured research methods. We just needed samples of live infections. What better place to find them than at ground zero: McLeod Ganj, India, the home of the exiled Tibetan spiritual leader, His Holiness the Dalai Lama?

Walton had established a reliable and trusting bond with Tibetan organizations over many years, undertaking numerous journeys to Dharamshala in northern India, the headquarters of the Tibetan government-in-exile, the Dalai Lama, and numerous Tibetan NGOs. Within these organizations, rumors were circulating of the potential interception of their communications and sensitive documents stored on computers. Individuals had been detained while traveling to mainland China and questioned about details that seemed to originate from internal emails. The Chinese government had advance knowledge of the Dalai Lama's travel itinerary—information typically known to only a few senior advisors. China would then exert pressure on foreign dignitaries not to meet with the Dalai Lama. How did the Chinese government get this information, if not through clandestine access to Tibetan computers?

Immediately after our Chiang Mai workshop, Walton returned to Dharamshala. At this time, the Citizen Lab collaborated with the Cambridge Security Group in the United Kingdom, headed by Professor Ross Anderson, as part of the OpenNet Initiative. Thinking we could use some additional technical muscle for this project, we enlisted one of Anderson's graduate students, Shishir Nagaraja, an Indian who was based in Bangalore at the time, to assist Walton in the Himalayan mountains. There they interviewed members of Tibetan organizations and observed their information security practices. They zeroed in on computers that contained the most sensitive information and, with the consent of the owners, effectively wiretapped them. That allowed us to gather packet captures (network traffic information) and observe any suspicious or unauthorized beaconing (data transfer) over the internet. Walton then traveled to Tibetan missions in London, New York, and Brussels, where he did the same work.

Our collaboration with the Cambridge team was eventually severed over an unfortunate misunderstanding. Nagaraja said he wanted to publish his own report with Anderson on data he had collected up to that point showing compromises on computers at the office of the Dalai Lama, cutting us out of the publication. Naturally, we objected to this proposal and tried to work out a different solution. Despite my attempts to forge a consensus, we went our separate ways, agreeing to release independent reports on an agreed date based on the evidence each of us had gathered independently.

Shortly thereafter, our team made an important discovery that eluded the Cambridge group. Digging through the packet captures collected from the field, Nart Villeneuve—now the lead technical researcher at the Lab—noticed a string of twenty-six characters. On a whim, he googled it. The results returned websites without any form of security or authentication, wide open for browsing. When he scouted these servers from our location in Toronto, he came across a control panel that listed many hacked computers, including their names (if they were given any) and commands to send these infected machines instructions. So much for "hacking"—

Villeneuve had merely browsed the internet. "It's all here," he told me, "the Dalai Lama's computers and a whole lot more."

It was truly a mind-blowing discovery—we had stumbled across a roster of high-profile victims of cyber espionage that included the ministries of foreign affairs of Bangladesh, Barbados, Bhutan, Brunei, Latvia, Indonesia, Iran, and the Philippines; the embassies of Cyprus, Germany, India, Indonesia, Malta, Pakistan, Portugal, Romania, South Korea, Taiwan, and Thailand; the Association of Southeast Asian Nations Secretariat, South Asian Association for Regional Cooperation, and Asian Development Bank; a mail server for the Associated Press; and an unclassified computer located at NATO headquarters. We waited and observed, for weeks, as the hacking operation unfolded in real time before our eyes. We were doing what I had set out to do when I founded the Lab: we were watching the watchers.

Early on in our research on this project, I contacted John Markoff, the senior technology correspondent for the *New York Times*. I had briefed him on our preliminary findings—that we had proof the office of the Dalai Lama had been hacked by what appeared to be China-based operatives—and he came to Toronto to interview some of our staff for his article. When Villeneuve made the discovery of the much larger group of victims, I immediately called Markoff: "Are you sitting down?" I asked. As I described our latest findings, he interrupted, "You guys! Unbelievable!"

The report, *Tracking GhostNet*, was published to coincide with Markoff's exclusive in the *New York Times*—the lead story on the front page and a full page inside, including a photo spread of our team.[18] As soon as the news hit the stands, my home phone erupted in nonstop calls from journalists who had somehow got hold of my number. The university organized a makeshift media scrum to accommodate the throngs who attended. Before long, the news was splashed over the front page of Canada's national newspaper, the *Globe and Mail*, as well as CNN, MSNBC, Fox News, and more.[19] We were catapulted into an unprecedented spotlight—a real game changer.

While most of the infrastructure for what we called "GhostNet" was taken down after we outed the operation, there were still some parts that were active. We also had new leads to follow, so Walton traveled back to Dharamsala to gather more packet captures and samples.

In this second round of investigations, we partnered with threat intelligence expert Steven Adair, who was affiliated with an independent group of cybersecurity experts known as the Shadowserver Foundation that possessed significantly more experience and resources than our small team. Together, we devised a strategy to sinkhole domains that we attributed to the operators. This approach—which involves capturing malicious network traffic destined for specific domains that we registered after their previous owners let them expire—enabled us to identify still-infected computers that were connecting to the command and control servers we now had under our control. Further research identified the owners of those computers—those who had been hacked but didn't know it.

Walton brought more packet captures and malware samples back to Toronto, and the team again analyzed the network traffic. Along with information streaming into the sinkholed domains, we again found ourselves peeking behind the scenes of yet another major cyber espionage operation. This time it was orchestrated by a different group of operators from the one likely responsible for GhostNet, but it was still based in China.

We titled our follow-on report *Shadows in the Cloud* because the operators used cloud services and social media platforms as part of their command and control infrastructure. They communicated instructions to compromised computers through disposable Twitter and Yahoo Mail accounts—a new strategy for cybercrime at the time. Within their infrastructure, we identified a "drop zone"—an account where stolen data was temporarily stored before moving to other locations on the network. Like some of GhostNet's infrastructure, this drop zone lacked authentication protection, allowing us to observe fragments of pilfered material as they passed through. Some items were difficult to comprehend, such as enigmatic Word documents or spreadsheets without context, but others could be reconstructed, enabling us to confidently associate them with specific organizations or individuals whose computers were hacked.

Piecing this stolen material together provided insights into the identities of some of the victims and revealed yet another extensive espionage operation. However, again like the GhostNet incident, identifying the responsible parties proved elusive. The culprits were aligned with the interests of the People's Republic of China, but we had no definitive evidence to establish who was steering it all. The closest we got was an email address that connected to an individual associated with the University of Electronic Science and Technology of China in Chengdu, Sichuan. We speculated that this person could be part of a patriotic hackers-for-hire operation—cybercriminals who moonlighted with the Ministry of State Security for extra income. Chengdu also happens to be the location of one of the People's Liberation Army's technical reconnaissance bureaus tasked with the collection of signals intelligence.

Whoever the hackers were, they managed to compromise computers in multiple locations around the world. The operators once again targeted computers at Tibetan institutions and the office of the Dalai Lama, resulting in the theft of sensitive data and approximately 1,500 private letters sent from the Dalai Lama's office between January and November 2009. This breach granted the spies the ability to monitor all email exchanges between the Dalai Lama's office, government stakeholders, and Tibetan offices and NGOs all over the world. The consequences of this clandestine eavesdropping are uncertain, but it is possible that such activities could have resulted in imprisonment or even loss of life. Tibetans residing in mainland China who communicate or collaborate with diaspora groups abroad are frequently punished by Chinese authorities for their advocacy or activism.

The vast majority of the victims were related to India: Indian government entities, including the Indian embassy in the United States, or adversaries of India. The Pakistani embassy in the United States was also compromised. We determined that computers at the Indian embassies in Kabul and Moscow, the Consulate General of India in Dubai, and the High Commission of India in Abuja, Nigeria, were all hacked too—almost a hundred documents had been stolen, including encrypted diplomatic correspondence, five documents marked as "restricted," and four documents marked as "confidential."[20] The stolen documents included personal, financial, and travel details of embassy and diplomatic staff, visa applications, passport office circulars, and country assessments and reports. Individuals not directly targeted by the attackers were also caught up in the espionage web, revealing potentially useful data on foreigners' travel plans and passport details. In today's networked world, in which a person's sensitive information is entrusted to multiple computers and travels over extended computer networks, we are only as secure as the weakest link in the chain.

Perhaps the biggest discovery was that a computer was hacked at India's top secret National Security Council, which is headed by the prime minister of India. It is the apex of India's national security state. Other documents provided national security assessments of India's security situation in the states of Assam, Manipur, Nagaland, and Tripura as well as information on the Naxalites, Maoists, and what was referred to in the materials as "left-wing extremism." All of it was extraordinarily sensitive.

As a team, we debated what to do with all this material. Did we have an obligation to let someone know ahead of publication of our report? With *GhostNet*, we did not notify anyone in advance, other than Markoff. This time, we decided to be more deliberate and proactive about notification. We let the Canadian government know about the Indian embassy in Afghanistan and our observations about Canadian visa applications and passport details that had been stolen. We also asked for help with contacts in the Indian government to notify parties there, but we received no response. Working with Adair and others, we connected with principals at India's signals intelligence agency, the ultra-secretive Research and Analysis Wing. We set up a Skype call with an Indian official to relay our discovery and communicate our intent to pass along details of hacked computers. We also asked for guidance on how to dispose of the classified documents we now had in our possession.

Our jaws dropped when the Indian official asked if we would join them to turn the tables on the Chinese and hack them back. We politely declined, explaining it would be inappropriate.

Once again, I brought in Markoff to cover this report, and we gave embargoed copies to a few other news organizations too. We published *Shadows in the Cloud* a little more than a year after *Ghost-Net*. As before, it was featured on the front page of the *New York Times* and made headlines around the world.[21]

These two reports catapulted the Citizen Lab into a global spotlight. There was a whirlwind of activity, and we suddenly found ourselves sought after by people in high places. We were invited to conferences and to speak on panels featuring senior intelligence and other government officials. I met former or current heads of the United States' National Security Agency and the CIA, the United Kingdom's Government Communications Headquarters and MI6, and Canada's Communications Security Establishment. Suddenly I found myself mingling in circles with personnel from agencies that once seemed distant and abstract. Some of these interactions were surreal. One time Nigel Inkster, the former head of foreign intelligence for Britain's MI6, invited me and another colleague to accompany him to a pub in London during a break in a major cybersecurity conference organized by the UK government. While we were eating and chatting, I noticed a bright flash and a commotion to our left. We saw one man reprimanding another in Chinese, presumably because his camera flash went off when they were trying to take photos of our meeting. Were they following Inkster, me, or both of us?

The big tech platforms were keen to engage too. Several months after we published *GhostNet* in December 2009, I was invited to Google headquarters in Silicon Valley as part of an internet censorship circumvention summit where I delivered a Google policy talk covering our research on information controls and targeted espionage. I heard that Sergey Brin, one of the cofounders of Google, wanted to talk to me, and while I was having lunch, he strolled across the cafeteria and shook hands. He proceeded to pepper me with detailed questions about our GhostNet investigation. I was impressed with his knowledge of intricate parts of the command and control infrastructure and the malware's functionality. It was clear he had read our report carefully.

When I returned to Toronto, he called again, this time on a Sunday morning while I was driving my sons to their hockey game. He apologized for the background noise because he too was driving—"with the roof down." I was struck by the contrast between my beat-up Dodge Durango, which I was driving through thick Canadian snow, and whatever luxurious Lamborghini or Maserati the then twenty-fourth-richest person in the world, with a net worth of around $17 billion, was cruising along the highways of Northern California.

"I need you to keep this strictly confidential," he began. "We have been seriously hacked in what appears to be something very similar to the GhostNet operation you guys uncovered." Our cafeteria conversation suddenly made a whole lot of sense. When we were speaking that day, he had just discovered that Google's systems had been breached by what appeared to be operators from mainland China. Brin asked if we would be willing to come back to Google with our team and help analyze the hack, but I demurred, thinking it might be inappropriate for us, a public interest research group, to get involved in investigating a hack of one of the world's wealthiest companies. A couple of weeks later, I learned he had brought in the US government and several high-profile antivirus companies, including McAfee, to work on "Operation Aurora." Google's acknowledgement that it had been hacked was a remarkable act of transparency.[22]

Because India had featured so prominently in both the *Ghost-Net* and *Shadows* reports, both as a victim and the jurisdiction in which others were victimized, the Citizen Lab had extensive and sometimes bizarre interactions with various elements of the Indian government. Sachin Pilot, a senior minister, and Dr. Gulshan Rai, the director general of the Indian Computer Emergency Response Team, traveled to Toronto to meet with me and my team at the university. Like the reception at Canada's Privy Council Office, this meeting did not go smoothly. Rai became furious as soon as we began talking and tried to intimidate me in front of Pilot, who, in contrast, remained composed and polite. Rai was ostensibly responsible for securing India's computer systems, so our report exposed him and his organization as incompetent. We provided them with the IP addresses of the infected computers we had discovered, along with a spreadsheet detailing the classified material we had recovered, and bid them both farewell.

The reaction from my own government at the Privy Council Office was the most puzzling. One possible reason was the diplomatic fallout of our investigations. Both reports exposed major cyber espionage campaigns that would have embarrassed many governments—China, the alleged perpetrator, but also India and all the other countries whose data were pilfered. No doubt the Canadian government was fielding a lot of complaints about an upstart research group at the University of Toronto that was beyond its control.

Another possible cause of our hostile reception was connected to a discovery we made while analyzing the Edward Snowden disclosures several years later. In a top secret 2012 Government Communications Headquarters document, reference is made to data that can be collected from "operational relay boxes"—insecure computers used by signals intelligence as covert hopping-off points to stage its activities while masking its identity or to plant false flags. As one example, the document listed GhostNet.[23] Perhaps, in publicizing GhostNet, we burned one of its assets. Or perhaps the core issue lay in the very nature of our work—we risked exposing secret operations in which all governments are to some extent complicit and intertwined. If we outed major China-based cyber espionage networks, who would be next?

Over time, I have come to believe the frosty reception may have originated primarily in the Stephen Harper administration, which was both conservative and somewhat mean-spirited. I suspect it had little sympathy for the human rights–motivated work of the Citizen Lab. Shortly after leaving office, Harper headed up an advisory committee and was a principal business partner of a Torontonian-Israeli private equity investor group among whose assets was a company selling facial recognition surveillance technology to the United Arab Emirates—one of the world's worst human rights offenders.[24]

Our unsettling encounter at the Privy Council Office lingered with me. Some years later, I submitted a formal access to information request about the meeting, to see what I could unearth about the tense atmosphere that day. Under the Canadian Access to Information Act, once a request is received, the government has a legal obligation to respond, usually within thirty days. My request read: "Any briefing notes, emails, reports, briefs, and / or 'after action' documents that followed and are related to a meeting held at the Privy Council Office on or around April 29, 2010, with Ronald Deibert and Janice Stein of the University of Toronto. The meeting was in regards to: the Citizen Lab at the Munk School of Global Affairs, cyber espionage, *Tracking Ghostnet* and *Shadows in the Clouds* reports released in 2009 and 2010."

The response from the Government of Canada Privy Council Office came back empty: "A thorough search of the records under the control of PCO was carried out on your behalf; however, no records relevant to your request were found."

No records? So, as far as the public is concerned, the meeting didn't happen? Was it a dream? Definitely not, as Stein can attest. Was it classified for some reason? To this day, I have no clue.

———

After we published our *GhostNet* and *Shadows* reports, many "threat intelligence" companies began to sprout up, some echoing our distinctive formatting and style. We had, for example, "branded" the threat actors by naming them "GhostNet" and "Shadows." Later, other industry threat reports gave the perpetrators clever code names such as Fancy Bear, Newscaster, or Vixen Panda.

Entrepreneurs smelled a profit potential in this new endeavor, and some gravitated to us for the payoff the association might bring. The now notorious data analytics firm Palantir Technologies, which at this time was just starting out, had provided our researchers with free access to one of its analytical tools in both investigations. We found it only marginally useful, however. One of our team members was shocked then to see a giant billboard on the subway in Washington, DC, that asked, "Want to know how Ghostnet was cracked?" "Palantir" was the answer. Shyam Sankar, a director at Palantir, gave a TED Talk in which he claimed that James Bond had Q and our team had Palantir.[25] I made sure we ditched Palantir after that. It was a fortuitous decision since the firm would go on to be implicated in many controversial defense and intelligence programs.

This commercialization hype reminded us how important it is to safeguard the Lab's independent mission. As authentic watchdogs, we must report the facts impartially, regardless of where they lead or whom they might offend. That role cannot easily coexist with business priorities, forever driven by profit.

Around 2011, there was a major turnover of personnel and research collaborations at the Citizen Lab. The release of our two reports fed into the excitement surrounding the "cyber gold rush." Inevitably, some of our team left for better salaries in the private sector or to establish their own for-profit companies. We who remained reaffirmed our commitment to fearlessly communicate the truth to those in power, never exaggerating or, worse, omitting details to win favor. We knew that, in this line of work, the absence of any real or perceived conflicts of interest is essential. And, as we soon discovered, there were plenty of well-funded individuals eagerly waiting for an opportunity to discredit us.

That ethical compass became, in turn, a magnet for those wanting to "do good." Highly skilled individuals were attracted to our work because of the unadulterated independence of our mission. We realized that our trusted relations with civil society groups around the world were extremely precious both for their own sake and for the data we could gather with their consent. A group like the Citizen Lab could obtain intelligence that is as good as or better than the information government intelligence agencies and corporations could supply, simply because many frontline human rights and political opposition groups are like canaries in the coal mine—and they trust us.

Our *GhostNet* and *Shadows* reports revealed the tips of an iceberg of state-based espionage operations that were growing in scope, scale, and sophistication. We suddenly had more cases to investigate than we could possibly handle.

————

During the same period when our recognition soared, three individuals—Niv Karmi, Shalev Hulio, and Omri Lavie—were laying the foundations for what would eventually become the most notorious mercenary surveillance firm in history: NSO Group. The name NSO is derived from the initials of their first names. According to their own accounts, Hulio and Lavie initially sought business opportunities in the United States, selling gadgets in shopping malls. When those endeavors failed to yield substantial returns, they returned to Israel and ventured into digital businesses selling products featured on popular TV shows, such as *Sex and the City*, and, later, a remote mobile device troubleshooting app. "The solution we proposed was to have the cell phone carrier send the customers a link, and with a few clicks they could authorize the carrier to remotely access their phones," Hulio explained. "The tech support center receives the authorization to remotely perform many actions, including version updates and training. Our technology helped a lot and saved resources."[26]

Hulio has claimed that a mysterious individual "from Europe" steered them toward using that same basic system to service intelligence agencies. "A European intelligence service heard what we were doing and approached us," he recalled. "'We saw that your technology works,' they told us, 'why aren't you using this to collect intelligence?'"[27] Later, in an Israeli café, they purportedly overheard someone discussing remote phone hacking, and they said they convinced that person to join their company.

It's impossible to assess the credibility of this account. In a 2015 interview, Hulio told a different story: "From the outset, we thought of creating a system that would allow all the intelligence and law enforcement bodies to be in control of telephones remotely, or to extract information from them, with or without the user's knowledge."[28] Was it "from the outset," as he said in 2015, or a tip from a mysterious European much later?

Regardless of the true story, NSO Group's business rapidly expanded without much apparent scrutiny regarding its customers' morals. At the very moment we were committing ourselves to the highest possible ethical conduct as the only possible way to succeed in our mission, it seems Hulio and his colleagues were setting off with a completely opposite compass bearing. Although our paths did not intersect for several years, in hindsight it seems inevitable that they would.

"We are a ghost," Lavie was once quoted as saying. "We are completely transparent to our goal and we leave no traces."[29] We soon proved him wrong.

– PART THREE –

SHADOWS EVERYWHERE

"Mátalo! Mátalo!"

MAY 2017

MEXICO

On May 15, 2017, at around noon, the Mexican investigative journalist Javier Valdez Cárdenas drove out of his office garage in his red Toyota Corolla.[1] A gregarious, plainspoken journalist, his warm smile, the glint in his eyes, and his trademark panama hat softened his razor-sharp analyses.

Being a journalist in Mexico is an extremely risky job. Although not technically a war zone, the endemic violence in the country is so dire it might as well be one. Violence emanates from the military, paramilitaries, the police, organized criminal gangs, and warlords. Murders are glorified extensively in gory videos and pop songs. Violence is always lurking in the background for journalists, especially those holding powerful elites to account. If you cover sensitive beats—military abuses, government corruption, drug cartels—you're playing with fire. And Valdez covered them all.

Valdez had cofounded *Ríodoce*, a feisty newspaper based in Sinaloa, home to one of the most notorious cartel leaders of all time, Joaquín "El Chapo" Guzmán. Earlier that year, El Chapo had been extradited to New York to face six separate criminal indictments, leaving a power vacuum in Sinaloa and a bloody struggle for control of the drug trade whose results could be counted in bodies on the streets of Culiacán.[2] Valdez's columns laid bare the corruption that was eroding Mexican politics and singled out the adult children of cartel leaders for their arrogance and entitlement. He spoke an uncomfortable truth: the drug lords were the ones really in charge. "Politicians no longer have to go to the narcos to seek their backing," he said. "Nowadays the narcos are the ones who create the politicians from the start, and then nurture and promote them."[3] Among the many enemies he racked up through his reporting, one of them finally decided Valdez had gone too far.

Outside the garage, a truck cut off Valdez's car, and two men dragged him out and executed him. Shell casings found indicate sixteen shots were fired, twelve of which entered his body. Photographs of the scene show Valdez face down, his trademark hat splayed next to him on the street.[4] His investigative files, laptop, and cellphones were all stolen from his vehicle.[5] Someone wanted not only to put an end to Valdez but to find out what he knew—and put an end to that.

Two days after Valdez's execution, Andrés Villarreal, a friend and colleague at *Ríodoce*, received an unsolicited text with a news alert: the killers had been identified. "NEWS," it read. "The Jalisco New Generation Cartel is responsible for the execution of the journalist in Culiacan. See report." It was no innocent news alert. The message had been carefully crafted with an exploit link designed to trick Villarreal into clicking on it. Had he done so, his iPhone would have been surreptitiously infected with NSO Group's Pegasus spyware.[6]

In the following days, the operators made several more attempts to infect not only Villareal's phone but also the one belonging to *Ríodoce*'s director, Ismael Bojórquez. They attempted to lure their targets by appealing to their curiosity, using *Ríodoce*'s investigations, family matters, and even allegations of affairs. Fortunately, neither of the targets took the bait.

The operators then zeroed in on Griselda Triana, Valdez's wife and a journalist herself.[7] Still grieving and in shock, she was cooperating with authorities while publicly demanding a thorough investigation into the execution. Whoever was sending the messages saw her as nothing more than a pawn in a violent game of chess. Their messages were designed to exploit her vulnerability in order to gain access to whatever valuable information she might have, to infiltrate her phone and uncover what she knew, whom she was talking to. Clearly, they had no conscience whatsoever.

Whenever principals at NSO Group were asked about abuses of their Pegasus spyware, they responded, "Our technology is essential to help governments investigate serious matters of crime and terrorism." They boasted that Pegasus had been used in the capture of El Chapo.[8] Regardless, it was also used to target Valdez's widow and colleagues after he was executed gangland style in what was likely a cartel-ordered murder. Why would Mexican authorities want to place these people under surveillance? Were they afraid of what they knew? What were they trying to cover up, and on whose behalf?

For a firm that has profited from the spread of digital repression worldwide, it seems fitting that NSO Group's first sales were to Mexico, a country plagued with corruption and abuse of power. For decades, the United States funneled billions of dollars of security assistance into Mexico as part of various initiatives, including the war on drugs, counterterrorism, and immigration and customs policing.[9] The Mexican military, which has been progressively assuming a larger role in domestic politics and public security, received most of these funds despite successive scandals, involvement in brutal massacres, endemic secrecy, and a culture of impunity. Typically, large sums of money must be spent within specific budgetary cycles, creating massive opportunities for graft and corruption in Mexico. Many private security firms, some of them with connections to Israeli entrepreneurs, rushed in to capitalize on the defense and intelligence gold rush.[10]

The tone in Mexico was set at the highest possible levels years before NSO Group was founded. Take Genaro García Luna, for example, convicted in the United States in February 2023 for taking millions in bribes from Sinaloa cartels.[11] From 2001 to 2012, he was Mexico's top security official—essentially, the head of Mexico's FBI. He was also, according to a prosecutor in his criminal trial, "the FedEx of cocaine."[12] In other words, the very person heading the government's top law enforcement and intelligence agencies, charged with bringing the narcos to heel and ultimately responsible for procuring and deploying the most advanced surveillance technology in aid of that mission, was himself on the cartel's payroll.

Thanks to García Luna's conviction in the United States, a lawsuit filed by the Mexican government in the state of Florida, and extensive reporting by the Mexican journalist Peniley Ramírez, we now have details on his bewildering, opaque circle of corruption.[13] Along with his wife, former spy Linda Cristina Pereyra, García Luna cultivated a relationship with Samuel Weinberg, another surveillance entrepreneur with Israeli connections. García Luna, Pereyra, and the Weinberg family colluded on a frenzy of secretive money laundering, bid tampering, and kickback schemes and created a network of shell companies that helped funnel millions of dollars from defense and intelligence contracts into bank accounts in the United States, Hong Kong, Barbados, Panama, Israel, the United Kingdom, and other countries.[14]

Some of the contracts were channeled through a mysterious Panamanian registered company, Nunvav, operated by a close associate of García Luna and Weinberg named Natan Wancier Taub (who once worked as a sales representative for another Israel-based surveillance vendor, NICE Systems).[15] From 2012 to 2018, Nunvav deposited close to a quarter billion dollars into its accounts, presumably funds coming from government contracts, kickbacks, or bribes paid to García Luna by El Chapo and the Sinaloa cartel. Nunvav then transferred portions of those funds to a potpourri of companies owned by the Weinberg family.

For all their clandestine training and experience, however, García Luna and his wife didn't do a very good job hiding their illicit wealth. They purchased fancy cars, motorcycles, and multiple luxury residences in Mexico and Florida—all implausible on a public servant's salary. After he retired from Mexico's top law enforcement agency in 2012, García Luna bought a five-thousand-square-foot residence in Golden Beach, Florida, for more than

$3 million, in cash.[16] They were no exception—simply high-end grifters following a well-trodden path in Mexico.

————

When NSO Group came to Mexico, therefore, the ground was already prepped for its founders' "anything goes" kind of entrepreneurialism. They slipped right into the mix with their own roster of oddball reprobates and criminal brokers.[17] As the journalist Oded Yaron once explained in the Israeli newspaper *Haaretz*, "Corruption is the real secret of NSO Group's success in Mexico, much more than the Pegasus spyware's capabilities."[18] Although they would later brag to the press about their "rigorous due diligence," NSO Group's actions have demonstrated an utter disregard for any such standard.[19]

NSO Group had Mexico on its radar as soon as the company was founded in January 2010, with an eye to peddling its phone-cracking technology as a solution to the BlackBerry messaging system, then widely used by the cartels.[20] The company hired Matan Caspi, a secretive Israeli entrepreneur with experience brokering tech deals in the Americas. He worked with Elliott Broidy, an American and founder of the Broidy Capital Management group, which had closed several lucrative business deals with Mexican military and intelligence agencies. Broidy had also pleaded guilty to paying $1 million in illegal gifts to New York state officials.[21]

Along for the ride was Caspi's associate from Israel, Eran Reshef. Broidy, in turn, connected Caspi, Reshef, and NSO Group to Jose Susumo Azano Matsura, a Mexican billionaire with Japanese heritage and a checkered history of personal corruption and shady connections to drug smuggling and influence peddling.[22] Known as "Mr. Lambo" (short for Lamborghini), Azano's job was to consummate deals with Mexican government officials while helping to create a network of intermediary and front companies, such as Security Tracking Devices, which was granted an exclusive license to sell NSO Group's spyware in Mexico in exchange for $500,000.[23] Azano was straight out of an episode of *Breaking Bad*, with convictions for transporting sixty-nine pounds of marijuana across the US-Mexico border and attempting to bribe the mayor of San Diego.[24] When Phil Halpern, a former assistant US attorney who prosecuted him, was asked whether Azano was trustworthy enough to handle sensitive military technology like Pegasus, he replied, "I wouldn't trust him to do my laundry."[25] But NSO Group appointed him as its first middleman in Mexico.

Another principal involved in NSO Group's plans for Mexico was Eric Banoun, who was well connected to the Israeli cybersecurity and intelligence community.[26] As a vice president of NICE Systems, he conducted extensive business with Mexican authorities.[27] Later, Banoun partnered with Erik Prince, founder of the mercenary firm Blackwater, to form Eitanium, another Israeli cybersecurity company.[28] He also helped found Circles, a surveillance company that marketed cellphone tracking and interception services to government clients.[29] For a time, Circles partnered with NSO Group under the umbrella of Q Cyber Technologies when a US-based private equity fund managed by Francisco Partners took over both companies.[30]

Azano allegedly demonstrated Pegasus to Mexico's president, Felipe Calderón, and landed NSO Group's first big sale for a reported $15 million.[31] The *New York Times* reported that the negotiations were convened at a strip club.[32] In addition to selling spyware to the Mexican Defense Ministry (SEDENA), Azano also helped secure a sole-source contract (without competitive bids) to build a grandiose command and control center to operate the spyware.[33] Documents would later reveal this headquarters to be the home of a secretive Mexican military intelligence center known by the acronym CMI.[34] Altogether, thanks to Azano's brokerage, NSO Group reaped a reported $500 million from Mexican sales between 2010 and 2012.[35]

Eventually, these sketchy individuals turned on one another. NSO Group cofounders Shalev Hulio and Omri Lavie had a falling out with Caspi, Reshef, and Banoun, leading to litigation. Ultimately, they settled on an unspecified compensation sum.[36] Caspi and Reshef then returned to Israel to cofound a surveillance conglomerate of their own, Rayzone Group, among whose products is Echo, which gathers location data from mobile phones and sells it to government intelligence agencies.[37] Before getting involved in Circles, Banoun offered assistance in Mexico to one of NSO Group's competitors, the Italian spyware firm Hacking Team.[38]

Broidy, meanwhile, was relegated to footnote status in NSO Group's origin story after being cut out of the business. But he continued to excel at his various ignoble pursuits: employing Donald Trump's personal lawyer, Michael Cohen, to pay hush money to women with whom he had affairs; pleading guilty to acting as an unregistered foreign agent for the People's Republic of China; and lobbying on behalf of a series of Russian-linked financial institutions and companies.[39] Broidy's emails were also allegedly hacked by the Qataris and leaked to journalists, exposing his shady business deals with Gulf entrepreneurs and lobbying efforts on behalf of Saudi Arabia and the United Arab Emirates.[40] He was eventually pardoned for his long list of crimes by former president Trump. If it's true that you are the company you keep, it's revealing that NSO Group chose a lowlife like Elliott Broidy as one of its key interlocutors for sales to its first government client.

After the disputes were settled, NSO Group hired new agents reading from the same old script. NSO Group brought in another Israeli middleman, Uri (Emmanuel) Ansbacher, to facilitate procurement contracts with Mexican clients.[41] He was an old friend of Hulio's and a member of his wedding party who acted as an intermediary for many other Israeli companies conducting business with government security agencies in Mexico and throughout Latin America.[42] Along with his business partner, Avishay Neria, Ansbacher has registered scores of companies with Hebrew acronyms as prefixes, such as BSD ("within the help of God") and KBH ("blessed be He"): KBH Track, KBH Geolocation Systems, KBH Applied Technology Group, KBH Aviation, Zaracota, BS.D Applied Technologies, and many more.[43] Ansbacher also established a Panamanian registered company, called Comercializadora de Soluciones Integrales Mecale SA de CV, which leaked documents that revealed it was involved as a front company in dozens of NSO Group's early sales in Mexico.[44] Registering this many companies for a single business venture is not normal; it is, rather, a suspicious signal that someone may be looking to hide assets, obscure ownership, and make it harder for authorities and investigators to track illegal activities—a tactic straight from the handbook on corruption.

Another key figure who got involved in NSO Group's Mexican sales was Tomás Zerón, former president Peña Nieto's national security advisor and former director of the attorney general's criminal investigation agency. According to *Haaretz*: "Zeron isn't a 'bad apple' but a typical figure in NSO's business dealings in Mexico—one link in a chain of dubious brokers, corrupt security and law agencies and officers allegedly affiliated to drug syndications."[45] Mathieu Tourliere of *Proceso* wrote that Zerón was "one of the key figures for the cyber-surveillance industry during Peña Nieto's term: he chose which systems were purchased, and from which suppliers, which allowed him to forge strategic alliances with businessmen from the sector."[46]

Zerón's name shows up repeatedly in Hacking Team's leaked emails from the early 2010s.[47] These emails provide sordid details about the mercenary spyware marketplace, including in Mexico. They reveal that Zerón's goal was to put a spyware system in the office of every local prosecutor in the country. Hacking Team had contracts with fourteen different federal and state agencies, including Mexico City's police, the army, the navy, the federal police, and others, even though many of these agencies had no authority under the constitution to undertake surveillance of Mexican citizens.[48] The state-owned oil company, Pemex, was even a customer. Hacking Team staffers were aware that one governor used the firm's technology to spy on political rivals, academics, and journalists and chose to continue making sales anyway.[49]

The leaked emails also show that Hacking Team staffers reported dubious front companies linked to the cartels that had set up installations on their own, while cartel members bragged about purchasing surveillance equipment that enabled them to intercept phones. Although we do not have as much detail on the inner workings and finalized contracts with Mexican agencies for NSO Group as we do for Hacking Team, they were no doubt similar.

The emails also reveal why Mexico is so attractive to surveillance vendors: the multitude of security agencies at the federal and state levels opened a bonanza of sales opportunities for which the two companies competed vigorously until Hacking Team's demise in 2015. Among the leaked emails is a revealing correspondence from Eric Banoun, who was then working for Hacking Team after falling out with NSO Group, to his managers: "A friend of mine, namely Rodrigo from Balam Security, one of the major player today in field of intelligence solutions in Mexico, will contact you early next week with an urgent request for proposal. His company was awarded a contract from PGR Mexico [the attorney general's office] for an infection-based system for mobiles based on 500 re-usable agents. Originally, the tender was tailored for another company, namely NSO Pegasus. Main issue is that Rodrigo is looking for a viable alternative in light of the exorbitant price set forth by NSO."[50]

A 2021 investigation by Mexico's chief anti–money laundering investigator suggests that between 2012 and 2018, the value of NSO Group's sales to Mexican clients was around $300 million—making the first eight years of its sales in the country close to a billion dollars in total (when the $500 million worth of Azano-brokered sales between 2010 and 2012 are factored in).[51] The investigator also found evidence that bills included excess payments channeled back to former government officials as kickbacks. Leaked documents support that claim.[52] A front company called Grupo Tech Bull SA de CV, which was set up to broker a $32 million contract for Pegasus with the Mexican government's attorney general's office, was established by individuals working for that very same office.[53]

It's also interesting to take stock of the precedent set by NSO Group's experiences in Mexico, home to its first foreign customers. Entering a market with that modus operandi, getting richly rewarded and not facing any serious consequences for crooked dealings, and greasing the palms of middlemen and corrupt officials means you're likely to follow the same formula in other markets. Before long, NSO Group did just that, opening up front companies and negotiating deals with crooks and despots in places like Ghana, Panama, Rwanda, Saudi Arabia, Thailand, the UAE, and Uganda.[54]

While NSO Group was surrounding itself in Mexico with what seemed like a cast from a Steven Soderbergh film adaptation of an Elmore Leonard crime novel, we were working with people from trusted communities dedicated to human rights, ethical behavior, and doing the right thing. What followed was a real David versus Goliath story: a small Canadian academic research group, some human rights NGOs, and a couple of indomitable reporters versus NSO Group and its various front companies, reprobate middle-men, and corrupt officials.

Among the most important and inspiring of our allies in Mexico was Luis Fernando García, a lawyer with the human rights organization Red en Defensa de los Derechos Digitales (R3D). After I introduced him to our senior researcher John Scott-Railton (JSR), they hit it off immediately and have worked together on multiple investigations for many years. Through him, we also joined a network with other Mexican organizations such as SocialTIC, Amnesty International's Americas team, and various investigative news organizations. We then collaborated with two journalists at the *New York Times*, Azam Ahmed and Nicole Perlroth, who went on to publish several high-profile articles on our collective investigations.

Pegasus spyware was at this time dependent on some kind of interaction with a target. Shortened links sent in text messages were the principal vectors but also NSO Group's Achilles' heel. We began by working with potential targets to systematically search through their message history. Some of the victims came to us via the digital rights organization Access Now. Although receiving a link was not proof positive of hacking (that data had been successfully exfiltrated from the device), it was definitive proof that someone sent the target a link meant to infect the device with Pegasus. (Back then, we did not have methods to examine crash logs, but later we could do retrospective analysis of infections thanks to these new forensic techniques.) The targeting messages were accompanied with time stamps, which allowed us to triangulate events coinciding with them. This way we were able to build a picture of digital targeting that went beyond technical evidence on a phone and also helped explain why and when people were targeted.

The cases began to emerge in trickles, each telling a devastating story of abuse of power, corruption, and sometimes murder. Our first case is noteworthy because the targets were not criminals or terrorists—the people NSO Group and other spyware vendors claim to expose. In August 2016, three Mexicans—Dr. Simón Barquera, Alejandro Calvillo, and Luis Manuel Encarnación Cruz—all received text messages containing NSO Group exploit links. Barquera is a respected researcher at the Mexican government's National Institute of Public Health. Calvillo is the director of El Poder del Consumidor, a consumer rights and health advocacy organization. Encarnación is the director of Coalición ContraPESO, a coalition of more than forty organizations that work on obesity prevention strategies. Their crime? They were all supporters of Mexico's soda tax, a public health measure to reduce the consumption of sugary drinks. The powerful food and beverage industry in Mexico took umbrage: in 2013, the CEO of Coca-Cola personally called Mexico's president to lobby against the tax.[55] Then someone, we don't know who, decided it was time to hack the advocates' phones.

The scientists and advocates whose phones we checked received numerous text messages laden with NSO Group exploit links. Once we plotted them against a timeline, it became clear that whoever was targeting them wanted to find out what they were planning to do.

The bait content contained in the messages was disturbing. Dr. Barquera received one claiming that his daughter had been in a serious car accident, with a link giving directions to the hospital where she was supposedly receiving treatment. The attackers even used the daughter's name. Other messages threatened violence and were highly emotional. One read: "You are an asshole Simon, while you are working i'm fucking your lady here is a photo." There's no other way to describe the scam but obscene.

This pattern repeated in several other cases we investigated over the coming years. Several prominent journalists and lawyers had their phones targeted dozens of times. The targets were all working on investigations into corruption involving the Mexican president or human rights abuses connected to federal authorities. A primary target was investigative journalist Carmen Aristegui, who was looking into corruption involving Mexico's president and First Lady. She received fake Amber alerts, crude sexual taunts, messages purporting to come from the US embassy in Mexico, urgent work-related messages, and fake phone-sex billing notifications. After trying repeatedly to entice her into clicking on NSO exploit links, the operators started to target her son, Emilio Aristegui, then a minor attending boarding school in the United States. They sent at least twenty-one messages with crude sexual taunts, information purportedly from the US embassy communicating urgent information about his visa, and sensational details about his mother. This onslaught made my blood boil.

The Pegasus hacking spree in Mexico and our reporting on it continued throughout 2017 and into 2018. We published case studies on the targeting of opposition politicians and lawyers representing the families of three Mexican women who had been slain execution style with shots to the head in July 2015 in the Narvarte neighborhood of Mexico City. Reports claimed they had first been tortured and sexually abused. The official investigation into the Narvarte case was widely criticized by Mexican civil society for being inept: many suspected the real culprit was connected to Governor Javier Duarte de Ochoa, who often issued threats to journalists and was accused of corruption. Given that NSO Group claims to sell its products only to government clients, who other than a Mexican official involved in a cover-up would have a motive to spy on the lawyers representing the families of the slain women?

Among many disturbing revelations, one of the most significant was the targeting of international investigators examining the unsolved disappearance of forty-three students—the Ayotzinapa case.[56] In 2015, these students commandeered buses to head to a protest. They were intercepted by Mexican police and then disappeared, presumably murdered. Tomás Zerón, the man responsible for procurement of NSO Group's Pegasus spyware in Mexico, headed the government's investigation, which went on to produce a highly dubious report.[57] After an outcry from the victims' families, the Inter-American Commission on Human Rights and representatives of the families successfully lobbied the Mexican government to agree to permit the Interdisciplinary Group of Independent Experts (GIEI) to investigate the disappearances. It produced a scathing report accusing Zerón himself of not only botching the investigation but engaging in a cover-up.[58] Video that was leaked showed him personally involved in torturing people into confessing a role in the massacre.[59] As part of our digging, we found that at least one GIEI investigator's phone was targeted with Pegasus exploit links a week after the group held a press conference claiming the Mexican government and, specifically, the attorney general's office, led by Zerón, were hampering their investigation.[60] We also found that several individuals from Centro PRODH, an organization representing families of the disappeared, had been targeted at the same time as well.[61]

These cases make a mockery of NSO Group's pledges around due diligence and claims it has rigorous checks and safeguards in place against government abuses. In this instance, Pegasus seemed to be used mostly to eavesdrop on government critics, political opposition, lawyers, and public interest investigators—as if abuses were the principal rationale for procuring the spyware in the first place. As all this madness was unfolding, our reports were like swarms of stinging bees. We peeled back the obfuscation, revealed dozens of innocent victims, and helped produce mounting calls for accountability. Four of our reports were featured on the front pages of the *New York Times* in one calendar year, leading to major national scandals in Mexico. But would they lead to justice?

———

Given the high level of corruption across all sectors of Mexican society, the prospect of public accountability is always dim, especially when the person responsible for the top law enforcement agency is also responsible for procuring and abusing the spyware that targets the people the agency should be protecting. García Luna is probably the most vivid example, but Zerón is a close second. He worked tirelessly to equip Mexican agencies and prosecutors' offices with the latest spyware, but then used those tools on investigative journalists and anti-corruption investigators looking into abuse of power in his own office. His bungled investigation and cover-up of the forty-three disappeared students case provided an example of the level of corruption in the country, as did the discovery that the people working for or associated with him tried to hack the devices of the international investigators examining the cover-up.

In 2019, we received a formal request from the RCMP acting as a liaison for the Mexican Attorney General's Office. A federal prosecutor assigned to the Office of the Special Prosecutor for Attention to Crimes Committed against Freedom of Expression arranged a visit to our Lab that fall. We invited Luis Fernando García along, as the legal counsel of Mexican victims, to balance the proceedings and allow him to observe the questions being asked.

Repeatedly, the prosecutor tried to persuade us to turn over the devices of the victims so they could be analyzed by the authorities, something we would not be able to do under our research ethics rules even if we wanted to. Why would victims entrust their personal phones to the agency likely responsible for targeting them? Who knows what these agents might do to absolve themselves of responsibility—would they plant something incriminating on the device to discredit a journalist or activist they themselves had tried to hack?

We explained to the prosecutor how a proper investigation should go: compel the cooperation of the telecommunications companies that would likely have a record of the text messages sent and received; mandate the cooperation of the agencies involved in procuring the spyware and cross-check their logs against that data to determine who was working and had control of the spyware at the time the targeting messages were sent. We knew that would never happen because the investigation would likely lead right back to the prosecutor's office, and it quickly became apparent that this meeting was pure theater. Such is the pursuit of justice in a country like Mexico. As Mario Ignacio Álvarez, a former deputy at the nation's attorney general's office, said, "It is highly likely that the political actors who were using this software are now keeping this investigation from making any progress at all. This is still a country where it is better to pray to the Virgin of Guadalupe for justice than to the authorities."[62]

To add to the absurdity of it all, shortly before we met the Mexican attorney general's representative, Tomás Zerón transited through Canada to Israel, where he remains in exile as a fugitive from Mexican law.[63] The hunter became the hunted, as evidence of the corruption of this once senior law enforcement officer began to accumulate. Because Mexico's current administration has been critical of Israel's human rights record in the United Nations, the possibility of his being extradited to face justice is almost certainly nil. He now lives in a swank apartment building in Tel Aviv owned by David Avital, who has a 31 percent share in a subsidiary of Rayzone, a technology firm with operations in Mexico, and for whom Zerón had negotiated extensive contracts.[64]

The president of Mexico from 2018 to 2024, Andrés Manuel López Obrador campaigned for office on the promise that his administration would cancel all the Pegasus contracts and never condone the type of spying that we and others uncovered in Mexico. "We are not involved with that," he assured Mexicans in a televised press conference in 2019. "When we were in the opposition we were spied on . . . now that is prohibited. We have not purchased systems for interceptions, among other things, because of the corruption that was involved in the purchase of all this equipment at very elevated prices to foreign companies . . . there is still unused equipment purchased in the previous government. We don't do that. And we don't do it because it is a matter of principle."[65]

While in opposition, López Obrador and at least fifty people in his circle, including several close members of his family, were selected for targeting with Pegasus between 2016 and 2017.[66] The fact that he made these promises (reiterated in 2021) and his office began to investigate Zerón and publicly produced spyware contracts from previous administrations were all promising steps toward some serious accountability and transparency.[67] Among the revelations was the shocking finding that the targeting of Carmen Aristegui might have been done from one of the offices of Ansbacher's KBH company, rather than from a formal Mexican government agency.[68] An individual working for the company, Juan Carlos García Rivera, was eventually arrested.[69] But corruption runs so deep in Mexico that many people speculated he was just a sacrificial lamb. Sure enough, in January 2024, a judge acquitted García Rivera, saying the prosecutors had not provided sufficient evidence to establish his guilt.[70] But the judge also made a point of underlining that Aristegui's phone had indeed been hacked, citing the Citizen Lab's JSR and Bill Marczak, who had traveled to Mexico to provide testimony during the trial.[71]

Despite some promising signs from the new administration, our teams soon discovered fresh evidence of yet more Pegasus targeting in Mexico. In the fall of 2022, R3D identified Pegasus infections against journalists, a human rights defender, and opposition politician Agustín Basave Alanís.[72] The targeting took place between 2019 and 2021. As usual, we provided the technical support for R3D's analysis and validated the forensic evidence. The big takeaway: despite López Obrador's promises and the seemingly endless series of abuse cases we had collectively unearthed over the years, one or more Mexican government agencies were likely still busy hacking people's phones with Pegasus spyware.

The investigation into the murder of Javier Valdez Cárdenas is yet another infuriating case. In 2020 and 2021, Heriberto Picos Barraza and Juan Francisco Picos Barrueta were convicted and given lengthy prison sentences for their involvement in the murder.[73] A third suspect, Juan Ildefonso Sánchez Romero, died in 2017 before he could face justice. According to reports, all three men were hired by Dámaso López Serrano, the son of a lieutenant of El Chapo's, who was later arrested and sentenced to five years in prison for drug conspiracy charges in the United States.[74] However, López Serrano and his father deny any involvement in Valdez's killing and claim they are being framed by El Chapo's sons and corrupt

Mexican officials. Some US law enforcement officials have anonymously supported their claims, but in Mexico, where investigations often lead nowhere or are intentionally stalled, it's hard to know the truth.[75] Ultimately, we are left wondering who had the means and motivation to send Pegasus exploit links to Valdez's widow and colleagues days after his murder in hope of snooping on their phones. As Luis Fernando García said, when loose ends never get tied by the relevant bodies, "it translates into still feeling vulnerable. When nothing happens, it emboldens those with this kind of technology to continue using it illegally."[76]

When I asked García who he thought was responsible for the targeting we observed, he said it was impossible to know. It could have been the prosecutors investigating the murder; it could have been Mexico's top intelligence agency, concerned that the aftermath of the murder was becoming a political headache for the government; or it could have been the army. But it could also have been "any one of them working on behalf of the killers and the cartels."

MARCH 2023

Luis Fernando García joins our group call. "Okay, what I'm going to show you is pretty gruesome, but it is important for the context around our case."

The YouTube video shows one end of a car chase, with shaky body-cam footage from the vehicle in the rear, which appears to be connected to the armed forces. The vehicle these occupants are chasing is a pickup truck, speeding and swerving dangerously. A hail of steady gunfire from automatic weapons pierces the half-lit nighttime streets of Nuevo Laredo, a city on the Rio Grande bordering the United States and mired for years in cartel-related violence. The pickup truck is eventually forced to a halt with a rain of bullets that seems to go on forever.

"Stop, stop," someone off camera can be heard pleading. But the gunfire goes on . . . bodies are lying prone near the truck.

"He's alive!" one officer yells in the video. *"Mátalo! Mátalo!"*

"Kill him!" another shouts.

García says that this video was published by a local Mexican newspaper. Before it surfaced, the Mexican government had told a completely different story about the incident: that the cartel had opened fire on the army first and that all those killed in the incident were cartel members. The body-cam footage shows a completely different story.

García explains the role of Raymundo Ramos, a former investigative journalist and now human rights defender, in the saga. Army abuse is his beat. He had spoken to relatives of three of the deceased who said that the men were definitely not members of the cartel; in fact, they were kidnapped by the cartel. When their bodies were recovered after the melee, they were dressed in casual clothes and had their hands and feet tied. They died by close-range execution: bullets to the head and chest.

Ramos had started to speak publicly about his investigations, and then the video surfaced. Soon after, Ramos received a notification from Apple warning him that his device had been hacked. He connected with R3D, who pointed him to our team. Our investigation revealed that at the exact time he first went public, his device was hacked with Pegasus spyware. We published a report about his hacking in October 2022, and although we had strong suspicions that some element of the Mexican government was behind the hacking, we had no smoking gun. All that changed when hacked documents surfaced thanks to a group calling itself Guacamaya.[77]

Guacamaya is a mysterious collective of international hackers motivated by anti-imperialism and environmental issues and focused mostly on Latin American countries and corporations. Among its targets before Mexico were major extractive companies in Guatemala, Colombia, Brazil, and Ecuador and the Joint Chiefs of Staff of Chile. In September 2022, the group released six terabytes of detailed information it had hacked from the Mexican Secretariat of National Defense. García and his R3D colleagues, Mexican investigative journalists, and others pored through the voluminous dump of raw emails, attachments, and contracts. Smoking guns are hard to come across in our line of work, but Garcia and R3D's search gave us direct attribution to the Mexican Army.

The details García provided as he walked us through the documents were mind-blowing. Our forensics had shown that Ramos's phone was hacked with Pegasus spyware in August and September 2020. In that window, documents showed, discussions were being held among senior army officials concerned that he was trying to "discredit the armed forces" through his questions about the assassination of the five men in Nuevo Laredo a few weeks earlier.

The documents revealed disclosures about the existence of the secretive military agency CMI, which was responsible for the use of Pegasus by the Mexican Army—the sole-source contract Azano had initially negotiated.[78] They provided a window into the inner workings of the army's deceit. The army is not allowed to spy on Mexican citizens, so it cannot disclose the existence of the CMI or the fact that it is the ultimate client for Pegasus software.

The leaked materials also showed there was an internal debate about Ramos's private correspondence that had been acquired by the infiltration of his device with Pegasus spyware. The army wanted to paint him as a stooge of the drug cartels, but nothing in the hacked material supported this allegation. All it had were his conversations with his sources. R3D was able to triangulate these references by tracking down individuals Ramos communicated with at the time to verify that they had indeed exchanged Telegram messages with Ramos, whose phone was then hacked with Pegasus, thus revealing their end of the correspondence to the military spies.

"For the first time," said JSR to the media after the reporting emerged, "it shows us how the operators took this man's private digital life, dumped it out on the table, and then tried to select the parts that would be most harmful to him." What is most damning is that the documents showed this type of skullduggery was known to and approved by the most senior person in the Mexican military, Secretary of Defense Luis Cresencio Sandoval González. A calendar entry included in the hacked materials shows that Sandoval met with senior military officials from the CMI the very day the internal report on Ramos's hacking was sent by email: September 2, 2020.

The documents also contradict assertions made by President López Obrador that his government would never engage in spying using Pegasus because it was "immoral" and "illegal." Either he was unaware of what his army was doing or he knew and was deliberately concealing it.

The case is noteworthy because, for the first time, we were able to establish the full arc of evidence leading to attribution. Most commonly, we know someone has been hacked and have strong circumstantial evidence pointing to a government client. Never before had we obtained such detailed information from inside the government, on government documents, to confirm who was responsible. As the *New York Times* put it, "This is the first time a paper trail has emerged to prove definitively that the Mexican military spied on citizens who were trying to expose its misdeeds."[79]

President López Obrador's response on March 10, 2023, to the undeniable facts was a sad reminder of just how little real accountability there is in the country.[80] He simply told reporters that our report was "made up." "The thing is," he said in another press conference, "we don't spy."[81]

Anarchy in the United Kingdom

AUGUST 2020

"Has anyone heard of a law firm called Payne Hicks Beach?" Bill Marczak, Citizen Lab senior researcher, asked. "I think I've seen some indications they've been compromised."

Another summer day in Toronto, another hot lead for the Lab.

Marczak was investigating targeted espionage against a United Arab Emirates dissident based in the United Kingdom. As he always does, he was also monitoring the command and control infrastructure of NSO Group and other spyware firms, using a variety of network measurement techniques. Occasionally, some converge to produce an unexpected result. That morning he observed that IP addresses associated with a prominent UK law firm were compromised and "checking in" to NSO Group's infrastructure.

In 2020, while most of the world's population came to a standstill during the pandemic, the Lab shifted into high gear. Ever since the Israel-based spies-for-hire firm Black Cube targeted us in 2019, we had noted a seemingly endless wave of digital targeting cases. Most of the Lab's staffers were used to working remotely, and by staying where we resided, we had more time to zero in on some pandemic-related digital security risks.

With remote work now the norm, the business video conferencing platform Zoom experienced a massive surge in users. Curious about its claims of being completely secure, we took a closer look and inspected the platform through a series of controlled experiments. Our research identified several major security issues.

Our team discovered we could intercept and reconstruct video calls completely, provided we had control over the network through which one end of the call was transmitted. Any Zoom calls conducted through a Wi-Fi connection under an attacker's management—at an airport or coffee shop, for example—would be susceptible to interception. Furthermore, we observed that in several of our experiments, the encryption keys used to secure the sessions originated from Zoom infrastructure located in mainland China. That posed a substantial security risk: if the keys resided in mainland China, the Chinese government could exert pressure on Zoom to surrender them, potentially exposing every Zoom call worldwide to Chinese government surveillance. As the pandemic pause continued, more and more governments, corporations, and organizations relied on Zoom for sensitive and confidential communications. UK prime minister Boris Johnson even convened cabinet meetings over Zoom.

After we published our report on the security risks we identified around the platform, we had a bizarre interaction with its CEO, Eric Yuan, over Zoom itself.[1] He thanked us for our work—then surprised us by asking if we would work for him. When we declined, he offered to donate money to the Citizen Lab, but we explained we cannot accept money from a corporation we are researching. Our integrity is far more important than the money a firm under investigation could offer us, and we seriously doubted it would have been extended without some kind of quid pro quo, implicit or otherwise. After our report and those of others identifying additional problems with the platform, the US Federal Trade Commission claimed that Zoom "engaged in a series of deceptive and unfair practices that undermined the security of its users." A settlement agreement was eventually reached that required Zoom to strengthen its security—a win for public interest research.[2]

Despite the COVID-19 lockdowns and stay-at-home orders, spies kept on spying, and many of the victims of digital espionage made their way to us. Our discovery that the phones of the inner circle around Jamal Khashoggi had been hacked by Pegasus spyware (chapter 5) drew people to our work, including many victims who were concerned about the security of their devices or their confidential communications appearing online. Other events amplified the topic: the security team around Jeff Bezos, for example, announced it had evidence that his phone had been hacked with Pegasus too.[3] As the owner of the *Washington Post*, and someone who had exchanged personal WhatsApp messages with Crown Prince Mohammed bin Salman (MBS) of Saudi Arabia, it was certainly plausible he would be targeted. However, the analysis commissioned by Bezos's head of security, Gavin de Becker, and performed by FTI Consulting contained many questionable assertions, so it's not clear whether his phone was in fact hacked.[4] Still, the publicity around his experience drew yet more attention to the topic and led to more cases crossing our desk.

Simultaneously, our forensic methods, thanks to Marczak's inventiveness, were becoming more refined. We were no longer limited to looking at artifacts of targeting—phishing texts or traces of communications in NSO Group infrastructure. We now had the ability to dig deep into the logs of a phone's operating system to find proof that someone had been hacked. Even better, this type of analysis opened the prospect of hunting retrospectively. Examining log files allowed us to go back in time and pinpoint precisely when someone's device had been infected with spyware, a fact we could correlate with events that were then happening in that target's life. It's a bit like rewinding the feed from a closed-circuit security camera and watching a crime in progress.

Many of the tips that came our way turned out to be dead ends. But not the one about the UK law firm. It led Marczak into a real doozy.

————

Marczak connected with human rights lawyer Martyn Day from the law firm Leigh Day, who helped with outreach to Payne Hicks Beach, the firm whose staff and associates we suspected were under surveillance with Pegasus spyware.[5] Marczak would eventually be commissioned to be an expert witness in the case that followed, which means that to this day, at the judge's order, some of the facts of his investigations cannot be publicly disclosed (and while the litigation was underway he was prohibited from sharing information about the case even with us). But the details that have now been made public through the court's eventual ruling are compelling enough on their own.

After further forensic investigation in consultation with the IT support staff at Payne Hicks Beach, Marczak determined that a total of six phones connected to the law firm and devices owned by individuals involved with one of the firm's highest-profile clients had been hacked using Pegasus.[6] To his amazement, the client at the center of it all was Princess Haya, estranged wife of Sheikh Mohammed bin Rashid al-Maktoum, prime minister of the United Arab Emirates and the absolute ruler of Dubai.

Sheikh Mohammed is, by many accounts, a misogynist tyrant. His always grim demeanor does little to help diminish that reputation. Princess Haya, the daughter of King Hussein of Jordan and the half sister of King Abdullah II, married the sheikh in 2004, becoming one of his several wives.[7]

Princess Haya projects a cosmopolitan aura: she was educated in the United Kingdom, is an Olympian horse jumper, and is close to members of the British royal family.[8] As a Jordanian royal, she was granted diplomatic immunity in the United Kingdom, which brought additional privileges. She lives in a palatial residence in the posh Kensington neighborhood of London, alongside other glitterati and foreign elites.[9]

The relationship between the sheikh and Haya deteriorated gradually and became fraught around 2017 or 2018, when she had an affair with one of her bodyguards.[10] When four members of her security team blackmailed her, the affair became public.[11] This discovery set in motion what the princess described in court testimony as a "campaign of fear and intimidation."[12] Several times a gun was placed on her bed—an unmistakable Mafia-style threat.[13] Anonymous written notes were left for her that threatened to seize her children or asserted her life would soon be over.[14] One day a helicopter landed in the Dubai palace where she lived, and security personnel tried to strong-arm her into getting on board, saying they were taking her to a prison in the desert.[15] Her young son clung to her legs, begging them not to take his mother—a plea the princess claims thwarted the kidnapping.[16]

Fearing for her safety, Princess Haya fled to the United Kingdom, to her Kensington residence. That didn't stop the sheikh. Threats were still issued, and at one point she discovered he was looking to purchase a neighboring property, presumably so his security detail could keep close tabs on her.[17] Eventually she petitioned the British High Court for a divorce and sole custody of her children—and so she contacted Payne Hicks Beach.[18]

The harassment and intimidation campaign against the princess followed the sheikh's usual modus operandi. In 2000, Sheikha Shamsa, one of his daughters by a different wife, fled the family's $134 million Longcross estate in Surrey, England.[19] It was no easy feat. The compound was guarded by extensive private security, and family members, especially young Shamsa, were continuously and closely monitored. Late one night, Shamsa snuck out of her bedroom and commandeered a black Range Rover, which she ditched at the gates of the estate, along with her mobile phone. Sheikh Mohammed helicoptered into the estate to oversee the frantic search. For two weeks, Shamsa hid with friends in London until, one day, she was apprehended on the street by four Emirati men who pulled her into their vehicle, drove to a private airport, sedated her, and flew her back to the United Arab Emirates. Although a police report was filed and a case opened by Cambridgeshire authorities about the kidnapping, the investigation sputtered because of lack of cooperation by the sheikh and the Longcross estate staff. Sheikha Shamsa has not been seen in public for the last twenty years.

Her sister Sheikha Latifa, who saw Shamsa for the first time in eight years in 2018, described her shocking condition: "She was in a very bad state. She had to be led around by her hand. She wouldn't open her eyes, I don't know why. They would make her eat, then give her a bunch of pills to control her basically. The pills made her like a zombie. Right now she's surrounded by nurses. They are in her room when she sleeps, they take notes of when she wakes up, when she sleeps, when she eats, what she eats, what she says, the conversation she says. These drugs control her mind, I don't know what they are. And so her life is totally controlled."[20]

Sheikha Latifa herself had endured her father's tyranny on multiple occasions and, like Shamsa, had made various attempts to escape. The most ambitious came in February 2018, when she orchestrated a bold getaway from the United Arab Emirates with the assistance of Tiina Jauhiainen, her Finnish personal fitness trainer. Jauhiainen and Latifa drove to neighboring Oman, where they crossed the border while Latifa hid in the trunk. Once through, they made their way to a beach in Muscat, inflated a raft they had brought with them, and then navigated to a prearranged rendezvous with a private yacht they had chartered, *Nostromo*, piloted by a French former naval officer Hervé Jaubert and bound for India.

The mission seemed to run smoothly for the first few days but ended abruptly when Indian commandos stormed the yacht, roughing up Jauhiainen and Jaubert. "Shoot me here! Don't take me back!" Latifa begged before the commandos drugged her and whisked her back to Dubai.[21]

There was speculation that the sheikh's security services employed sophisticated digital surveillance technology to locate the yacht.[22] Although Jaubert had insisted on no cellphones and a communications blackout during the escape, Latifa had brought her mobile phone and sent several messages anyway, even posting and then deleting some on Instagram. The report suggests that the Emirates' signals intelligence agency may have capitalized on these operational security lapses thanks to the Israeli vendor Rayzone, chaired by Yohai Bar Zakay Hasidoff, the former second-in-command of Israel's elite signals intelligence agency, Unit 8200.[23] Among Rayzone's products is a system called Echo, the marketing for which boasts of providing its government customers with the ability to geolocate mobile devices anywhere in the world: "You can run, you can hide, but you can't escape your own echo," proclaims the firm's marketing material—an eerie tagline considering Latifa's fate that day.[24]

Data reviewed by the Bureau of Investigative Journalism show that a series of signals sent via mobile networks in Jersey, Guernsey, Cameroon, Israel, Laos, and the United States designed to reveal mobile device location were sent to a US-registered mobile belonging to Jaubert the day before the Indian commandos stormed *Nostromo*.[25] Such signaling messages are consistent with the kind of exploitation of the global SS7 protocol that companies such as Rayzone do. However, Jaubert insists he did not bring a mobile device on the escape mission, and Rayzone claims that "any attempt to associate our company with activities that could have been performed by others, is misleading and untrue."[26]

Other reports say the sheikh issued an urgent plea for help to the FBI, saying Latifa had been kidnapped.[27] The FBI then obtained data about the yacht's location from a marine internet service provider, KVH Industries, a Rhode Island–based company, and provided it to the Dubai government. It, in turn, shared it with Indian authorities, to provide a target for the commandos. If this story is accurate, it shows another type of impropriety: the FBI didn't obtain a warrant for the data. "Rather than seek a subpoena for *Nostromo*'s location," claimed the *USA Today* report, "agents contacted the internet provider and said they needed help because of a public safety emergency."[28] This story seems plausible, as law enforcement often cajoles information informally out of internet service providers and telecommunications companies using the stature of public authority, as it's done for decades.

Regardless of whatever means were employed to locate the yacht (state intelligence agencies use numerous techniques of "maritime domain awareness," and the UAE has a penumbra of surveillance systems at its disposal thanks to the commercial surveillance industry), Sheikha Latifa never reached her intended destination.[29] Occasionally over the last few years, she has sent out videos filmed surreptitiously in her bathroom or other secret locations where she claims she is being kept a prisoner, explaining her plight and horrible treatment and pleading for help.[30] "Every day, I'm worried about my safety and my life. I don't know if I'm going to survive this situation," she said in one video.[31] Lately, photos have circulated purporting to show Latifa moving around freely and enjoying travel to Spain and

other countries. Her legal representatives have issued statements re-
questing privacy on her behalf, saying she just wants to be left alone.
She may well have met the same fate as her sister Shamsa.

That the UAE would use Pegasus spyware to hack the phone
of Princess Haya is entirely consistent with the regime's abusive
practices and the sheikh's obsessiveness. He's a control freak—an
autocratic despot with billions of dollars and a retinue of private
intelligence firms at his disposal; a husband and father who ruthlessly exercises his power over the women in his life; someone who
is long accustomed to getting whatever he wants with the snap of a
finger and never being held to account for it.

––––––––––

Marczak's investigation determined the phone of Baroness Shackleton of Belgravia, Haya's lawyer and a sitting member of the UK
House of Lords, had also been hacked (along with the mobile devices of Haya's security team, her personal assistant, and another
lawyer on Shackleton's staff).[32] While hacking the phone of a Gulf
princess in the United Kingdom was crossing numerous lines,
hacking the phone of a sitting member of the House of Lords was
nothing short of brazen. Fiona Sara Shackleton is a high-priced
lawyer who has represented numerous members of the British
royal family, including King Charles and Prince Andrew, as well as
celebrities like Paul McCartney in his divorce proceedings against
Heather Mills.[33] Imagine the angst that rippled through London
high society when it was revealed that the mobile phone of a lawyer
many of them had retained had been hacked by a Gulf autocrat.

NSO Group markets Pegasus as a tool that is sold to government clients and strictly controlled to help those governments
investigate serious matters of crime and terrorism. Here, it was
employed at the direction of a billionaire sheikh to spy on his wife,
her security team, and her solicitor. This act was at once a major
abuse of power, a violation of legal privilege, a criminal act, and
a potential violation of international law. That's the thing about
autocrats who get used to committing dirty deeds with no conse-

quences: there's virtually no line they won't cross in the service of their own corrupt ends.

————

One of the more remarkable developments to surface from the court proceedings concerned a late-hour intervention in the espionage Marczak had uncovered. Several hours after Marczak, via human rights lawyer Martyn Day, reached out to the UK law firm to notify it of his findings, an unexpected and high-profile third party did the same: Cherie Blair, wife of former UK Labour prime minister Tony Blair, called Baroness Shackleton to alert her about the hacking of her devices.

Since Tony Blair left office, the couple has built enormously profitable consulting businesses servicing dubious autocrats and multinational corporations.[34] One of his contracts involved helping Saudi Arabia "modernize"—whatever that means for a kingdom that still employs medieval-era beheadings as a form of capital punishment.[35] In another case, he brokered oil deals between Chinese oligarchs and Saudi princes.[36] For her part, in 2010, leaked private emails showed that Cherie Blair lobbied Secretary of State Hillary Clinton on behalf of another Gulf regime: "As you know I have good links to the Qataris," she wrote.[37]

The United Kingdom has gained a well-deserved reputation as the "butler to the world," as author Oliver Bullough described it.[38] The establishment has profited by serving the interests of dictators, kleptocrats, and oligarchs who take advantage of the country's favorable tax laws, exorbitant real estate market, and entourage of costly lawyers and PR consultants to launder their assets and enhance their public image. The Blairs are part of this unprincipled venality—raking in millions of pounds, jetting around the world, and glad-handing some of the world's biggest offenders of human rights and liberal democracy.

One of the clients of Cherie Blair's firm, Omnia Strategy, was NSO Group.[39] Facing relentless media scandals, most of which were generated by our investigations, NSO Group and its various investors have sought, instead of dealing with the root of the problem, to gloss it over with the help of a coterie of well-known, seemingly reputable advisors and consultants. They have included former Obama official Juliette Kayyem, former US Homeland Security chief Tom Ridge, former French ambassador to the United States Gèrard Araud, and Cherie Blair.[40]

According to an affidavit Blair submitted as part of the legal proceedings surrounding Princess Haya, NSO Group called her in the early hours of the morning on August 5, 2020, to say that "it had come to their attention that their software may have been misused to monitor the mobile phones of Baroness Shackleton and HRH Princess Haya."[41] NSO Group asked her to reach out and warn them, which she promptly did.

As an important aside, despite NSO Group's public but vague criticisms of the technical accuracy of our research, the fact it contacted Shackleton soon after Marczak did substantiates the accuracy of the Lab's methods. Left hanging is the obvious question: Why did NSO Group choose to prompt Cherie Blair at precisely this time, immediately after Marczak provided his own discreet notification to the law firm he discovered had been hacked?

There are several possible answers. First, we could take NSO Group at its word and believe it discovered the misuse of its spyware—and that the timing so close to Marczak's outreach was just coincidental. If that's true, however, it means its public assertions that it has no visibility into its clients' use of its spyware are false—something we and others have long suspected.

Another possibility is that NSO Group (or someone aligned with the firm or one of its government clients) had tapped Marczak's mobile and was observing the ongoing investigations, so intervened to try to limit the fallout from what he had discovered. This explanation is plausible, given that one of NSO Group's principal adversaries is the Lab, and it is well known that Marczak leads our technical investigations. The Mossad or Unit 8200 could also have cast a surveillance net around Marczak and discovered what he had stumbled into—and tipped NSO Group off. NSO in turn activated Blair to try to limit the diplomatic fallout. Given that all our devices are routinely inspected using the same techniques we employ to detect infections on high-profile victims, though, this scenario seems unlikely.

Another plausible explanation is that whoever was undertaking the espionage on the UAE side learned of our outreach because the devices of the people we notified had been hacked. The Emiratis then could have alerted NSO Group that their operation had been exposed, and the firm decided to intervene using Cherie Blair's services. Whichever scenario is true, Blair's sudden appearance in the saga turned what was already an unreal experience into something out of a Fellini movie.

But the bizarre findings around this case didn't end there. While investigating the UAE government operator behind the spying as well as Pegasus operators he attributed to India, Cyprus, and Jordan, Marczak began to identify what he suspected were infected devices coming from IP ranges that were associated with the UK Foreign, Commonwealth, and Development Office. Then, a little later, the same Emirati operator who had hacked Princess Haya and her associates hacked what appeared to be a device located at 10 Downing Street, the official residence of the UK prime minister—at the time, Boris Johnson.

How to handle these findings? We had routinely uncovered instances of governments using Pegasus to spy on each other—another contravention of the ways in which NSO Group and other mercenary spyware firms advertise their wares. If the industry is so poorly regulated that governments use spyware to hack the devices of journalists and activists, they're also going to take liberties and use them to spy on each other. Our mandate, however, is to provide a kind of counterintelligence capacity for civil society, so, typically, we park discoveries of government-on-government espionage to one side, interesting to observe but not within our mission to do anything about. Our job is to act as government watchdogs, not as subordinates. Furthermore, governments should have their own capabilities to investigate and defend themselves without our help.

But this situation seemed exceptional. There were several cases of serious litigation involving redress for spyware victims or, in the case of Princess Haya, domestic abuse and child custody in which one of the parties, Sheikh Mohammed, had used spyware to gain an unfair advantage in the proceedings. Moreover, although our visibility into the hacked device in 10 Downing Street was limited, we could observe that it was sending data to the spies' servers late one Saturday night. As best we could tell, Johnson was there that weekend, and few other people were likely around at that time whose devices would be of interest to UAE's spies. We may have stumbled upon espionage against Johnson himself, which would make this discovery the second serious case of insecurity at the highest levels of the UK government we had a role in uncovering (the other being that Johnson held cabinet meetings over Zoom when the platform was susceptible to eavesdropping).

Our findings were still tentative and incomplete. We could observe only traces of infections, and although we had strong suspicions about which government operators were behind them, our analysis was constrained without further means of gathering information. So instead of publicizing what we knew, we sent a quiet notification to the UK authorities. As a courtesy, I also notified contacts in the Canadian government. We hoped the case might, finally, prompt a serious reckoning with the fact that an unregulated market for mercenary spyware poses not only serious human rights risks but national security risks as well. A few years later, the *New Yorker* journalist Ronan Farrow reported on the discovery we made and received confirmation from the UK government about the compromised devices.[42]

Gulf espionage against UK targets wasn't limited to just the upper establishment. The same government spies were aggressively targeting dissidents and human rights defenders too. Ghanem Almasarir, for example, a Saudi dissident, had applied for and received political asylum in the United Kingdom. Much like Canada's Omar Abdulaziz (chapter 5), he is an exiled critic of the Saudi regime who has used his popular social media platform to criticize Saudi Arabia, and MBS in particular, and has paid the price for it.[43] We determined his device had been targeted with Pegasus via malicious

SMS texts in 2018 by the same Saudi government operator who had targeted Abdulaziz, an unnamed Amnesty International staffer, and another UK-based Saudi dissident named Yahya Assiri.[44]

Much like other victims of transnational repression, Almasarir was routinely harassed from abroad, including one case where two unnamed assailants tracked him down and beat him outside Harrods in London's exclusive Knightsbridge district. "Who are you to talk about the family of al-Saud?" they shouted at him on the street.[45]

Almasarir replied, "This is London," meaning not Riyadh.

"Fuck London, their Queen is our slave and their police are our dogs," one of the men shouted. Closed-circuit TV footage from the assault showed that one man was wearing a gray suit and a wired earpiece.

Afterward, Almasarir condemned the UK government for being too subservient to Gulf autocrats, inviting such malfeasance and acts of violence. "I had never thought they would attack me here. . . . This is the area where I feel most safe."[46]

One of the most heartbreaking stories of Gulf espionage against dissidents exiled in the United Kingdom concerned the case of Alaa al-Siddiq, a young Emirati activist who died in a car accident there in June 2021.[47] In January 2020, al-Siddiq reached out to us because she was concerned about her digital security. Eight years earlier, her father, Mohammed al-Siddiq, had signed a pro-democracy petition, alerting the authorities to the family. After her father was arrested, Alaa al-Siddiq left the UAE and sought refuge in Qatar. Her case caused a diplomatic dispute between the two Gulf rivals when the Emiratis demanded she be repatriated and the Qataris refused. In 2015, when al-Siddiq was stripped of her UAE citizenship, she moved to the United Kingdom. There, much like other dissidents and refugees, she was relentlessly harassed over social media, including being called a "terrorist" for her support of the Arab Spring.

When al-Siddiq contacted us, we set her phone up on a VPN (virtual private network) that routed all her network traffic through a Citizen Lab–controlled server for detailed analysis. This technique allowed us to observe all the device's communications over the internet, including malicious and unauthorized communications. Marczak noted that on July 12 and August 3, 2020, al-Siddiq's iPhone downloaded approximately 2.4 megabytes of encrypted data from servers associated with two domain names he had previously identified as belonging to NSO Group. Her device was hacked, in other words, while we were watching.

Marczak instructed al-Siddiq to send crash logs and a full backup of her device. After analyzing that data, he determined that her device had been hacked multiple times with Pegasus spyware beginning in 2015, when she was living in Qatar, and then intermittently ever since. "They were trying to hack her 24/7," Marczak later told the *Guardian* reporter Stephanie Kirchgaessner.[48]

As with many victims, al-Siddiq initially chose not to speak publicly about her hacking experiences, fearing for her safety. But the knowledge she had been under constant surveillance traumatized her. In interviews she conducted with colleagues at Forensic Architecture and with filmmaker Laura Poitras that were not published until after her death, she described the risks of being a human rights activist and how the hacking of her phone put her friends and colleagues at risk by association. "In this case, this kind of violation is not changeable, and I cannot protect them," she said. "It is a sad thing to feel."[49] She told Marczak that she was especially worried about the private family photos stored on her device, now accessible to UAE authorities. She worried they would be used in a campaign to discredit and embarrass her—an experience shared by many women in conservative societies who are targeted by autocratic regimes.

On June 19, 2021, al-Siddiq was traveling in a BMW with two friends and a child. Their car collided with a Land Rover at an intersection in Oxfordshire. Al-Siddiq was declared dead on the scene.[50] She was thirty-three years old. At first, many people suspected foul play, but an investigation determined there was none.[51] There is no doubt, however, that the fear of being under constant threat weighed heavily on her: she changed her habits, including the routes she traveled on the tube, and took care not to stand close to the edge of the platform.[52] She had found no peace in exile in the United Kingdom: her tormentors still tracked her down and hounded her.

———

For years, the UK establishment has ingratiated itself with Gulf autocrats, making everyone rich in the process. This Faustian bargain has involved rolling out the red carpet, facilitating money laundering through the best and most opaque corporate registration processes wealth can buy, and welcoming massive real estate transactions that have driven property costs to astronomical levels.[53] All the while, it has turned a blind eye to the sinister origins of the amassed wealth: stolen public assets, fossil fuel extraction, and corruption. It has enabled oligarchs and heads of state to park their funds in Britain's football teams, educate their children in the country's elite boarding schools and universities, and use the UK's legal system to launch aggressive defamation suits against legitimate democratic opposition, journalists, and critics. Meanwhile, these oligarchs have been able to hobnob with the royal family and other doyennes of the upper crust to boost their pedigree and polish their public reputation.

Consider Sheikh Mohammed himself. His extensive British property portfolio "ranges from mansions, stables and training gallops across Newmarket, to white stucco houses in some of London's most exclusive addresses and extensive moorland including the 25,000-hectare Inverinate estate in the Scottish Highlands," making him one of the single largest landowners in the United Kingdom.[54] Determining the exact scale of his holdings is difficult because "most of the properties connected to him are owned via offshore companies in the tax havens of Guernsey and Jersey." He also owns an "illustrious and hugely successful [horse] racing and bloodstock operation," Godolphin stables, which brought him into Queen Elizabeth's inner circle.[55] Given such substantial reservoirs of wealth continuously flooding the English system—hotels, law firms, real estate companies, and brokers—it should be no surprise that Gulf autocrats are embraced with open arms and allowed to carry on with an air of invincibility.

And who pays the price? Those who have escaped their despotism and fled to the United Kingdom hoping for safety, expecting that the words about protecting human rights and safeguarding democracy actually mean something. They watch in fear while rich sheikhs and their family members drive through the streets of London in their Rolls-Royces and Lamborghinis as if they own the place—which, in a very real sense, they do.

————

Fortunately, there have been some small but important victories in the United Kingdom. In 2019, Ghanem Almasarir filed a civil legal claim for misuse of private information, harassment, and trespass to goods against the Kingdom of Saudi Arabia.[56] His case rested largely on the research the Lab had conducted showing that his device had been targeted and hacked with Pegasus spyware. In August 2022, the UK High Court dismissed Saudi Arabia's attempt to use state immunity provisions to block his claim, allowing the case to proceed.[57]

In 2021, the University of Cambridge announced it had broken off talks with the United Arab Emirates over what would have been a record £400 million donation, citing the Gulf state's use of Pegasus spyware.[58] The decision was made by Vice-Chancellor Stephen Toope, formerly my colleague at the University of Toronto. At his request, I kept him apprised of the Citizen Lab's work once he became vice-chancellor, and I like to think that my updates on the UAE-related hacking played some role in his decision to refuse such an enormous sum of money.

In late 2021, Sir Andrew McFarlane, president of the Family Division of the UK's Courts and Tribunal Judiciary, published his final decision with respect to the divorce of Princess Haya and Sheikh Mohammed.[59] He ruled that Sheikh Mohammed bin Rashid al-Maktoum inflicted "exorbitant" domestic abuse against his ex-wife, awarded her sole custody of the children, and imposed a staggering £554 million ($730.5 million) payment for the children's long-term security and maintenance.[60] He stated that the sheikh had "consistently displayed coercive and controlling behaviour" toward his wife and children. Marczak's analysis featured prominently in the ruling. Citing his research, which was peer-reviewed by an independent expert and found to be sound, the judge said that "the mobile phones of the mother (Princess Haya), two of her solicitors, her personal assistant and two members of her security staff had been the subject of either successful or attempted infiltration by surveillance software. The software used is called Pegasus software and was that of an Israeli company, the NSO Group."

To see one of our team members' work cited in such a prominent case against one of the world's richest authoritarians responsible for so much harm and trauma was extremely satisfying, but the celebration did not last long. A couple of years later, Sheikh Mohammed was welcomed alongside other visiting dignitaries at Queen Elizabeth's funeral, as if his "campaign of fear and intimidation" and "domestic abuse" against his ex-wife and family were a distant memory.[61] It was a stark reminder of the carte blanche that such extreme wealth and power provide and that impunity for despotism will continue as long as unprincipled political elites benefit by it.

– 13 –

"Can You Sit on Your Phone?"

"Hey Ron," the Amnesty International staffer messaged, "I was hoping we could meet in person. I have something very sensitive I want to brief you on. Best we do it face to face."

This request was unusual: COVID-19 dominated our lives, and, as a second wave of the virus swept through Toronto, a new public shutdown order had just been enacted.[1] Everyone was still being extremely cautious about in-person meetings. We also had fairly secure options for communicating online that we used regularly, so I was curious about what had prompted this heightened level of vigilance. The Amnesty staffer lived a few hours away and offered to drive close to my neighborhood. We arranged to meet at a spot along the waterfront and found a park bench to talk where no one would hear us.

"Do you have your phone with you?" she asked.

"Of course, but I can turn it off if you want or remove the battery."

"Why don't you sit on it—that should be enough."

I complied. "Okay, what's up?"

The staffer explained Amnesty had "something huge" coming up.

"What can you tell me about it?" I asked.

"Unfortunately, I can't say much. It's about NSO Group, that's about all I can say."

Now I was confused. Why had she asked to meet me in person to discuss something highly sensitive and driven several hours to meet me, only to say she couldn't tell me anything?

"I can say we are planning on releasing our methodology for detecting Pegasus in full," she continued, "and were wondering if you guys would consider doing an independent peer review, to make sure it's sound?"

"Peer-review your methodology?"

"Yes, and perhaps a selection of devices that we have determined are infected with Pegasus."

"It shouldn't be a problem to do the peer review and check the findings on those devices. I'll talk to the team," I replied.

And that was that.

Although I felt a little frustrated to go through this fuss for such limited information, I empathized with the staffer's predicament. Practicing operational security is difficult, especially for civil society groups that have limited resources and professional support. Sometimes it makes sense to take all the precautions you can. The appropriate risk mitigation measures for every circumstance are never always clear either. Suggesting that I sit on my phone would at least limit the microphone's exposure, should my iPhone be compromised, and meeting face-to-face is prudent whenever confidential matters are in play.

It's also nerve-racking to be entrusted with highly sensitive information, especially if you are—as was this person—part of a larger network of collaborators with a lot hanging in the balance. You don't want to be the one who spoils it for the entire group. You don't want to be that weakest link, especially if lives are at risk. There's a lot at stake, and everyone is trying to do their best in what can be a very stressful context.

We had inklings something was going on related to NSO Group with Amnesty International and a few other organizations. Journalists were reaching out to us with odd questions. One asked what I thought of work done by Amnesty International's tech lab. "It's great," I responded. We had toiled largely alone investigating mercenary spyware for years and had produced the first reports on it. With the case, in 2016, of Ahmed Mansoor, the human rights defender in the United Arab Emirates, we had found the first forensic evidence of Pegasus infections. That same year, former Citizen Lab research fellow Claudio Guarnieri joined Amnesty International as a technology fellow, and in 2019, the group founded a security lab, modeled to some extent on the Citizen Lab. We were stretched thin ourselves, so we welcomed these additional contributions to the field.

Later, as I read through *Pegasus*, Laurent Richard and Sandrine Rigaud's book about the collaboration the Amnesty staffer felt reluctant to tell me about, I got the sense that some kind of competitive dynamic may have been at play that sidelined us from fully participating in what would come to be known as the "Pegasus Project" disclosures.[2] This is not surprising—it's natural and sometimes healthy to have groups working independently and holding their cards close to their chest. For our part, we offered what we could to be helpful and waited for the big reveal.

———

On July 18, 2021, the news broke about the Pegasus Project, a consortium of investigative journalists, the news collective Forbidden Stories, and Amnesty International.[3] This group had been working together for about a year on a leaked data set—a "list of numbers"—that purported to show individuals who had been "selected" for Pegasus infections by NSO Group's government clients. The stories were released in a staggered fashion and distributed among multiple news organizations, including the *Guardian* and the *Washington Post*.[4] The main findings reinforced what had been apparent from the reporting and investigation on mercenary spyware up to that point: without effective international safeguards, the mercenary spyware market had been providing highly invasive tools to government clients, and they were being widely abused to spy on journalists, human rights defenders, lawyers, government officials, and others.

The Citizen Lab simultaneously published a peer review of Amnesty International's forensic methodology and an independent validation of the forensic analysis Amnesty's Security Lab had made on a selection of victims' devices.[5] We confirmed that its methodology was sound and its findings of infections on the devices were accurate. We continued doing this kind of independent validation for each other in numerous other cases.

Amnesty International also released a mobile verification tool-kit (MVT), a diagnostic tool intended for distribution and use as a "checker" to detect potential Pegasus infections. In principle, it was a commendable idea, enabling potential victims to discover malicious hacking attempts and, by empowering them, to avoid bottle-necks within groups such as the Citizen Lab. But MVT turned out to be challenging for novices to run and then interpret the results. Moreover, because it was also easy for NSO Group to evade, the Lab has continued to use our own closely guarded methods and signatures instead. Despite these challenges, we regard MVT as an asset to the ecosystem and recommend it to some targets, or those assisting them, as an initial step in the triaging process—much like a COVID home test. If it yields a positive result, you should exercise caution and conduct further diagnostics.

Initially, there was considerable confusion within the digital security and rights community regarding several aspects of the Pegasus Project. This confusion was undoubtedly a result of the need to maintain confidentiality around the investigations and protect the source of the shared data. But many civil society partners, like us, were not briefed on the full details beforehand, and the announcement caught many by surprise. That ruffled feathers and left some people wondering what it meant for their constituencies. Numerous human rights and other NGOs worldwide, for example, received a flood of inquiries from concerned individuals asking if their names were on the list and what implications it held for them. There appeared to be no process in place to funnel such questions to someone with access to the data.

There was also a lot of confusion around the leaked information—the "list of numbers." Despite a short explanation published by the *Guardian*, there was still uncertainty about what the list pertained to, how it was hypothetically used by NSO Group's government clients, and what it meant if someone's number was on it.[6] The sensational headlines focused on the names of those associated with numbers on the list and the capabilities of the spyware, but not all the people whose phone numbers were on the list were actually infected with Pegasus.

As for me and others who closely follow mercenary spyware and international espionage, we assumed that the list of numbers referred to one of the many vendors operating in the shadowy world of mobile network surveillance and security. A dirty open secret of the telecommunications industry is that there is gross insecurity at the most fundamental level of mobile communications around data roaming and especially the SS7 protocol (chapter 4). Using these protocols, any network operator with a telecommunications license can ask for details on users of other networks anywhere in the world, revealing their locations and the make, model, and other identifiers of their mobile devices, and enabling the operator to intercept SMS and voice messages. Home Location Register (HLR) lookups, for example, provide the precise geolocation of any mobile device anywhere in the world.

In decades past, as part of the "do not speak" clandestine world, state intelligence and law enforcement agencies developed cozy partnerships with their national telecommunications companies, enabling them to take advantage of such lookups almost completely outside public scrutiny.[7] (Remember all the blinking lights tracking phones on maps in films such as *Enemy of the State* or the *Bourne* series?) Today, many private firms can provide such services to any paying government client. Not surprisingly, a flood of abuses has followed. One such firm is Circles, whose poorly configured firewall allowed us to enumerate its government clients around the world—a list that included authoritarian regimes, military agencies associated with acts of torture, and some of the worst offenders of human rights (chapter 4).

The level of insecurity at the heart of the global telecommunications system, exploited by firms offering "tracking" as a "service," is nothing short of jaw-dropping, especially considering how reliant we are on it. Any government security agency anywhere in the world can contract with a surveillance vendor and, using the services of a company in, say, Vanuatu, Tonga, or Fiji, pinpoint where you and your device are *right now*. It can acquire your unique device identifier, potentially intercept your text messages and calls, spoof a message, and deny you mobile service. If you own a device and connect to a cellular service anywhere in the world, you're trackable.

Some efforts have been made to publicize SS7 insecurities. In November 2017, Canada's French news organization Radio-Canada initiated an investigative report in which it paid a German firm to exploit SS7 protocols to track the location and intercept the phone calls of a sitting member of Parliament, the New Democratic Party's Matthew Dubé.[8] When he was shown a map plotting his device's movements, he responded, "Good thing I wasn't doing anything inappropriate." But the story came and went, without any public outcry or Canadian government action to fix the root of the issue.

In 2021, Gary Miller joined the Lab as a part-time fellow. He had worked for years in the mobile security industry, growing increasingly disturbed by the abuses he could see in the SS7 protocol and phone lookup system and the failure of anyone in a position of authority to do anything about them. In a business meeting he had in 2017 with NSO Group's senior executives, including founders Shalev Hulio and Omri Lavie, the firm offered his employer, Mobileum, a deal to provide NSO clients with phone lookup capabilities.[9] Lavie told them that the NSO Group would pay for their services with "bags of cash"—a sure sign of shady practices.

That meeting, along with other similar episodes, prompted Miller to reconsider his professional life. In 2021, a month before the Pegasus Project story broke, he filed a whistleblower complaint to the US Department of Justice, the Securities and Exchange Commission, the Federal Communications Commission, and members of the US Congress. Miller joined the Citizen Lab shortly after and briefed us on the deep insecurities within the infrastructure we rely on for entertainment, business, health, and, really, everything we do. Together, we published several detailed reports on SS7 insecurities, including one that revealed evidence of millions of malicious network requests sent from Saudi Arabia to geolocate the phones of Saudi users who were traveling in the United States—a chilling discovery in light of that regime's deadly clandestine activities abroad.[10]

When I read the Pegasus Project details, I had a hunch about what was going on with the "list of numbers": NSO Group had probably established a bespoke service, either in-house or contracted out to a third party, in which its clients could first query a phone number before firing Pegasus exploits in its direction. Doing so is extremely valuable because the government client would have several questions: Is this person in a jurisdiction where it is safe for me to hack (not in the United States, for instance, where Pegasus is not supposed to work)? Is this person using a cellphone that is susceptible to the type of exploit I have in my arsenal? Where is this person right now? Are they in a high-value meeting that could yield some important bits of intelligence? It's the equivalent of stalking a target before mugging them.

When I asked Miller about the Pegasus Project list, he reminded me that "it's not realistic to assume all NSO clients would have the ability to strike separate deals with a single HLR query provider. It's more likely that the NSO Group constructed a feature that could be accessed at each customer location using an API [application programming interface] call to a centralized location (say, an NSO Group software cloud in Israel), which sent the request to a single HLR query provider." As an important aside, if this explanation is accurate, and the HLR requests go through a cloud maintained by NSO Group, the firm's claims about not knowing in advance whom its government clients are targeting is not accurate. NSO Group's lookup services would be a one-stop portal to the advance scouting its government clients perform—and NSO Group's engineers would see it all.

———

Once the full scope of what was contained in the Pegasus Project leaks became apparent, it revealed a snapshot in time of worldwide cyber espionage enabled by a single mercenary company—NSO Group. According to the consortium, the data covered five years

(2016–21) and contained around fifty thousand phone numbers.[11] There seemed to be information in the leaks about at least ten government clients: Azerbaijan, Bahrain, Hungary, India, Kazakhstan, Mexico, Morocco, Rwanda, Saudi Arabia, and the UAE. This list corresponded to the research the Citizen Lab had already done on NSO Group's government client base, so the match was compelling. Some of the countries did a lot of lookups. Mexico selected the most—around fifteen thousand—followed by Morocco and the UAE selecting about ten thousand each.[12] All these governments have poor human rights track records, almost nonexistent oversight of their state security agencies, and long histories of corruption and authoritarianism. Giving their spy agencies access to a lookup service is like providing murderers with "find my phone" capabilities for anyone anywhere in the world. What could go wrong?

The bulk of the Pegasus Project's investigative work went into tracking down the identities behind the phone numbers on the list. Once those identities started to emerge, it was clear that a global reconnaissance of high-profile targets had occurred. Those whose phone numbers were checked spanned forty-five countries across four continents.[13] In Europe alone more than one thousand numbers had been selected by NSO Group clients.[14] Among the highlights, the circle of people around Jamal Khashoggi had been targeted, including his wife, Hanan Elatr, and his fiancée, Hatice Cengiz.[15] Forensic analysis done by the Citizen Lab and Amnesty International later confirmed infections on devices belonging to both women (chapter 5).[16]

In Hungary, the phones of at least ten lawyers, an opposition politician, and five journalists were queried—including Szabolcs Panyi's phone immediately after he questioned President Viktor Orbán about corruption in a news conference.[17] Amnesty International subsequently confirmed that his device had been repeatedly infected with Pegasus.[18]

Also on the list was the phone number of Adrien Beauduin, a Canadian-Belgian PhD student at Central European University in Hungary—a university funded by philanthropist billionaire George Soros.[19] Beauduin, who studied gender (a "woke" topic targeted for

repression by Orbán's regime), had participated in political demonstrations and had once been detained by Hungarian police. Amnesty's analysis of his phone showed evidence of targeting, but it
couldn't determine whether the device had actually been infected.[20]
Soon after, the Orbán government dismantled not only gender
studies but Central European University as a whole. In 2019, the
university moved to Vienna.[21]

Other revelations showed how the Orbán government used Pegasus to stifle a free press in the country. Attendees of a private meeting organized by a Hungarian media mogul, Zóltan Varga, were
selected for potential hacking.[22] Varga is the owner of the news site
24.hu, one of Hungary's last remaining independent media outlets.
In 2018, concerned about growing media repression in the country, he organized a dinner with several prominent friends in the
industry to discuss a possible media venture.[23] After the invitations
were extended but before the gathering, all seven participants were
added to the phone list, and, according to a forensic examination, at
least one person's phone was successfully infected with Pegasus and
another bore traces of a Pegasus hacking attempt.

In India, the phone numbers of more than forty reporters, major
opposition figures, and even serving ministers in the Modi government were discovered on the list.[24] Days after a Supreme Court
staffer accused the chief justice of sexual harassment, her phone,
her husband's phone, and several of her family members' phones
were selected.[25] Another set of numbers on the list was associated
with Prime Minister Narendra Modi's main opponent in the 2019
national elections, Rahul Gandhi of the famed Gandhi family.[26]
During the campaign, two of his phones were selected along with
those belonging to five of his friends and several other members of
his Congress Party. As if to underscore the corruption and abuse
of power, after the India-related Pegasus Project stories were published, police barged into the offices of one of the consortium partners, Indian news organization the *Wire*, as part of a drummed-up
fraud investigation.[27] Two founding editors, its diplomatic editor,
and two of its regular contributors were all found on the Pegasus
Project list.[28]

The Citizen Lab had published numerous reports on cyber espionage targeting Tibetans and the office of the Dalai Lama since 2009.[29] Most of them attributed the cyber espionage to China or groups affiliated with the People's Republic of China. But we always assumed the Indian government also kept close tabs on the Dalai Lama's inner circle, given that he was headquartered in Dharamsala, India. Sure enough, the phone numbers of these people appeared on the list, notably in a period before and after a private meeting between the Dalai Lama and US president Barack Obama.[30]

Before the Pegasus Project disclosures, we had unearthed a raft of espionage against journalists in numerous countries. The list confirmed this type of abusive targeting. More than 180 reporters and editors around the world were on it, including Azerbaijan's leading investigative journalist, Khadija Ismayilova.[31] Phones belonging to a network of her family, friends, and associates were also on the list. Forensic investigation by Amnesty International showed that Ismayilova's device had been hacked with Pegasus for two years.[32] Notably, she had been subjected to numerous smear campaigns that involved publication of private information and attempts to blackmail her with sex tapes.[33]

Also on the list were three French journalists, and ANSSI, France's national agency for information systems security, confirmed that their phones had been hacked.[34] French prosecutors announced they would launch an investigation into the hacking, with Morocco as the prime suspect.[35] (Ironically, a few years later France supported draft European Council legislation that would legalize the hacking of journalists' phones.)[36]

In the years leading up to the Pegasus Project, the Lab had undertaken a series of reports on abusive spyware hacking in Mexico. The Pegasus Project's list reinforced those findings. One of the most dramatic of the findings concerned journalist Cecilio Pineda Birto, who was getting death threats for reporting on official collusion with a cartel capo.[37] His private conversations with a source and a colleague were published verbatim in a national newspaper. Shortly after his phone number was looked up, he was assassinated.

Also in Mexico, at least fifty people close to President López Obrador (his wife, family members, drivers, aides, and others) were found to be on the list while he was campaigning in the two years leading up to his election as president in 2018.[38] López Obrador didn't use a phone regularly, so whoever was surveilling him followed those close to him, including his chief of staff, Alfonso Romo Garza; his legal counsel, Julio Scherer Ibarra; his communications coordinator, Jesús Ramírez Cuevas; and his cardiologist, Patricio Heriberto Ortíz Fernández. Mexican media had carried leaked reports about López Obrador's health, including details about his 2013 heart attack.[39] Was the hacked phone of his cardiologist the ultimate source of those details?

Ironically, although López Obrador included pledges in his platform never to spy and promised to end the Mexican government's purchase of spyware, we later discovered that his administration went on its own Pegasus hacking spree, one that led to the highest levels of his government and continues today (chapter 11).[40]

We had already found victims of Rwandan surveillance before the Pegasus Project list, including several who had been victims of the 2019 WhatsApp attacks (chapter 1).[41] So it was no surprise that several members of the Rwandan diaspora who had fled Paul Kagame's regime were on the list too. The publication of these cases caught the attention of family members of Paul Rusesabagina, the man who inspired the Academy Award–nominated film *Hotel Rwanda* and had been kidnapped and jailed because of his opposition to the president.[42] Although the phone number for Carine Kanimba, one of Rusesabagina's daughters, was not on the list, the Citizen Lab and Amnesty International later discovered she was targeted with a flurry of Pegasus infections (chapter 18).[43] Journalist Michela Wrong, who introduced me to several Rwandans experiencing this type of repression, said that the Pegasus Project revelations about Rwanda being a client of NSO Group reinforced existing suspicions among Rwandans living abroad. "Many Rwandans are so intensely suspicious of all modes of electronic communication they will only stray beyond the prosaic and banal when sitting face to face," Wrong explained. "In that way, the mere knowledge of Pegasus's existence has had a chilling effect on freedom of thought in this small but influential central African nation."[44]

It came as no surprise that a lot of phone numbers on the list related to the United Arab Emirates, including that for Princess Haya (chapter 12).[45] Princess Latifa's phone number was selected on February 25, 2018, one day after her attempted escape from her father's clutches.[46] She discarded that phone in a café and replaced it with a new phone and SIM card.[47] Also on the list were several of Latifa's friends, selected during the days of her attempted escape.[48]

Perhaps most shocking of all were the government officials whose phone numbers were selected for targeting. The Pegasus Project list included ten prime ministers, a king, and three presidents, including French president Emmanuel Macron.[49] Time stamps in the data showed that seven former prime ministers were targeted while they were still in office: Yemen's Ahmed Obeid bin Daghr, Lebanon's Saad al-Hariri, Uganda's Ruhakana Rugunda, France's Édouard Philippe, Kazakhstan's Bakytzhan Sagintayev, Algeria's Noureddine Bedoui, and Belgium's Charles Michel.[50] As we knew from our own research, Pegasus and other spyware tools were routinely used by governments to spy on each other—something NSO Group and other similar firms did not advertise.

Also on the list were the phone numbers of several US diplomats and Robert Malley, the chief US negotiator in the Iran nuclear talks.[51] (Several years later, Malley was placed on leave and his security clearance suspended over concerns about his possible mishandling of classified material.)[52] Alongside previous disclosures of US government personnel whose devices were targeted or hacked, or individuals whose phones were eavesdropped on while in meetings with US officials, these revelations angered the US Congress and, later, the Biden administration. They began to clamp down hard on NSO Group and other mercenary spyware vendors.[53]

NSO Group and its investors were blindsided by the revelations. Instead of owning up to them, the firm gave its usual response to reports of abuse of its spyware: it tried to turn the tables on those who made the allegations. This time, however, it played a new card:

NSO Group was the real victim! "Enough Is Enough" headlined its statement to reporters.[54] Calling the Pegasus Project a "well-orchestrated media campaign" that was "vicious and slanderous," NSO Group took particular issue with the fifty thousand phone numbers on the list. "You won't reach 50,000 Pegasus targets since the company was founded," said CEO Shalev Hulio.[55]

Will Cathcart, the CEO of WhatsApp, delivered a stinging rebuke of NSO Group's mathematics, pointing out that the size of the Pegasus Project's list of phone numbers is entirely consistent with the two-week period of targeting his company had discovered (and the Citizen Lab helped investigate). More than 1,400 phone numbers were targeted in that two-week period. "That tells us that over a longer period of time, over a multi-year period of time, the numbers of people being attacked are very high," Cathcart said.[56] He also noted that the same kinds of victims were found then as now: politicians, lawyers, journalists, human rights defenders, and senior government officials. "The reporting matches what we saw in the attack we defeated two years ago," he said, and "it is very consistent with what we were loud about then."

Although NSO Group flat-out denied any connection between its operations and the list of phone numbers, forensic data proved it wrong. Amnesty International reached out to sixty-seven people on the list to undertake forensic analysis. Of those, twenty-three phones showed signs of infections, and another fourteen showed infection attempts.[57] The forensic data proved that the infections or targeting happened mere seconds after the location queries were sent to the victims' devices. That powerful correlation helped substantiate the relationship of the list to NSO Group's government clients. Once again, NSO Group was busted.

———

While the Pegasus Project unfolded, we were engaged in our own highly sensitive project stemming from the 2019 WhatsApp investigation. In the fall of 2019, as we undertook our victim notification, several Catalans whom we had notified reached out to Elies Campo, an individual well known in Spanish civil society for his work in the technology industry. Campo, formerly employed by WhatsApp, was currently lending his expertise to Telegram, the increasingly popular messaging application used by activists worldwide, including in Spain. (Coincidentally, the phone number of the founder and CEO of Telegram, Pavel Durov, was on the Pegasus Project list.) The targeted Catalans asked Campo to check with WhatsApp to make sure that the notifications and the Citizen Lab were legitimate. He responded that he had verified who we were and recommended they follow the instructions we had given to them to better secure their devices.

Campo didn't give the issue much thought again until July 2020, when the *Guardian* published its exposé of the Catalan victims of the WhatsApp exploitation we had unearthed (chapter 1).[58] Until then, none of them had gone public with their experiences. Campo says he was confused by the victims' profiles because they were not, in his opinion, the most likely targets of espionage. He suspected there must be more.

After reading the *Guardian* report, Campo contacted John Scott-Railton (JSR), who had led our team on the WhatsApp investigation. They agreed that our discoveries were almost certainly only a fraction of the espionage in Spain. Campo asked how he could assist us in further investigations. Eager to dig deeper, we connected Campo to Luis Fernando García of Mexico's R3D (chapter 11). JSR had worked closely with him in our extensive investigations in Mexico, and his trusted relationships with victims and targets had proved essential there. We felt we could apply the same model that García and the Lab had developed in Mexico to Campo in Catalonia.

We connected the two experts, and they talked at length about the process of investigation. García explained to Campo the type of conversations to have with victims, to be empathetic and talk them through what they were experiencing. Together, we tutored Campo on how to undertake the "snowball" method of discovery, in which confirmed victims are asked who in their immediate circles were most likely to be targeted. Campo could then reach out to them through their colleagues to see if they would participate in the research process. In this way, the net is cast in increasingly wider circles. Sure enough, as we began systematically checking in this manner, the cases in Spain mounted higher.

By the time the Pegasus Project revelations were announced, we were well on our way to unearthing a major domestic espionage scandal in the heart of Europe. The timing couldn't have been better. NSO Group was reeling from the Pegasus Project revelations, and media attention had catapulted the topic into the news. A drumbeat of stories on mercenary spyware was catching the attention of policymakers, including in Europe and the United States. We focused in earnest on the Catalan cases, with JSR leading the sleuthing, and prepared ourselves for a major publication.

As always, though, another unexpected discovery found its way to the Lab—one that dramatically changed the landscape around mercenary spyware and briefly consumed our team's attention.

– 14 –

"A Very Special Guest"

One of the most inspiring people I've encountered in the course of our research is Loujain al-Hathloul, who resides in Saudi Arabia but studied at my alma mater, the University of British Columbia (UBC), from 2008 to 2013.[1] Like many activists from the Gulf and Middle East regions, she became active on the internet and social media as she watched the street demonstrations and other tumultuous events during the Arab Spring. The courage shown by those demonstrators inspired her to take to the internet and engage in political activism for women's rights.

Like many women from conservative societies who speak their minds online, al-Hathloul soon encountered hostility. Trolls began posting derogatory comments and threats on her Facebook account, and taunts arrived in direct messages and emails, some of which contained repulsive pornographic content. Al-Hathloul reported these incidents to UBC security administrators, but they took no action, unsure at the time how to address this targeted harassment campaign from supporters of a distant sheikhdom. For al-Hathloul, these distressing encounters were soon followed by more sophisticated hacking operations and harrowing experiences.

When al-Hathloul completed her program at UBC and returned to Saudi Arabia, she continued her activism despite the harassment. An archaic law still prohibited women from driving a car—part of the sexist system of paternalistic control over women in the country. Al-Hathloul became the public face of a woman's right to drive.[2] She broadened her activism to demand an end to the entire guardianship system in Saudi Arabia in which women are legally treated as the property of the men in their lives.[3] Even punishments are applied in a way that's inherently discriminatory. In 2013, for example, instead of penalizing her directly for her stand, the Saudi regime punished her father. "I felt insulted and furious towards such a decision, which sent a clear message: you, women, don't exist," she said.[4]

In 2014, she photographed and videotaped herself defiantly driving a car.[5] Her mission was to cross the border from the United Arab Emirates, where she had a valid driver's license, into Saudi Arabia, where the ban prohibited women from driving, filming the entire journey. But she was stopped by Saudi authorities before she could officially enter her home country and imprisoned for seventy-three days.[6] Other women who followed her lead were arrested as well.[7] Saudi Arabia was "not ready" for women drivers, said Mohammed bin Salman (MBS), the crown prince.[8] Al-Hathloul was getting under the skin of the rising autocrat.

Al-Hathloul routinely received messages threatening to expose sensitive personal information. She reported these threats to Saudi authorities through an online portal set up by the government for precisely this purpose. After three days she received a notice saying the case was closed—probably because the harassment she reported had been engineered by Saudi authorities themselves. A major disinformation campaign then began in which she was portrayed as an agent of Qatar, Saudi Arabia's geopolitical rival.[9]

Starting around 2016, the targeting became more focused and clandestine. Al-Hathloul began to get hints that her devices or accounts may have been compromised. One happened while she was attending a conference in Madrid for women activists in the Middle East and North Africa. As part of the proceedings, security trainers explained to attendees how to check their Gmail accounts for evidence of unauthorized access. Al-Hathloul found that her account had been accessed one time from the UAE for fifteen consecutive hours during that visit to Spain. She reported the incident to the security trainers, but it proved difficult to find out who had access. Google gives out only general warnings, so no help could be found there. The trainers advised her to harden her account by setting up multi-factor authentication and to notify colleagues and friends to be on guard. The suspicious targeting of her email account did little to daunt her activism as she continued to press for change in Saudi Arabia. She soon became the worldwide face of a major political movement—and thus a nagging thorn in the regime's side.

Things took a dramatic and more serious turn in March 2018 while al-Hathloul was registered in a master's program in Abu Dhabi.[10] When she tried to leave for a conference abroad, she was informed by officials at the airport gate that she was not allowed to leave the country and was prevented from boarding the plane. It's one thing to be denied entry to a country but quite another to be told you cannot leave. There's one place you can go, the officials told her: back to Saudi Arabia.

Al-Hathloul left the airport and called her then husband to explain the situation. She decided that with only two months left in her program in Abu Dhabi, she would stay to complete the degree and then return to Saudi Arabia. But someone was listening in on that call. A few days later, al-Hathloul was suddenly intercepted on the highway by two large black sport utility vehicles.[11] "They blocked me in the middle of the highway . . . and took me in," she explained to me. "They never informed me of their identities." They drove her to a private place that was decorated with the logo of the Abu Dhabi police. "It was impressively quiet," she said. "Isolated and feeling as if it was haunted."

Four hours later, they locked her in an inmate partition cage in one of the vehicles and drove to a private airstrip. A camera pointed at her face the entire time. "I was literally in a tiny cell in that big car with the camera in front of me. When they opened the door, I was in front of a private jet, the most luxurious jet I've ever seen in my life." She was introduced to the crew as a "very special guest"— and soon was in the air on her way to Riyadh, Saudi Arabia.

On arrival, al-Hathloul was arrested and sent to a detention center. Her husband, who at the time was in Jordan, was arrested and returned to Saudi Arabia, where he was interrogated—no doubt reprimanded for failing to control his "property" (his wife). Curiously, both were released after three days. However, three months later, on May 15, 2018, al-Hathloul was arrested again—the highest profile of a wave of arrests across the country.[12] This time the detention was longer and the treatment far harsher. She was held in two separate detention centers for three years, one of which was a "secret prison." She described it as a converted Saudi officers' club—a combination of leisure and torture that seems befitting for an autocratic regime with a barely concealed sadistic side.

The timing of al-Hathloul's detention was no coincidence. MBS had been planning to announce a new "women's rights" initiative meant to burnish the reputation of the kingdom in the eyes of the world.[13] In fact, it was a cynical PR move meant to apply some camouflage over the regime's gender discrimination and widespread inequality. Although women would be allowed to drive by June 2018, they would still be required to obtain a guardian's permission to work or to travel.[14] MBS's widely trumpeted measures also did nothing to resolve endemic domestic violence and systemic discrimination against women and girls inside Saudi Arabia, or the transnational repression MBS and his security team practiced against women dissidents based outside the country.[15] (One can't help but wonder whether Tony Blair and his firm helped conjure up this initiative when they were contracted to help MBS "modernize" Saudi Arabia.)[16] As if to underscore how superficial the measures were, MBS made sure that al-Hathloul—widely recognized as the face of women's rights in Saudi Arabia and unlikely to let the kingdom's PR go unquestioned—was effectively neutralized by being rendered back to the country and imprisoned.

"They didn't want us to be part of it," she told me some years later. "So when they heard me on the phone saying I would stay in the UAE until I finished my studies in the summer, there was no option for them—they needed to bring me by force to the country. I assume that's why they kidnapped me from the UAE. I assume also that the UAE really were invested in my calls and my communications, and they communicated it to the Saudis immediately because they wouldn't have kidnapped me if the Saudis didn't ask them to bring me."

Al-Hathloul's ordeal in prison was grim. She was repeatedly tortured and subjected to intense interrogation, including the use of electric shocks, waterboarding, flogging, and threats of rape and death; Saud al-Qahtani, the "Lord of the Flies" who had personally overseen the execution of Jamal Khashoggi (chapter 5), was a participant in the gruesome proceedings.[17] According to the testimony of Loujain's sister Alia, al-Qahtani "laughed at her, sometimes he threatened to rape and kill her and throw her body into the sewage system. Along with six of his men, . . . [he] tortured her all night during Ramadan, the Muslim month of fasting."[18]

Early on, the interrogators seized her phone and forced her to turn over her passwords, so they could copy the contents. She was presented with information about her past private communications with friends and family that could only have come from remote access to one of her older devices. The interrogators mocked her use of Telegram, saying it was hardly as secure as she thought, now that they had access to all her chats. They questioned her about some of her contacts and pressured her to turn over names to implicate others. They told her sister they had incriminating and embarrassing photos of al-Hathloul—a bluff, she believes, that was meant to pressure the extended family to keep their mouths shut.

In 2019, while al-Hathloul was still in prison, Reuters journalists Joel Schectman and Christopher Bing published their investigation into DarkMatter, the UAE hacking firm.[19] Among the revelations they learned from the whistleblowers was that al-Hathloul was one of the targets of Project Raven—the operation we exposed in 2016 that was executed by former NSA contractors hired by the Emiratis (chapter 3). She was categorized as a "national security risk" by the UAE authorities. Their report described how DarkMatter used a zero-day exploit to pry open Apple's iMessage operating system and hack into her phone. The spyware, called Karma, remains elusive to researchers even today. The new evidence was an aha moment for her: it provided an explanation for the surveillance she had felt but couldn't explain while studying in Abu Dhabi, as well as for the way her Saudi interrogators had learned some of the personal details that could only have come from her hacked device.

———————

After years of beatings, torture, threats, and other ill-treatment, al-Hathloul was finally freed from prison in February 2021.[20] It was not an unconditional release. She was prohibited from traveling outside Saudi Arabia—a travel ban that continues at the time of writing. But that wasn't enough for the regime. Shortly after being released from prison, she received a warning from Google saying her device had once again been targeted by what the firm referred to vaguely as "state-sponsored" espionage actors.[21]

Al-Hathloul reached out to her brother, Walid, and asked him for advice. Living in Canada and aware of our work, Walid recommended that she connect with the Lab.[22] It was yet another of those extraordinary opportunities that came our way and ended up having enormous implications. We were familiar with her activism and her ordeals, and so we gladly dove in to investigate.[23]

We realized that this case was exceptionally sensitive. Al-Hathloul was at great personal risk, having just endured three years of imprisonment and now subjected to countrywide arrest. We wanted to make sure not to give the authorities any excuse to touch her. We also assumed she would be under at least one if not several overlapping layers of surveillance, electronic and physical. We treat these individuals with our equivalent of what intelligence agencies call "sensitive compartmented information"—keeping information within the Lab restricted on a need-to-know basis and taking every possible precaution to avoid drawing attention to the work we are doing on their cases.

With al-Hathloul's consent, Bill Marczak set up a dedicated VPN for her devices that would route all communications in and out of her phone through a server we controlled. Doing so would, in theory, allow us to inspect the traffic, flag anything suspicious, and then dig deeper. For about six months, we detected nothing unusual, but that was not surprising. Targeted espionage had evolved to become more like a "smash-and-grab" operation: hack the device, gather as much data as you can, especially any credentials and passwords to valuable platforms and cloud accounts, then get out before you are caught. To detect anything significant in progress, by sheer good luck our VPN monitoring would have to be set up at the right place and the right time—and even then we had no way of spotting what might have happened in the past.

Meanwhile, Marczak was developing a new approach to forensic analysis that involved scrutiny of crash logs and processes contained in device backups. This approach allowed us to effectively "travel back in time." We could scan processes going back months and even years and observe any anomalies that suggested nefarious intrusions—whether of the "smash-and-grab" variety or those that are more persistent. Marczak instructed al-Hathloul to send us a full backup of her device so we could scan through it. He quickly ran into an explosive discovery. The backup revealed that her device had been hacked several months before, and specific process names in the crash logs showed the device had been infected with Pegasus spyware. But that wasn't all Marczak found: he discovered a copy of some of the highly sensitive ingredients used in the hack.

Before loading a copy of something like Pegasus onto a target's device, spyware companies use exploits to open Apple's operating system via flaws in the software architecture that even Apple is unaware of. These zero-day exploits are the most precious assets in a mercenary spyware company's arsenal. They are either developed internally or purchased from exploit developers or brokers in the shadowy market for such commodities. A zero-day exploit targeting an Apple device can run into the millions of dollars. To avoid "burning" zero-day exploits, companies like NSO Group engineer them to effectively self-destruct, erasing their tracks at the scene of the crime. This feature allows exploits to be reused for longer periods and prevents meddlesome groups like ours from tracking them down and disclosing them to the tech platforms so they can be fixed. Marczak found, however, that the process in al-Hathloul's device had malfunctioned, and a copy of some malicious image files that were used as part of the exploitation process had failed to self-destruct. Once again, NSO Group had slipped up. "It was a game changer," said Marczak. "We caught something that the company thought was uncatchable."[24]

What Marczak located were the blueprints for what was, at that time, the most sophisticated attack against Apple products in circulation. He called the exploit ForcedEntry. Looking back over one of our previous investigations, Marczak recognized elements of processes involved in ForcedEntry exploits in a massive espionage campaign we had discovered, and published about in a December 2020 report, in which the devices of more than thirty-six journalists, producers, and other staff at Al Jazeera were hacked with Pegasus.[25] We now had evidence of the tools used to silently load Pegasus on those devices, something we could see only remnants of in the data we gathered from the Al Jazeera victims' devices at the time.

In addition to being a zero-day exploit, ForcedEntry was also a "zero-click" version of the spyware, which means that no interaction is required between spyware operators and victims to hack a device. There is no need to trick someone into clicking on a link or opening an attachment. All an operative has to do is send the phone a message (which itself can be silent and traces of it then removed), and the exploit does the rest. One minute a target is blissfully going about their business as usual with a perfectly clean phone; the next, the spyware client is embedded inside, allowing the spies to watch every move, listen to every call, film surroundings, eavesdrop on private meetings, and read texts and emails.

Marczak and one of our colleagues at Amnesty International's tech lab, Donncha Ó Cearbhaill, developed a metric they called the "observed update deficit" to calculate the length of time a zero day is typically active before a company such as Apple provides a patch to fix the flaw.[26] With ForcedEntry, the deficit was about 131 days. That means that for more than four months, every single Apple user everywhere in the world was vulnerable to a silent Pegasus exploitation by NSO Group's government clients. No matter how diligent users were in updating their iOS and taking other precautions, no matter how suspicious they were about unsolicited emails, messages, and attachments, they were defenseless against

ForcedEntry. For 131 days, well over a billion people who use Apple products were sitting ducks for cyber espionage. Al-Hathloul was one of them. So were the thirty-six journalists, producers, and other staff at Al Jazeera—and countless numbers the world over.

———

For the second time in five years, we had disarmed a mercenary and disrupted a thief in the middle of an ongoing heist, thanks to al-Hathloul's cooperation. "We had the shell casing from the crime scene," Marczak said triumphantly.[27] As soon as we realized what we had in our hands, we did the right thing: we reached out to Apple and made a responsible disclosure.

On September 7, 2021, we forwarded the artifacts of the exploit to Apple's security team. Exactly five days later, Apple confirmed that the files included a zero-day exploit against iOS, MacOS, and even WatchOS. The team designated the ForcedEntry exploit CVE-2021-30860 and described it as "processing a maliciously crafted PDF [that] may lead to arbitrary code execution."[28] It swiftly pushed out an emergency patch that improved the security of more than a billion Apple users worldwide.

After the patch was released, Google's elite Project Zero team, with whom we had also shared a copy of ForcedEntry, published a detailed technical analysis of the exploit.[29] "Based on our research and findings," team members wrote, "we assess this to be one of the most technically sophisticated exploits we've ever seen, further demonstrating that the capabilities NSO provides rival those previously thought to be accessible to only a handful of nation states." "It's pretty incredible, and at the same time, pretty terrifying," they continued, referring to the fact that there is no need to prompt a target into clicking on a malicious link or attachment. "Short of not using a device," they wrote, "there is no way to prevent exploitation by a zero-click exploit; it's a weapon against which there is no defense."

The global news covered both the disclosure and the patch, drawing attention once again to the perils of the mercenary spyware market. But a key piece of the story was missing: the victim's name, Loujain al-Hathloul. After consulting with us and her family, she decided to remain anonymous. We described her in our reporting and our comments to the media as a "Saudi activist." Our overarching priority had to be her safety: she was under countrywide arrest and the object of intense scrutiny, and she had been arrested and tortured numerous times. We all knew that MBS could be vindictive and cutthroat.

————————

With the news of the Apple patch still resonating, I received an outreach from Ivan Krstić, head of security engineering and architecture at Apple. Among internet circles, Apple is notorious for being tight-lipped. Although we had interacted professionally with its threat teams during two responsible disclosures, the reaction on the other side of the Apple wall was always a mystery to us.

When Krstić contacted me, therefore, I was curious. He said our disclosure of ForcedEntry was a game changer for the firm. Despite spending considerable resources scouring its infrastructure looking for the holes in the systems that were being exploited by NSO Group, it had failed—until we handed Apple the blueprints for ForcedEntry.

Krstić explained he was enraged by companies like NSO Group and felt strongly that Apple had a duty to protect its users from the scourge. Much to my surprise, he laid out three initiatives Apple was about to take. First, it would announce a lawsuit against NSO Group in US courts. That was huge: Apple—a company valued at $2.9 trillion—would follow Meta and WhatsApp in suing NSO Group in the same US district court.[30]

Second, Apple would donate $10 million, plus whatever damages were awarded as part of the litigation, to an independent fund that would support cybersecurity research of the sort the Lab was doing.[31] This was also welcome news, especially as the Citizen Lab, like Amnesty International and other NGOs, does not accept direct funding from companies like Apple that may be the focus of our research. Krstić understood this principle. As he was conveying the news, I was aware that one of our research teams was busy undertaking two separate critical reports about Apple's censorship policies with respect to mainland China—precisely the type of independent research we wouldn't want to jeopardize with a conflict of interest. Although we applauded Apple's initiatives in the spyware field, we were not about to let it off the hook for its actions infringing on rights and freedoms in other areas of its operations.

Third, Krstić told me that Apple planned on notifying the victims it had discovered had been hacked through its platform by Pegasus or another spyware. This step was monumental, similar to the notifications to a selection of victims WhatsApp undertook in 2019 with the Citizen Lab's assistance (chapter 1). We knew that tech companies such as Apple, Google, and Meta could "see" a lot of malicious stuff happening on their networks, but for various reasons—fear of legal liability or threat to their bottom line—they were reluctant to chase that malfeasance down. Now, however, Apple was not going to sit back and let spyware companies target its customers. It was going on the offense big-time.

The practical consequences of these notifications were enormous. Apple shook a fruit tree worldwide, and the victims fell into our laps. As my Citizen Lab colleague John Scott-Railton described it, they helped "laser in on places where there may be bad things going on."[32] Users whose devices Apple determined had been hacked received notifications through email and iMessage alerts with instructions on further measures they could take to safeguard their devices. The messages also recommended that users reach out to Access Now's 24/7 digital security helpline. Cases flooded in, some directly to us, others to Amnesty International or Access Now. Before long, we were investigating major abuse cases in various parts of the world thanks to Apple's actions.

In El Salvador, after several journalists received Apple's notifications, they contacted Access Now or local NGOs for help. Together with Front Line Defenders, SocialTIC, and Fundación Acceso, we started analyzing crash logs and backups obtained from those who received the notifications to confirm Apple's findings (chapter 15). We then used the snowball technique in which we asked each confirmed victim to introduce us to others in their organization or orbit who might also have been infected. In the end, we were able to confirm thirty-five cases of El Salvadorian journalists and members of civil society whose phones had been successfully infected with NSO Group's Pegasus spyware between July 2020 and November 2021.[33]

A similar process played itself out in Thailand. After receiving Apple's notifications, Thai civil society victims turned to Access Now, the Citizen Lab, and local NGOs. After forensically analyzing those devices, we undertook more snowballing techniques to find other victims. Working with Thai NGOs iLaw and DigitalReach, we forensically confirmed that at least thirty individuals had been infected with NSO Group's Pegasus spyware between October 2020 and November 2021, a period of time coinciding with intense pro-democracy demonstrations in the country.[34] It wouldn't be long before similar cases would emerge in Mexico, Armenia, Serbia, and numerous other countries, thanks to Apple's alerts.[35]

One of the biggest consequences of Apple's first round of notifications came about after several serving US foreign officers based in Africa, working on issues related to Uganda, received notifications from the tech giant that their devices had been hacked.[36] This disclosure echoed our earlier discovery that the devices of foreign service officers in the United Kingdom and a device based at 10 Downing Street had been hacked. It supported our warning that an unregulated mercenary spyware market was not just a privacy or human rights issue but a national security issue as well. NSO Group had made a serious error. Allowing its customers to recklessly target the personal devices of serving American officials was the surest way to annoy the US government. This discovery soon mobilized senior national security officials and policymakers in the United States to take action against both NSO Group and the entire mercenary spyware industry.

That November, not coincidentally, the US Commerce Department added NSO Group (alongside Candiru and several other hack-for-hire firms the Lab had outed) to its designated entity list—a serious trade restriction and a stomach punch to the firms.[37] Once a foreign individual, entity, or government is placed on the list, it is prohibited from doing business with Americans and with American companies. Although the designation would be mostly an inconvenience for NSO Group, it meant a huge loss of reputation and a warning message from the US government to all potential investors and customers. NSO Group's valuation immediately plummeted, and the firm was downgraded by the credit-rating agency Moody's.[38] The table was turning on NSO Group and others in the sector. We began to feel we were making progress.

––––––––

After further reflection, al-Hathloul changed her mind about discussing her role in the discovery of ForcedEntry and decided to go public. She gave a lengthy interview to Reuters journalists Schectman and Bing describing her activism, her prison ordeal, and her decision to come forward.[39] Shortly before the interview, she filed a lawsuit against the UAE cyber offensive firm DarkMatter and three US citizens who worked for it.[40] These people had recently entered into a deferred prosecution agreement with the US Department of Justice for violation of the Arms Export Control Act, the International Traffic in Arms Regulations, and the Computer Fraud and Abuse Act.[41] The US-based Electronic Frontier Foundation represents her in the lawsuit.[42] Although progressing through the legal system is a long and complicated journey to justice, it's important to exercise that path whenever possible, if for no other reason than to show those responsible—whether governments or the mercenaries that service them—that victims won't just grit their teeth and bear it.

"It's good to have accountability," she said to me. "At least the public would know that they have some sort of power of stopping these monsters. They are backed by governments and military groups. But they are not gods. We still can and will do something to stop them."

The interrogations, the beatings, the torture, and the threats have all taken a major toll on al-Hathloul. She still experiences physical effects such as panic attacks and horrifying flashbacks. She told me that one day while driving in Riyadh, she noticed the sign for the Saudi officers' club that housed the "secret prison." Her heart started to race, her throat tightened, and she had to pull to the side of the road to settle herself. She continues to fear being spied on and now hesitates to use her device to communicate with people or to log on to social media. "I hate phones," she told me. "They made me hate any sort of device. When I have my phone around, I am always aware that I might be attacked." Most other people would quite justifiably retreat into isolation after going through something like what al-Hathloul experienced, but not her. She carries on: "I may not win immediately, but I will definitely win."

The Coolest Dictator in the World

2019–2024

EL SALVADOR

Ever since NSO Group began to communicate publicly, it has claimed that it operates a strict customer vetting process.[1] Government clients it considers too risky are passed over, and those guilty of abuse are dropped. Over the years, NSO has released pieces of this vetting process as "evidence" of its risk mitigation process, usually in the form of "human rights frameworks" circulated to friendly journalists and lawmakers the firm is courting.

While NSO Group's promotional materials may seem convincing to some on first blush, for those of us investigating the company and its spyware malfeasance, the claims contained in them are easily falsified. NSO Group not only sold its spyware to authoritarian governments with appalling human rights records (such as Saudi Arabia and the United Arab Emirates) or rampant corruption (such as Mexico) but did so repeatedly, even after abuses were documented and brought to its attention.[2] Its purported "strict vetting" is nothing but a shameless farce. No better illustration of this hypocrisy can be found than in the case of El Salvador and its mercurial, authoritarian-leaning president, Nayib Bukele.

For decades, El Salvador has been mired in violence, civil war, and endemic crime and corruption. From roughly 1970 to 1992, the country was torn apart by the Salvadoran Civil War, which pitted a right-wing military junta against a coalition of left-wing guerrilla groups operating under the banner of the Farabundo Martí

National Liberation Front (FMLN).[3] There were devastating and frequent human rights violations, including numerous extrajudicial killings, mass disappearances, and civilian massacres. Some of these egregious acts were attributed to "death squads" allegedly trained and supported by US military advisors.[4]

The aftermath of this violent and authoritarian era led to a culture of impunity and corruption within El Salvador's political system, police agencies, and armed forces. The subsequent increase in organized crime and corruption fostered the growth of inadequately regulated and unaccountable private security firms. The consequent scar on the country's social fabric is still visible today.

Bukele projects a kind of strongman chic with a millennial twist.[5] He favors backward baseball caps, aviator shades, and leather jackets. He celebrates digital technology, especially social media.[6] His X (formerly Twitter) account has become a launching pad for major policy initiatives announcements and criticism of dissenters.

In step with the digital hipster persona, Bukele is also a vocal champion of cryptocurrency and has even promoted Bitcoin as the legal tender.[7] He has installed hundreds of Bitcoin ATMs throughout the country and given every Salvadoran a $30 credit, even though most have no clue what to do with it. He even spoke about powering the mining of Bitcoin by tapping geothermal energy from volcanoes.[8] According to Salvadoran journalist Nelson Rauda Zablah, Bukele's crypto boosterism is just another means to whitewash his government's alt-right tendencies—a way to ingratiate himself with apolitical crypto billionaires who visit the country and sing his praises, oblivious to his shredding of democratic institutions. "By using his Bitcoin antics to distract from the truth," wrote Rauda, "Mr. Bukele dodges culpability for his regime's actions."[9]

Despite his antics, Bukele's popularity is undeniable—the highest in the region by far, according to an October 2022 CID Gallup poll that asked people in thirteen Latin American countries to rate their presidents. Bukele came out on top, with 86 percent approval. His ratings have never dipped below 70 percent since he's been in power and usually hover around 90 percent.[10] "Bukele's success relies on millennial authoritarianism: an innovative political strategy combining traditional populist appeals and classic authoritarian behavior with a youthful and modern personal brand built on social media," as Manuel Meléndez-Sánchez put it.[11] Among those Bukele has been compared with is Mohammed bin Salman of Saudi Arabia, another aficionado of digital despotism.[12] Any responsible firm would think twice about providing heads of state of this ilk with the most sophisticated tools of espionage available in the world. But not NSO Group.

Nayib Bukele was born in San Salvador.[13] His father, Armando Bukele Kattán, was a Muslim of Palestinian descent and a serial entrepreneur.[14] He opened the first McDonald's franchise in El Salvador and owned a public relations firm, Obermet, which his son later ran. One of Obermet's main clients was the FMLN (the guerrilla group transitioned into a left-leaning political party after the 1992 peace agreement).[15]

Perhaps inspired by this client, Bukele ventured into politics in 2011.[16] Running on the FMLN ticket, he was first elected as mayor of the small town of Nuevo Cuscatlán and was mayor of San Salvador from 2015 to 2018.[17] Even then, warning signs of his authoritarian personality were evident. Although he helped spearhead major revitalization efforts in San Salvador, he disregarded permits and zoning ordinances, withheld information from the city council, and paid inflated prices to contractors—all early signs of corrupt intent.[18]

During the formative stages of his political career, Bukele began experimenting with influence operations carried out over social media. Annoyed by mainstream news coverage of his work as mayor, he "started building an alternative media landscape: TV programs, a network of trolls on Twitter, an army of YouTubers, and several publications that posted pro-Bukele stories on Facebook."[19] Bukele hired a small team of contractors, operating from offices in San Salvador, who monitored his critics and flooded them with disinformation and online threats.[20] They frequently reported critics to Twitter for alleged violations of the platform's terms of service, hoping to get them banished from the public platform. One contractor alone sent more than nine hundred abuse complaints in a single month.

Buoyed by their success, Bukele has continued to support these influence operations and online harassment campaigns ever since.[21] Reuters journalist Sarah Kinosian was granted access to an internal February 2022 US State Department assessment of his manipulation of El Salvador's media landscape, which explained that his strategy is "to flood El Salvador with propaganda, demonize the institutions charged with debunking that propaganda—the free press and civil society—dominate public narratives, and repress dissent."[22] Bukele employs dozens of social media workers to use the latest techniques of online propaganda "to amplify the president's messaging and deride opponents and journalists perceived as hostile to his administration." As with autocrats the world over, Bukele has fully embraced the opportunities for covert operations that the social media ecosystem serves up.

In 2019, Bukele was elected president with a majority, in what most observers agreed was a free and fair election.[23] He was the youngest head of state in Latin America. Almost immediately, though, he began flirting more openly with authoritarianism. In a shocking incident on February 9, 2020, he confronted lawmakers opposed to a new $109 million "territorial control" bill by entering the legislative assembly flanked by armed soldiers while thousands of his supporters chanted outside.[24] "If we wanted to press the button, we would press the button," he said, implying he would not hesitate to remove legislators by force.[25]

When COVID infections reached El Salvador, Bukele issued a state of emergency, but like many authoritarians he used the excuse to bolster his power.[26] He detained thousands of people in detention centers under the pretense of COVID quarantines. Even though the Supreme Court of Justice of El Salvador declared his measures unconstitutional, he ignored the rulings and threatened the judges instead. "If I really were a dictator, I would shoot all of them," he said.[27] He publicly commanded the police and the military to make more arrests, in contravention of the judges' orders, and enthusiastically encouraged the use of violence to do so.

The Bukele-backed party in the country's legislature fired Supreme Court magistrates and the country's attorney general, replacing them with judges and acolytes who, among other things, allowed Bukele to run for a second term even though the constitution forbids it.[28] His Nuevas Ideas party, which has a majority in the assembly, has passed laws that enable those newly appointed judges and his handpicked attorney general to fire lower-level judges and prosecutors.[29] It's all part of Bukele's not-so-secret plan to remake the country's institutions to enable centralization of power and dissolve any checks and balances that might hinder his personal ambitions—in other words, to be a dictator.

A key feature of this growing despotism has been persistent attacks on the media. Bukele has systematically stifled independent journalism in the country through a strategy of rewards and punishments. He has bought off journalists working for independent outlets and brought them to pro-regime state media, where they parrot his propaganda.[30] In one case, thirty journalists from *La Prensa Gráfica*, one of the country's largest independent newspapers, resigned and switched to a pro-Bukele media outlet.[31] The country's independent press association said the government now controls almost all the mass media television and radio stations in El Salvador. All of them sing his praises while pounding his critics.

Bukele routinely harasses journalists and others critical of his policies on his X account and in fiery public speeches delivered at rallies that resemble rock shows. Not surprisingly, El Salvador's ranking in the standard press freedom indexes has plummeted.[32] "The media are among the victims of El Salvador's widespread violence," says Reporters Without Borders's assessment. "Since taking office in June 2019, President Nayib Bukele has attacked and threatened journalists critical of his government. Outspoken media outlets are harassed and journalists covering security issues and gangs are criminalised. The use of trolls reinforces the government's narrative, and state-held information has been kept confidential since the pandemic."[33]

In February 2020, when Bertha Deleón, his former attorney, criticized Bukele on Twitter, the reprisals came immediately. The government launched a smear campaign accusing her of working for the gangs and criminals, and the army of trolls followed suit.[34] After colleagues told her she was under official investigation, she fled to Mexico, where she was granted asylum.

Bukele's authoritarian-chic personality has attracted followers outside of El Salvador too. His X account is full of fans from the alt-right illuminati, such as Roger Stone and Michael Flynn.[35] Jack Posobiec, a notorious alt-right, white supremacist political activist, gushed to his two million followers that Bukele should be named "Man of the Year." Before being dismissed from Fox News, Tucker Carlson interviewed Bukele and fawned over him.[36] He is, in the words of journalist Zach Beauchamp, "the MAGA movement's new favorite autocrat."[37] Much like Donald Trump, he's an illiberal who has fashioned a strongman cult of personality based on being tough on crime and dismissive of conventional restraints on power. He's also not afraid to mock traditional institutions that are normally respected. After the US government sanctioned his handpicked judges for corruption, Bukele changed his X biography to "the coolest dictator in the world."[38]

Bukele's clampdown on gangs in El Salvador is probably the most important reason for his popularity. As with many autocratic leaders, his tough-on-crime stance is a relief for many citizens who have suffered the gangs' indiscriminate violence, extortion, and murder. But the story is more complicated than the "new sheriff in town" mythology he likes to present.

At the time of writing, a common motif of Bukele's X feed are pictures and videos of near-naked, tattooed MS-13 gang members with their hands shackled over their shaved, bowed heads and lined up closely back-to-back. Many of these gang members may deserve to be locked up for the violence and mayhem they have caused, but their right to a fair trial seems to have been abandoned in the mass roundups.

Human Rights Watch and numerous other rights organizations have documented the lack of due process around Bukele's crackdowns and mass incarcerations.[39] Thousands of individuals with no apparent connection to criminal activity have been swept up by the police and held for months without trial.[40] Their anxious families have even been forced to pay for their clothing and food while they are in detention—a cruel cost-cutting measure.

There's also a seamier side. Although Bukele has portrayed himself as a bulwark against organized crime, his administration has been caught in secret negotiations with MS-13 and other gangs to bolster his popularity and support his rule.[41] That's how you survive politically or even physically in El Salvador, where numerous presidents and mayors have done under-the-table deals with gangs. What's different with Bukele is how contrary these negotiations seem to his well-crafted tough-on-crime persona.

Journalist Carlos Martínez, of the independent El Salvador news organization *El Faro*, published an article that showed, based on leaked audio recordings, that MS-13 gang members had negotiated with the president for special treatment, including private hospital transfers and government-issued IDs.[42] They even had a code name for him: "Batman."[43]

El Faro's reporting was corroborated by the US government. In December 2021, the US Treasury Department sanctioned two Bukele cabinet members for negotiating with and offering financing to MS-13 gang members.[44] And a September 2022 US Justice Department indictment of MS-13 gang members showed that the gangs negotiated with Bukele for privileges and good treatment in exchange for their help in reducing the perception of murders and thereby delivering the votes he needed.[45] The indictment describes how the El Salvador government refused to cooperate with US extradition requests and protected gang members sought by US authorities while dismissing the attorney general and other judicial officials to prevent the extradition.

Bukele didn't like this type of criticism and pushback. Although he couldn't influence the United States in its actions, especially once Trump lost the 2020 election, he could take his wrath out on local investigative journalists. He suggested that *El Faro* was involved in money laundering—the type of inflammatory accusation dictators like to use before unleashing a baseless state investigation.[46] He started attacking *El Faro* and its journalists by name.[47] Pro-Bukele state-controlled media organizations did the same. The slow drip of disinformation and smear campaigns wore people down: many *El Faro* journalists were forced to leave the country, and some reports suggest that many Salvadorans are beginning to believe that the agency's reporting is biased.[48]

Given Bukele's millennial authoritarianism, fascination with social media, and digital influence operations, it was obvious that he would almost certainly abuse spyware for his own crooked purposes. But, as we soon found out, NSO Group had apparently ignored all those warning signs.

———

Once Apple started, in November 2021, to notify the victims who had been hacked through its platform by Pegasus or other spyware, we waited in suspense as calls trickled in to Access Now's helpline and then to us (chapter 14). We didn't have to wait long for calls for help from El Salvador. One of the first sets of victims we heard about were journalists, including several working for *El Faro*.

We had already been in touch with some of the targets because, before the Apple notifications, some of them had run Amnesty International's mobile verification toolkit (MVT) and reached out to us, and we had begun the process of deeper forensic analysis. By the time they received their warnings from Apple, we were already in touch with a key group of victims and with partners at Access Now whose helpline staff (some based in the region) became indispensable partners in the data collection process.

Based on our ongoing internet scanning and DNS cache probing methodology, we had strong suspicions that El Salvador was using Pegasus for domestic spying. We first identified what we believed to be a Pegasus operator focusing almost exclusively within El Salvador in early 2020—and gave that operator the code name Torogoz, after the country's national bird. The domain names associated with this operator appear to have been registered as early as November 2019 (five months after Bukele assumed office). We also had evidence of a Salvadoran client of Circles—the NSO Group–affiliated company that offers SS7 geolocation and cellphone interception capabilities. Our scans showed it had been operational since at least 2015. Given these bits of information, we were not surprised to discover hacking of civil society in the country.

We employed the same snowballing method of discovery as in other cases. Once we had confirmation of a single victim, we interviewed that person and established who else in their network might also be a target for hacking. Every one of these "human subjects" is protected under a research ethics protocol approved by the University of Toronto's Research Ethics Board and designed to keep their personal data confidential and secure. This process, though time-consuming, is especially critical in El Salvador—one of the most dangerous places to be an independent journalist or human rights defender.

Once the results were delivered to the victims, we helped them think through the risks of making the findings public. Any exposure could have severe repercussions not only for themselves but for their loved ones, colleagues, and friends. It could also result in stigmatization: Who would want to associate with someone under state surveillance? Your job as a journalist could be toast with that cloud hanging over your head.

As our investigation closed, we knew we had a blockbuster. What we discovered was another hacking spree and a domestic espionage operation of epic proportions, thanks to NSO Group's services. We confirmed thirty-five individual cases of journalists and members of civil society whose phones were successfully infected with NSO's Pegasus spyware between July 2020 and November 2021.[49] Our colleagues at Amnesty International independently confirmed the veracity of a selection of the findings using their own technical methodology.

This brazen hacking scheme took place during the time when the targeted organizations were reporting on sensitive issues involving Bukele's administration, including on the pact between the president and MS-13 gangs and on corruption involving COVID infrastructure funds.[50] Targets included virtually all the remaining independent news organizations and journalists in El Salvador, including victims working at *El Faro, GatoEncerrado, La Prensa Gráfica,*

Disruptiva, Diario El Mundo, and *El Diario de Hoy.* We found that the phones of two independent journalists were also hacked. Civil society targets included Fundación Democracia, Transparencia y Justicia (DTJ), Cristosal, and another NGO that chose to remain anonymous. Basically, all those whose job it was to hold power accountable in the country were systematically targeted.

Although the number of individual victims was large, it was the flurry of hacks that stood out in El Salvador—more than 250 infections by our count.[51] That was likely an underestimation of the full scope of the espionage, given the limitations of our snowball methodology and the lack of visibility into hacks on Android devices, which typically do not preserve enough data for us to be able to do thorough forensic analyses in the way we do with iPhones. Some of the victims were hacked relentlessly. The phone of *El Faro*'s editor in chief, Carlos Martínez, was infiltrated an astonishing forty-two separate times.

The hacking answered a lot of questions for the targets, who had long suspected they were under surveillance and had already taken as many precautions as they could to protect themselves and their sources. *El Faro*'s journalists told the *New Yorker*'s Ronan Farrow, who covered the investigation, how they joked about not discussing sensitive topics in the newsroom in case the country's intelligence chief, Peter Dumas, was listening in.[52] Despite these precautions, the government seemed to know what was going on. "Now we have an explanation," Martínez said. "We were hacked."

It's always striking to hear the victims piece together what was going on in their professional and personal lives once we tell them the specific day and time their device was hacked. Journalist Julia Gavarrete of *El Faro* recalled arranging a meeting with a source via text messages. When she arrived at the location, she was met by a group of military officers who questioned her and her source. "That confirmed to me that they are reading our messages," she told Farrow.[53] We found that Gavarrete's phone was hacked eighteen times. Another *El Faro* journalist, Roman Gressier, had his phone hacked multiple times, the first after he covered the US State Department's decision to place one of Bukele's cabinet members on a list of corrupt officials.[54] The second time corresponded to a column he published about the May 2021 ouster of the five Supreme Court magistrates and the attorney general. Gressier, who is bisexual, panicked at the prospect of government spies knowing the details of his sexuality in a country where harassment against the LGBTQ+ community is routine.[55] He left El Salvador for good and now works for the agency from abroad.

All the journalists we consulted with immediately thought of the risk to their sources. It's common for journalists to feel this sense of guilt, even though there's little that could protect them against a zero-click version of Pegasus spyware. "Sources, they were very upset with me," said Martínez, "and they have the right to be. They just trusted me. And I failed them."[56] Another victim described how journalism was much harder after the revelations. "When news of the hacking broke," *El Faro*'s Nelson Rauda Zablah said, "a few sources jokingly answered our calls by greeting the good people who might be listening. But many more picked up the phone only to say we should stop calling them, and most simply didn't respond at all."[57]

As with most other espionage investigations, we could deduce who the government operator might be based only on circumstantial evidence. In this case, however, we identified a Pegasus operator focusing exclusively on domestic surveillance and El Salvador–based targets, and that fact strongly supported the thesis that the operator was part of Bukele's administration. What other government would want to spy so extensively on Salvadoran targets?

While a lot of the attacks we observed employed zero-click versions of Pegasus, one journalist was targeted with a one-click version of the spyware, with the links contained in SMS bait messages. The domain name in the text messages matched one of our fingerprints for a Pegasus URL shortener website. Those texts contained El Salvador–themed bait content, including "District attorney's office against journalists from El Faro" and "Nuevas Ideas [Bukele's political party] eclipses their opponents."[58] It's highly unlikely any other government but El Salvador would be behind these targeted bait messages.

The sheer volume of abuse was astonishing. Pegasus was used not to investigate criminals or security risks but to brazenly hack the devices of regime critics, journalists, and political opposition. What else should we expect from the "world's coolest dictator"?

———

We published our report in January 2022—a joint investigation with Access Now in collaboration with Front Line Defenders, SocialTIC, and Fundación Acceso. It was widely covered in the world's press.

"Pegasus Spyware Used in 'Jaw-Dropping' Phone Hacks on El Salvador Journalists," said the *Guardian*.[59]

"Journalists in El Salvador Targeted with Spyware Intended for Criminals," exclaimed the *New York Times*.[60]

The official government responses were muted. Bukele passed the job to his spokeswoman, Sofía Medina, who said that "El Salvador is no way associated with Pegasus and nor is it a client of NSO Group."[61] Then in a surprising twist, Medina said that some of Bukele's own cabinet members had received Apple notifications alerting them that they were targeted, including the justice minister and also herself.[62] She added that the Lab and other organizations could not be trusted to do impartial investigations because we "are favoring the agenda of the groups behind the attacks."[63] That was a head-scratcher. Was she implying that the civil society victims had used Pegasus to spy on Bukele's cabinet? I don't think the truth really matters to people in these circumstances.

Although we were not in a position to check Medina's phones and those of Bukele's cabinet members, it's possible they did receive those Apple notifications. Autocrats are typically hardwired to be paranoid of those around them, so Bukele may well have spied on his own administration. That is what happened in Mexico, after all.[64]

NSO Group issued its usual earnest but completely implausible explanation of the findings: "While we have not seen the report mentioned in your inquiry, and without confirming or denying specific customers, NSO's firm stance on these issues is that the use of cyber tools in order to monitor dissidents, activists and journalists is a severe misuse of any technology and goes against the desired use of such critical tools."[65] So, you entrusted your technology to the "world's coolest dictator," whose brazen assaults on press freedom are part of his social media schtick, and you thought it wouldn't be misused? *Right . . . gotcha.*

There were other important consequences to the report, some quite illuminating. In March 2022, public hearings began before the Inter-American Commission on Human Rights.[66] Margarette May Macaulay, one of the commissioners, said, "This was a serious attack on democracy and democratic standards . . . so many rights were violated."[67] In the same hearing, the Salvadoran state representative said, "An extensive investigation is underway," but blamed the victims for not cooperating with the investigation—again, just as in Mexico.[68] What victim in their right mind would hand their phone over to the very government responsible for the hacking in the first place?

Although no smoking gun emerged to definitively prove El Salvador purchased Pegasus from NSO Group, leaked information soon surfaced that had that sulfurous smell of gunpowder. *El Faro* journalist Jimmy Alvarado combed through the voluminous Guacamaya leaks—the same ones that Mexican organizations dug through to find evidence of Pegasus contracts with the Mexican Army—and discovered some tantalizing information. On October 19, 2020, the director of the Salvadoran police approved the purchase of three surveillance tools from a firm called EyeTech Solutions: an IMSI catcher, which simulates a cell tower in order to geolocate phones in the vicinity and store their unique identifiers; a product called Wave Guard Tracer, which "converts raw cellular network data into actionable real-time intelligence, tracking voice calls, SMS, data applications and many more non-call events with extremely high accuracy"; and Web Tangles, a social media open-source intelligence (OSINT) analysis tool.[69]

Alvarado also discovered that the middleman for the deal, Yaniv Zangilevitch, was an Israeli businessman based in Mexico and a friend of Nayib Bukele's.[70] Zangilevitch's résumé on LinkedIn states he was a special operations officer in the Israel Defense Forces who then worked as a "counter terror specialist" for Israel's prime minister, Benjamin Netanyahu.[71] *El Faro* published videos of Bukele attending Zangilevitch's wedding ceremony in Mexico. Tagging alongside was the head of El Salvador's intelligence agency, Peter Dumas.[72] Zangilevitch's EyeTech was reportedly involved in brokering sales of Circles surveillance systems to the Mexican government—the same Circles that is a close partner to NSO Group.[73]

————

As much as our investigation was a bombshell, it didn't change much on the ground or alter El Salvador's steep descent into authoritarianism. In fact, shortly after the report was released, Bukele's administration passed legislation that reformed the code of criminal procedure to legalize the use of information obtained via surveillance technologies.[74] The new legislation says police may "carry out 'digital undercover operations' at the request of the Attorney General's Office, and does not establish the need for judicial authorization to do so. It also allows digital documents, electronic messages, images, videos, data and any type of information that is stored, received or transmitted . . . through any electronic device to be accepted as evidence in criminal proceedings."[75] El Salvador's police, in other words, are free to hack whomever they please.

And then, in March 2022, Bukele imposed a state of emergency in the country.[76] After a spate of gang murders allegedly in reprisal for his failure to live up to promises to the gangs, Bukele went on a major counteroffensive, rounding up close to one hundred thousand detainees within the next year and a half, many of whom reportedly have no connection to gang activity.[77] El Salvador's Congress has voted to allow the government to conduct mass trials, prosecuting as many as nine hundred individuals at a time, in defiance of basic due process norms.[78] Numerous accounts circulated of individuals swept into a Kafkaesque nightmare of months in detention with no apparent hope of a fair hearing.[79]

According to the Associated Press, "Under the state of exception, the right of association, the right to be informed of the reason for an arrest and access to a lawyer are suspended. The government also can intervene in the calls and mail of anyone they consider a suspect. The time someone can be held without charges is extended from three days to 15 days."[80] Human rights abuses by the police and military have been documented throughout the country. *El Faro*, meanwhile, has moved its operations entirely out of El Salvador to Costa Rica.[81] As Martínez said, "This time we have no choice but to leave because it's not one group that is after us. It is the entire state."[82]

None of this repression hurt Bukele's popularity, which reached a 90 percent approval rating.[83] He ran for an unprecedented second term in February 2024, in defiance of the constitution, and won a supermajority.[84] In preparation, he gerrymandered the electoral districts in his favor.[85] Meanwhile, his strongman shenanigans continued. While making the announcement of the redrawn political map at the legislative assembly, he played a video showing a real-time bust of a former politician from a rival party accused of fraud—precisely the kind of spectacle a dictator loves.[86]

Others in the region and around the world are taking note of his formula for popularity. Honduran president Xiomara Castro declared a state of emergency to fight gangs in that country and extended it twice.[87] One of Guatemala's candidates for president has vowed to build huge prisons, echoing Bukele.[88] Observing the chaos and gang violence that has erupted in Haiti, Bukele offered to "fix" the problems but would require a UN Security Council resolution first "and all the mission expenses to be covered."[89] One wonders what types of ulterior motives and techniques of repression will be shared among these countries outside the public eye. Perhaps soon the Lab will discover them.

In November 2022, fifteen journalists and other members of *El Faro* filed a lawsuit in US federal court against NSO Group.[90] They are represented by the Knight First Amendment Institute, based at Columbia University, whose director, Jameel Jaffer, is a Canadian by birth and a fellow at the University of Toronto's Munk School of Global Affairs & Public Policy, where the Lab has its headquarters. The lawsuit relies extensively on the forensic investigation we performed along with our colleagues and partners in El Salvador. "These spyware attacks were an attempt to silence our sources and deter us from doing journalism," said *El Faro*'s Carlos Dada in explaining the rationale for the suit. "We are filing this lawsuit to defend our right to investigate and report, and to protect journalists around the world in their pursuit of the truth."[91]

Another victim, Nelson Rauda Zablah, elaborated: "I can assure you we're not in this for the money: if we wanted to be rich, we wouldn't be independent journalists. We're doing this as a progression of our everyday work in El Salvador to expose official wrongdoing. We're doing this in the United States because we've exhausted all legal avenues in El Salvador's co-opted institutions."[92]

Litigation can be frustratingly slow, enormously complicated—and a double-edged sword. As we discovered with the spies-for-hire Black Cube operation (chapter 6), litigation can prompt underhanded measures by the accused parties, especially if they are already well accustomed to thriving in the world of dirty tricks and professionalized subversion. Judges can make unfavorable rulings too, as the plaintiffs in this case discovered in March 2024 when the district court granted NSO's motion to dismiss the case on the basis of forum non conveniens—legal terminology for the case being brought in the wrong jurisdiction.[93] NSO Group's lawyers argued that Israel, not California, is the appropriate venue for the litigation—an obviously convenient one for the firm given the way the Israeli government has cast a cloak of secrecy over other spyware-related litigation underway there.[94] At the time of writing, the lawyers for the victims are intending to file an appeal.[95] Even if suits like these succeed and firms are held accountable, it's not uncommon for them to go insolvent and then rebrand under a different name to evade liabilities—a process known as "phoenixing."

But in a world in which Bukelism is spreading far and wide, it's important to exercise whatever legal avenues are available to fight repression and to remind millennial authoritarians like Bukele and their enablers that there are those who still defend the rule of law. Before long, we can all hope, justice will be served.

"Finally a European State"

MAY 10, 2022

I stepped off the plane in Barcelona–El Prat Airport after traveling from Canada via Frankfurt. My trip was the digital equivalent of a sensory deprivation tank because I had to disconnect and wipe all my electronic devices in Toronto before departure. For many hours, I was truly in the dark.

Our *CatalanGate* report, detailing a massive domestic espionage campaign targeting Catalans that we uncovered, had been splashed over the news in Spain for the previous three weeks—a stream of outrage, demands for investigations, and government denials and deflections.[1] I was eagerly awaiting the latest installment as I approached a news ticker just past the arrival gate.

There it was: "Spain Dismisses Spy Chief in Pegasus Phone Spyware Scandal."[2] I stared at the headline, my mouth agape. The head of Spain's intelligence agency had been fired in the wake of our report. Paz Esteban headed Spain's CNI, the country's equivalent of the CIA, FBI, and NSA all wrapped into one organization. Only a few days earlier, I learned from sources, she had been bad-mouthing us and our report in a meeting of government officials and congresspeople.

Never before had our reporting been linked to the firing of such a senior national intelligence official. Incredibly, it would not be the last that year. It was another reminder that we had ceased being spectators of world politics and become players in the game—a huge responsibility.

The news was both surreal and unnerving. This trip was especially risky coming soon after our report had caused a national fiasco in Spain, which was also in the middle of a constitutional crisis. Here I was, the director of the organization that had dropped a bombshell exposing a massive secret espionage operation in the heart of Europe, walking into the eye of the storm we had created. I wasn't as concerned about my own physical safety as I was about someone planting false incriminating information on my device or in my hotel room that could be used as a pretext to detain me or as an excuse to discredit me and the work of the Citizen Lab.

There was also the prospect of someone following me to discover whom I was meeting in the city. As a victim-centric organization, we are obliged to protect the people who participate in our research, and any physical surveillance or unwanted scrutiny would complicate our work. Barcelona, like Geneva or Vienna, is replete with foreign espionage, so the likelihood of my being watched was high.

The firing of Paz Esteban suddenly made all these threats more acute. Ever since Donald Trump made the term "deep state" more popular, it has been used a lot and is usually laughed off by reasonable people as a conspiratorial joke. But with Spain, there does seem to be something approximating it stretching back to Franco's time—a network of influential individuals within Madrid's government bureaucracy, intelligence agencies, and the military who employ personal networks and patronage systems to shape government policies and decision-making behind the scenes regardless of changes in elected leadership.[3]

I suspected that the people who worked for the organization Esteban had headed would be unhappy with the Lab's report and might well decide to take measures if they knew I was in Spain. Some of those responsible for the espionage might even take it personally. Although I knew we had done nothing illegal, that's not how it might be construed by someone with the power to mount an obstruction of justice charge.

As I walked through the airport that morning, my laptop and phone were still nonfunctioning bricks, leaving me with no communication with my team back home. Once I found a private location outside of the airport, I opened my backpack's electronics gear bag to follow the steps needed to get connected to the internet, reboot my devices, and set up the digital security profile I'd carry with me for the trip.

There is a paradox at the heart of this setup: I must be able to communicate, yet I must keep as discreet an electronic profile as possible. I can't be entirely off the grid, but I must not draw attention to myself or to those with whom I'm meeting. I must secure the Lab's data by connecting and communicating only in strictly controlled ways. State security agencies in a NATO country such as Spain have extraordinary capabilities at their disposal, including spyware, as we had discovered. Leaked documents we had reviewed showed that Spain's intelligence agency also had access to other technology and equipment that could be used to track my cellphone, its SIM card, and other identifiers. It could even intercept electronic emissions that may emanate from my devices and listen in to calls using directional microphones if it really desired to do so.[4] For all these reasons, I checked my setup frequently and followed the recommendations of my technical team as diligently as possible.

I cannot travel on an assumed identity, so I use my real name to book transport and hotels and use my own passport. I realize this openness makes me vulnerable against a determined government or agency, but, again, I take precautions. After I check in at a hotel, I assume the room may be bugged so find an excuse to request a change to a different room—a slight evasion that buys some time and may upend any advance preparation that was done there. I use the hotel only to sleep and shower, and I never connect to any Wi-Fi network. When I leave the hotel, my electronics and other valuables come with me and never leave my side for the entire trip. The system's not perfect, but it's the due diligence I am required to do.

Once I got connected and oriented in Barcelona, I touched base with Elies Campo, the Citizen Lab research fellow working under our supervision who helped coordinate our investigation in Spain, and arranged for a place and time to meet. I had a big week ahead of me.

_____

Our research on this project began in the fall of 2019, after our notification to several prominent Catalan victims who were targets of the 2019 WhatsApp/Pegasus case (chapter 1). At the time we made the notifications, those victims chose to remain anonymous. However, in July 2020, they started to go public, beginning with Roger Torrent, the former speaker of the Catalan regional parliament who was targeted with Pegasus while he was in office.[5] He was followed shortly after by Ernest Maragall, political leader of a pro-Catalan independence party; activist Jordi Domingo; Sergi Miquel i Gutiérrez, who worked for the Catalan president; and Anna Gabriel, a former pro-independence politician who had been living in Switzerland since the 2017 referendum.[6] When Campo heard stories about their ordeal, he reached out to us (chapter 13). Our investigations on targeted espionage against Catalans began in earnest, with Campo assisting with outreach to potential victims, first as a volunteer and then as a Citizen Lab research fellow working closely with John Scott-Railton (JSR), our senior researcher who led the Catalan investigation.

Our investigation went on for months. To gather data for forensic analysis, we had to follow consent processes with each person and organization, a necessary but time-consuming endeavor to protect research participants. The evidence of targeting and hacking began to accumulate slowly. We discovered more victims, including many prominent people in Catalan civil society. Before long, we realized we were slowly peeling back the layers on a major domestic espionage operation targeting Catalans.

We knew we were treading into a complicated political minefield. Catalonia is an autonomous region within Spain whose population has for centuries expressed desires for greater independence. As a Canadian who came of age during the constitutional crises of the 1970s and 1980s and growing calls for Quebec's sovereignty, I saw the obvious parallels. Both cases have been covered in standard political science courses on constitutionalism and international law. Still, there were key differences. Spain, with its long history, endured a wrenching civil war in the 1930s, followed by a brutal dictatorship under the fascist regime of General Francisco Franco until his death in 1975. Catalan culture and politics were systematically quashed under Franco's heavy hand.

The Statute of Autonomy of Catalonia of 1979 divested significant powers to the region.[7] Calls for independence waxed and waned over the following decades, with pro-independence parties occasionally pushing for and sometimes holding referenda as Spain's central authorities pushed back.[8] Courts would strike down various unilateral declarations of independence as unconstitutional—incompatible with the "indissoluble unity" clause of Article 2 of the 1978 Spanish Constitution.[9] As written there, only Spain itself has the power to decide whether regions can become sovereign—a paradox of sorts (at least for Catalans) that has been extensively debated among international legal scholars for years.

The movement for secession in Catalonia reached a tipping point in September 2017, when the Catalan parliament voted to hold another referendum on independence.[10] Although the Spanish Supreme Court declared the referendum illegal, the Catalan government, led by President Carles Puigdemont, went ahead with it. Turnout was low, around 43 percent of the population, with 90 percent voting for independence. The disappointing turnout was attributed to reports of police intimidation and the seizure of ballots by Spanish police.[11] Riots ensued when police clashed with peaceful voters and around nine hundred people were injured.[12] Human Rights Watch, Amnesty International, and other rights groups condemned the Spanish police for using excessive force.[13] The UN high commissioner for human rights, Zeid Ra'ad al-Hussein, called for an independent investigation into the violence.[14]

Spain's central government, led by Prime Minister Mariano Rajoy, then dissolved Catalonia's parliament, fired Puigdemont, and called for regional elections (which produced another pro-independence majority in the region).[15] Several prominent Catalan politicians, including Puigdemont, fled into exile in Belgium and other countries, while others were arrested and sentenced to lengthy jail terms for sedition, misuse of public funds, or other public order offenses.[16]

The crackdown on Catalans triggered more waves of public anger. This time a tech-savvy grassroots movement called Tsunami Democràtic, using the Telegram app extensively, emerged to help digitally organize flash protests, nonviolent civil disobedience, and other demonstrations.[17] The authorities responded with yet more harsh crackdowns. Reports of excessive and inappropriate police force garnered mounting international condemnation.

Meanwhile, international organizations and NGOs condemned the sentencing of Catalans involved in the referendum and independence movement and denounced the violations of basic rights around freedom of expression and peaceful assembly and association. The Council of Europe passed a resolution calling on Spain to reform the criminal provisions related to sedition, pardon the convicted leaders, and drop extradition requests against the Catalans who had fled Spain.[18] On June 22, 2021, the Spanish government pardoned the nine Catalans convicted of sedition and granted them immediate release from prison.[19] In the fall of 2021, the Catalan and Spanish governments resumed their negotiations.[20] They remained largely gridlocked until February 2022, when Catalonia's president, Pere Aragonès, pledged to kick-start them again.[21]

It was against this political backdrop that we published the *CatalanGate* report in April 2022, exposing perhaps the biggest domestic targeted espionage operation ever uncovered in post–Cold War European history.

––––––––––

In all our years studying cyber espionage, what we found in Spain was among the most audacious spying operations in scope and scale—an attempt to subject a large cross-section of Catalan civil society to targeted surveillance. Our research uncovered at least sixty-five Catalans, many working at the highest levels, whose devices had been hacked or who had received bait messages that could have infected their phones with spyware. Victims were hacked with "zero-click" WhatsApp or iMessage exploits or via malicious texts that were sent to their phones. Pegasus spyware was used in most of the hacking we uncovered, while a few devices were targeted or hacked with a mercenary spyware product associated with another Israeli firm, Candiru. Almost all these incidents took place between 2017 and 2020, although we had traces of targeting going back to 2015 in at least one case. Most significantly, the hacking involved a purely domestic political matter, and it happened not in an authoritarian regime but in Spain, a liberal democracy in Europe.

Every Catalan president since 2010 had been hacked while in office, before election, or after retiring. President Aragonès's phone had been targeted with SMS messages while he was involved in what he thought were honest negotiations with Madrid. In other words, the Spanish government was secretly eavesdropping on its negotiating partner on the Catalan side.

The phones of numerous elected officials of Catalonia's government had also been hacked or targeted, as was almost every Catalan member of the European Parliament who supported independence. In addition, we found several politicians whose staff and lawyers had been targeted or had their phones hacked. For example, we found that eleven people around Puigdemont, including his spouse, key staff members, lawyers, and close associates, had all been targeted with Pegasus between 2019 and 2020. It's difficult to fathom what type of warrant would allow such extensive hacking of individuals close to a principal target even assuming that the person was under some kind of judicially authorized investigation. The operations of Spain's security agencies are supposed to be overseen by the judiciary and the relevant minister, but it's a stretch to believe the spying we uncovered was approved in any legitimate oversight process.

The hacking extended beyond Spain into other countries, such as Switzerland, following targets as they relocated. This type of surveillance raised the issue of appropriate conduct for lawful cross-border investigations. Bait messages containing links to spyware sent to targets even impersonated real NGOs, news organizations, companies, and other entities, again raising questions of misbehavior.

Although we did not attribute this campaign to a single government client (or clients), numerous circumstantial pieces of evidence pointed to a strong nexus with the government of Spain, including the kinds of victims and targets, the timing, and the fact that Spain was reported to be a government client of NSO Group. In 2020, *El País* confirmed that the Spanish government was an NSO Group customer and that its intelligence agency, the CNI, was using spyware.[22] That same year, a former NSO Group employee told *Vice* that the firm was "actually very proud of [Spain] as a customer."[23] "Finally a European state," the anonymous source recalled the company executives saying.

Some messages included in the targeting of victims contained content that likely could have been sourced only by a government's intelligence agency. For example, one victim, Jordi Baylina, an IT specialist who had worked on digital voting projects, was targeted multiple times with Pegasus. In one attempt, he received a text message masquerading as a boarding-pass link for a Swiss International Air Lines flight he had purchased. This authentic information indicates that the Pegasus operator may have had access to Baylina's passenger name record compiled by the airline or a travel agency, or perhaps to his email inbox where he may have kept a confirmation of the ticket. Another text he received contained a portion of his actual official tax identification number, which most likely would be accessible only to a Spanish government agency.

Hypothetically, it was possible that another government client of NSO Group could have undertaken this hacking, but it was extremely unlikely. It would be highly risky for another government to hack the phones of numerous high-profile individuals within Spain's jurisdiction not just once but dozens of times over a period of several years. Should it be discovered, it would lead to serious diplomatic and legal repercussions for the country. In any event, these hypotheticals and confidence-level assessments became irrelevant once Spain itself acknowledged it was responsible for at least a sizable portion of what we uncovered.[24]

This unrestrained hacking raised many questions about the necessity and proportionality of the surveillance we discovered. It was the type of extensive domestic espionage usually associated with a dictatorship or an autocratic regime, not a democracy. Most of the victims whose phones we determined had been hacked were not even charged with crimes, nor were they, by any reasonable definition of the terms, serious criminals and certainly not terrorists—the typical justifications mercenary surveillance companies employ for sales of their spyware to government clients. These targets exemplified democracy at work: they were peaceful protestors, members of NGOs, and politicians organizing for self-governance (as well as their legal representatives and family members).

I couldn't help but make comparisons to Canada and Quebec. I imagined what the fallout might have been had it been discovered that the RCMP or another Canadian intelligence agency, in the middle of the 1980 Quebec referendum, was tapping the phones of several former Quebec premiers, the currently serving one, and numerous members of their cabinet, as well as Quebec-based sitting members of Parliament. And not just the politicians either—their lawyers, friends, and family members too. Who knows, maybe they were—or tried to, anyway. But times were different then. There were no mobile phones that were portals into the most intimate details of their personal lives, private communications, movements, and social networks. I'm sure that had such an operation been mounted and then exposed, most Canadians would have been outraged, and the federal government would not have survived the scandal.

By contrast, the reaction to the *CatalanGate* report in Spain was muted, dismissive at senior levels, and largely indifferent outside Catalonia itself. I got the sense that most non-Catalan Spaniards didn't really care or chalked it up to the usual back and forth between secessionists and central authorities. I learned there was resentment about Catalans' desire for self-rule, which I found to be alarming considering that what we uncovered was as much about abuse of power by Spanish agencies in general as it was about any particular political movement.[25]

What was even more shocking was that our revelations were almost certainly the tip of the iceberg. Our snowball method, in which we asked one victim to introduce us to others in their network who might be willing to have their phones checked, was inherently only a sampling of the population. In fact, part of the reason for my visit was to reengage that process in a more comprehensive manner.

Furthermore, most Spaniards use Android devices to communicate—around 80 percent—but our forensic methods for detecting spyware are far more advanced for iOS systems.[26] Our report's overall findings therefore almost certainly vastly under-counted the actual number of individuals whose devices had been hacked or targeted.

———————

Our report was published on April 18, 2022. We had heard some of the victim groups using the term "CatalanGate" to refer to the espionage campaign we uncovered, and we liked the allusion, so we decided to adopt it as the title of our report. (That choice would eventually become fodder for one of the ridiculous red herrings used by a pro-Spain disinformation campaign to suggest some kind of political bias.) We hired a Barcelona-based graphic design company to assist in creating a portal to the report that provided a snap-shot of the high-level findings and victim profiles.[27] At the request of the victims, we gave Ronan Farrow of the *New Yorker* an exclusive embargo for an article, and numerous other media worldwide took up the story.[28] The *Washington Post*'s editorial board posted a commentary in reaction to our report, saying, "Democracies shouldn't surrender to a future of limitless surveillance."[29]

The publication of the *CatalanGate* report generated intense reactions in Catalonia. President Aragonès told the *Guardian* that the spying we uncovered constituted a violation of individual rights, an attack on democracy, and a threat to political dissent.[30] He called for an immediate impartial investigation.[31] He said negotiations with Spain's prime minister, Pedro Sánchez, had been "dynamited."[32] He and other senior Catalan officials called for immediate resignations, saying that Defense Minister Margarita Robles, nominally in charge of Spain's CNI, was "unfit" for office.[33]

The official Spanish government reaction was puzzling. At first, there were denials and attempts to shoot the messenger. In Spain's national congress, Robles mocked the Citizen Lab's report as nothing more than "insinuations" and "accusations" without "any proven facts" (ignoring the extensive technical data we published).[34] Bizarrely, she made the irrelevant comment that she had never heard of the *New Yorker* magazine.[35]

Then some partial admissions were floated. In another congressional session, Robles seemed to justify the spying, saying, "What should a state, a government do, when someone violates the constitution, someone declares independence, when someone blocks off roads, when someone leads public disorder, when someone has relations with leaders of a country that has invaded Ukraine?"[36] Journalists started hearing from confidential sources that the spying had in fact been authorized by Spanish judges. Lines in the sand were shifting in real time.

At that point the Spanish government dropped a bombshell of its own.[37] On May 2, 2022, it announced that it had discovered that the phones of Sánchez, Robles, Fernando Grande-Marlaska (minister of the interior), and Luis Planas (minister of agriculture) had all been hacked with Pegasus too.[38] That news took what was already a major controversy and turned it into a kind of absurdist drama.

Was this a wild attempt at deflection? The timing certainly seemed suspicious. Had our report perhaps prompted someone to do more thorough checks on government phones? That's not inconceivable. But if the claims were true, who was responsible for the hacking? The government never said. Theories pointed to Morocco, another Pegasus client state. There were many ongoing disputes between the two countries, and Planas had served as ambassador to Morocco.[39] The hackers may well have been some rogue element within Spain's "deep state," spying on its own government. Considering how weak Spain's oversight of its intelligence agencies appears to be, this theory was plausible.

More admissions came by way of convening an Official Secrets Committee of the Spanish Congress (Comisión de Secretos Oficiales del Congreso)—an infrequently exercised process held in private in which the head of the CNI, Paz Esteban, delivered a confidential briefing on the affair to a select group of elected officials from multiple parties.[40] Although the participants are sworn to secrecy, many told journalists what they heard. Later, when I met several of the attendees, they all independently substantiated the same details.

In the meeting on May 5, 2022, Esteban confirmed that the Spanish government had spied on eighteen of the sixty-five cases we had uncovered—and, she claimed, with appropriate judicial authorization.[41] She offered no information on the other victims. She cast aspersions on the Citizen Lab, saying our investigation contained unspecified errors and was part of a "Russian influence operation," and that we were "funded by the Chinese government."[42]

These charges were ludicrous. Only a few years earlier we had published an extensive exposé, *Tainted Leaks*, on a major Russian-organized hack-and-leak operation, and at that very time we were engaged in a deep-dive investigation into Russia's domestic surveillance apparatus.[43] We were also investigating exiled Russian journalists that were victims of cyber espionage, reports around which would eventually be published in collaboration with Access Now over the following two years.[44] In 2024, the Munk School of Global Affairs & Public Policy, the institutional home of the Citizen Lab, would be designated by the Kremlin as an "undesirable organization."[45] We had also undertaken pathbreaking reports on China's censorship and surveillance practices, including a detailed investigation into security flaws in the official app for the Beijing Olympics;[46] pioneering studies exposing surveillance on China's WeChat platform;[47] and a high-profile report exposing Zoom's insecurity because of its reliance on China-based infrastructure to secure video calls.[48] More to the point, we had published the first report on China-based cyber espionage and had collaborated extensively with Tibetan victims for over a decade (chapter 10). I had met with the Dalai Lama, enemy number one of the People's Republic of China, and just a few months before CatalanGate, I was warned by the Canadian government that I was on a list of enemies and should never travel again to either Hong Kong or mainland China.

Soon after the convening of the Official Secrets Committee, Esteban was fired.[49] Her smears, however, were a taste of what was to come.

Campo, an easy target because he was a Catalan by birth, bore the brunt of the first waves of disinformation and harassment. Critics charged that he, along with others in the Catalan movement, had manipulated evidence, even though his work was closely supervised by JSR, who led our targeted threats team, and me, as director. The actual forensic work on the targeting and infections of phones was done by our technical team, not by Campo.

One of those leading the disinformation campaign was Jose Javier Olivas Osuna, a Spanish academic. After *CatalanGate* was published, he started an X (formerly Twitter) thread that, at the time of writing, is well over eight hundred posts long.[50] Those that contain obsessive references to me, Campo, JSR, or the Citizen Lab are full of baseless and defamatory statements. Olivas accused me of "lying," of being on the payroll of Apple, WhatsApp, and other big tech platforms, and of being a "don" for some kind of organized cartel of human rights groups in cahoots with Edward Snowden and Russian intelligence agencies—none of which is true.

To further his spurious claims, Olivas teamed up with a miscreant troll named Jonathan Villareal, who changed his name to Jonathan Scott. Scott had published numerous false allegations about the Citizen Lab's work going back to the Beijing Olympics app. His modus operandi was to post "white papers" in PDF format that initially appeared to be technical and credible but were riddled with nonsense, obvious factual inaccuracies, and logical flaws. (He was later expelled from his PhD program because of his white paper about *CatalanGate* and social media activity about it.) Occasionally these rants were picked up and referenced by unwitting individuals on social media, careless or technically uninformed journalists, or, as in this case, disingenuous people like Olivas. Scott may have been what is referred to in espionage parlance as a "useful idiot"—a person who unknowingly or unintentionally serves the interests of bad-faith actors while believing they are acting on their own volition. Regardless of their competence or credibility—or perhaps precisely because of their lack of both—their smears were amplified by NSO Group's Shalev Hulio and trumpeted on pro-Spanish far-right tabloids that paid no attention to basic journalistic norms around fact-checking.[51]

Olivas also worked closely with a group called the Foro de Profesores, a pro-government academic organization in Spain that professes to "share a commitment to the unity of Spain" and opposes the Catalan independence movement.[52] Carlos Conde Solares, the chair, said explicitly in a video presentation to his group that our publication was a "sneak" and "a real scam of a report." He implied that it was part of a seditious conspiracy involving Russia and stated that the goal of his organization was to actively resist and counter our research to prevent bad publicity at the time of the upcoming NATO summit in Madrid. About a hundred Foro members signed a petition calling for an "investigation" into the Citizen Lab—a call the University of Toronto promptly dismissed.

Another key ally in what appeared to be an organized smear campaign was Jordi Cañas, a Spanish member of the European Parliament. He too sent letters to the University of Toronto asking questions and demanding an investigation.[53] He amplified Olivas's and Scott's claims dozens of times, commissioned Olivas to publish a defamatory report full of errors and misleading accusations, and made liberal use of the hashtag #Catalanfake, suggesting our investigation had been manufactured as part of a separatist conspiracy.[54] Later, he made numerous efforts to block the European Parliament's official investigation into the Catalan affair and went so far as to push for Olivas and one of Olivas's allies, a bumbling computer scientist named Gregorio Martin, to appear as expert witnesses.[55] Martin "peer-reviewed" one of Scott's white papers that tried to discredit our research and then delivered embarrassingly incompetent testimony to the committee.[56] A flood of protests prevented Olivas from appearing, until Cañas engineered a separate hearing for him in an empty hall that was broadcast over the internet.[57] It received zero attention from credible press outlets.

We responded publicly and in good faith to a letter Cañas sent to the University of Toronto, answering all his questions as well as those raised by Olivas and the Foro.[58] But the smears and harassment continued. Olivas went on to file several access to information requests with the university, hoping to find some kind of smoking gun of our corruption. The university's Freedom of Information and Protection of Privacy Office dutifully responded to these requests, and no such evidence ever materialized. Truth didn't matter to Olivas, though. Even after receiving an unambiguous statement that we were not paid by Apple, he would go on to publicly accuse me of lying about it, repeatedly stating, falsely, that I was on its payroll.[59]

Although it was a minor nuisance for us and others, the low-level disinformation took its toll in a variety of ways. We were alarmed that such an amateur disinformation campaign could creep into official proceedings and spread shadows of incredulity over otherwise credible findings. It was repeated enough that doubts began to circulate in various quarters, including within the European Parliament's official investigation into Pegasus.

One goal of the campaign appeared to be to overwhelm the University of Toronto and the Citizen Lab with a large volume of specious claims, partial truths, misrepresentations, and lies. When we responded to and debunked the assertions and insinuations, the perpetrators either dropped and replaced them with variations or simply continued to repeat them. The impact on the university, the Munk School, and the Citizen Lab's staff was substantial. Each time someone was tagged or received a letter from the campaign, we were obliged to respond and repeat the same explanation.

Perhaps that was the ultimate intent: to grind us down while raising doubts among those who do not have the time to separate fact from fiction. It's a clever tactic. Almost all the journalists who were sent this information and who spent time analyzing it dismissed it out of hand. But some contacted us with questions that required thoughtful, time-consuming answers. I was proud that our team responded professionally to these requests, despite the nuisance they were. Ultimately, the experience helped fortify our resolve to continue our mission.

Across the Atlantic, however, the relentless attacks on Campo affected him and his family deeply. His picture was splashed all over the far-right tabloids, with defamatory content and hints that he was under investigation or about to be arrested. At one point, Spanish tabloids even printed photos of Campo and his friend that were taken clandestinely by Spain's authorities and leaked to the press, proving that he was being followed by agents as he arrived in Barcelona Airport.[60] Part of the reason for my trip to Spain was to show my support for Campo and help to deflect the malicious muck that swamped him. While the attacks on the Citizen Lab were easy to parry as self-evident nonsense, those on Campo were personal and profoundly hurtful to him and his family.

Underneath the absurdity of it all may have been a more serious strategy. While the European Parliament's investigation into spyware abuses in Europe, including Spain, was underway, the calls for an investigation into the Citizen Lab may have been intended to create the appearance of dueling investigations and to distract from spyware victims and the need to regulate the technology. If successful, this strategy would reduce pressure on the Spanish government while simultaneously casting doubts on the credibility of the Lab's research. As we would soon learn, however, it was not only the Spanish government that would benefit by such tactics.

———

Disinformation campaigns aside, my trip to Spain was also motivated by the desire to track down victims we missed the first time around. I spent days in Barcelona and then in Madrid having meetings morning to night with one group of victims after another, all of whom told similar stories. Most of the victims assumed the government was watching them, but they had no idea the scrutiny would be so persistent and intrusive. Some of those whose devices had been hacked merely because they had some association with a principal target were outraged at the invasion of their private lives and the abuse of power.

I met with Pere Aragonès, the president of Catalonia, in his official residence in the center of old Barcelona. He described how he felt about being spied on during negotiations with Spain. We had experienced some difficulty obtaining data from Aragonès's devices in the first phase of the investigation, but my visit helped open the door to more evidence that led to additional findings yet to be reported at the time of writing. This detailed data from his device backups showed that he had been hacked an incredible thirteen times over a period of more than a year (July 2018–October 2019) while he was serving as vice president and minister of economy and finance. The infections and SMS targeting coincided with significant political events, cabinet meetings, important congressional votes, and other activities in which he was involved.

Another person I met in Barcelona was Joan Matamala, who runs a bookstore promoting the Catalan language and culture that his father had cofounded and ran for decades in defiance of Franco's dictatorship. Matamala also helped start a foundation to promote open-source software based on the campus of the University of Girona.

We had determined that Matamala's phone was infected with Pegasus in July 2020 and documented the details around this case for our forthcoming report. Separate from our Catalan investigation, we were simultaneously monitoring the infrastructure of the spyware firm Candiru when we noticed a live infection on an institutional network used by a consortium of Catalan universities. Campo recognized the IP address from the previous investigation into Matamala's hacking and, working with the IT department at the university consortium, resolved the infection down to Matamala's campus of the University of Girona. We directed Campo to call Matamala and persuade him to discreetly step outside into the hallway, where Campo called him back on a different device. He told Matamala about our discovery and instructed him to return to his office, unplug the computer, and wrap it in tinfoil to create a DIY Faraday cage—an enclosure designed to block all electromagnetic transmissions. JSR was in touch with Campo in real time while these events unfolded.

We shipped a cloned copy of Matamala's hard drive to Marczak, whose forensic analysis showed it had been infected with Candiru. We were able to recover artifacts of the malware from the computer, and we shared forensic traces of the spyware with Microsoft's Threat Intelligence team. Its analysts did their own investigation and determined that what we found was evidence of two separate zero days exploiting Microsoft's operating system.[61] They issued a security patch and continued their investigation, eventually discovering more than one hundred victims across ten countries who had also been targeted with Candiru, including "politicians, human rights activists, journalists, academics, embassy workers, and political dissidents."[62]

Once again, the discovery showed how one victim and some dogged forensic research could improve the practical security of billions of people worldwide.

At the time of our initial report on Candiru, Matamala's identity was not disclosed, but he agreed to be named for the *CatalanGate* report. Our forensic analysis of Matamala's devices showed he had been infected at least sixteen times with Pegasus between August 2019 and July 2020. Spanish authorities were apparently determined to get inside his digital life and stay there for close to a year, employing the spyware of at least two separate mercenary spyware vendors to do so.

Over coffee, Matamala described how he felt about being spied on, though he was not surprised it was happening. He had lived through the Franco period, with the discrimination and repression against Catalans that characterized the regime. I found that many Catalans were resigned to constant surveillance, especially those in older age brackets. For them it was politics as usual—a familiar feeling of being the underdog constantly mistreated by Madrid.

I met with numerous lawyers whose devices we found had been hacked, including Gonzalo Boye, who represents Puigdemont and was targeted at least eighteen times with infection attempts between January and May 2020. Some of the messages masqueraded as tweets from organizations such as Human Rights Watch, the *Guardian*, *Columbia Journalism Review*, and *Politico*. Other lawyers I met whose devices had been hacked were Andreu van den Eynde, who represented several prominent Catalans, and Jaume Alonso-Cuevillas, who also represented Puigdemont and was a member of the Parliament of Catalonia, former dean of the Barcelona Bar Association, and former president of the European Bars Federation.[63]

When I asked the lawyers how they felt about the surveillance of their devices, they all responded that it violated a basic tenet of attorney-client privilege that is respected in democracies around the world. It was an outrageous violation of due process. In addition, each lawyer's privileged communications with other clients were also exposed. There can be no justifiable reason under international human rights standards to place a lawyer's entire data profile and communications under such extensive surveillance.

We also discovered that Campo and members of his family had been targeted for surveillance. Once we enlisted his help in the investigation, Campo searched back through his SMS history and located a well-crafted message purporting to be from Barcelona's Mercantile Registry containing factual information about a company he administered. The message included an alarming warning that a similarly named company was registered in Panama.

At the time, Campo's phone had a US SIM card, which may have prevented a successful infection of his device. Reports then circulating indicated that most Pegasus customers were not permitted by NSO Group to target numbers starting with the US country code (+1) for fear of provoking US authorities. However, the phones of Campo's parents had Spanish numbers, and they were targeted on the day Campo flew back to Spain from the United States—presumably to try to gain information about him and his whereabouts. It was another outrageous example of what we called "relational targeting," which allows an attacker to gather information about a primary target without necessarily maintaining access to that person's device.

I met with Campo's family over lunch at the hospital where his mother, Maria, and father, Elias, are employed as physicians. It was readily apparent that while both were knowledgeable about politics and the world, they were not politically active, particularly around Catalan secession. If nothing else, they were too busy: Campo's mother is a senior oncologist, and his father is an internationally recognized, award-winning professor of pathology at the University of Barcelona and a staff member at the hospital.

As they described the type of highly confidential patient data contained on their phones, it infuriated me that spies would have hacked their phones. Campo's parents said how ironic it was that they and their fellow physicians must follow extremely strict rules around protecting health information according to Spanish and EU privacy laws, yet someone, somewhere, decided it was fine to hack their phones and be privy to the information they held. Campo's mother said her phone was used to communicate extremely serious health diagnoses with patients and contained X-ray photos of her patients and other highly sensitive, personal information. Although most of their colleagues were empathetic, they could sense that others were now distant or paranoid about associating with them.

Campo's sister, another Maria, a lawyer, was also at the lunch. Days before, we had checked her phone and discovered it too was hacked—details that have also yet to be reported at the time of writing. Like her parents, she was concerned that the discovery of the hacking would jeopardize her professional life and that clients might hesitate to associate with her.

Near the end of the lunch, Campo's mother described the history of Spain and the difference in worldview between Madrid and Barcelona. According to her, Barcelona, situated on the Mediterranean coast and thriving on trade, embraced a more open and global perspective. Madrid, located in the interior and surrounded by landowners and farmers, has traditionally been fortified by walls and nearby castles to fend off outsiders' encroachment. One culture looked outward, while the other was secretive, hierarchical, and focused on safeguarding against the outside world. This insight resonated with me and shed light on the complex struggle for greater autonomy and the resistance to it. What we were witnessing was the latest chapter in an old story, this time intertwined with highly sophisticated digital surveillance technologies and a group of Canada-based watchdogs.

As I approached the end of my fieldwork in Spain, I felt motivated to speak out against the abuses we had unearthed and the prejudices I had encountered. I also felt it was my duty to express my feelings about the smears and harassment against Campo.

I contacted two separate news organizations, *El País* and the *Guardian*, and arranged for interviews under the agreement that their stories would be embargoed until I left Spain.[64] I considered the *Guardian*'s Sam Jones to be objective but had concerns about the *El País* journalists. One of them was a well-known "access journalist" with close ties to Spain's intelligence agencies. His questions were more hostile and clearly influenced by the misinformation that had circulated ever since Esteban's Official Secrets Committee proceedings.

The principal message I wanted to communicate was the need for an impartial and independent investigation into the abuses. Clearly, the surveillance we uncovered was inappropriate and raised questions about Spain's compliance with international human rights norms. Our investigation showed serious problems with Spain's oversight regime. What type of legal entity would authorize the hacking of numerous relatives, friends, and associates of principal targets, with no regard for the collateral information unrelated to Catalan issues that would be collected? As far as we knew, most of the victims were not charged with serious crimes—the typical justification mercenary surveillance companies employ for sales of their spyware to government clients. At most, some seem to have been under investigation for allegations of criminal offenses related to independence and peaceful political activities, allegations that were highly controversial outside Spain.

I also emphasized we had likely uncovered only a fraction of the individuals who had been hacked. Referencing the puzzling nonchalance that seemed to greet the *CatalanGate* report among some Spaniards, I said it would be a gross mistake to view this scandal through the prism of separatist politics. What it was really about, in my opinion, was the type of abuses that security agencies could undertake in the absence of appropriate safeguards. Such powerful capabilities could easily be used for purposes of blackmail or extortion or even to plant evidence against anyone, anywhere, who appeared on the security agencies' enemy list.

The *El País* journalist asked questions about the soundness of our methodology, seemingly confused by our nuanced explanation in the report around attribution to the Spanish government. I used an analogy to a crime scene investigation: we had discovered a murder and could tell definitively—with 100 percent confidence—what bullet and weapon had been used to execute it. But we had only circumstantial evidence about who pulled the trigger, although the subsequent partial admission by the government itself made that circumstantial evidence now much stronger. If you want to get to the bottom of what has gone on, I said, then an independent inquiry would be the only way to do it.

Spain did convene an investigation of sorts, as did the European Parliament, which formed a "Committee of Inquiry to investigate the use of Pegasus and equivalent surveillance spyware" (known as the PEGA committee) a few weeks before we published the *CatalanGate* report.[65] Perhaps not surprisingly, Spain's intelligence agencies refused to cooperate. Appearing before the PEGA committee, the new head of Spain's intelligence agency, Esperanza Casteleiro, infuriated members by trotting out worthless platitudes that were apparently designed to deflect direct questions.[66] Spanish authorities then blocked the committee from visiting Madrid.[67] Spain's own official investigation into Pegasus hacking in the country seemed to peter out when Israel refused to cooperate—a very convenient way to bury the issue.[68] Then, in April 2024 Spain's High Court signaled that it would reopen the case after receiving new, unspecified information from France. However, the investigation seems focused on the alleged hacking of Spanish government officials rather than the Catalans we identified.[69]

To this day, not a single government official in Spain has reached out to us in a formal capacity to learn more about the details of our investigation, although I remain hopeful that will change.

———————

At the time of writing, over two years after the publication of our report, details have emerged of a new hack-for-hire company based in Spain called Variston.[70] My sources tell me it has become the successor to DarkMatter in the United Arab Emirates, working closely with an Emirati firm called Protect Electronic Systems. A story in *Intelligence Online*, which specializes in insider espionage information, said that Barcelona was emerging as a "new cyber offensive hub in Europe."[71]

Part of the reason may be that, following US sanctions, Israeli surveillance entrepreneurs feel pressured to migrate to more "friendly" jurisdictions. Is the country that thoroughly abused mercenary spyware now the place du jour for mercenary spyware vendors looking to set up shop? NSO Group once bragged that it had a European customer; now spyware vendors can rightfully brag that they not only have European clients but are firmly based in Europe too.

Following my visit to Spain, we have continued to gather more evidence of hacking yet to be reported at the time of writing. We have unearthed new details on victims and uncovered other cases of spying that we were unaware of at the time of our first report. The abuses may be continuing, in other words. But so is our hunting.

Europe Flooded with Watergates

2022–2024
GREECE, HUNGARY, AND POLAND

On August 5, 2022, the Associated Press headline read: "Greece: Intelligence Chief Resigns amid Spyware Allegations."[1] Another European spyware scandal had been precipitated by our investigations, and another head of intelligence had been dismissed. This time it was Panagiotis Kontoleon, head of the secretive state intelligence agency Ethniki Ypiresia Pliroforion (EYP), founded in 1953 and modeled after the CIA.[2] Judging by his grim face splashed all over the world news, Kontoleon didn't look happy about it either. This organization is not used to being exposed to sunlight. Its motto, Λόγων ἀπορρήτων ἐκφορὰν μὴ ποιοῦ, means "Do not discuss confidential affairs."[3]

Unlike his colleague from Spain, Paz Esteban (chapter 16), Kontoleon was not the only sacrificial lamb. Along for the slaughter was a curious accomplice: Grigoris Dimitriadis, general secretary of the prime minister's office and the nephew of Prime Minister Kyriakos Mitsotakis.[4] Nepotism at the highest levels of government is usually a sign of disreputable pursuits, and his case would prove to be no exception.

Our role in Greece's surveillance scandal started innocently enough with a report we published in late 2021, *Pegasus vs. Predator*, which seemed only marginally related to Greece.[5] There we described how Ayman Nour, an exiled Egyptian politician living in Turkey, had his phone hacked not once but twice, and not with one spyware tool but two: the infamous Pegasus and another spyware variant called Predator. To top it off, we determined that the hacking was done by two government clients: Egypt and the United Arab Emirates. A single victim's device hacked by two different government operators using two different spyware products was a first on both counts.

By this time Pegasus was widely known, but Predator was not a household name. For this report, our team had to investigate the complicated maze of corporate structures behind Predator. We found a bewildering array of individuals, corporate registries, holding companies, and corporate alliances with operations in Greece, Cyprus, Hungary, and the Republic of Ireland and roots that reach back into Israel and the multiple intelligence services there.

Digging through these arrangements was like entering a labyrinth populated with sketchy individuals and dubious private intelligence and mercenary surveillance companies spread across several jurisdictions. As we tried to chase down registrations in each jurisdiction, for instance, we found subtle shifts in names and different principal shareholders. These ownership obfuscation techniques, like those used by plutocrats and money launderers, are designed to evade public accountability—to make everything that much harder to pin down.

Predator was originally developed by a firm called Cytrox, reportedly founded in North Macedonia in 2017 (and also registered at various times as Cytrox EMEA Ltd., Cytrox Software Ltd, Balinese Ltd., Peterbald Ltd, and Cytrox Holdings Zrt). We found it was connected to a young entrepreneur named Ivo Malinkovski whose thin social media presence included tech-bro selfies and at least one picture at the pyramids in Egypt and another with a T-shirt emblazoned with the message "More Money."[6] After we published our report, he purged his LinkedIn and other social media profiles, disappeared from the spyware industry, and retreated to promoting his father's luxurious wineries.[7] One theory is that he was merely a convenient placeholder in someone else's larger corporate scheme.

Around 2018, Cytrox was integrated into the business of another mercenary surveillance firm called Intellexa—an opaque and ever-changing constellation of firms positioning itself as a competitor to NSO Group. It offers various surveillance products and services from different subsidiary vendors, presenting itself as the "Star Alliance" of mercenary surveillance.[8]

The branding is clever: it suggests a one-stop shop for a full suite of intelligence arsenal and, by appropriating the trademark of the well-known airline rewards program, it implies a degree of corporate legitimacy. Intellexa once described itself with pride as "EU-based and regulated, with six sites and R&D labs throughout Europe."[9] It's a telling boast. The European Union's lack of regulation around state intelligence practices, along with the huge appetite for surveillance technology among its numerous government security services, is one of the major factors behind the world's gnawing mercenary spyware problem.

It was difficult to pin down exactly who was behind Intellexa, Cytrox, or the other holding companies that orbited around them. However, one highly dubious individual repeatedly peeked out from behind the curtains: Tal Dilian. Before our investigation, the resourceful *Forbes* journalist Thomas Fox-Brewster had scooped an exclusive interview with Dilian as he showed off a souped-up surveillance van from which he peddled his interception gear, as if straight out of James Bond's Q laboratory.[10] Predictably, Dilian is a veteran of Unit 8200, but he left Israel to run his business in Greece so he would be located in Europe.[11] There he could evade oversight processes by the Ministry of Defense that Israeli companies are obliged to follow, however weak those may be. As one industry source commented, "Ethically both this firm [NSO Group] and the Israeli policy were questionable as sales were made to oppressive regimes—but it was regulated. Intellexa on the other hand does not follow Israeli law and sells to similar but also worse clients—including those that are a risk to Israel's own national interest. A company that does not abide by Israeli law and is not subject to any regulator is de facto a pirate organisation."[12]

We had already seen hundreds of innocent victims of state surveillance facilitated by NSO Group, including several cases undertaken by governments involved in targeted assassinations. How could any company be "ethically worse" than that? NSO Group once claimed it had passed up around $300 million from deals because of human rights concerns.[13] If true, maybe Cytrox picked them up.

Dilian also marketed a mobile phone interception technology based on cell-site simulators (WiSpear/Passitora Ltd.) and was one of the founders of Circles—the notorious SS7 surveillance vendor we had picked apart and exposed in a 2020 report—which had links to NSO Group (chapter 4). Although he initially based his operations in Cyprus, his revealing interview with *Forbes* magazine cost him dearly. Authorities opened an investigation into his operation, so Dilian moved on to Greece.[14]

These constantly morphing ownership arrangements are designed to frustrate regulators and exhaust investigators. But Dilian left digital trails behind for researchers like us. Predator's telltale indicators were stamped on the phone logs of the Egyptian politician, giving us clues about the firm's spyware and its network of global clients.

Empirical evidence of yet another firm involved in spyware abuse is always an important discovery. Attention had focused on Pegasus, thanks in part to the widespread publicity around the Pegasus Project. But we knew the market was bigger than one firm, and every report on a new vendor confirmed that the problem went beyond Shalev Hulio and NSO Group. Their shady clients and unaccountability are not an exception: it's an industry syndrome. So, when Marczak identified Predator spyware on Nour's device, we were energized to get the word out.

As we acquired forensic data on the functionality of the spyware from his phone, we learned about active installations of Predator worldwide. Our network scanning determined that Armenia, Egypt, Greece, Indonesia, Madagascar, Oman, Saudi Arabia, and Serbia were likely government clients of Cytrox. It was another disquieting list of human rights abusers, authoritarian regimes, and illiberal or corrupt governments.

Cytrox's infrastructure abused WhatsApp for delivering its exploits, so we reached out to Meta's threat intelligence team to see if it too was interested in investigating the firm. Despite our reservations about a company like Meta, we found common ground with this team in our fight against the spyware scourge. The individual members almost always "got" what we were doing and supported us in whatever way they could. These types of cooperative engagements are also appropriate to the independence of our mission, since sharing information involves no strings attached.

We discovered Meta's security team had also been tracking Predator's infrastructure, though without the empirical evidence of the exploit we had recovered from a victim's infected device.[15] It had its own ground truths, though. Meta and other social media are like incubating pods in which bad actors of all kinds metastasize their influence operations and digitized subversion schemes. If those firms choose to look inside, they can find a lot. The problem is they rarely do. Threat teams, while talented and enjoying extraordinary visibility into their users' behavior and armed with a whole range of expensive security tools, are perennially under-resourced because, fundamentally, they act at cross-purposes to the platform's overarching goal of driving engagement: the outcome of their investigations is almost always to clean house, which invariably reduces subscribers. Many of them now also face pressure, as tech platforms cut costs and lay off safety and security teams. But a few dedicated individuals in these companies continue to make productive contributions—and they did so in this case.

Our report was published simultaneously with Meta's announcement that it had removed about three hundred Facebook pages and Instagram accounts it had discovered were linked to Cytrox.[16] Meta's independent investigation corroborated what we found with respect to likely Cytrox customers in Armenia, Egypt, Greece, Oman and Saudi Arabia. To that list, it added Colombia, Côte d'Ivoire, Germany, the Philippines, and Vietnam. Meta also confirmed it had observed Cytrox's customers engaged in the abusive targeting of civil society.

Like us, Meta published some technical indicators linked to Cytrox's operations. Among those we published were domains used by Cytrox's customers for Predator targeting—websites set up by the company for its clients and used to trick victims into clicking on malicious links. They could be included in shortened links or links that appeared to be something enticing to a target, such as a news site, an NGO's site, or something else familiar and tailored to particular classes of victims.

The purpose of publishing these technical indicators was to encourage others to explore leads, have their IT team scan their systems, or simply check their own message history to see if they had been targeted too. And that's precisely what happened next.

————

As in so many of our investigations, one case led to another discovery. In 2020, Greek investigative journalist Thanasis Koukakis was covering his usual beat, which revolved around sketchy financial deals and Greek government corruption.

That July, a source within the Greek intelligence community met with Koukakis and handed him a printed document.[17] In it was a verbatim transcript of a conversation Koukakis had had with a colleague at the *Financial Times* with whom he was working on a story about a major Greek banking scandal. The conversation took place over Koukakis's mobile phone while he was waiting to pick up his daughter from school, and parts of the transcript were marked "unintelligible" where the background noise of children playing had drowned out the conversation for those listening in. It was an extreme invasion of privacy not just for him but for his colleague at the *Financial Times* too.

Koukakis started to investigate. On August 12, 2020, he filed a complaint with the Hellenic Authority for Communication Security and Privacy (ADAE), asking whether he was a target of government surveillance.[18] "I am writing to your Authority to investigate my complaint that my mobile phone and possibly my conversations via VoiceIP applications or my landline are being monitored," he wrote. "I am making this complaint following information conveyed to me by a third party relating to the existence of transcripts of my conversations relating to my telephone conversations from 15 May 2020 to 30 May 2020. Due to the accuracy of the words contained in the transcripts, and also due to the fact that some of the conversations recorded have taken place outdoors, it follows effortlessly that they have resulted from eavesdropping."

Although it took some time, eventually the response came back: "No event was found to constitute a violation of the law."[19] It was a sneaky answer. Unbeknownst to Koukakis, the Greek authorities had actually amended a law not long after his request to prohibit the sharing of information with citizens who are the targets of surveillance.[20] It wouldn't be the first time that regulations were changed after an event to effect a cover. The Greek authorities were not telling the truth because the new law they created prevented them from doing so. As if sarcastically, they also sent him a link to a website with details on "protecting smartphone devices."

After the Citizen Lab's and Meta's reports on Cytrox were published in December 2021, referencing Cytrox's and Intellexa's connections to Greece, investigative journalists started digging in. One of them, Eliza Triantafyllou, writes for *Inside Story*, the Greek investigative journalism outlet.

Triantafyllou found that a person named Felix Bitzios had been appointed to a senior administrative role in three firms in Greece: Apollo Technologies, Hermes Technologies, and Intellexa.[21] Bitzios was well known to financial crimes reporters like Koukakis because he was involved in a shady bank scandal in Greece that Koukakis was covering.[22] When Koukakis read Triantafyllou's report about Bitzios's links to Intellexa, he figured he better get his phone checked. He reached out to the Lab for help.

In March 2022, we gathered forensic data from Koukakis, and Bill Marczak scoured through it. Sure enough, he discovered that the phone had been hacked with Predator spyware between July 12 and September 24, 2021. Forensic analysis showed that it was first hacked at approximately 10:01 GMT on July 12, when a developer certificate we had previously identified as connected to a sample of Predator spyware was added to it.

The likely vector for the infection was a text message Koukakis received that we determined arrived two minutes before the installation of the Cytrox developer certificate. "Thanasis you know about this matter," read the message, which was accompanied by a link to a URL that we had been able to attribute to Cytrox's command and control infrastructure. It was the first case we discovered of a European being targeted and his phone infected with Predator spyware.

Koukakis was aware his beat was controversial, and that he was likely being scrutinized by powerful people, but the discovery that his phone had been hacked came as a shock. "Although I had been aware since 2020 that the national intelligence service of Greece was monitoring me using conventional surveillance technology," Koukakis told me, "it never occurred to me that this surveillance had not only continued but had been escalated to include such invasive methods."

When we gave Koukakis this confirmation, he decided to go public with the story on April 11, 2022.[23] He was certain that if he was being spied on, other journalists were too, and he felt obligated to raise alarms. "The fact that a Greek journalist with over twenty-five years of experience, who had also served as a correspondent for major international media outlets, was targeted by Predator spyware strongly suggested that other journalists, including those in more senior positions, were also at risk," he said to me. A spokesperson for the Greek government denied any involvement, saying it was likely the work of a "private individual."[24]

Four days later, on April 15, 2022, documents surfaced, thanks to a group of independent investigative journalists called Reporters United, showing that Greece's intelligence service, the EYP, had indeed been monitoring Koukakis's phone at least as far back as 2020.[25] The documents stated that the surveillance was justified for unspecified "national security" reasons. "How is national security compromised by a financial reporter investigating the interests of private banks and bankers?" the Reporters United journalists asked. That very good question received no answer.

The documents also revealed that when Koukakis made his complaint to the ADAE in August 2020, the surveillance was temporarily halted, suggesting the spies themselves were spooked by his inquiry. "One hypothesis is that because the authorities were 'listening' to Koukakis, they knew he was planning to turn to ADAE," the journalists speculated. "[Koukakis] himself explained to Reporters United that, before filing the complaint, he had contacted the independent Authority by phone to find out about the procedure he had to follow in order to submit it. EYP was able to listen to these conversations."

It was around this time, Reporters United also explains, that the authorities began pushing for a revision to the laws on disclosure to prevent those under government surveillance from having their cases disclosed by the ADAE.[26] The regulation had retroactive effect and covered Koukakis's wiretapping, generating that sneaky response to his query. The Greek government's edifice of denial was gradually crumbling.

There were signs that other Intellexa products might have also been deployed against journalists in the country. Greek journalist Tasos Telloglou claimed he was stalked by unnamed individuals over several months.[27] In one case, he confronted the person following him, who then ran away.[28] A parking attendant at a lot he routinely used warned him that he spotted police trying to gain access to his vehicle.[29] In June 2022, an intelligence source gave him a photograph taken of him and Koukakis in an Athens café and told him authorities were using cellphone signals to track his movements.[30] The type of technology the source described matches that supplied by WiSpear, one of Dilian's Intellexa-branded services.

Alerted by news of the Predator hacking of journalists in Greece and the earlier reports the Citizen Lab and Meta published, the European Parliament's security team initiated a search of the phone messages of a group of its members, looking for a match with the domains we had published. Among them was one positive find, sent to the device of Nikos Androulakis, a Greek socialist opposition party leader and member of the European Parliament.[31]

The security check showed Androulakis's phone received a text message on September 21, 2021, shortly before the start of confidential proceedings of his party, known as PASOK.[32] The message, which read "Let's get a little serious, man, we've got a lot to gain," contained a link to a website that matched a domain published in our December 2021 report. Fortunately, Androulakis didn't click on the link, but the message proved someone was intent on spying on his device. The dam was beginning to burst wide open: a journalist had been wiretapped, and now a senior figure in the political opposition had been targeted too.

————

The press quickly dubbed the slew of wiretaps "Greece's Watergate." The reactions followed a familiar script. First, the government denied any involvement, suggesting it was the work of lone individuals or a foreign party. In the words of the government's official spokesperson, Yiannis Economou, "The Greek authorities do not use the specific software described in these complaints, and therefore the Greek state does not deal with any of the companies that manufacture or market such software."[33] It was a lie.

Gradually, partial admissions were made. Kyriakos Mitsotakis, the prime minister—who, coincidentally, had changed the structure of the country's intelligence service to report directly to his office in 2019—eventually disclosed that the hacking had happened and was lawful, although "wrong."[34] He seemed to be pointing the finger at others in his administration. Scapegoats were offered up: the head of intelligence, Panagiotis Kontoleon, was dismissed; so was Mitsotakis's nephew, Grigoris Dimitriadis, but without much explanation.[35]

The government claimed that the surveillance it undertook was more like a conventional wiretap and that it had never used Predator. But the forensic data doesn't lie, and although it was impossible to establish attribution to the Greek government based on that forensic data alone, the circumstantial evidence was strong and growing more so every day, pointing closer and closer to the government's intelligence agency. A major *New York Times* story signaled that indeed a national scandal was in full swing.[36]

————

Greece's Watergate was not the only one in Europe. Scandals arising from the work of the Pegasus Project, Amnesty International's tech lab, Access Now, and the Citizen Lab were growing in leaps and bounds across the continent. Some of the victims came to our attention directly, reaching out to us individually or through third parties. Some checked themselves using preliminary diagnostic tools, such as Amnesty International's MVT checker, and then approached one of our organizations for a follow-up. Others heard they were hacked when they received notifications from WhatsApp or Apple and reached out to one of us for assistance and diagnostics. We soon realized that Europe was in the grips of a major spyware abuse problem that reflected a disturbing lack of political accountability.

First, there was Hungary—a country that for years had been backsliding into authoritarianism. Led by the superhero of the alt-right, Viktor Orbán, Hungary has clamped down on press freedom, eroded liberal democratic institutions, forced a shutdown of Central European University as part of a campaign against liberal educational programs, and centralized management over secretive intelligence agencies under Orbán's direct control.[37] Oversight around the country's intelligence services is among the weakest in Europe. The country's national security services act enables the state's security services to carry out covert surveillance against any victim they choose. Its vaguely worded provisions fail to define the types of crimes that are subjected to state surveillance. This broad legal framework around secret intelligence gathering has brought Hungary into conflict with the European Court of Human Rights, which on one occasion expressed concern over "unfettered executive power."[38]

Orbán's regime has a strong appetite for surveillance technology. In July 2015, leaked files revealed that the Hungarian secret services were a client of the Italian spyware company Hacking Team.[39] Our research into Candiru, an Israel-based surveillance company, uncovered a government operator of that spyware in Budapest too.[40] We also found that the mercenary spyware developer Cytrox had a corporate presence in Hungary.[41] But it was Orbán's use of Pegasus that caused the most controversy.[42]

When the Pegasus Project was published, the telephone numbers of around three hundred Hungarian nationals figured among the leaked list.[43] Subsequent investigations by the Hungarian non-profit news organization Direkt36, probably the last such independent group in the country, revealed that the potential targets' numbers belonged to journalists, businessmen, an international student, and a foreign minister, among others.[44] Some of the people on the list were close to Orbán and even part of his administration, signaling paranoia on the part of the prime minister—a trait common to autocrats.[45] Hungary was the only EU country on the Pegasus Project list of ten suspected government clients. Amnesty International approached some of those targets, offering to check their devices, and the team verified that several had had their phones hacked with Pegasus spyware, thereby corroborating the list of leaked phone numbers.[46]

The Lab's entry into Hungary came via investigative photojournalist Dániel Németh, who works for Direkt36. He operates below the radar, with no X (formerly Twitter) profile, so the subjects of his investigations won't easily recognize him. On one project he set out to photograph the rich cronies and oligarchs around Orbán. He studied their travel itineraries, using open-source information and tips from sources, then booked low-cost flights to follow them to their vacation destinations, photographing them as they partied on Orbán's yachts.

Németh was reasonably suspicious about surveillance, given the nature of his work. He asked his friends to buy his flight tickets for him and purchased a new phone, assuming it might insulate him from surveillance. He then reached out to us through a mutual friend and asked if we could check his device. After examining his phone's logs, we determined it was hacked in July 2021 while he was back in Hungary after a trip to southern Italy.[47] There he had taken photographs of Lőrinc Mészáros, whose personal wealth had inexplicably exploded after his friend Orbán rose to power in 2010.[48] It was a familiar story: Pegasus had not been used to track a criminal or a terrorist but to spy on an investigative journalist digging into Orbán's circle of corruption.

The revelations about widespread Pegasus abuse in Hungary triggered public outrage. A regional prosecutor's office launched a probe into the matter after receiving complaints.[49] In Budapest, around one thousand protestors marched from the House of Terror museum, which commemorates victims of Nazism and communism, to the government's party headquarters.[50] Opposition MPs demanded a full inquiry.[51]

Although the authorities initially denied all knowledge of Pegasus, partial admissions gradually came—just as in Greece. Sándor Pintér, the minister of the interior, acknowledged Hungary's use of Pegasus to European Parliament representatives during a delegation visit of the Committee on Civil Liberties, Justice and Home Affairs.[52] Lajos Kósa, the ruling party's vice president, acknowledged there was surveillance but denied that any tools were used inappropriately.[53] A former NSO Group employee then confirmed to journalists that Hungary was among the company's clients in Europe.[54]

Meanwhile, investigations by Direkt36 discovered that the decision to acquire Pegasus was made during a closed session of the Hungarian parliament's national security committee on October 11, 2017.[55] The vote was held shortly after a country visit by Israeli prime minister Benjamin Netanyahu that summer.[56] The Special Service for National Security requested Pegasus, specifying that the purchase should be exempted from public procurement announcements. The committee vote was unanimous. Direkt36 also discovered the usual myriad middlemen and front companies that were used to broker the procurement for Hungarian intelligence, including individuals with close ties to the government's security services. The journalists even discovered that Hungary hired a person linked to Mercury Public Affairs—the same lobbying firm used by NSO Group in Washington, DC.[57]

More details of sketchy surveillance transactions emerged in bits and pieces. *Intelligence Online* reported that Hungary's intelligence agencies had been mandated to investigate European parliamentarians after the European Union withheld several billions in aid dollars earmarked for Hungary.[58] The agencies were then rewarded with a huge budgetary increase.[59] In September 2022, the Avnon Group—another Israel-based surveillance firm—confirmed that it had plans to sell social media tracking software to the Hungarian government.[60]

————

Next came Poland. There are haunting similarities between Poland and Hungary: the systematic erosion of an independent press, the deliberate reining in of judicial independence, populist reactionary measures against rights for LGBTQ+ people and other minority groups—and the use of Pegasus. We forensically examined the mobile phones of several Polish victims and confirmed they were hacked with Pegasus.[61] Some received Apple notifications and then reached out to us, while others had other suspicions or indications that concerned them, and they too contacted us.

First there was Ewa Wrzosek, a prosecutor formerly at the Warsaw-Mokotów District Prosecutor's Office and a member of Lex Super Omnia, a group involved in fighting government attempts to rein in the independence of the judiciary.[62] Wrzosek received an Apple notification and asked us for assistance. Our forensic analysis of her device confirmed it was infected with Pegasus spyware.[63]

Next up was Roman Giertych, a lawyer who represented, among others, the former president of Poland and a senior member of Poland's political opposition, Donald Tusk.[64] We confirmed his device had been hacked with Pegasus at a time when he was Tusk's attorney, showing yet another case of the violation of attorney-client privilege.

Senator Krzysztof Brejza of the opposition Civic Platform party had messages stolen from his phone during the exact period in which we forensically verified that his device had been hacked with Pegasus.[65] The messages were misleadingly presented out of context and used in a smear campaign against him on the state broadcaster TVP. His children, wife, and mother have all been traumatized by the relentless smears.

We discovered Michał Kołodziejczak's phone had been hacked with Pegasus ahead of a fall election in which he was hoping to have his group, AGROunia, become a formal political party—a risk for

Poland's ruling regime.[66] We uncovered that the phone of author Tomasz Szwejgiert had been hacked while he was writing a book on Poland's security services.[67] We also confirmed the device of Andrzej Malinowski, the former president of an organization called the Employers of Poland, had been hacked with Pegasus.[68]

Were any of these individuals suspects in a legitimate criminal or "terrorist" investigation? On the face of it, it seems unlikely. The Polish government's lack of transparency meant that there was almost no public accountability around such matters, just as in Greece, Hungary, and Spain. Everything was shrouded in state secrecy.

———

As the scandals unfolded in Europe, the investigations continued. Formal inquiries and probes were launched, but the results were varied.

In November 2022, investigative journalists published a detailed story showing that Greece had authorized exports of Intellexa spyware to Sudan, among other problematic countries.[69] The delivery of highly sophisticated software to the war-ravaged African country represented a particularly acute case of abuse: the spyware was sold to Mohamed Hamdan Dagalo, known as Hemedti, Sudan's richest man and the leader of the notorious militant group the Rapid Support Forces (RSF), known for its genocidal rampages.[70]

The investigation, undertaken jointly by *Haaretz*, Lighthouse Reports, and *Inside Story*, originated when journalists discovered a social media post from an Intellexa engineer that identified an eight-seater Cessna owned by Dilian and used by Intellexa for visits to potential government clients.[71] (In a confusing unrelated twist, the Cessna's parking spot in Cyprus was at a facility called the Pegasus Flight Center.) The journalists scoured through dozens of passenger lists and other open-source data to connect the plane to Tal Dilian and to the RSF in Sudan, where Predator spyware was sold. They also determined that the Cessna flew to other prospective clients in the United Arab Emirates, Saudi Arabia, Mozambique, Angola, Kenya, and Equatorial Guinea—the last recognized as one of the most corrupt, authoritarian, and repressive regimes in the world.[72]

Following these disclosures, in December 2022 the Greek police raided Intellexa's offices in Athens—but Dilian and the firm had already packed up and moved elsewhere.[73] Some suspect the raid was largely theatrics—the government showing it was doing something about the scandal when in fact it was dragging its heels.

Also in November 2022, another investigation by Reporters United showed that Grigoris Dimitriadis, the prime minister's nephew who had been dismissed after the first Predator revelations emerged in Greece, had business ties with individuals connected to Intellexa, including the shady entrepreneur Felix Bitzios, who owned a 35 percent stake in the mercenary firm.[74] Dimitriadis promptly filed a defamation suit against the journalists, a case that was widely condemned by press organizations as another example of a SLAPP suit: abusive litigation filed by powerful entities aimed at silencing and intimidating legitimate journalism.[75] Among those named in the suit by Dimitriadis was Thanasis Koukakis, who simply retweeted the Reporters United post about the story. "The fact that Dimitriadis is linked in a business way to Intellexa would maybe mean nothing if he wasn't responsible for the National Intelligence Service. The fact he was, that he is in the scandal and has connections with these people, this is something the public should know," said one of the Reporters United journalists.[76]

In the same month, the news organization *Documento* obtained a list of dozens of individuals who had been placed on the government surveillance list, including opposition figures, journalists, businessmen, politicians, and publishers close to Prime Minister Mitsotakis.[77] According to *Documento*'s sources, these individuals were first placed under surveillance by the EYP to understand their movements and relations, and then the high-value targets were hacked with Predator spyware. Logistically, this distinction makes sense because using spyware to hack phones is expensive and carries the risk of exposure if done improperly.

The leaked list led the Lab to yet another discovery. When Artemis Seaford, a dual American-Greek citizen who was working as a trust and safety manager for Meta, the parent company of Facebook, discovered her name was on the list, she turned to us for assistance. She was involved in numerous discussions with Greek officials as part of her job. We analyzed her device and discovered it had been hacked with Predator spyware in September 2021 for at least two months.[78] Sources who spoke to the *New York Times* confirmed she was under EYP surveillance for a period stretching from about August 2021 until several months into 2022.[79] "In my case, I do not know why I was targeted, but I cannot see any reasonable national security concerns behind it," Seaford said.[80] Insidiously, the text that was used to deliver the exploit to her device was a message appearing to come from the government's state vaccine agency and mimicked a link to confirm her COVID vaccination appointment.[81]

As Greece's Watergate unfolded, the Hellenic Data Protection Authority—an independent public watchdog—launched an inquiry of its own. As it kicked off, agents reached out to interview us about what we had found and asked for recommendations on how they might further investigate. We suggested the best course of action would be to contact internet service providers and other entities in Greece that might have access to the envelope information around messages that were sent to target individuals—who sent the messages, who received them, and when they were sent. And that's presumably just what the Greek DPA did next. After a lengthy investigation, the agency disclosed it had discovered that more than two hundred Predator-linked SMS messages were sent to ninety-two individuals in the country.[82] No doubt some of them will make their way to us for further forensic analysis.

As positive as these investigations have been, they have run up against a hard-nosed Greek response. A parliamentary commission that was formed to investigate the Predator scandal was made up mostly of members of the ruling party.[83] Its proceedings were held almost entirely behind closed doors, and many of the key witnesses and victims who had been identified were not even consulted. The government passed a law banning the private sale, use, and possession of spyware, but human rights organizations and privacy advocates widely criticized the law for legitimating its use by the Greek government and not building in safeguards such as proper oversight.[84] Finally, in July 2024, a widely criticized Supreme Court investigation absolved the government of any wrongdoing, announcing that four individuals tied to Intellexa and its businesses will instead be prosecuted for "misdemeanors" relating to the spying.[85] Despite the scandal, in other words, it was business as usual for Greece: more cover-ups and abuses of power.

In Hungary and, for a time, under the then ruling party in Poland, the official responses followed similar trajectories. Both governments officially denied the hacking, but sometime later they begrudgingly acknowledged they had in fact used spyware, though they claimed the surveillance was legally authorized. They talked vaguely of official investigations but didn't initiate them. No one expected much accountability to come from regimes that would ultimately be investigating themselves.

Despite minimal progress at national levels, many human rights advocates pinned their hopes on regional accountability mechanisms. In early 2022, the European Parliament convened its official investigation into mercenary spyware in Europe with the formation of the PEGA committee.[86] Considerable excitement attached to its investigations, and many victims testified, as did the Lab's senior researchers John Scott-Railton and Bill Marczak. The hearings produced important findings on abuses, which were documented in a comprehensive report.[87]

However, the proceedings were also bogged down by political machinations and stonewalling. Greece, Hungary, Poland, and Spain were all noncooperative in various ways. Key witnesses from the governments' national intelligence bodies either did not comply with requests to testify or offered platitudes that shed no light on what was really going on.

When the PEGA committee visited Poland, it was snubbed. Requests to meet with representatives of the Ministry of the Interior and the Ministry of Justice, the likely operators of the spyware, were both declined, prompting the members of the European Parliament to hold a press conference and issue a critical joint statement with some stinging rebukes to the Polish government.[88]

Spain was next in line to assume the presidency of the European Council, and other states seemed deferential to the government's maneuvering. A visit to Spain by the PEGA committee was blocked there too.[89] Spanish members of the European Parliament, led by disinformation peddler Jordi Cañas, did their best to water down the final PEGA committee report and used smears and false accusations to cast shade on the reliability of the Citizen Lab's and Amnesty International's forensic methodologies (chapter 16).

Just as the PEGA committee was wrapping up its proceedings and issuing its final report, a scandal was uncovered that undercut some of the credibility of the European Parliament as a whole. Several members were charged with accepting bribes to curry favor with certain countries, including Morocco and in the Gulf.[90] Bags of cash were found stashed away in closets.[91] The scandal took some of the luster off the PEGA committee's report, but ultimately it made little difference: the European Parliament has not much real authority of its own and can only make recommendations to governments to implement as they see fit. Many governments had, by that time, asserted that surveillance was not only a national-level concern but a national security issue too. "As soon as national security is invoked, transparency doesn't apply anymore, citizens' rights don't apply anymore. Parliamentary scrutiny or judicial scrutiny doesn't apply anymore. It's basically an area of lawlessness," remarked Sophie in 't Veld, the chair of the European Parliament's PEGA committee.[92] Proving her point, in 2022, the European Commission put forward a proposed regulation meant to prevent spyware targeting of journalists in the region, but the law contained a huge exemption in cases of "national security"—a loophole that legitimized the very spying it ostensibly was designed to prevent.[93] It's as though the government security agencies were saying, "It's none of anyone's business but our own."

This mixed bag of responses to the spying scandals that were uncovered in Europe is a stark reminder of the complicated political dynamics around government surveillance and the industries that support it. To be sure, many people and policymakers want to do something to restrain abuses and bring the sector under principled democratic oversight. But the security agencies and their allies in the industry have enormous influence, both behind the scenes and elsewhere—influence that increases as corruption and authoritarianism deepen. As the screws tighten on the spyware industry in Israel, many entrepreneurs are migrating to Europe, and firms are sprouting up in Italy, Spain, and elsewhere in the region. Without doubt, business for private intelligence is open and thriving in Europe.

It's a vicious cycle: right-leaning securocrats seek out the latest surveillance technology; mercenary vendors migrate to the region and profit; together, they sink deeper into the shadows; and the intelligence acquired is like crack cocaine. Once you hack an opposition politician's phone, you crave more information. Discoveries of abuses lead to yet more cycles of abuse as the phones of lawyers, judges, and journalists are tapped to neutralize investigations. Accountability suffers, and the pillars of liberal democracy begin to crumble.

The different aftermaths around Greece's and Poland's Watergates are microcosms of these complex dynamics. The disclosures made a huge splash in Greece, and some heads rolled. But the crisis didn't affect Mitsotakis at the ballot box. On May 21, 2023, his center-right New Democracy party trounced its opponents in the election, securing more than 40 percent of the vote.[94] Many thought the spying scandal would cause the government's fall, but the opposite happened.

Some people with whom I've spoken about the lack of consequences for what was uncovered in Greece and elsewhere in Europe explain it as exhaustion with digital surveillance and a feeling of resignation around government espionage and abuse of powers. As In 't Veld said, "People tend to shrug a little bit like 'oh, yeah, political parties are spying on others. What's new?' I think if we are that careless about democracy and the rule of law, then we don't deserve to live in a free world anymore."[95] Thanasis Koukakis told me part of the reason "lies in the right-wing government's extensive control over a large portion of the Greek media since late 2019," which was "secured through generous state funding and advertising, contributing to Greece's decline in international press freedom rankings."

In Poland, in contrast, still-functioning democratic processes helped to tip the scales in favor of public accountability. In December 2023, Donald Tusk—whose attorney's device we found had been hacked with Pegasus when he was in opposition—secured enough votes in the Polish parliament to be elected prime minister, returning to rule after a nine-year absence.[96] Among his first acts was to publicly disclose confidential contracts and other material that "one hundred percent confirm the purchase and illegal use of Pegasus."[97] In April 2024, the Polish justice minister disclosed that under the previous government nearly six hundred people had been placed under targeted surveillance, many of them for the reason that they were simply "inconvenient" to the ruling party.[98] As we suspected, the abuse cases we surfaced were just the tip of a massive iceberg of government corruption. An investigation was launched into the matter by the Polish Senate too, which is ongoing at the time of writing.[99]

While progress toward some kind of accountability in Europe around mercenary spyware was mixed, the story was different across the Atlantic Ocean. In July 2023, the US Department of Commerce added Cytrox and Intellexa to the designated entity list, alongside NSO Group, Candiru, and other hack-for-hire firms.[100] Less than a year later, the US Department of the Treasury, through the Office of Foreign Assets Control, went further, placing sanctions on Dilian and his ex-wife and business partner, Sara Hamou, as well as five corporate entities involved in the Intellexa-Cytrox Star Alliance consortium.[101] The designation came a few months after the Citizen Lab discovered that Cytrox technology was used yet again to target Predator spyware at the Egyptian opposition politician Ahmed Eltantawy's phone.[102] As part of that investigation, we worked with Google's Threat Analysis Group and captured copies of Predator's exploit chain and the first stage of its spyware, which we determined included three separate Apple zero days. Our responsible disclosure led to yet another Apple emergency security patch for its billions of users worldwide.[103]

We also identified that the equipment of a Canadian-headquartered company, Sandvine, was implicated in the attempted malware injection onto Eltantawy's device. (Sandvine had once threatened to sue the Citizen Lab for a previous report we had published on the use of its PacketLogic devices to inject malware in Turkey and Egypt [chapter 4]). Afterward, the US Commerce Department added the Canadian firm to its designated entity list too. It was an embarrassing indictment of Canada's poor regulations around its own industries' surveillance exports.[104] Then, in September 2024 the US Treasury Department's Office of Foreign Assets Control slapped Felix Bitzsios and five others involved in Intellexa's sketchy business ventures with yet more sanctions.[105]

As I read the news of these US-led initiatives, I imagined how distressing and frustrating it must be for the European lawmakers who care about rights and democracy. Intellexa, Cytrox, and the other related entities were European companies, and the scandals unleashed by the discovery of abuses connected to both Pegasus and Predator spyware had boiled over in Europe, causing regional crises. Yet it was the US government that was able to get its act together and start to hold the private sector mercenary spyware industry accountable. One hopes that the new Polish government's investigations into spyware abuses will prompt similar European-wide remediation efforts. As always in politics, however, everything depends on who's in power—both overtly and in the shadows.

Ms. Kanimba Goes to Washington

JULY 2022
WASHINGTON, DC

The setting is familiar to anyone even remotely interested in politics, as seen on television broadcasts of the Watergate, Iran-Contra, or Trump impeachment hearings. Those testifying are seated at a large polished wooden table with a microphone in front of them. They face a raised dais with rows of seats arranged in a wide semicircle, each occupied by a congressperson. At the back and center is the chair; today it's Representative Adam Schiff. Seated next to him is the ranking member, Representative Mike Turner. Along the back row are the congressional staff. The public gallery is full. Cameras are positioned throughout the well-lit room, and the entire affair is being streamed live over C-SPAN.

Seated at the witness table is John Scott-Railton (JSR), who leads our targeted threats research team. Next to him is Shane Huntley from Google's Threat Analysis Group, known by the acronym TAG. And next to him is Carine Kanimba, a dual Belgian-American citizen whose father, Paul Rusesabagina, was portrayed by actor Don Cheadle in the Academy Award–nominated film *Hotel Rwanda*. Kanimba, who wanted to be identified publicly, is one of the many human subjects in our targeted threats research. We had recently confirmed that her device was hacked with Pegasus spyware.[1] Her presence here gives the subject of the hearing both a dramatic and a human touch. The panel represents well the different components of investigations into cyber espionage against civil society: researchers, tech platforms, and victims.

The powerful House Intelligence Committee oversees the eighteen intelligence agencies that make up the entire US intelligence apparatus.[2] If your aim is to regulate mercenary spyware, there are not many more influential forums than this one. It controls the budget strings, sets the priorities, decides when to open inquiries, issues subpoenas, and compels legal testimony. With a few sentences in a budgetary bill, it can move institutional mountains or, with a nod, it can alter structural incentives in the United States and internationally too. Other governments and especially allies frequently follow US legislative priorities. In an era of extreme polarization, it seems both major US political parties realize they must do something about spyware and digital transnational repression.

Representative Schiff began the hearing on July 27 with these words:

> Today we are convening a public hearing on the acute and rapidly evolving threat posed by foreign commercial spyware. Public reports have shined a bright light on the robust market for powerful spying tools that are sold on the open market, essentially offering sophisticated signals intelligence capabilities as an end-to-end service. . . .
>
> The availability of these tools in the hands of governments who previously lacked robust surveillance capabilities is truly a game-changer for U.S. national security, which makes it an issue of particular concern to this committee.[3]

After Representative Turner made his opening remarks, Schiff introduced the witnesses and concluded with: "Mr. Scott-Railton, you are recognized for your opening remarks."

JSR, never one to disappoint, described the unchecked growth of the mercenary spyware industry and the harms the Citizen Lab and others had documented. He outlined the functionality of the latest and most powerful versions of zero-click software, such as the one we had recently acquired from Loujain al-Hathloul's hacked device and shared with Google and Apple (chapter 14).

"This isn't about sitting in a café and connecting to unsecured WiFi," he testified. "Your phone can be on your bedside table at two in the morning. One minute your phone is clean; the next minute the data is silently streaming to an adversary a continent away. You see nothing."[4]

One of the most powerful parts of his testimony was about the security risks around mercenary spyware sales, which are often mediated by shady firms and corrupt individuals. To illustrate the point, he showed a slide of Pegasus equipment located in "a privately owned heavy machinery warehouse in a dusty industrial section of Accra, Ghana." The equipment was discovered during a police raid related to corruption charges. So much for NSO Group's strict controls.

Everyone at the Lab was tuned in to the hearings, as were many allies throughout the human rights community. Finally, we felt vindicated, after all the frustrations we'd endured over the years—the ridiculous denials, defamatory trolling, and covert targeting.

When one of the congressional members asked JSR what could be done, he reframed the problem as a national security risk. He said that if the weight of the US government were brought to bear on the mercenary surveillance industry, that alone would expose and curb the industry's abuses. "There is a powerful host of tools, both legislative and in terms of empowering the Intelligence Community, to disrupt and degrade the capabilities of problem actors," he testified, adding, "If the U.S. Intelligence Community, with its considerable capabilities, identified the zero-days that were being used by problem actors—and it could—and submitted them to big tech, you could burn their [mercenary spyware firms'] house down."[5]

Up next was Shane Huntley from Google's TAG. He described how his group has tracked more than thirty mercenary spyware vendors worldwide. He talked about the sophistication of the ForcedEntry exploit that we'd shared with Google (chapter 14).

"We assessed this to be one of the most technically sophisticated exploits we had ever seen," he said, "and the ability for an end user to protect themselves from such a threat is very minimal."[6]

Then it was Carine Kanimba's turn—heart-wrenching testimony from a victim who has suffered disturbing and consequential harms from surveillance. In 1994, her father, Rusesabagina, was the manager of a hotel in Kigali. He gave refuge to 1,268 people, risking his life to resist a machete-wielding militia waiting outside. Not a single person who took refuge in his hotel was murdered.[7]

Kanimba was born in Rwanda just before the horrific 1994 genocide. Both her birth parents were among the first of the nearly one million people who were killed, leaving her and her sister, Anaïse, orphans. Rusesabagina and his wife found them in a refugee camp and raised them as their own, even though the sisters are ethnically Tutsi and Rusesabagina is Hutu.[8] That difference didn't matter to the family, but it was eventually used as ammunition by pro-Kagame disinformation actors in one of the many smear campaigns launched against Rusesabagina and his family.[9]

Rusesabagina eventually fell out with Paul Kagame, the president of Rwanda. In 2005, when President George W. Bush awarded Rusesabagina the Presidential Medal of Freedom, Kagame was furious.[10] Things got worse when Rusesabagina started using his newfound profile to speak out against human rights and other abuses in the country. "[There were] assassination attempts against my father's life in Belgium, house break-ins, and intimidation attempts," Kanimba testified.[11] Rusesabagina moved his family to Texas, hoping for better opportunities and safety, but the harassment and threats continued.[12]

In 2020, Rusesabagina was invited to a conference in Burundi. During a layover in Dubai, he was lured onto a private jet chartered by the office of the Rwandan president and illegally rendered to Rwanda.[13] He was then sentenced to twenty-five years in prison on trumped-up terrorism charges in a mass trial full of procedural improprieties.[14] His sentence was widely condemned by governments and human rights organizations worldwide, including the Clooney Foundation for Justice and the American Bar Association, as well as by several UN special rapporteurs.[15] This treatment was straight out of Kagame's playbook of repression: brook no opposition, hunt people down who embarrass and criticize you, spy on them, kidnap them, throw them in jail—or, worse, snuff them out.

After his abduction, Carine and Anaïse Kanimba became full-time advocates for their father's release. They met regularly with elected officials in Europe and the United States to advocate for US intervention. Although these government officials did occasionally apply pressure on Kagame to secure Rusesabagina's release, con-flicting interests complicated their efforts. Situated in the heart of the Great Lakes region of Africa, which is rich in minerals critical to the digital economy, Rwanda is a strategically important ally to a lot of Western governments, many of which have funneled billions in aid there.

Rwanda has been a heavy consumer of high-tech surveillance equipment and, seemingly, an enthusiastic customer of NSO Group. During the networking scanning we performed in 2017 and 2018, we discovered a Pegasus operator, whom we codenamed GrandLacs, targeting phones in Rwanda, Kenya, Uganda, and South Africa.[16] We strongly suspected that the operator was the Rwandan security services because the targeting matched the type of transnational espionage Rwanda was known to be involved in regionally. Not long afterward, as part of the investigation we per-formed in cooperation with WhatsApp, we discovered and noti-fied several Rwandans who were targeted with Pegasus spyware, some in exile.[17] Once again, victim confirmation provided a kind of ground truth to our high-level infrastructure reconnaissance.

Among the victims were individuals who had experienced hor-rible episodes of harassment and threats, followed by fear and paranoia once they learned their phones had been hacked. Some of them had friends or colleagues who had been murdered by Kag-ame's death squads. Our discovery provided a window into a dread-ful campaign of digital transnational repression that Kagame's security services were mounting.

As part of my outreach for these investigations, I connected with

Michela Wrong, the British author and Rwandan expert, who had read about the 2019 WhatsApp cases. Wrong suggested we contact Kanimba and her sister, as well as other Rwandans at risk she had encountered. She had just published *Do Not Disturb*, a book on Kagame's political murders, whose title she took from the death of the former Rwandan intelligence chief Patrick Karegeya, who was strangled in his Johannesburg hotel room while hiding in exile.[18] The assassins had hung the sign on his door to buy time as they fled the country. Wrong herself had experienced seemingly endless streams of vicious slander, sexist harassment, and even death threats. She was well known among the Rwandan diaspora for her courageous reporting and, for the same reason, was frequently targeted by Kagame's goon squads.

Coincidentally, around this time, members of the Pegasus Project reached out to Kanimba. A staff researcher from Amnesty International's office in Berlin discreetly contacted her while she was living in Brussels and arranged to meet her—to ask if she would give Amnesty her phone for forensic analysis. Kanimba was understandably wary to entrust her phone to someone she had never met before, but she overcame her trepidation and turned it over. Amnesty's forensic analysis showed evidence that her device had been compromised with Pegasus multiple times from late 2020 to the summer of 2021.[19]

In the spring of 2022, the Citizen Lab participated in the Oslo Freedom Forum in Norway, a major human rights conference. We decided to organize a pop-up booth in which we could triage for phones that had been targeted or infected with spyware among the sprawling group of dissidents, activists, and journalists who were attending the event. Kanimba came by our booth, and we checked her phone. Our analysis confirmed that it had indeed been hacked, substantiating Amnesty International's earlier analysis. Later, when she gave one of her devices to Belgian intelligence, the agency further substantiated it had been penetrated with Pegasus spyware.[20]

Kanimba was living in a house in Belgium with her cousin Jean Paul Nsonzerumpa. He too came by our booth at the forum and gave us his phone to check. We discovered it had been hacked multiple times over a period of weeks in the fall of 2020.[21] "I watched in horror, last year, as we discovered that my cousin Carine's phone had been infected with the Pegasus spyware," he said. "I felt the need to protect her and our family not knowing that the Rwanda government had also infected my phone and that we were not safe at all."[22]

Kanimba's testimony to the House committee was riveting, particularly because of the time frame around which her device was hacked with Pegasus. "The forensics reports [of Amnesty and the Lab] have been presented to this committee, and they show that the spyware was triggered as I walked in with my mom into a meeting with the Belgian Minister of Foreign Affairs," she said. "It was active during calls with the U.S. Presidential Envoy for Hostage Affairs team and the U.S. State Department, as well as U.S. human rights groups."[23] That seemed to touch a raw nerve with the committee members. Nothing wakes up US policymakers more than hearing that foreign governments are eavesdropping on the private meetings of their government officials.

In her witness statement, Kanimba described how she had "lost all sense of security in my private actions and my physical surroundings."[24] Like many victims, she had become wary of the device that is meant to be her portal to the world. "I am a 29-year-old woman and I use my phone quite often, not only in the efforts to secure my father's release but on my social, my private conversations with my friends, and the fact that the same government that tortured my father, that is holding him hostage, and that has been trying to silence him all these years now also has access to my private messages and my conversations and my location, it is very, very scary."[25]

As part of her testimony, she entered the Citizen Lab's and Amnesty International's forensic analyses of her hacked devices into the congressional record as well as the separate forensic analysis obtained from the Belgian General Intelligence and Security Service.

As we interacted with Kanimba, al-Hathloul, Omar Abdulaziz, and other victims, we couldn't help but be struck by the enormous psychological and emotional toll the spying took on their lives. Starting around 2019, we decided we should devote research time to better understand and systematically investigate that toll. We developed a qualitative project on digital transnational repression—the phenomenon of states applying repressive policies by digital means such as spyware or social media–based harassment campaigns to silence or coerce nationals located outside their territorial borders. The research team involved in this project, which continues as of the time of writing, is led by two talented and devoted Lab researchers, Noura Aljizawi and Siena Anstis.

Aljizawi not only studies digital transnational repression but has been a victim of it herself.[26] In 2011, inspired by the events of the Arab Spring, she joined in activities against the Assad regime in Syria. She was arrested by authorities in Damascus in 2012 and detained in a horrific prison where she and her fellow prisoners were brutally tortured and subjected to electric shocks and sexual assaults. After six months she was released and fled to Turkey, eventually making her way to Canada and to the Lab as a full-time researcher.

Anstis is a lawyer by training who previously worked with refugees and immigrants who suffered harassment after fleeing Iran, Syria, Uganda, Sri Lanka, and other repressive countries. On her first day at the Lab as a senior legal advisor and researcher, October 1, 2018, our blockbuster report on the hacking of Abdulaziz was published, and then came news of the astounding connection between Jamal Khashoggi and Abdulaziz, who has since feared for his own life (chapter 5). Despite it all, Anstis remained unflappable. Her meticulous attention to detail and ethics, combined with a passion for justice and rights, has made her essential to the Lab's success.

We realized that the hacking and its calamitous results had left a huge emotional and psychological scar on Abdulaziz. With little empirical research on the topic, we set out to investigate ourselves. We received approval from the University of Toronto's Research Ethics Board for the project, enrolled our first human subjects into the study, and began to interview them.[27] Many interviews lasted for hours as we learned about the enormous stress and anxiety the victims had endured after authoritarian regimes hunted them down from abroad. Although the victims originated from countries all over the world, their experiences seemed nearly identical, whether they were being spied on and harassed by China, Iran, Russia, Rwanda, Saudi Arabia, or some other despotic regime. This transnational phenomenon of crime and repression appeared to be growing exponentially.

Some individuals had their phones hacked by security services they thought they had escaped. They experienced fear and intense anxiety after they learned about the largely invisible violation of their privacy. We listened as victims recounted how their ordeals touched their friends, family, and work, sometimes in ways that brought unintended risks to them all. We documented the nightmarish ways in which electronic and physical surveillance are often combined.

Women, especially those coming from conservative societies, faced awful discrimination and were subjected to sexualized taunts, threats of rape, and other vile attacks. We found many whose phones had been hacked and their private photos published online or threatened with publication in attempts to blackmail or extort them. Some even had their photos doctored and manipulated. In one case, a victim reported to us that China's Ministry of State Security had produced a four-part documentary series that was posted to YouTube detailing an entirely fictional account of her sex life.

We also learned about the impact digital transnational repression had on the victims' friends and family members—an occurrence that happened so often that we coined the term "relational targeting" to describe it. We routinely ask victims if their inner circle or family would like to get their phones checked. These people are often extorted or threatened to pressure the victims, especially if they still live in the country from which the victim fled. One woman we interviewed explained that her father was told by his supervisor at work that he had to "discipline" his daughter or someone would kill him.

Many of the victims reported physical effects alongside the emotional and psychological harms they experienced. "I lost even the ability to write," one of the subjects told us. "I started to associate the motion of writing with trauma and pain . . . I tried everything. I feel a bit better, but still not 100 percent myself." Al-Hathloul described panic attacks stemming from the torture and espionage she experienced.

Nearly all victims recounted a feeling of futility when they tried to react, whether they reported their experiences to the tech platforms or to law enforcement and other local government agencies. Most of the harassment and targeting we documented took place over social media, but victims uniformly said they rarely received any useful assistance when they lodged complaints with the companies. X (formerly Twitter), Meta, and other social media firms are notoriously ill-equipped to curb online harassment campaigns, especially those emanating from the non-English-speaking world, and they are progressively dismantling their safety teams to cut costs. Many victims have simply dropped out of social media—a pernicious silencing of voices arising from the fear of inevitable harassment in the toxic discussions online. What better way to censor your critics?

As for reports to local police and other government agencies, almost all the subjects we interviewed said there was no follow-up. When they filed reports with the police, most didn't know how to respond so ended up doing nothing or advising subjects to turn to a private investigator. In some cases, victims chose not to file reports because they feared being deported. Some of the worst accounts came from individuals who lodged complaints with Canada's security and intelligence agency, CSIS, whose agents tried to recruit them as intelligence assets. Freed from the clutches of one spy agency, they would end up in the arms of another.

Kanimba consented to be interviewed as part of our project, and her stories aligned with what we heard from other victims. She was regularly threatened and harassed over social media and in numerous phone calls and unsolicited emails. Almost any time she tweeted something, trolls would descend with vicious slander and lies. One time, she was threatened on X by one of President Kagame's top advisors, saying she deserved a "golden machete"—a particularly cruel taunt because both her parents had been murdered in the Rwandan genocide in which the main tool of slaughter was the machete.[28]

These personal attacks typically escalated after Rwandan government officials gave speeches—for example at youth rallies—and fired up the online trolls. Pro-Kagame accounts photoshopped pictures of her to present her in a vulgar light. They dug through old images in her Instagram posts to try to embarrass and discredit her. When the images included her friends, they too were subjected to the same online harassment. "I don't think there's a single day that I could go on social media and not see something that attacks my character, my looks, a picture of me that is photoshopped," Kanimba told us, "and it takes a toll on me emotionally."

The precarious position of her father in Rwanda while serving his terrorism sentence was also used as a tool to intimidate and harass Kanimba. She recalled purchasing a clean phone, suspicious of surveillance on her other devices. One day a Rwandan official called her on that phone. When she asked how he found the number, he told her he got it from her father—but she hadn't given him that number. Obviously, the official was able to get it through some other means of unknown surveillance.

Kanimba also experienced physical stalking. "I went to a café to meet a friend who was in town from the US . . . we noticed two Rwandan government agents sitting at the table next to us." Belgian police warned her several times about this type of physical surveillance, but she was unclear what measures she should take to protect herself and her family. These experiences were deeply unsettling because Kagame had a track record of sending assassins to murder critics.

As Kanimba testified before the US Congress, she made a deep impression on the committee members. "Ms. Kanimba's experience should serve as a stark warning of the future that awaits us if countries and the private sector do not ban[d] together to act decisively to rein in foreign spyware companies," House committee chair Adam Schiff said.[29]

————

As if to validate her claims about the continual harassment she faced, almost immediately after her testimony aired, Rwandan trolls pounced like hyenas on Kanimba. Like other illiberal regimes, Kagame's Rwanda has gone all in on information operations aimed at subverting political opposition, ranging from hacking to human intelligence, to social media trolling, to outsourced dark PR campaigns and even targeted assassinations. Our interviews with Rwandan victims were full of stories about this type of harassment—sometimes crude, always cruel. Kanimba was no exception.

The outer layer of such campaigns are social media trolls with accounts seemingly cobbled together overnight. On first glance, they almost always appear amateur: few followers, spelling errors, and poor grammar. But dismissing them misses the point. With enough traction and reinforcement from local partisan media outlets, the disinformation starts to stick—and hurt. Trolls swarm in, some just cynical and spiteful hecklers along for the spectacle. In the algorithmically rage-driven universe of most social media platforms, it's all gas, no brakes.

For victims, the onslaught is difficult to ignore when they're tagged repeatedly for days on end, called names, and subjected to horrible smears and lies. The only alternative is to unplug and turn away, which may be the ultimate intent. The more victims drop their online engagement, the less effective they are in their advocacy. Kanimba's high moment testifying before the US Congress, streamed live before the world, was inevitably tarnished by the muck of toxic disinformation and online harassment that followed.

And then, as if on cue, and to the surprise of no one on our team, some familiar figures piled on. First came Jonathan Scott (aka Jonathan Villareal), the purveyor of seemingly endless nonsense aiming to discredit the work of the Citizen Lab and others in our space (chapter 16). He reached out privately to Kanimba, claiming he was a PhD student studying mercenary spyware and was interested in learning more about the forensic work on her phone. It wasn't the first time Scott had pulled this stunt: he had tried before with Ewa Wrzosek, the Polish prosecutor whose phone we determined was hacked (chapter 17). Wrzosek refused to cooperate with Scott after checking in with us, but Kanimba, not realizing his malicious intent, shared her material with him. He immediately used it in a vicious, mean-spirited online harassment campaign against her. He prepared yet another "white paper" with highly inaccurate, misleading, and confused technical details claiming to "prove" that Kanimba was not targeted with Pegasus.[30] He said the forensic analysis of her phone was really part of a "smear campaign" against Rwanda.

Next, to discredit and embarrass Kanimba, Scott tweeted screenshots of his private X and email conversations with her.[31] He tagged numerous Rwandan individuals on X, including Rwandan media as well as accounts believed to be linked with pro-government coordinated inauthentic activity. Scores of trolls pounced on his posts and amplified them further. They portrayed Amnesty International and the Citizen Lab as "frauds," and Scott threatened to call the FBI on us for "lying" to the US House Intelligence Committee. Meanwhile, he continually harassed Kanimba privately in messages she later shared with us.

Suspiciously, Rwandan government officials engaged with Scott's tweets, including the high commissioner for Rwanda to the United Kingdom. The director general of communication and partnership at the Rwandan Ministry of National Unity and Civic Engagement "liked" his posts. Scott himself said he was working in coordination with the Rwandan foreign ministry. In December 2023, Scott registered as a foreign agent, in accordance with the US Foreign Agents Registration Act, claiming he was doing work on behalf of the Rwandan government.[32] For supporting material, he attached a WhatsApp and a Twitter exchange with what appeared to be a job offer from a Rwanda National Police officer.[33] A review of that account showed the officer in question had previously visited

Russia for police training.[34] Things took a bizarre turn when the Rwanda National Police issued a press release disavowing Jonathan Scott's claims and distancing itself from him.[35] What remained unclear, however, was what a Russian-trained Rwanda National Police officer was doing connecting with such a disingenuous troll in the first place. A similar dynamic unfolded with Scott and claims about Morocco's abuse of spyware. He appeared in Rabat, Morocco, at a government-organized press conference to denounce Amnesty International and the Citizen Lab—later admitting, after being publicly questioned about it, that the government of Morocco paid for his expenses during his trip.[36]

More harassment against Kanimba ensued. Scott hosted an X Spaces session entitled "Facts: The Carine Kanimba False Positive Spyware Case & CatalanGate," which repeated his many false claims about Kanimba, with an added dose of conspiracy theories and false claims about our *CatalanGate* report.[37] They in turn activated Jose Javier Olivas Osuna, the pro-Spanish conspiracy theorist and author of numerous defamatory claims about the Citizen Lab and me (chapter 16). Olivas amplified Scott's false accusations and claims over social media numerous times.[38] Although Scott's "white papers" had been universally condemned by experts as lacking any credibility, Olivas retweeted links to them anyway. Their combined actions resulted in yet more pro-government Rwandan trolls directing their harassment against Kanimba—harassment that Olivas and Scott, in turn, then amplified. X did nothing, and observers who pointed to errors, such as the highly regarded independent digital security expert Runa Sandvik, were themselves subjected to misogynistic slurs from Olivas and Scott.[39] It was a disgusting turn of events.

And then to top it all off, a right-wing Israel-based newspaper, *Israel Hayom*, published a lengthy article promoting the widely discredited views of Olivas, Scott, and a third individual named Irina Zuckerman, who now goes by Irina Tsukerman.[40] That article openly denounced the Citizen Lab's research while attempting to exonerate NSO Group, portraying the company as a "victim" of a plot in which we are somehow central. The journalist reached out to me for comment only a couple of hours before his deadline. I wrote a detailed reply despite the short turnaround, but the journalist never published my remarks in the main article (and only a distorted excerpt in a preview), suggesting the intent was a hit piece.[41] The article contained defamatory statements that the Citizen Lab's research is financially supported by Qatar (which it is not), among other false claims.

Tsukerman then published a "white paper" of her own with an outlandish conspiracy theory suggesting that the Citizen Lab was part of a Russian-organized influence operation.[42] She produced a diagram resembling the map of an organized crime syndicate in which I was positioned in the center, with links between me and Glenn Greenwald, Edward Snowden, Julian Assange, and, to top it off, the Russian FSB, who were pulling the strings. Olivas and Scott have both claimed that the Lab, Amnesty, and others are part of an organized cartel in which I am the powerful "capo."[43] Astonishingly, the piece was picked up and broadcast on prime-time Polish state television under the conservative government, demonstrating how even the most ridiculous nonsense can gain traction in today's media ecosystem.[44]

It's hard to say what motivates these people. Scott appears to be obsessed with the Citizen Lab and Amnesty International. With each "white paper," he gathers a coterie of miscreants, like Olivas, who find his half-brained "reports" and "analyses" tactically useful. One of NSO Group's sales executives praised him for his "genuine, independent and bold perspective."[45] It feeds him the attention he desperately craves. Olivas and his MEP benefactor Jordi Cañas seem to lack any moral or ethical compass and will say or support anything to discredit the Lab, Amnesty International, and others because it serves their ulterior purpose to combat Catalan self-determination. They're Spanish nationalists.

Tsukerman, meanwhile, is a widely known merchant of propaganda who was permanently banned on Twitter (a ban she has falsely accused the Citizen Lab of engineering along with Qatar).[46] She trolled critics of Mohammed bin Salman when Jamal Khashoggi was executed and has routinely attacked researchers and investigative journalists who have outed Saudi wrongdoing. Her name has been linked to numerous lobbying efforts on behalf of foreign governments, suggesting that her motives are probably pecuniary.[47]

Is this harassment part of a coordinated campaign? Are the Spanish, Rwandan, Moroccan, and Saudi governments providing financial support? Is money being exchanged? Is NSO Group or its dark PR firms involved in some way? It's impossible to say without further evidence, which one day may materialize as part of an indictment for violation of the Foreign Agents Registration Act.

JUNE 2023

COSTA RICA

"Hello, Ron!" Carine Kanimba said with a wide smile, alongside her sister, Anaïse. Although we had communicated over Signal and video conference, we were meeting for the first time in person.

The sisters were beaming. Only a few months before, their father, Paul Rusesabagina, had been released from prison in Rwanda and was now safely back in the United States.[48] It was a rare success at the end of a long and tiring campaign.

The Lab had set up another booth, this time at RightsCon in San José, Costa Rica, to do spot checks on phones that might turn up fresh evidence of hacking. It was at one of these booths in Norway, a year before, that we discovered evidence of Pegasus infections on the phones of Carine Kanimba and her cousin Jean Paul.

"Want to get your phones checked?" I offered. While I walked her and Anaïse through the steps to generate bug reports from their devices, we reminisced about her appearance before the US House Permanent Select Committee on Intelligence. "You were amazing, a true hero," I told her. I explained we had watched it glued to the screen and cheered along with her testimony. "Do you realize the impact your testimony had?" I asked.

After those hearings, the US government passed the 2023 Intelligence Authorization Act.[49] In it were measures designed to focus the vast US intelligence apparatus on mercenary spyware firms such as NSO Group. The US government has also undertaken several broad initiatives that cut across several government agencies, designed to deal with the problem of digital transnational repression. The machinery of government was moving slowly toward creating a legal environment in which the harassment and spying she experienced would be criminalized.

"Anaïse, your phone is clean," said the Citizen Lab's Bahr Abdul Razzak, seated behind us, who was doing real-time forensic analysis on the device logs I had just obtained and sent over to him for analysis. "Carine, you're positive, but you know that already."

There was a momentary pause as we all tried to evaluate what Abdul Razzak meant. Carine was using a new phone, different from the one we'd previously checked. Was this a new infection?

"This is your old infection. It still shows up on your backup."

I watched as the two sisters walked away from the booth on their way to a keynote interview Carine was about to do on the main stage. I was thrilled to meet them in person and see their smiling faces. Brave people like them inspire us to do our job.

Fight the Future

SEPTEMBER 2023
SWEDEN

The Thirteenth Global Investigative Journalism Conference, held in Gothenburg, Sweden, in September 2023 was a perfect opportunity for another Citizen Lab spyware-checking booth. More than 2,100 investigative journalists from 132 countries attended the event—reportedly the largest gathering of its kind in history—and I was invited to deliver the keynote address. We knew many high-risk targets would be there, so the Citizen Lab's Bahr Abdul Razzak, Siena Anstis, and John Scott-Railton (JSR) accompanied me to staff the booth.

I opened my talk with a reference to our recent discovery, in collaboration with Access Now, that the device of exiled Russian investigative journalist Galina Timchenko had been infected with Pegasus spyware earlier that year. She was the cofounder, CEO, and publisher of Meduza, a prominent Russian independent media outlet that had been labeled "an undesirable organization" by the Kremlin, prompting the staff to move Meduza's operations to Latvia.[1] Our forensic analysis showed her phone was hacked one day before she was scheduled to attend a private meeting in Berlin with other exiled Russian independent media in Europe to discuss how to manage threats and censorship by Vladimir Putin's regime.[2]

As with many of our investigations, we found it challenging to prove who pulled the trigger. We could only make educated guesses. One obvious potential culprit was Russia, given Putin's hostility toward Meduza. However, it is highly unlikely that Russia is a client of NSO Group (Israel wouldn't allow it), and we had not seen any indications from our research to suggest it is (although one can never rule out Russian spies stealing Pegasus from NSO Group or one of its clients).[3] The hacking could have been undertaken by any number of European government security agencies armed with Pegasus. Latvia, Estonia, Germany, and the Netherlands were all known to be NSO Group customers, and it is conceivable that one of their intelligence services had decided to keep tabs on the exiled Russian journalist.[4] Some prominent European officials, including the president of the Czech Republic, Petr Pavel, had publicly stated that all Russians living in the West should be put under "strict surveillance" because of Russia's war against Ukraine, and Latvia had declared another Russian independent media organization, TV Rain, to be a "threat to the national security and public order"[5] and revoked its license.[6] Certain government operators of Pegasus allied with Russia, such as Azerbaijan or Kazakhstan, might also have been doing Putin's dirty work.[7] Europe was replete with poorly regulated intelligence agencies armed to the teeth with surveillance technology, so any of these scenarios was possible.

I reminded the assembled crowd of reporters why they were all potential targets and explained the risks of the latest "zero-click" versions of spyware: one minute you're fine, and the next your adversaries have all your notes and recordings, information on your confidential sources, advance knowledge of stories you are filing, and the ability to silently track your movements and turn on your camera and microphone at will. Their work inherently put them in the crosshairs of some dangerous, well-resourced despots and oligarchs. If anyone had reason to worry about spyware risks, it was the group assembled here.

The message seemed to sink in. Over the next several days, our booth was flooded with journalists looking to have their phones checked. It was like a roll call of abuse cases we had investigated over the previous decade, including reporters covering the Gulf and Middle East, Mexico, Indonesia, India, and numerous European countries—Armenia, Greece, Hungary, Poland, and Spain. Each conversation provided a window into a local story of corruption or abuse of power and the brave reporting that sought to uncover it all.

Early one morning, David Kaplan, the executive director of the Global Investigative Journalism Network and the host of the event, pulled me aside for an update. The event organizers had received a disturbing message threatening the lives of two exiled Russian journalists who had planned on participating in the conference, Alesya Marokhovskaya and Irina Dolinina. The message was unambiguous: "You know who to tell this to: they can't go to Gothenburg. Not even for a day. It's known where to look for them. Trust me."[8] Ominously, a second message followed containing precise details on the two journalists' flight information, seat numbers, hotel reservations, and hotel room numbers—the type of information likely available only to a well-resourced state intelligence agency. The conference ramped up security measures, and warnings went out to all participants to exercise extreme caution.

It wasn't the first reminder, nor would it be the last, that our world is a dangerously unpredictable place.

OCTOBER 7, 2023

The assault began at dawn with waves of rocket barrages into southern Israel.[9] Off-the-shelf, Chinese-manufactured quadcopter drones were then employed to drop explosives on towers along the border wall, disabling communications, surveillance, and automatic weapons installations. Bulldozers smashed through fences, making way for waves of heavily armed Hamas fighters to stream in. Fan-powered paragliders flew over barriers under the cover of rocket fire, bringing more of the same.[10] A bloody slaughter followed. Around 1,200 Israeli citizens and soldiers were massacred in their homes, at a music festival, on military bases, or driving through the streets.[11] Several hundred others, including numerous children, were taken hostage and spirited back to Gaza's vast network of tunnels.[12] Parts of the carnage were gruesomely filmed with GoPro cameras and streamed over Telegram channels.[13] It was by far the worst terrorist attack in Israel's history.

Despite its world-renowned surveillance capabilities and the asymmetric advantage it enjoys because of its extensive control over Palestinian infrastructure, the Israeli government was caught off guard.[14] Much like the September 11, 2001, terrorist attacks on the United States, the failure appears at least in part to be a human one. Numerous warnings were given to Israeli authorities that "something big" was about to happen, including from Egyptian and US intelligence agencies.[15] Personnel in Israel Defense Forces units tasked with monitoring Hamas's movements and preparations warned of an impending assault too.[16] But the warnings were ignored or minimized by those higher up the chain. For its part, Hamas had evolved improved operational security tactics, including communicating via hardwired phone lines embedded in the tunnels under Gaza, thereby evading Israel's advanced phone-hacking tools.[17] Although a full reckoning will come only after a formal investigation, it is likely that some of the blame will also be laid on the Netanyahu administration, distracted by the mounting investigations into its far-reaching corruption.[18]

The response to the terrorist attack was predictably brutal. The IDF unleashed a massive air and ground campaign that obliterated huge parts of the Gazan urban infrastructure, turning already impoverished areas into a rubble-filled, unlivable moonscape.[19] There have been extensive civilian casualties, at the time of writing rising to the tens of thousands.[20] As of August 2, 2024, investigations by the Committee to Protect Journalists showed that at least 113 journalists and media workers were among the multiple thousands killed.[21]

Although the IDF made a pretense to warn civilians and direct them into "safe zones," its military campaigns were widely condemned as excessive and deliberately targeting refugee camps, schools, and hospitals.[22] Senior Israeli officials used inflammatory, dehumanizing language to describe their actions, which prompted fears of how far they would go and what their ultimate objectives would be.[23] The South African government filed charges of genocide against the Israeli government in the International Court of Justice, and the court ruled that Israel must take steps to "prevent and punish incitement of genocidal acts" and "allow civilians access to humanitarian aid."[24] In May 2024, the chief prosecutor of the International Criminal Court (ICC) applied for arrest warrants for Israeli prime minister Benjamin Netanyahu and Hamas leader Yahya Sinwar, for war crimes and crimes against humanity.[25] That same month, a *Guardian* investigation described a decade-long covert hacking and surveillance campaign by Israeli intelligence against senior members of the ICC. The report alleged that the former head of the Mossad, Yossi Cohen, surreptitiously monitored an ICC chief prosecutor's family members and threatened the chief prosecutor during secret meetings unless the ICC abandoned its war crimes investigations.[26] It was an eerily familiar episode for us at the Lab, given our brush with Black Cube and our investigations into clandestine ops.

This entire conflict was a demoralizing relapse into yet another cycle of never-ending subterfuge, cruelty, violence, and death.

———

With the world in such turmoil, it's easy to overlook the progress against cyber espionage we have made. After years toiling alone, the Citizen Lab is now part of a growing community that is conducting the type of digital accountability investigations we pioneered. Our forensic methods are becoming more refined, allowing us to automate the process of checking crash logs for evidence of targeting and infections. Our technical capacity is growing as talented people gravitate to us—some of them leaving threat intelligence teams at the tech platforms to do so. As we unearth abuses in every region of the world, advocacy groups push for governments to act against the scourge.

Big tech platforms are also getting into the mix, some in a substantially positive way. Although we are definitely strange bedfellows, it is encouraging to see the abuses of the mercenary spyware industry squarely on the radar of almost all of the major tech companies now, including Google, Meta, WhatsApp, Apple, and others. Reports from their threat intelligence divisions outing bad actors, either in cooperation with us or on their own, are now fairly routine. Many of them include detailed indicators that help fuel our collective investigations while others root out the inauthentic accounts used in coordinated disinformation campaigns. Among these firms, Apple has gone the furthest since its 2021 announcement of a series of measures it would take against companies like NSO Group, precipitated by our ForcedEntry disclosure (chapter 14). The tech giant began routinely sending batches of notifications to users it determined had been either targeted or hacked.[27] In doing so, it is effectively triaging work for groups like ours. An Apple notification is proof of something tangible that warrants further investigation. Many users who receive these notifications make their way to us directly or to one of our partners, including Access Now's 24/7 Digital Security Helpline.[28] Others publicize that they have received them, and then we try to contact them for further investigation. The notifications and the follow-ups have led, in turn, to several blockbuster discoveries of yet more national espionage campaigns, including in El Salvador and Thailand.[29] Apple has also introduced an optional security feature intended for high-risk targets, Lockdown Mode, which reduces the attack surface (and some functionality) of their iPhones.[30] While somewhat inconvenient to use, we have yet to observe a victim's phone being hacked with the feature turned on.

On top of these measures, Apple has donated $10 million to set up a spyware accountability fund operated by an independent foundation.[31] The fund's purpose is to seed research, advocacy, and remedial efforts into spyware abuses. Other philanthropies and public interest groups soon followed with their own contributions.[32] Alongside representatives from Access Now, Amnesty International, and other organizations in the community, I was invited to serve on the fund's advisory board and helped to publicize it.[33] To avoid any conflict of interest, we were required to recuse ourselves from considerations of any potential funding for our respective organizations. A more diverse and distributed digital accountability network is about to blossom and spread, bringing yet more civil society watchdogs to the global arena.

Governments are beginning to act too, especially the United

States. In late 2021, the US Commerce Department added NSO Group, Candiru, and other firms to an official designated entity list, prohibiting them from undertaking business with US individuals and entities.[34] The sanctions are no magic solution to the harms of the mercenary spyware industry but, rather, a major source of irritation for the firms and their investors. Firms on the list become toxic brands, signaling they have crossed a line into inappropriate territory and lost the lucrative US market.

As the consequences of those sanctions were being felt by the industry, we published a report on yet another Israel-based mercenary spyware vendor, QuaDream.[35] We discovered several civil society victims whose phones had been hacked with QuaDream's exploits, and our network scanning showed its systems were being operated from Bulgaria, the Czech Republic, Ghana, Hungary, Israel, Mexico, Romania, Singapore, the United Arab Emirates, and Uzbekistan—another collection of flawed democracies, dictatorships, and corrupt regimes. When our report was published in April 2023, the company folded, explaining to journalists that the Citizen Lab's investigation was "the last nail in its coffin."[36] A few months later, the US Commerce Department added Intellexa and Cytrox, two more mercenary surveillance entities whose operations we had exposed, to its designated entity list.[37] Eventually, the US government imposed personal sanctions and visa restrictions as yet more punishments on those profiting from spyware abuses.[38]

Also in spring 2023 came a major blockbuster: the Biden administration passed an executive order that prohibits US federal agencies from procuring spyware if it can be shown "a foreign actor uses the commercial spyware against activists, dissidents, or other actors to intimidate; to curb dissent or political opposition; to otherwise limit freedoms of expression, peaceful assembly or association; or to enable other forms of human rights abuses or suppression of civil liberties."[39] The order also restricts operational use if a company sells spyware to a foreign government that is credibly reported to clamp down on dissent or engage in repression. In other words, you don't have to prove that a government is using the spyware to undertake inappropriate actions; it's enough to have proof that a firm sold spyware to a repressive regime that has a track record of human rights abuses.

The executive order was an epic loss for NSO Group and companies like it. For years they had been maneuvering to gain a toehold in the US market. A contract with any American government agency would not only legitimize their business with investors and other potential government clients around the world but would allow them to tap into almost endless pools of procurement contracts. There are eighteen federal intelligence agencies in the United States and thousands of law enforcement agencies at state and local levels, most with huge budgets for the latest spying gear. All, potentially, would be long-term customers with renewable licenses and costs scaled to target numbers. That dream had all but evaporated now.

To be sure, the executive order wasn't perfect. It didn't ban the use of spyware altogether—something many in our community had advocated. And it applied only to US federal agencies, not those operating at local and state levels. The order also did nothing to prevent US agencies from using spyware procured from a firm not on a designated entity list. A cynical take would be that the measures were introduced only out of self-interest, to preserve the US government's hegemony in digital surveillance. Innovation in this area would continue and would gradually seep into the broader global market through informal alliances or corporate partnerships. Spyware firms could also simply write off the US market, set up shop in friendly jurisdictions, and continue to earn revenues from the world's growing number of autocrats and despots. Or they could merely rebrand and seek to enter the American market in a different guise.

Still, this ruling was a big deal. To have the president of the United States sign an order using language that could have come straight out of one of our opinion pieces and targeting the exact problem we have been raising alarms about for years was a huge victory for the Citizen Lab, Amnesty International, Access Now, numerous investigative journalists, and the entire community of which we are a part. For me personally, as a trained political scientist, it was like capturing a professional holy grail. We knew that none of these restrictions would have been introduced if US intelligence agencies had not substantiated our technical findings behind closed doors. Even though we had no formal acknowledgement, it was enormously gratifying to realize that this sort of verification was done—that our reports were taken seriously and cross-checked at the highest possible levels by agents with access to all sorts of classified technology. My visit with JSR to the White House in December 2022 suddenly took on a deeper meaning: the senior official from the National Security Council had explained that the experts there had great respect for the work of the Citizen Lab.

In addition to the executive order, ten other governments signed on to a joint statement pledging to counter the proliferation and misuse of commercial spyware: Australia, Canada, Costa Rica, Denmark, France, New Zealand, Norway, Sweden, Switzerland, and the United Kingdom.[40] Not long after, an announcement was made at the 2024 Summit for Democracy that Finland, Germany, Ireland, Japan, Poland, and the Republic of Korea had joined the club.[41] Then Austria, Estonia, Lithuania, and the Netherlands announced they were joining the global regime too, bringing the number of countries pledging to uphold the initiative to twenty-one. Although the statement is merely words and many governments are not included in the pledge, the mere utterance of support for greater accountability around the sector was encouraging. The pledges now provided goalposts for us to measure against as well as commitments.

Then, in May 2024, Canada joined with the United Kingdom, the United States, Estonia, Japan, and Finland to issue an advisory warning on digital threats to civil society, adopting language almost identical to what we had been using for well over a decade to describe the risks around targeted digital espionage. The release even cited the Citizen Lab's reporting and advised those who may be targeted with spyware to reach out to Access Now's Digital Security Helpline.[42]

It was truly remarkable to witness a multilateral arms control regime emerging around spyware, considering the inspiration for the Lab's work came via my experiences in the 1990s observing the development of the International Monitoring System to monitor for nuclear tests. Who could have predicted back then that we would come so far?

Meanwhile in Europe, though progress was mixed overall, formal inquiries and commissions into spyware abuses were launched in Poland and Spain, respectively.[43] National elections in both countries led, in Poland, to a new regime under Donald Tusk and, in Spain, to a controversial coalition government in which Prime Minister Pedro Sánchez found himself forming an alliance with the Catalan independence parties his government had previously put under surveillance (chapter 16).[44] The Citizen Lab was invited to provide testimony to the Polish Senate (and, barring unforeseen developments, expects to receive invitations to inquiries in Madrid and Barcelona). I relished the opportunity to get the facts we had unearthed on formal public record in a way that might foster greater accountability and justice.

All these developments rattled the top firms in the mercenary spyware arena. NSO Group's stock value dropped precipitously.[45] The company soon found itself wallowing in at least $400 million in debt.[46] Competitors were circling around, and staff had reportedly begun to flee to competitors or other lines of business. Shalev Hulio stepped down as CEO, and the company began an embarrassing public spat with a private equity management fund that was issued a court order to manage the firm's finances and described NSO Group as essentially "valueless."[47] Responding to the US regulatory measures, the Israeli minister of defense began to scale back approvals for spyware export licenses.[48] The freewheeling days of arming dictators and despots seemed to be coming to an end—at least for the Israel-based companies.

Simultaneously, throughout 2023 the Netanyahu administration —widely viewed as supportive of the sector—found itself reeling from and distracted by daily protests.[49] The prime minister was embroiled in corruption scandals and, in 2019, was indicted for breach of trust, bribery, and fraud.[50] Netanyahu's government took steps to rein in the independence of the judiciary and impose government control over judicial appointments.[51] Tens of thousands of Israelis took to the streets every weekend to protest this dangerously undemocratic and patently corrupt move.

In my wildest dreams, I could never have imagined the Citizen Lab's mission to serve as "counterintelligence for civil society" would actually bring about the dismissal of heads of state intelligence, precipitate national scandals and special investigations in several jurisdictions, help find and patch software vulnerabilities that protect billions of internet users multiple times over, practically bankrupt billion-dollar firms, and trigger worldwide regulatory measures. The community of research and advocacy of which we are a part was starting to feel optimistic for the future. Light could be seen at the end of a long dark tunnel through which we had all journeyed together. A constellation of political forces seemed to be aligning in our favor.

Then came the events of October 7 and all that followed—a sobering reminder of the unpredictable nature of geopolitics and how quickly the currents can shift. As often in times of war and national security crises, Israeli citizens rallied around the government and its offensive against Hamas, at least in the short term. A December 2023 poll taken by the Israel Democracy Institute found two-thirds of Israelis didn't think the military should scale back its bombardment of populated areas in Gaza, despite mounting civilian casualties.[52] Criticism of the government's actions was equated with disloyalty and even racism.[53] The ultranationalist right-wing factions with which Netanyahu had aligned himself were now pushing hard for extreme actions against Palestinians, including proposing the resettlement of Gaza.[54] Eventually the conflict spread to Lebanon and Iran, risking a wider regional war.

NSO Group quickly jumped on the crisis to pitch its product as a potential tool for finding hostages, conveniently ignoring the fact that they were being held underground in tunnels without reception and almost certainly no longer had their mobile phones. Hulio used the opportunity to raise millions in investments for a new start-up, Dream Security, which he claimed would be used only for "defensive purposes."[55] He made the announcement while wearing military fatigues, with an assault rifle strung across his shoulder.[56] (Another cofounder of Dream, Sebastian Kurz, is on trial in Austria for perjury.)[57] NSO Group pressed the US government to have its sanctions lifted, contracting several high-priced DC-based law firms, PR companies, and lobbyists to approach lawmakers in the US Congress.[58] It passed around copies of yet another "human rights due diligence framework," which soon proved to be worthless when, a few weeks later, Access Now, working with the Citizen Lab and Amnesty International, discovered that Pegasus had been used to hack into the phones of dozens of Jordanian journalists and activists.[59]

Although NSO Group was embroiled in numerous lawsuits around the world, it wasn't all bad news for the firm. A California judge dismissed the suit brought against NSO Group by the journalists working for *El Faro* for jurisdictional reasons (a ruling that, at the time of writing, they intend to appeal). And then in September 2024, Apple announced it was withdrawing its lawsuit against NSO Group, citing concerns that their sensitive threat intelligence methodology, used to hunt for spyware infections and alert innocent victims, could not be protected in the discovery process and might end up helping firms like NSO Group circumvent Apple's measures and hide their tracks. These concerns were legitimate: Apple cited a *Guardian* investigation showing that the Israeli government had been colluding with NSO Group's lawyers in the US litigation cases—surreptitiously accessing legal documents marked "attorney's eyes only" and forbidding NSO Group from sharing its own internal materials in the process.[60]

We had anticipated that the firm and its lawyers would attempt to undermine our work with "lawfare," using legal interventions to try to damage us. Sure enough, they embarked on a full-scale fishing expedition. As part of the discovery process in the WhatsApp case, NSO's lawyers served a subpoena to our senior researcher Bill Marczak, who lives in California. It tried to do the same for John Scott-Railton (JSR) but had difficulties locating him. An affidavit filed in the court proceedings showed that NSO Group had retained the services of licensed investigator Dan Whelan, "a Special Agent of the United States Federal Bureau of Investigation for 25 years."[61] Whelan testified that among the unsuccessful attempts to serve a writ to JSR, he arranged for a colleague from his team to park outside an address they discovered was once associated with JSR and run the plates of all the vehicles parked there. He also described using "other investigative techniques," though ominously didn't elaborate on what those might have entailed. The disclosure that a private investigator was hired by NSO Group's counsel to do this type of personal tracking was an eye-opener, in light of our prior experiences being subjected to a covert op.

Finding me proved challenging too, though in a different way. To issue a subpoena in Canada from the United States requires going through a complicated and lengthy jurisdictional process called "letters rogatory." So NSO lawyers took a flier and sent a request to me and the Citizen Lab's senior legal advisor, Siena Anstis, directly asking whether we would "spare the relevant courts and interested parties the burdens associated with that process and . . . agree to provide the requested documents and witness testimony voluntarily." Naturally, we declined to do so, referring them to our lawyers for all future communications. NSO's counsel then filed a letters rogatory request, which demanded we turn over, as part of discovery, information and communications that went far beyond our role in the WhatsApp case. It included "related investigations Citizen Lab has undertaken concerning NSO, Pegasus, [and] individuals allegedly targeted using Pegasus." In other words, NSO's lawyers were hoping to find out details of our closely held forensic methodologies used to detect Pegasus and highly sensitive details on victims whose identities we are obliged to protect. How convenient for them that would be. Our lawyers filed a vigorous rebuttal arguing that "the consequences of permitting NSO's overreach are grave."[62] Fortunately the judge saw their attempts for what they were and dismissed them summarily. However, the experience was a clear lesson in the potential risks of litigation for a group like ours and the imperative to have seasoned legal counsel.

The drama around the litigation is also an important reminder: while we can claim impressive victories related to our work, it is impossible to deny the dark forces that continue to build and threaten to overturn them. There is no doubt that spaces for civil society are shrinking daily as despotism continues to thrive and spread worldwide. There are major armed conflicts in the Middle East and in the heart of Europe that show no signs of abating, gnawing humanitarian crises in failed states like Haiti and Sudan, and omnipresent risks of nuclear war. Dictators, like Putin, are becoming more aggressive, risking the normalization of assassinations and violations of other international norms. To top it all off, Donald Trump, a convicted felon who faces dozens of indictments in several ongoing criminal investigations, has stunned the world by being reelected as the forty-seventh president of the United States.[63] There is no varnishing it: his victory is an unmitigated disaster for human rights and the rule of law and a major victory for like-minded authoritarians across the globe. At the time of writing, he has yet to be sworn into office. However, his administration's plans include quashing those criminal investigations and retaliating against his political adversaries and journalists with a vengeance. There is now a very real prospect of a fascist dictatorship taking root in the world's greatest superpower. All of the progress that has been made in the United States combating transnational repression and regulating spyware abuses is now at risk of reversal too—a terrible omen for human security the world over.

Meanwhile, the mercenary spyware industry appears poised to enter a new and dangerous phase. Reports indicate a migration of companies and talent away from Israel, seeking jurisdictions with less stringent oversight than even that provided by the Israeli Ministry of Defense and unbound by burgeoning spyware regulations enacted by like-minded governments. New firms untainted by associations with the NSO Groups of the world have established operations in European locales, eager for the prestige and legitimacy of being based in the region.[64] Other ventures are taking off in the Gulf, lured by the lavish incentives and huge investments bestowed by the region's oligarchs and ruling families.[65] These firms will adapt, learning from the experiences of the past ten years to avoid publicity and operate under the radar as much as possible.

To add to the mix, new AI-enabled tools are proliferating, making the art and practice of subversion cheaper and more effective.

Dozens of companies now openly offer a new kind of machine-enabled dark PR for any paying client. Authentic-looking synthetic images, videos, and audio recordings are flooding the infosphere, pushing disinformation, overwhelming fact-checkers, and silencing dissent—a despot's dream. A ceaseless torrent of information derived from data-sucking apps now floods through an almost entirely unregulated and opaque market of firms selling advertising intelligence ("ADINT" in industry parlance) tailored to government security agencies. Highly detailed dossiers on targets can be compiled in real time, thanks to the digital exhaust around surveillance capitalism: precise information on residences, places of work, friends, interests, movements—all served up on a platter to ruthless, vindictive spies and the autocrats they serve.

It is daunting to contemplate the future, considering the deteriorating political condition and the numerous weapons in the arsenal of those who conduct digital transnational repression. Sometimes it feels like the walls are closing in and the ever-present risks are magnifying to the point where the Lab's very existence may be in jeopardy. But I worry less about those risks now that the community of digital accountability research and advocacy has grown and matured. Our collective efforts go far beyond any individual or organization. We truly are a global movement, and our resilience grows daily. It is our collective mission to push back against tyrants and to resist the tidal wave of despotism with rigorous, evidence-based public interest research. The future may be bleak, but who's to say you cannot fight the future?

————

"Hello, Ron, how are you doing? It's been a while. I hope you are doing well. I don't know what to tell you, but I think I have been hacked again. How could I check that out?"

It was early and the coffee had not yet hit the bloodstream, so I was still bleary-eyed when the message from Omar Abdulaziz came in.

Since learning from us that his device had been hacked with Pegasus by Saudi operators and that the surveillance of his communications may have contributed to the execution of his friend and colleague Jamal Khashoggi, Abdulaziz had been in high demand (chapter 5). Researchers were keen to get in touch with him. Law enforcement and intelligence agencies in Canada and elsewhere wanted to learn more about his targeting. And journalists all over the world wanted his compelling story.

Abdulaziz was generous with the interviews. He was featured on CNN and other platforms and even in a major film, *The Dissident*, directed by Bryan Fogel.[66] Abdulaziz spent time with the production team and hoped the film would have an impact on the plight of people like him, but distribution proved to be difficult. Despite Fogel's Academy Award–winning résumé, distributors initially balked at taking the film, fearful it would offend the Saudi regime. Eventually, after an independent streaming service accepted it, Apple picked it up. But the politics around the film's distribution was a reminder of the intrigue that accompanied anything to do with the Saudi regime.

In that film, and in his various media appearances, Abdulaziz relived in detail the discovery of the hacking, the personal conversations he'd had with Khashoggi leading up to his murder, the Saudi-paid trolls that harassed him on social media, and the impact they had on his personal life and activism. The whole affair weighed heavily on Abdulaziz. Although he continued his criticism of the Saudi regime on social media, he realized he could be the next victim, and he often disappeared for long periods. Journalists looking to contact him sometimes reached out to me asking for help. I realized Abdulaziz's emotional scars were deep—an often overlooked consequence of the type of spying we were documenting.

"Hi, Omar," I replied after moving him to a more secure means of communication. "I'm sorry to hear you think you've been hacked. We can check it out for you. Did something suspicious occur?"

Abdulaziz told me three of his friends with whom he was in regular communication over the internet had just been arrested in Saudi Arabia. He wondered whether their arrests had anything to do with his phone being under surveillance again.

I included Bahr Abdul Razzak on the call, and we instructed Abdulaziz on how to pull logs from his phones. They all came back negative, and we recommended that we also check his circle of friends and associates. Eventually, all their logs came back negative too.

These types of null results get far less attention than the published reports unearthing espionage, but they happen much more frequently. They are just as rewarding as the flashy news coverage, although few people outside the Lab hear about them. For a few minutes, you are giving victims a little relief.

Abdulaziz reacted with a heart emoji, and we bid each other goodbye.

By the time the analysis on Abdulaziz's phone was done, it was late in the evening in the Lab and I was the only person still there. I looked around at desks full of notepads, assorted pieces of equipment, and other evidence of recent activity. I thought about how lucky I was to be surrounded by many talented and dedicated people. Every day, an exciting new adventure surfaces—adventures that help save lives.

Suddenly, I felt a vibration in my pocket—an encrypted message from JSR.

"Got a second?" he wrote. "I think I've come across something huge . . ."

Here we go again.

Notes

A curated archive of sources for *Chasing Shadows* can be found at https://chasingshadowsbook.ca

THE WHITE HOUSE

1 US Department of Commerce, "Commerce Adds NSO Group and Other Foreign Companies to Entity List for Malicious Cyber Activities," press release, November 9, 2021, https://www.commerce.gov/news/press-releases/2021/11/commerce-adds-nso-group-and-other-foreign-companies-entity-list.

2 Adam Schiff, "Wyden, Schiff, Meeks and Maloney Lead House and Senate Democrats in Calling for Magnitsky Act Sanctions against Companies That Enable Human Rights Abuses," press release, December 15, 2021, https://schiff.house.gov/news/press-releases/wyden-schiff-meeks-and-maloney-lead-house-and-senate-democrats-in-calling-for-magnitsky-act-sanctions-against-companies-that-enable-human-rights-abuses.

3 US House of Representatives Permanent Select Committee on Intelligence, "Full Committee Hearing—Combatting the Threats to U.S. National Security from the Proliferation of Foreign Commercial Spyware," accessed May 29, 2024, https://docs.house.gov/Committee/Calendar/ByEvent.aspx?EventID=115048.

4 Carine Kanimba, "Statement of Carine Kanimba," US House of Representatives Permanent Select Committee on Intelligence, July 27, 2022, https://docs.house.gov/meetings/IG/IG00/20220727/115048/HHRG-117-IG00-Wstate-KanimbaC-20220727.pdf.

5 Mehul Srivastava and Kaye Wiggins, "Israel's NSO Bets Its Future on Netanyahu's Comeback," *Financial Times*, December 6, 2022, https://www.ft.com/content/88379bcd-2d99-427f-86e1-bcc841cb609f.

CHAPTER 1: A NEAR-PERFECT HACK

1 Simon Kemp, "Digital 2023 October Global Statshot Report," DataReportal, October 19, 2023, www.datareportal.com/reports/digital-2023-october-global-statshot.

2 Ronen Bergman and Mark Mazzetti, "The Battle for the World's Most Powerful Cyberweapon," *New York Times*, January 28, 2022, www.nytimes.com/2022/01/28/magazine/nso-group-israel-spyware.html.

3 Ronen Bergman and Mark Mazzetti, "Israeli Companies Aided Saudi Spying

Despite Khashoggi Killing," *New York Times*, July 17, 2021, www.nytimes.com/2021 /07/17/world/middleeast/israel-saudi-khashoggi-hacking-nso.html; Drew Harwell, "Dubai Ruler Used Pegasus Spyware to Hack Princess's Phone, U.K. Court Rules," *Washington Post*, October 6, 2021, www.washingtonpost.com/technology/2021 /10/06/pegasus-dubai-princess-haya-court-ruling/; Natalie Kitroeff and Ronen Bergman, "How Mexico Became the Biggest User of the World's Most Notorious Spy Tool," *New York Times*, April 18, 2023, www.nytimes.com/2023/04/18/world /americas/pegasus-spyware-mexico.html.

4 Raphael Satter, "Undercover Spy Exposed in NYC Was 1 of Many," Associated Press, February 11, 2019, www.apnews.com/general-news-9bdbbfe0c8a2407aac14a 1e995659de4.

5 Ronen Bergman and Patrick Kingsley, "Despite Abuses of NSO Spyware, Israel Will Lobby U.S. to Defend It," *New York Times*, November 8, 2021, www.nytimes .com/2021/11/08/world/middleeast/nso-israel-palestinians-spyware.html.

6 Alex Kane, "How Israel Became a Hub for Surveillance Technology," *Intercept*, October 17, 2016, www.theintercept.com/2016/10/17/how-israel-became-a-hub -for-surveillance-technology/.

7 Patrick Howell O'Neill, "Israeli Hacking Company NSO Group Is on Sale for More Than $1 Billion," CyberScoop, June 12, 2017, www.cyberscoop.com/nso -group-for-sale-1-billion-pegasus-malware/; Yasmin Yablonko, "Novalpina Capital and Founders Buy NSO at $1b Co Value," Globes, February 14, 2019, en.globes.co .il/en/article-novalpina-capital-and-founders-buy-nso-for-1b-1001273312.

8 Jeremy Herb, Katelyn Polantz, Evan Perez, and Marshall Cohen, "Flynn Pleads Guilty to Lying to FBI, Is Cooperating with Mueller," CNN, December 1, 2017, www.cnn.com/2017/12/01/politics/michael-flynn-charged/index.html; "Michael Flynn: Trump Pardons Ex–National Security Adviser," BBC, November 25, 2020, www.bbc.com/news/world-us-canada-55080923.

9 Ryan Johnston, "How Michael Flynn Helped Cybersecurity Firms before His White House Stint," CyberScoop, June 19, 2017, cyberscoop.com/flynn-dabbled -private-sector-government-appointment-form-shows/.

10 Adam Entous, Greg Miller, Kevin Sieff, and Karen DeYoung, "Blackwater Founder Held Secret Seychelles Meeting to Establish Trump-Putin Back Channel," *Washington Post*, April 3, 2017, www.washingtonpost.com/world/national-security/black water-founder-held-secret-seychelles-meeting-to-establish-trump-putin-back -channel/2017/04/03/95908a08-1648-11e7-ada0-1489b735b3a3_story.html; "Mueller Report Findings: Mueller Rejects Argument That Trump Is Shielded from Obstruction Laws," *Washington Post*, April 18, 2019, https://www.washingtonpost .com/politics/mueller-report-russia-investigation-findings/2019/04/18/b07f4310 -56f9-11e9-814f-e2f46684196e_story.html; Robert S. Mueller III, *Report on the Investigation into Russian Interference in the 2016 Presidential Election*, vol. 1 (Washington, DC: US Department of Justice, March 2019), https://www.justice. gov/archives/sco/file/1373816/dl; Erin Banco, "Mueller Exposes Erik Prince's Lies about His Rendezvous with a Top Russian," *Daily Beast*, April 18, 2019, https://www.thedailybeast.com/mueller-exposes-erik-princes-lies-about-his -seychelles-rendezvous-with-top-russian-kirill-dmitriev.

11 Wendy Siegelman, "Eitanium Ltd Chart: Erik Prince and Directors and Their Network of Cyber Surveillance Related Companies," Medium, March 21, 2021, wsiegelman.medium.com/eitanium-ltd-chart-erik-prince-and-directors-and-their-network-of-cyber-surveillance-and-related-16e6b28c0379.

12 Amnesty International, "Pegasus Project: Rwandan Authorities Chose Thousands of Activists, Journalists and Politicians to Target with NSO Spyware," press release, July 19, 2021, www.amnesty.org/en/latest/press-release/2021/07/rwandan-authorities-chose-thousands-of-activists-journalists-and-politicians-to-target-with-nso-spyware/; Julian E. Barnes and David E. Sanger, "Saudi Crown Prince Is Held Responsible for Khashoggi Killing in U.S. Report," *New York Times*, February 26, 2021, www.nytimes.com/2021/02/26/us/politics/jamal-khashoggi-killing-cia-report.html; Bill Marczak and John Scott-Railton, *The Million Dollar Dissident: NSO Group's iPhone Zero-Days Used against a UAE Human Rights Defender*, Research Report No. 78, Citizen Lab, University of Toronto, August 24, 2016, www.citizenlab.ca/2016/08/million-dollar-dissident-iphone-zero-day-nso-group-uae/.

13 Emma Graham-Harrison, "Missing Emirati Princess 'Planned Escape for Seven Years,'" *Guardian*, December 4, 2018, www.theguardian.com/world/2018/dec/04/missing-emirati-princess-latifa-al-maktoum-had-planned-escape-for-seven-years.

14 Shane Huntley, "Buying Spying: How the Commercial Surveillance Industry Works and What Can Be Done about It," Google Threat Analysis Group, February 6, 2024, https://blog.google/threat-analysis-group/commercial-surveillance-vendors-google-tag-report/.

15 "FSB Team of Chemical Weapon Experts Implicated in Alexey Navalny Novichok Poisoning," Bellingcat, December 14, 2020, www.bellingcat.com/news/uk-and-europe/2020/12/14/fsb-team-of-chemical-weapon-experts-implicated-in-alexey-navalny-novichok-poisoning/.

16 Andy Greenberg, "Signal Is Finally Bringing Its Secure Messaging to the Masses," *Wired*, February 14, 2020, www.wired.com/story/signal-encrypted-messaging-features-mainstream/.

17 Bill Marczak, John Scott-Railton, Sarah McKune, Bahr Abdul Razzak, and Ron Deibert, *Hide and Seek: Tracking NSO Group's Pegasus Spyware to Operations in 45 Countries*, Research Report No. 113, Citizen Lab, University of Toronto, September 18, 2018, www.citizenlab.ca/2018/09/hide-and-seek-tracking-nso-groups-pegasus-spyware-to-operations-in-45-countries/; "Azerbaijan Suspected of Spying on Reporters, Activists by Using Software to Access Phones," Radio Free Europe/Radio Liberty, July 18, 2021, www.rferl.org/a/azerbaijan-pegasus-spying-nso/31365076.html.

18 Raeesa Pather, "The Botched Investigation into Rwanda's Murdered Spy Chief," *Mail & Guardian*, January 25, 2019, www.mg.co.za/article/2019-01-25-00-murdered-spy-boss-probe-botched/.

19 John Scott-Railton, Siena Anstis, Sharly Chan, Bill Marczak, and Ron Deibert, *Nothing Sacred: Religious and Secular Voices for Reform in Togo Targeted with NSO Spyware*, Research Report No. 129, Citizen Lab, University of Toronto, August 3, 2020, www.citizenlab.ca/2020/08/nothing-sacred-nso-sypware-in-togo/.

20 John Scott-Railton, Elies Campo, Bill Marczak, Bahr Abdul Razzak, Siena Anstis,

Gözde Böcü, Salvatore Solimano, and Ron Deibert, *CatalanGate: Extensive Mercenary Spyware Operation against Catalans Using Pegasus and Candiru*, Research Report No. 155, Citizen Lab, University of Toronto, April 18, 2022, www.citizenlab.ca /2022/04/catalangate-extensive-mercenary-spyware-operation-against-catalans -using-pegasus-candiru/.

21 "Read the WhatsApp Complaint against NSO Group," *Washington Post*, October 29, 2019, www.washingtonpost.com/context/read-the-whatsapp-complaint-against -nso-group/abc0fb24-8090-447f-8493-1e05b2fc1156/.

22 Will Cathcart, "Why WhatsApp Is Pushing Back on NSO Group Hacking," *Washington Post*, October 29, 2019, www.washingtonpost.com/opinions/2019/10/29/why -whatsapp-is-pushing-back-nso-group-hacking/.

CHAPTER 2: HUNTING A STEALTH FALCON

1 "UAE: Investigate Threats against 'UAE 5,'" Human Rights Watch, November 25, 2011, www.hrw.org/news/2011/11/25/uae-investigate-threats-against-uae-5.

2 Juhie Bhatia, "Journalist's Tweets Give Voice to Libya Uprisings," Women's eNews, March 22, 2011, www.womensenews.org/2011/03/journalists-tweets-give-voice-libya -uprisings/.

3 Marc Owen Jones, "Social Media Fuelled the Arab Spring, then Helped Dictators Quash It," *New Arab*, January 12, 2021, www.newarab.com/opinion/tech-fuelled -arab-spring-then-helped-quash-it.

4 Cora Currier and Morgan Marquis-Boire, "Leaked Files: German Spy Company Helped Bahrain Hack Arab Spring Protesters," *Intercept*, August 7, 2014, www .theintercept.com/2014/08/07/leaked-files-german-spy-company-helped-bahrain -track-arab-spring-protesters/.

5 Marwa Fatafta, "From Free Space to a Tool of Oppression: What Happened to the Internet since the Arab Spring?," Tahrir Institute for Middle East Policy, December 17, 2020, www.timep.org/2020/12/17/from-free-space-to-a-tool-of -oppression-what-happened-to-the-internet-since-the-arab-spring/.

6 "How BAE Sold Cyber-Surveillance Tools to Arab States," BBC, June 14, 2017, www .bbc.com/news/world-middle-east-40276568; Ronen Bergman and Mark Mazzetti, "The Battle for the World's Most Powerful Cyberweapon," *New York Times*, January 28, 2022, www.nytimes.com/2022/01/28/magazine/nso-group-israel-spyware.html.

7 Ian Black and Sarah Carr, "Egyptians Prise Open Secrets of Hosni Mubarak's State Security Headquarters," *Guardian*, March 7, 2011, www.theguardian.com/world /2011/mar/07/egypt-state-security-mubarak-cairo.

8 Karen McVeigh, "British Firm Offered Spying Software to Egyptian Regime— Documents," *Guardian*, April 28, 2011, www.theguardian.com/technology/2011/apr /28/egypt-spying-software-gamma-finfisher.

9 Ramy Raoof, "Egypt: How Companies Help the Government Spy on Activists," Global Voices Advox, May 7, 2011, advox.globalvoices.org/2011/05/07/egypt-how-com panies-help-the-government-spy-on-activists/; David Pegg, "Bahraini Arab Spring Dissidents Sue UK Spyware Maker," *Guardian*, October 11, 2018, www.theguardian .com/world/2018/oct/11/bahraini-arab-spring-dissidents-sue-uk-spyware-maker.

10 "The Spy Files," WikiLeaks, December 1, 2011, www.wikileaks.org/spyfiles/list
    /releasedate/2011-12-08.html.

11 Vernon Silver, "Cyber Attacks on Activists Traced to FinFisher Spyware of Gamma,"
    Bloomberg, July 25, 2012, www.bloomberg.com/news/articles/2012-07-25/cyber
    -attacks-on-activists-traced-to-finfisher-spyware-of-gamma.

12 Morgan Marquis-Boire and Bill Marczak, *From Bahrain with Love: FinFisher's Spy Kit
    Exposed?*, Research Report No. 9, Citizen Lab, University of Toronto, July 25, 2012,
    www.citizenlab.ca/2012/07/from-bahrain-with-love-finfishers-spy-kit-exposed/.

13 Morgan Marquis-Boire, *Backdoors Are Forever: Hacking Team and the Targeting of
    Dissent?*, Research Report No. 12, Citizen Lab, University of Toronto, October
    10, 2012, www.citizenlab.ca/2012/10/backdoors-are-forever-hacking-team-and
    -the-targeting-of-dissent/.

14 Tu Thanh Ha, "Middle Eastern Activists Being Cyber-Spied On: U of T Report,"
    Globe and Mail, October 10, 2012, www.theglobeandmail.com/news/world/middle
    -eastern-activists-being-cyber-spied-on-u-of-t-report/article4601322/.

15 Nicole Perlroth, "Ahead of Spyware Conference, More Evidence of Abuse," *New
    York Times*, October 10, 2012, archive.nytimes.com/bits.blogs.nytimes.com/2012
    /10/10/ahead-of-spyware-conference-more-evidence-of-abuse/.

16 Bill Marczak and John Scott-Railton, *Keep Calm and (Don't) Enable Macros: A New
    Threat Actor Targets UAE Dissidents*, Research Report No. 75, Citizen Lab, Univer-
    sity of Toronto, May 29, 2016, www.citizenlab.ca/2016/05/stealth-falcon/.

17 Bryan Burrough, "How a Grad Student Found Spyware That Could Control
    Anybody's iPhone from Anywhere in the World," *Vanity Fair*, November 28, 2016,
    www.vanityfair.com/news/2016/11/how-bill-marczak-spyware-can-control-the
    -iphone.

18 Bill Marczak and John Scott-Railton, *The Million Dollar Dissident: NSO Group's
    iPhone Zero-Days Used against a UAE Human Rights Defender*, Research Report No.
    78, Citizen Lab, University of Toronto, August 24, 2016, www.citizenlab.ca/2016/08
    /million-dollar-dissident-iphone-zero-day-nso-group-uae/.

19 Nicole Perlroth, "iPhone Users Urged to Update Software after Security Flaws
    Are Found," *New York Times*, August 25, 2016, www.nytimes.com/2016/08/26
    /technology/apple-software-vulnerability-ios-patch.html.

CHAPTER 3: ALOHA FROM HAWAII

1 PowerfulJRE, "Joe Rogan Experience #1536—Edward Snowden," September 15,
   2020, video, 2:28:39, www.youtube.com/watch?v=_Rl82OQDoOc; Citizen Lab
   (@citizenlab), "Have you heard about us on @joerogan thx to @Snowden? youtu
   .be/_Rl82OQDoOc Check out Security Planner! Gives hints on how to make
   your online experience more secure: securityplanner.org. Also see our friends @
   EFF's surveillance self-defence guide t.co/eYe7EZFpKC," X, September 15, 2020,
   https://x.com/citizenlab/status/1306013241483685893.

2 Christopher Bing and Joel Schectman, "Inside the UAE's Secret Hacking Team of
   American Mercenaries," Reuters, January 30, 2019, www.reuters.com/investigates
   /special-report/usa-spying-raven/.

3	Jill Ann Crystal and J.E. Peterson, "United Arab Emirates," *Encyclopedia Britannica*, February 4, 2024, www.britannica.com/place/United-Arab-Emirates.

4	Maggie Michael and Michael Hudson, "Pandora Papers Reveal Emirati Royal Families' Role in Secret Money Flows," International Consortium of Investigative Journalists, November 16, 2021, www.icij.org/investigations/pandora-papers/pandora-papers-reveal-emirati-royal-families-role-in-secret-money-flows/.

5	"The UAE Defense Market—Budget Assessment and Drivers 2022," GlobalData, February 21, 2022, www.globaldata.com/reports/the-uae-defense-market—budget-assessment-and-drivers-2022/; "Military Expenditure (Current USD)," World Bank Group, accessed February 4, 2024, https://data.worldbank.org/indicator/MS.MIL.XPND.CD?skipRedirection=true&view=map.

6	Rajiv Chandrasekaran, "In the UAE, the United States Has a Quiet, Potent Ally Nicknamed 'Little Sparta,'" *Washington Post*, November 9, 2014, www.washingtonpost.com/world/national-security/in-the-uae-the-united-states-has-a-quiet-potent-ally-nicknamed-little-sparta/2014/11/08/3fc6a50c-643a-11e4-836c-83bc4f26eb67_story.html.

7	Craig Whitlock and Nate Jones, "UAE Relied on Expertise of Retired U.S. Troops to Beef Up Its Military," *Washington Post*, October 18, 2022, www.washingtonpost.com/investigations/interactive/2022/uae-military-us-veterans/.

8	Jonathan Swan, Kate Kelly, Maggie Haberman, and Mark Mazzetti, "Kushner Firm Got Hundreds of Millions from 2 Persian Gulf Nations," *New York Times*, March 30, 2023, www.nytimes.com/2023/03/30/us/politics/jared-kushner-qatar-united-arab-emirates.html.

9	Matthew Cole, "The Complete Mercenary: How Erik Prince Used the Rise of Trump to Make an Improbable Comeback," *Intercept*, May 3, 2019, theintercept.com/2019/05/03/erik-prince-trump-uae-project-veritas/.

10	Patricia Hurtado and David Voreacos, "'Trump Is the Man': Barrack Touted Friendship to UAE in 2016," *Bloomberg*, September 29, 2022, www.bloomberg.com/news/articles/2022-09-29/-trump-is-the-man-barrack-touted-his-friendship-to-uae-in-2016.

11	Matthew Cole, "UAE Adviser Illegally Funneled Foreign Cash into Hillary Clinton's 2016 Campaign," *Intercept*, January 16, 2022, theintercept.com/2022/01/16/uae-2016-election-trump-clinton-george-nader/.

12	Devon Pendelton, Ben Bartenstein, Farah Elbahrawy, and Nicolas Parasie, "Secretive Gulf Family's $300 Billion Fortune Is about More than Oil," *Bloomberg*, December 6, 2022, www.bloomberg.com/features/2022-worlds-richest-family-abu-dhabi-royals-al-nahyans/.

13	Simeon Kerr and Andrew England, "The Abu Dhabi Royal at the Nexus of UAE Business and National Security," *Financial Times*, January 24, 2021, www.ft.com/content/ce09911b-041d-4651-9bbb-d2a16d39ede7; Bill Marczak, "A Breej Too Far: How Abu Dhabi's Spy Sheikh Hid His Chat App in Plain Sight," Medium, January 2, 2020, www.medium.com/@billmarczak/how-tahnoon-bin-zayed-hid-totok-in-plain-sight-group-42-breej-4e6c06c93ba6; "Former Senai Exec Roy Shloman Blossoms in Israeli Cyber," *Intelligence Online*, June 8, 2023, www.intelligenceonline.com/surveillance—interception/2023/06/08/former-senai-exec-roy-shloman-blossoms

-in-israeli-cyber,109991921-art; "UAE Cyber-Offensive Firm Beacon Red's Russian Hackers Disillusioned," *Intelligence Online*, May 18, 2023, www.intelligenceonline .com/surveillance—interception/2023/05/18/uae-cyber-offensive-firm-beacon-red -s-russian-hackers-disillusioned,109975806-art.

14 Noa Landau and the Associated Press, "UAE Issues Decree Ending Israel Boycott after U.S-Brokered Deal to Normalize Ties," *Haaretz*, August 29, 2020, www .haaretz.com/israel-news/2020-08-29/ty-article/uae-issues-decree-ending-israel -boycott-after-u-s-brokered-deal-to-normalize-ties/0000017f-e7d7-da9b-a1ff -efff118a0000.

15 "Full Text of the Abraham Accords and Agreements between Israel and the United Arab Emirates/Bahrain," CNN, September 15, 2020, www.cnn.com/2020/09/15 /politics/israel-uae-abraham-accords-documents/index.html; Sean Gallagher, "UAE Buys Its Way toward Supremacy in Gulf Cyberwar, Using US and Israeli Experts," *Ars Technica*, February 1, 2019, arstechnica.com/information-technology/2019/02/uae -buys-its-way-toward-supremacy-in-gulf-cyberwar-using-us-and-israeli-experts/.

16 "UAE Used Israeli Spyware to Gather Intel on Qatari Royals, Lawsuits Claim," *Haaretz*, August 31, 2018, www.haaretz.com/israel-news/2018-08-31/ty-article/uae -used-israeli-spyware-to-track-qatari-royals/0000017f-f2b9-d5bd-a17f-f6bb091 f0000.

17 David D. Kirkpatrick and Azam Ahmed, "Hacking a Prince, an Emir and a Jour-nalist to Impress a Client," *New York Times*, August 31, 2018, https://www.nytimes .com/2018/08/31/world/middleeast/hacking-united-arab-emirates-nso-group .html?searchResultPosition=1.

18 Chaim Levinson, "With Israel's Encouragement, NSO Sold Spyware to UAE and Other Gulf States," *Haaretz*, August 25, 2020, www.haaretz.com/middle-east-news /2020-08-25/ty-article/.premium/with-israels-encouragement-nso-sold-spyware -to-uae-and-other-gulf-states/0000017f-dbf3-d856-a37f-fff3a4ba0000.

19 "Israeli Group Uses South African Agent," *Intelligence Online*, August 28, 2013, www.intelligenceonline.com/corporate-intelligence/2013/08/28/israeli-group-uses -south-african-agent,107973676-art.

20 Shuki Sadeh, "A Shady Israeli Intel Genius, His Cyber-Spy Van and Million-Dollar Deals," *Haaretz*, December 31, 2020, www.haaretz.com/israel-news/tech-news /2020-12-31/ty-article-magazine/.highlight/a-shady-israeli-intel-genius-his-cyber -spy-van-and-million-dollar-deals/0000017f-f21e-d497-a1ff-f29ed7c30000.

21 "Karl Gumtow," *Maryland Daily Record*, May 31, 2023, thedailyrecord.com/2023/05 /31/karl-gumtow-2/.

22 "CyberPoint Exports Know-How," *Intelligence Online*, November 28, 2012, www .intelligenceonline.com/corporate-intelligence/2012/11/28/cyberpoint-exports -know-how,107934137-art.

23 Joel Schectman and Christopher Bing, "White House Veterans Helped Gulf Monarchy Build Secret Surveillance Unit," Reuters, December 10, 2019, www .reuters.com/article/idUSKBN1YE1PE/.

24 Lee Fang, "Adviser to Cyber Program at NYU's UAE Campus Linked to Spy Tech Used to Repress Activists," *Intercept*, July 8, 2015, www.theintercept.com/2015/07 /08/nyu-spyware-uae/.

25 Alexander Cornwell, "Emerging Gulf State Cyber Security Powerhouse Growing Rapidly in Size, Revenue," Reuters, February 1, 2018, www.reuters.com/article /idUSKBN1FL451/.

26 Ronald Deibert, "Cyberspace Confidential (*Globe and Mail* Essay)," Ronald Deibert, August 9, 2010, deibert.citizenlab.ca/2010/08/cyberspace-confidential-globe-and -mail-essay/.

27 chabermu, "RIM CEO Mike Lazaridis Ends BBC Interview," May 11, 2011, video, 1:28, www.youtube.com/watch?v=Q6iGe7vuGeQ.

28 "DarkMatter Inaugurates R&D Centre Based in Toronto, Canada," PR Newswire, April 13, 2016, www.prnewswire.com/news-releases/darkmatter-inaugurates-rd -centre-based-in-toronto-canada-575520061.html; "Eugene Chin," social media profile, LinkedIn, accessed February 4, 2024, ca.linkedin.com/in/eugenechincanada.

29 Matt Johnson, dir., *BlackBerry*, 2023; Toronto: Elevation Pictures, 2023. Online video.

30 Eli Yarhi, "Jim Balsillie," *The Canadian Encyclopedia*, February 26, 2012, www .thecanadianencyclopedia.ca/en/article/jim-balsillie.

31 Mark Mazzetti, Adam Goldman, Ronen Bergman, and Nicole Perlroth, "A New Age of Warfare: How Internet Mercenaries Do Battle for Authoritarian Governments," *New York Times*, March 21, 2019, www.nytimes.com/2019/03/21/us/politics /government-hackers-nso-darkmatter.html.

32 Catalin Cimpanu, "US Fines Former NSA Employees Who Provided Hacker-for-Hire Services to UAE," *Record*, September 13, 2021, therecord.media/us-fines -former-nsa-employees-who-provided-hacker-for-hire-services-to-uae.

33 Office of Public Affairs, "Three Former U.S. Intelligence Community and Military Personnel Agree to Pay More than $1.68 Million to Resolve Criminal Charges Arising from Their Provision of Hacking-Related Services to a Foreign Government," press release, US Department of Justice, September 14, 2021, www.justice .gov/opa/pr/three-former-us-intelligence-community-and-military-personnel -agree-pay-more-168-million.

34 Hiba Zayadin, "The Persecution of Ahmed Mansoor," Human Rights Watch, January 27, 2021, www.hrw.org/report/2021/01/27/persecution-ahmed-mansoor /how-united-arab-emirates-silenced-its-most-famous-human.

35 "Tribute to Artur Ligęska, Former Prisoner in UAE," Human Rights Watch, June 7, 2021, www.hrw.org/news/2021/06/07/tribute-artur-ligeska-former-prisoner-uae.

36 "Digital14 Picks Up Darkmatter's Key Activities, Including the Vulnerabilities Researcher xen1thLabs," *Intelligence Online*, January 21, 2021, www.intelligenceonline .com/surveillance—interception/2021/01/21/digital14-picks-up-darkmatter-s-key -activities-including-the-vulnerabilities-researcher-xen1thlabs,109636378-gra.

37 John Hudson, Ellen Nakashima, and Liz Sly, "Buildup Resumed at Suspected Chinese Military Site in UAE, Leak Says," *Washington Post*, April 26, 2023, www .washingtonpost.com/national-security/2023/04/26/chinese-military-base-uae/; "UAE Cyber-Offensive Firm Beacon Red's Russian Hackers Disillusioned," *Intelligence Online*, May 18, 2023, www.intelligenceonline.com/surveillance— interception/2023/05/18/uae-cyber-offensive-firm-beacon-red-s-russian-hackers -disillusioned,109975806-art.

CHAPTER 4: BREAKFAST IN UZBEKISTAN

1 Amir Rapaport, "The Cyber Technology Market Is Endless," *Israel Defense*, December 15, 2015, https://www.israeldefense.co.il/en/node/24622.

2 "Elbit Systems Buys Nice's Cyber Unit for up to $158 Mln," Reuters, May 21, 2015, www.reuters.com/article/idUSL5N0YC0XF/.

3 Elbit Systems, "Elbit Systems to Reorganize the Business of CYBERBIT," press release, September 18, 2017, elbitsystems.com/pr-new/elbit-systems-reorganize -business-cyberbit/.

4 "World Report 2015: Uzbekistan—Events of 2014," Human Rights Watch, 2015, www.hrw.org/world-report/2015/country-chapters/uzbekistan.

5 "Ethiopia," Minority Rights Group, June 2019, www.minorityrights.org/country /ethiopia/; Laetitia Bader, "Ethiopia's Other Conflict," Human Rights Watch, July 4, 2022, www.hrw.org/news/2022/07/04/ethiopias-other-conflict.

6 "Ethiopia," Reporters without Borders, rsf.org/en/country/Ethiopia; Felix Horne and Cynthia M. Wong, "They Know Everything We Do," Human Rights Watch, March 25, 2014, www.hrw.org/report/2014/03/25/they-know-everything-we-do /telecom-and-internet-surveillance-ethiopia.

7 Morgan Marquis-Boire, Bill Marczak, Claudio Guarnieri, and John Scott-Railton, *You Only Click Twice: FinFisher's Global Proliferation*, Research Report No. 15, Citizen Lab, University of Toronto, March 13, 2013, www.citizenlab.ca/2013/03/you-only -click-twice-finfishers-global-proliferation-2/; Bill Marczak, John Scott-Railton, and Sarah McKune, *Hacking Team Reloaded? US-Based Ethiopian Journalists Again Targeted with Spyware*, Research Report No. 50, Citizen Lab, University of Toronto, March 9, 2015, citizenlab.ca/2015/03/hacking-team-reloaded-us-based-ethiopian -journalists-targeted-spyware/.

8 Bill Marczak, Geoffrey Alexander, Sarah McKune, John Scott-Railton, and Ron Deibert, *Champing at the Cyberbit: Ethiopian Dissidents Targeted with New Commercial Spyware*, Research Report No. 102, Citizen Lab, University of Toronto, December 6, 2017, citizenlab.ca/2017/12/champing-cyberbit-ethiopian-dissidents-targeted -commercial-spyware/.

9 Elbit Systems Ltd., US Securities and Exchange Commission, December 31, 2011, www.sec.gov/Archives/edgar/data/1027664/000117891312000998/R10.htm.

10 "C4 Security Ltd.," Israel Export Institute, 2023, https://pitchbook.com/profiles /company/268044-58#overview.

11 "Hacking Team," WikiLeaks, July 8, 2015, wikileaks.org/hackingteam/emails/.

12 "Cyberbit Caught Up in Zambian Financial Crisis," *Intelligence Online*, October 24, 2018, www.intelligenceonline.com/corporate-intelligence/2018/10/24/cyberbit -caught-up-in-zambian-financial-crisis,108329307-art.

13 Office of Public Affairs, "Israel's Largest Bank, Bank Hapoalim, Admits to Conspiring with U.S. Taxpayers to Hide Assets and Income in Offshore Accounts," press release, US Department of Justice, April 30, 2020, www.justice.gov/opa/pr /israel-s-largest-bank-bank-hapoalim-admits-conspiring-us-taxpayers-hide-assets -and-income.

14 Agence France-Presse, "Israel's Bank Hapoalim Pays $900 Mn over Tax Evasion,

FIFA Cases," *Barron's*, April 30, 2020, www.barrons.com/news/israel-s-bank
-hapoalim-pays-900-mn-over-tax-evasion-fifa-cases-01588285508.

15 Peter Bouckaert, "'License to Kill': Philippine Police Killings in Duterte's 'War on
Drugs,'" Human Rights Watch, March 2, 2017, www.hrw.org/report/2017/03/02
/license-kill/philippine-police-killings-dutertes-war-drugs.

16 "Thailand: Events of 2022," Human Rights Watch, 2023, www.hrw.org/world
-report/2023/country-chapters/thailand.

17 "Vietnam Jails Dissident for Eight Years over Facebook Posts," Reuters, November
18, 2022, www.reuters.com/world/asia-pacific/vietnam-jails-dissident-eight-years
-over-facebook-posts-2022-11-18/.

18 Cheryl Reed, "Citizen Journalist's Arrest Decried by Media Rights Advocates,"
Eurasianet, July 5, 2022, eurasianet.org/kazakhstan-citizen-journalists-arrest-decried
-by-media-rights-advocates.

19 Victoire Ingabire Umuhoza, "Rwanda Has to Investigate Killings of Opposition
Members," Al Jazeera, March 24, 2023, www.aljazeera.com/opinions/2023/3/24
/rwanda-has-to-investigate-killings-of-opposition-members; "Rwanda Classified,"
Forbidden Stories, accessed May 29, 2024, https://forbiddenstories.org/projects
_posts/rwanda-classified/.

20 Fatima Hussein, "US Is Sanctioning the Pro-Russian Head of Serbian Intelligence
for Alleged Corruption," Associated Press, July 11, 2023, www.apnews.com/article
/serbia-sanctions-treasury-vulin-russia-6b8e01b5595fc114094c4a3a3cf9eab5.

21 "Nigeria: Events of 2022," Human Rights Watch, 2023, www.hrw.org/world-report
/2023/country-chapters/nigeria.

22 John Snow, "Shodan and Censys: The Ominous Guides through the Internet of
Things," *Kaspersky Daily* (blog), February 29, 2016, www.kaspersky.com/blog
/shodan-censys/11430/.

23 Morgan Marquis-Boire and Bill Marczak, *From Bahrain with Love: FinFisher's Spy Kit
Exposed?*, Research Report No. 9, Citizen Lab, University of Toronto, July 25, 2012,
citizenlab.ca/2012/07/from-bahrain-with-love-finfishers-spy-kit-exposed/.

24 Bill Marczak, Claudio Guarnieri, Morgan Marquis-Boire, and John Scott-Railton,
Mapping Hacking Team's "Untraceable" Spyware, Research Report No. 33, Citizen
Lab, University of Toronto, February 17, 2014, www.citizenlab.ca/2014/02/mapping
-hacking-teams-untraceable-spyware/; Bill Marczak, Claudio Guarnieri, Morgan
Marquis-Boire, and John Scott-Railton, *Hacking Team and the Targeting of Ethiopian
Journalists*, Research Report No. 32, Citizen Lab, University of Toronto, February 12,
2014, www.citizenlab.ca/2014/02/hacking-team-targeting-ethiopian-journalists/; Bill
Marczak, Claudio Guarnieri, Morgan Marquis-Boire, John Scott-Railton, and Sarah
McKune, *Hacking Team's US Nexus*, Research Report No. 35, Citizen Lab, University
of Toronto, February 28, 2014, www.citizenlab.ca/2014/02/hacking-teams-us-nexus/.

25 Irene Poetranto, "Open Letter to Hacking Team," Citizen Lab, University of
Toronto, August 2014, citizenlab.ca/2014/08/open-letter-hacking-team/.

26 "Hacking Team," WikiLeaks, July 8, 2015, wikileaks.org/hackingteam/emails/;
"Eight Things We Know So Far from the Hacking Team Hack," Privacy International, July 9, 2015, http://privacyinternational.org/news-analysis/1395/eight
-things-we-know-so-far-hacking-team-hack.

27 Morgan Marquis-Boire and Cora Currier, "A Detailed Look at Hacking Team's
     Emails about Its Repressive Clients," *Intercept*, July 7, 2015, www.theintercept.com
     /2015/07/07/leaked-documents-confirm-hacking-team-sells-spyware-repressive
     -countries/.

28 David Vincenzetti, "URGENT: Yet Another Citizen Labs' Attack," email, June 24,
     2014, www.wikileaks.org/hackingteam/emails/emailid/179377, in "Hacking Team,"
     WikiLeaks, July 8, 2015.

29 David Vincenzetti, "Re: URGENT: Yet Another Citizen Labs' Attack," email, June 30,
     2014, www.wikileaks.org/hackingteam/emails/emailid/171363, in "Hacking Team,"
     WikiLeaks, July 8, 2015.

30 Lorenzo Franceschi-Bicchierai, "Hacking Team Founder: 'Hacking Team Is Dead,'"
     Vice, May 26, 2020, www.vice.com/en/article/n7wbnd/hacking-team-is-dead.

31 Lorenzo Franceschi-Bicchierai, "Founder of Spyware Maker Hacking Team
     Arrested for Attempted Murder: Local Media," *TechCrunch*, November 29, 2023,
     techcrunch.com/2023/11/29/founder-of-spyware-maker-hacking-team-arrested
     -for-attempted-murder-local-media/. Charges against Vincenzetti are still pending
     at the time of writing.

32 Vice TV, "An Interview with Hacker 'Phineas Fisher' as a Puppet | CYBERWAR,"
     July 20, 2016, video, 5:45, www.youtube.com/watch?v=BpyCl1Qm6Xs.

33 Jakub Dalek, Lex Gill, Bill Marczak, Sarah McKune, Naser Noor, Joshua Oliver,
     Jon Penney, Adam Senft, and Ron Deibert, *Planet Netsweeper*, Research Report No.
     108, Citizen Lab, University of Toronto, April 25, 2018, www.citizenlab.ca/2018/04
     /planet-netsweeper/.

34 Ronald Deibert, "Ottawa Needs to Act on Global Censorship of LGBTQ2+
     Content," *Hill Times*, August 2, 2018, www.hilltimes.com/story/2018/08/02/ottawa
     -needs-act-global-censorship-lgbtq2-content/262275/.

35 Jakub Dalek, Ron Deibert, Sarah McKune, Phillipa Gill, Adam Senft, and Naser
     Noor, *Information Controls during Military Operations*, Research Report No. 66,
     Citizen Lab, University of Toronto, October 21, 2015, citizenlab.ca/2015/10/infor
     mation-controls-military-operations-yemen/; Ron Deibert, "On Research in the
     Public Interest," Citizen Lab, University of Toronto, July 26, 2016, citizenlab.ca
     /2016/07/research-interest/.

36 Protection of Public Participation Act, 2015, S.O. 2015, c. 23—Bill 52, www.ontario
     .ca/laws/statute/s15023.

37 Morgan Marquis-Boire, Jakub Dalek, Sarah McKune, Matthew Carrieri, Masashi
     Crete-Nishihata, Ron Deibert, Saad Omar Khan, Helmi Noman, John Scott-
     Railton, and Greg Wiseman, *Planet Blue Coat: Mapping Global Censorship and Surveil-
     lance Tools*, Research Report No. 13, Citizen Lab, University of Toronto, January
     15, 2013, citizenlab.ca/2013/01/planet-blue-coat-mapping-global-censorship-and
     -surveillance-tools/.

38 Jakub Dalek and Adam Senft, *Behind Blue Coat: Investigations of Commercial Filtering
     in Syria and Burma*, Research Report No. 1, Citizen Lab, University of Toronto,
     November 9, 2011, citizenlab.ca/2011/11/behind-blue-coat/.

39 Bill Marczak, Jakub Dalek, Sarah McKune, Adam Senft, John Scott-Railton, and
     Ron Deibert, *Bad Traffic: Sandvine's PacketLogic Devices Used to Deploy Government*

Spyware in Turkey and Redirect Egyptian Users to Affiliate Ads?, Research Report No. 107, Citizen Lab, University of Toronto, March 9, 2018, citizenlab.ca/2018/03/bad-traffic-sandvines-packetlogic-devices-deploy-government-spyware-turkey-syria/.

40 Linda R. Rothstein, letter to Lyndon Cantor, CEO of Sandvine, March 8, 2018, citizenlab.ca/wp-content/uploads/2018/03/UofT-Sandvine-Letter-to-Lyndon-Cantor-signed-8-March-2018.pdf.

41 Bill Marczak, John Scott-Railton, Daniel Roethlisberger, Bahr Abdul Razzak, Siena Anstis, and Ron Deibert, "Predator in the Wires: Ahmed Eltantawy Targeted with Predator Spyware after Announcing Presidential Ambitions," Citizen Lab, University of Toronto, September 22, 2023, citizenlab.ca/2023/09/predator-in-the-wires-ahmed-eltantawy-targeted-with-predator-spyware-after-announcing-presidential-ambitions/.

42 "About the Security Content of iOS 17.0.1 and iPadOS 17.0.1," Apple Support, November 15, 2023, support.apple.com/en-us/106369.

43 Office of the Spokesperson, "The United States Adds Sandvine to the Entity List for Enabling Human Rights Abuses," press release, US Department of State, February 28, 2024. https://www.state.gov/the-united-states-adds-sandvine-to-the-entity-list-for-enabling-human-rights-abuses/.

44 Bill Marczak, John Scott-Railton, Siddharth Prakash Rao, Siena Anstis, and Ron Deibert, *Running in Circles: Uncovering the Clients of Cyberespionage Firm Circles*, Research Report No. 133, Citizen Lab, University of Toronto, December 1, 2020, www.citizenlab.ca/2020/12/running-in-circles-uncovering-the-clients-of-cyber espionage-firm-circles/.

45 Mark W. Zacher with Brent A. Sutton, *Governing Global Networks: International Regimes for Transportation and Communications*, Cambridge Studies in International Relations 44 (Cambridge: Cambridge University Press, 1995), https://doi.org/10.1017/CBO9780511521812; Josie Middleton, "Propelling Women in Tech across Emerging Markets: Our Reflections on Female Entrepreneurship," GSMA, June 18, 2019, https://www.gsma.com/mobilefordevelopment /blog/propelling-women-in-tech-across-emerging-markets-our-reflections-on-female-entrepreneurship/; SAP, "Who Run the Telco World? Gender Disparity in the Telecommunications Sector," http://www.sapevents.edgesuite.net/previewhub /women-in-telco/pdfs/Women%20In%20Telco%20Slideshare.pdf.

46 Nils Putnins, "Research on Signaling System 7 (SS7)—Risks, Attacks and Precautions," *SEQ Cybersecurity Blog*, September 15, 2022, web.archive.org/web /20220915101054/blog.seq.lv/research-on-signaling-system-7-ss7/.

47 Robert Krulwich, "Playful Pranks from Apple's Founder," NPR, January 3, 2009, www.npr.org/templates/story/story.php?storyId=98977379.

48 Sergey Puzankov, "Back to the Future: Cross-Protocol Attacks in the Era of 5G," Positive Technologies, accessed February 7, 2024, i.blackhat.com/asia-20/Friday/asia-20-Puzankov-Back-To-The-Future-Cross-Protocol-Attacks-In-The-Era-Of-5G .pdf.

49 Putnins, "Research on Signaling System 7 (SS7)."

50 Al Araby, August 31, 2018, https://web.archive.org/web/20190409205521/https:/ www.alaraby.co.uk/file/get/4749a75b-fc46-4917-85d3-7f8b41d4b34a; Ogala Emman-

uel, "How Governors Dickson, Okowa Spend Billions on High Tech Spying on Opponents, Others," *Premium Times* (Nigeria), June 9, 2016, www.premiumtimesng .com/investigationspecial-reports/204987-investigation-governors-dickson-okowa -spend-billions-high-tech-spying-opponents-others.html.

51 "Thailand: Investigate Alleged Army Torture," Human Rights Watch, November 22, 2016, https://www.hrw.org/news/2016/11/23/thailand-investigate-alleged-army -torture.

52 John Scott-Railton, Bill Marczak, Claudio Guarnieri, and Masashi Crete-Nishi-hata, *Bitter Sweet: Supporters of Mexico's Soda Tax Targeted with NSO Exploit Links*, Research Report No. 89, Citizen Lab, University of Toronto, February 11, 2017, www.citizenlab.ca/2017/02/bittersweet-nso-mexico-spyware/; John Scott-Railton, Bill Marczak, Bahr Abdul Razzak, Masashi Crete-Nishihata, and Ron Deibert, *Reckless Exploit: Mexican Journalists, Lawyers, and a Child Targeted with NSO Spyware*, Research Report No. 93, Citizen Lab, University of Toronto, June 19, 2017, www.citizenlab.ca/2017/06/reckless-exploit-mexico-nso/; John Scott-Railton, Bill Marczak, Bahr Abdul Razzak, Masashi Crete-Nishihata, and Ron Deibert, *Reckless Redux: Senior Mexican Legislators and Politicians Targeted with NSO Spyware*, Research Report No. 94, Citizen Lab, University of Toronto, June 29, 2017, www.citizenlab .ca/2017/06/more-mexican-nso-targets/; John Scott-Railton, Bill Marczak, Bahr Abdul Razzak, Masashi Crete-Nishihata, and Ron Deibert, *Reckless III: Investigation into Mexican Mass Disappearance Targeted with NSO Spyware*, Research Report No. 96, Citizen Lab, University of Toronto, July 10, 2017, citizenlab.ca/2017/07/mexico -disappearances-nso/; John Scott-Railton, Bill Marczak, Bahr Abdul Razzak, Masashi Crete-Nishihata, and Ron Deibert, *Reckless IV: Lawyers for Murdered Mexican Women's Families Targeted with NSO Spyware*, Research Report No. 98, Citizen Lab, University of Toronto, August 2, 2017, citizenlab.ca/2017/08/lawyers-murdered -women-nso-group/; John Scott-Railton, Bill Marczak, Bahr Abdul Razzak, Masashi Crete-Nishihata, and Ron Deibert, *Reckless V: Director of Mexican Anti-Corruption Group Targeted with NSO Group's Spyware*, Research Report No. 99, Citizen Lab, University of Toronto, August 30, 2017, citizenlab.ca/2017/08/nso-spyware-mexico -corruption/; John Scott-Railton, Bill Marczak, Bahr Abdul Razzak, Masashi Crete-Nishihata, and Ron Deibert, *Reckless VI: Mexican Journalists Investigating Cartels Targeted with NSO Spyware Following Assassination of Colleague*, Research Report No. 116, Citizen Lab, University of Toronto, November 27, 2018, citizenlab .ca/2018/11/mexican-journalists-investigating-cartels-targeted-nso-spyware -following-assassination-colleague/; John Scott-Railton, Bill Marczak, Siena Anstis, Bahr Abdul Razzak, Masashi Crete-Nishihata, and Ron Deibert, *Reckless VII: Wife of Journalist Slain in Cartel-Linked Killing Targeted with NSO Group's Spyware*, Research Report No. 117, Citizen Lab, University of Toronto, March 20, 2019, citizenlab.ca /2019/03/nso-spyware-slain-journalists-wife/.

53 "UPR Submission—Nigeria 2018," Front Line Defenders, April 7, 2018, www .frontlinedefenders.org/en/statement-report/upr-submission-nigeria-2018.

54 "Individuals Using the Internet (% of Population)," World Bank Group, accessed February 7, 2024, https://data.worldbank.org/indicator/IT.NET.USER.ZS?skip Redirection=true&view=map; Marczak, et al., *Champing at the Cyberbit*.

55 Stephanie Kirchgaessner, "More Polish Opposition Figures Found to Have Been Targeted by Pegasus Spyware," *Guardian*, February 17, 2022, https://www.theguardian.com/world/2022/feb/17/more-polish-opposition-figures-found-to-have-been-targeted-by-pegasus-spyware.

56 Bill Marczak, John Scott-Railton, Sarah McKune, Bahr Abdul Razzak, and Ron Deibert, *Hide and Seek: Tracking NSO Group's Pegasus Spyware to Operations in 45 Countries*, Research Report No. 113, Citizen Lab, University of Toronto, September 18, 2018, www.citizenlab.ca/2018/09/hide-and-seek-tracking-nso-groups-pegasus-spyware-to-operations-in-45-countries/.

CHAPTER 5: "TRUST ME, I AM THE ONE"

1 يقظة (@YakathahChannel), YouTube channel, accessed February 12, 2024, https://www.youtube.com/@YakathahChannel.

2 Mike Armstrong, "Saudi Dissident in Quebec Says People Who Ordered Khashoggi's Killing Were Also after Him," Global News, October 22, 2018, https://globalnews.ca/news/4583529/saudi-dissident-omar-abdulaziz-jamal-khashoggi/.

3 Matthew Braga, "A Quebecer Spoke Out against the Saudis—Then Learned He Had Spyware on His iPhone," CBC News, October 1, 2018, https://www.cbc.ca/news/science/omar-abdulaziz-spyware-saudi-arabia-nso-citizen-lab-quebec-1.4845179.

4 Jillian Kestler-D'Amours, "Saudi Dissident Vows to 'Keep Fighting' after Year of Intimidation, Arrests and Murder," *Middle East Eye*, December 28, 2018, https://www.middleeasteye.net/news/saudi-dissident-vows-keep-fighting-after-year-intimidation-arrests-and-murder.

5 Tim Adams, "Khashoggi Confidant Omar Abdulaziz: 'I'm Worried about the Safety of the People of Saudi Arabia,'" *Guardian*, February 20, 2021, www.theguardian.com/film/2021/feb/20/me-jamal-khashoggi-mohammed-bin-salman-omar-abdulaziz-the-dissident-netflix.

6 Nina dos Santos and Michael Kaplan, "Jamal Khashoggi's Private WhatsApp Messages May Offer New Clues to Killing," CNN, December 4, 2018, https://www.cnn.com/2018/12/02/middleeast/jamal-khashoggi-whatsapp-messages-intl/index.html.

7 Shane Harris and Souad Mekhennet, "Saudi Crown Prince Exchanged Messages with Aide Alleged to Have Overseen Khashoggi Killing," *Washington Post*, December 2, 2018, www.washingtonpost.com/world/national-security/saudi-crown-prince-exchanged-messages-with-aide-alleged-to-have-overseen-khashoggi-killing/2018/12/01/faa43758-f5c3-11e8-9240-e8028a62c722_story.html.

8 David Ignatius, "The Khashoggi Killing Had Roots in a Cutthroat Saudi Family Feud," *Washington Post*, November 27, 2018, www.washingtonpost.com/opinions/global-opinions/the-khashoggi-killing-had-roots-in-a-cutthroat-saudi-family-feud/2018/11/27/6d79880c-f17b-11e8-bc79-68604ed88993_story.html.

9 Leyland Cecco, "Saudi Foreign Minister Demands Canada Stop Treating It like a 'Banana Republic,'" *Guardian*, September 28, 2018, www.theguardian.com

/world/2018/sep/28/saudi-foreign-minister-demands-canada-stop-treating-it-like
-a-banana-republic.

10 "Saudi Arabia Arrests Sister of Imprisoned Blogger," CBC News, August 1, 2018,
    https://www.cbc.ca/news/canada/montreal/samar-badawi-arrested-1.4770268.

11 Foreign Policy CAN (@CanadaFP), "Canada is gravely concerned about additional
    arrests of civil society and women's rights activists in #SaudiArabia, including Samar
    Badawi. We urge the Saudi authorities to immediately release them and all other
    peaceful #humanrights activists," X, August 3, 2018, https://x.com/CanadaFP/status
    /1025383326960549889.

12 Mark Gollom, "Saudi Arabia 'Allergic to Criticism,' Making Example out of Canada,
    Analysts Say," CBC News, August 8, 2018, https://www.cbc.ca/news/politics/saudi
    -arabia-sanctions-canada-ambassador-1.4776502.

13 Foreign Ministry (@KSAmofaEN), "#Statement | The negative and surprising
    attitude of #Canada is an entirely false claim and utterly incorrect," X, August 5,
    2018, https://x.com/KSAmofaEN/status/1026241364604932096; Foreign Ministry
    (@KSAmofaEN), "#Statement | KSA through its history has not and will not accept
    any form of interfering in the internal affairs of the Kingdom. The KSA considers
    the Canadian position an attack on the KSA and requires a firm stance to deter who
    attempts to undermine the sovereignty of the KSA," X, August 5, 2018, https://x
    .com/KSAmofaEN/status/1026241371361996800?lang=en.

14 Foreign Ministry (@KSAmofaEN), "#Statement | Any other attempt to inter-
    fere with our internal affairs from #Canada, means that we are allowed to inter-
    fere in #Canada's internal affairs," X, August 5, 2018, https://x.com/i/web/status
    /1026241374516113409.

15 Ryan Patrick Jones, "Saudi Arabian Group Apologizes for Posting Image Appearing
    to Threaten Canada with 9/11-Style Attack," CBC News, August 6, 2018, www
    .cbc.ca/news/canada/toronto/saudi-arabian-group-apologizes-for-posting-image
    -appearing-to-threaten-canada-with-9-11-style-attack-1.4775509.

16 Eric Lichtblau and James Risen, "9/11 and the Saudi Connection," *Intercept*,
    September 11, 2021, theintercept.com/2021/09/11/september-11-saudi-arabia/;
    Daniel Benjamin and Steven Simon, "New 9/11 Evidence Points to Deep Saudi
    Complicity," *Atlantic*, May 20, 2024, https://www.theatlantic.com/ideas/archive
    /2024/05/september-11-attacks-saudi-arabia-lawsuit/678430/.

17 Jeremy Nuttall, "Case against Saudi Crown Prince by Toronto Resident Dismissed
    in U.S. Court," *Toronto Star*, October 27, 2022, www.thestar.com/news/canada/case
    -against-saudi-crown-prince-by-toronto-resident-dismissed-in-u-s-court/article
    _6fc786a9-2056-5806-843f-3bf79243a430.html.

18 Bill Marczak, John Scott-Railton, and Ron Deibert, *NSO Group Infrastructure
    Linked to Targeting of Amnesty International and Saudi Dissident*, Research Report No.
    110, Citizen Lab, University of Toronto, July 31, 2018, citizenlab.ca/2018/07/nso
    -spyware-targeting-amnesty-international/.

19 Bethan McKernan, "Jamal Khashoggi Murder: Timeline of Key Events," *Guardian*,
    December 23, 2019, https://www.theguardian.com/world/2019/dec/23/jamal-khash
    oggi-timeline-of-key-events.

20 Karen Attiah, "Let the World Hear Jamal Khashoggi's Last Words in Arabic," *Washington Post*, September 29, 2019, https://www.washingtonpost.com/opinions/2019/09/30/let-world-hear-jamal-khashoggis-last-words-arabic/.

21 David Hearst, "Jamal Khashoggi's Killing Took Seven Minutes, Turkish Source Tells *MEE*," *Middle East Eye*, December 10, 2018, https://www.middleeasteye.net/news/jamal-khashoggis-killing-took-seven-minutes-turkish-source-tells-mee.

22 Gul Tuysuz, Salma Abdelaziz, Ghazi Balkiz, Ingrid Formanek, and Clarissa Ward, "Surveillance Footage Shows Saudi 'Body Double' in Khashoggi's Clothes after He Was Killed, Turkish Source Says," CNN, October 23, 2018, https://www.cnn.com/2018/10/22/middleeast/saudi-operative-jamal-khashoggi-clothes/index.html.

23 Cassandra Garrison, "A High-Five from Putin and That Awkward Photograph—Saudi Prince's G20 Summit," Reuters, December 2, 2018, https://www.reuters.com/article/idUSKCN1O1047/.

24 Kestler-D'Amours, "Saudi Dissident Vows to 'Keep Fighting.'"

25 Ben Hubbard, "The Rise and Fall of M.B.S.'s Digital Henchman," *New York Times*, March 13, 2020, www.nytimes.com/2020/03/13/sunday-review/mbs-hacking.html.

26 "'Saudi Arabia's Steve Bannon,' Saud al-Qahtani, Still Active despite 'Firing' over Khashoggi Murder," *New Arab*, February 12, 2019, https://www.newarab.com/news/saud-al-qahtani-still-active-despite-firing-over-khashoggi-murder.

27 Michael Forsythe, Mark Mazzetti, Ben Hubbard, and Walt Bogdanich, "Consulting Firms Keep Lucrative Saudi Alliance, Shaping Crown Prince's Vision," *New York Times*, November 4, 2018, https://www.nytimes.com/2018/11/04/world/middleeast/mckinsey-bcg-booz-allen-saudi-khashoggi.html.

28 Kate Conger, Mike Isaac, Katie Benner, and Nicole Perlroth, "Former Twitter Employees Charged with Spying for Saudi Arabia," *New York Times*, November 6, 2019, https://www.nytimes.com/2019/11/06/technology/twitter-saudi-arabia-spies.html.

29 Katie Paul, "Twitter Suspends Accounts Linked to Saudi Spying Case," Reuters, December 20, 2019, https://www.reuters.com/article/idUSKBN1YO1JU/.

30 "New Disclosures to Our Archive of State-Backed Information Operations," *X Blog*, December 20, 2019, blog.x.com/en_us/topics/company/2019/new-disclosures-to-our-archive-of-state-backed-information-operations.

31 Shane Harris, Greg Miller, and Josh Dawsey, "CIA Concludes Saudi Crown Prince Ordered Jamal Khashoggi's Assassination," *Washington Post*, November 16, 2018, www.washingtonpost.com/world/national-security/cia-concludes-saudi-crown-prince-ordered-jamal-khashoggis-assassination/2018/11/16/98c89fe6-e9b2-11e8-a939-9469f1166f9d_story.html.

32 Lesley Stahl, "CEO of Israeli Spyware-Maker NSO on Fighting Terror, Khashoggi Murder, and Saudi Arabia," CBS News, May 14, 2019, https://www.cbsnews.com/news/interview-with-ceo-of-nso-group-israeli-spyware-maker-on-fighting-terror-khashoggi-murder-and-saudi-arabia-60-minutes/.

33 Dana Priest, "A UAE Agency Put Pegasus Spyware on Phone of Jamal Khashoggi's Wife Months before His Murder, New Forensics Show," *Washington Post*, December 21, 2021, https://www.washingtonpost.com/nation/interactive/2021/hanan-elatr-phone-pegasus/.

34 Bill Marczak, John Scott-Railton, Siena Anstis, Bahr Abdul Razzak, and Ron Deibert, "Breaking the News: *New York Times* Journalist Ben Hubbard Hacked with Pegasus after Reporting on Previous Hacking Attempts," Citizen Lab, University of Toronto, October 24, 2021, https://citizenlab.ca/2021/10/breaking-news-new-york -times-journalist-ben-hubbard-pegasus/.

35 Ben Hubbard, "Someone Tried to Hack My Phone. Technology Researchers Accused Saudi Arabia," *New York Times*, January 28, 2020, www.nytimes.com/2020 /01/28/reader-center/phone-hacking-saudi-arabia.html.

36 Ben Hubbard, "I Was Hacked. The Spyware Used against Me Makes Us All Vulnerable," *New York Times*, October 24, 2021, www.nytimes.com/2021/10/24/insider /hacking-nso-surveillance.html.

37 Amnesty International, "Massive Data Leak Reveals Israeli NSO Group's Spyware Used to Target Activists, Journalists, and Political Leaders Globally," press release, July 19, 2021, https://www.amnesty.org/en/latest/press-release/2021/07/the-pegasus -project/.

38 "Pegasus: Who Are the Alleged Victims of Spyware Targeting?," BBC, July 22, 2021, https://www.bbc.com/news/world-57891506.

39 Office of the Director of National Intelligence, "Assessing the Saudi Government's Role in the Killing of Jamal Khashoggi," February 11, 2021, https://www.dni.gov /files/ODNI/documents/assessments/Assessment-Saudi-Gov-Role-in-JK-Death -20210226v2.pdf.

40 "'Antithesis of Justice': Khashoggi Verdict Roundly Condemned," Al Jazeera, December 24, 2019, https://www.aljazeera.com/news/2019/12/24/antithesis-of-jus tice-khashoggi-verdict-roundly-condemned.

41 Office of the Director of National Intelligence, "Assessing the Saudi Government's Role."

42 Warren P. Strobel, "CIA Intercepts Underpin Assessment Saudi Crown Prince Targeted Khashoggi," *Wall Street Journal*, December 1, 2018, www.wsj.com/articles /cia-intercepts-underpin-assessment-saudi-crown-prince-targeted-khashoggi -1543640460.

43 Robert Tait, "Biden Accused of Betrayal of Khashoggi over Push to Deepen Saudi Ties," *Guardian*, October 7, 2023, https://www.theguardian.com/us-news/2023/oct /07/biden-saudi-arabia-mohammed-bin-salman-jamal-khashoggi.

44 Darren Major, "Canada, Saudi Arabia Agree to Restore Relations 5 Years after Diplomatic Feud," CBC News, May 24, 2023, https://www.cbc.ca/news/politics /canada-saudi-arabia-restoring-diplomatic-relations-1.6853285.

45 Steven Chase, "Saudi Arabia Is Top Export Destination for Canadian Arms after United States in 2022," *Globe and Mail*, June 4, 2023, https://www.theglobeandmail .com/politics/article-saudi-arabia-canadian-arms-exports/.

46 Omar Abdulaziz v. Twitter Inc., Case No. 19-cv-06694-LB (N.D. Cal. Feb. 18, 2021).

47 Oliver Holmes and Stephanie Kirchgaessner, "Israeli Spyware Firm Fails to Get Hacking Case Dismissed," *Guardian*, January 16, 2020, www.theguardian.com /world/2020/jan/16/israeli-spyware-firm-nso-hacking-case.

48 "Bindmans Launches Legal Action in the United Kingdom on Misuse of Pegasus

Spyware," Bindmans, April 19, 2022, www.bindmans.com/knowledge-hub/news
/bindmans-launches-legal-action-in-the-united-kingdom-on-misuse-of-pegasus
-spyware/; Hanan Elatr Khashoggi v. NSO Group Technologies Limited and Q
Cyber Technologies Limited, Case No. 1:2023cv00779—Document 50 (E.D. Va.
Oct. 26, 2023), https://law.justia.com/cases/federal/district-courts/virginia/vaedce
/1:2023cv00779/539227/50/.

49 Adams, "Khashoggi Confidant Omar Abdulaziz."

50 Stephanie Kirchgaessner, "Saudi Dissident Warned by Canadian Police He Is a
Target," *Guardian*, June 21, 2020, https://www.theguardian.com/world/2020/jun
/21/exclusive-saudi-dissident-warned-by-canadian-police-he-is-a-target.

51 Douglas Quan and Nadine Yousif, "He Claimed Asylum in Canada and Spoke Out
against the Saudi Regime. So Why Has Ahmed Alharby Gone Home?," *Toronto
Star*, February 19, 2021, https://www.thestar.com/news/canada/he-claimed-asylum
-in-canada-and-spoke-out-against-the-saudi-regime-so-why-has/article_2c28e941
-f7b7-5715-bcb1-c55efb917aa8.html.

52 Douglas Quan, Alex Boutilier, and Nadine Yousif, "Canada Needs to Investigate Saudi Dissident's Mysterious Return to Homeland, Critics Say," *Toronto
Star*, February 23, 2021, https://www.thestar.com/news/canada/canada-needs-to
-investigate-saudi-dissident-s-mysterious-return-to-homeland-critics-say/article
_ef4e3459-c2f9-5457-9d8c-a67558753746.html.

53 Kestler-D'Amours, "Saudi Dissident Vows to 'Keep Fighting.'"

CHAPTER 6: "HOW OFTEN DO YOU PRAY?"

1 Bill Hicks, "From Torture Victim to Human Rights Student," BBC, October 17, 2017,
www.bbc.com/news/business-41639458; Melissa Petro, "After Surviving Torture,
Noura al-Jizawi Is Fighting for Other Syrian Prisoners," *Vice*, January 6, 2017, www
.vice.com/en/article/gyxgaw/noura-al-jizawi-profile-syrian-female-prisoners.

2 John Scott-Railton, Bahr Abdul Razzak, Adam Hulcoop, Matt Brooks, and Katie
Kleemola, *Group5: Syria and the Iranian Connection*, Research Report No. 76, Citizen
Lab, University of Toronto, August 2, 2016, citizenlab.ca/2016/08/group5-syria/.

3 David D. Kirkpatrick, "Israeli Software Helped Saudis Spy on Khashoggi, Lawsuit
Says," *New York Times*, December 2, 2018, www.nytimes.com/2018/12/02/world
/middleeast/saudi-khashoggi-spyware-israel.html.

4 Ed Pilkington, "Harvey Weinstein Hired Black Cube to Block *New York Times*
Article, Jury Hears," *Guardian*, January 30, 2020, https://www.theguardian.com/film
/2020/jan/30/harvey-weinstein-black-cube-new-york-times.

5 Raphael Satter, "A Conversation with a Spy," Associated Press, www.documentcloud
.org/documents/6426634-John-Scott-Railton-s-Conversation-with-Michel#docu
ment/.

6 Adam Entous and Ronan Farrow, "Private Mossad for Hire," *New Yorker*, February 11,
2019, www.newyorker.com/magazine/2019/02/18/private-mossad-for-hire; Ronald
J. Deibert, "Subversion Inc: The Age of Private Espionage," *Journal of Democracy* 33,
no. 2 (April 2022): 28–44, https://www.journalofdemocracy.org/articles/subversion
-inc-the-age-of-private-espionage/.

7 Hagar Shezaf and Yaniv Kubovich, "Israeli Army Conducted Online Psy-Op against Israeli Public during Gaza War," *Haaretz*, March 22, 2023, www.haaretz.com/israel-news/security-aviation/2023-03-22/ty-article-magazine/.premium/israeli-army-conducted-online-psy-op-against-israeli-public-during-gaza-war/00000186-f972-df90-a19e-f9fff22a0000.

8 Mike Dvilyanski, David Agranovich, and Nathaniel Gleicher, "Threat Report on the Surveillance-for-Hire Industry," Meta, December 16, 2021, about.fb.com/wp-content/uploads/2021/12/Threat-Report-on-the-Surveillance-for-Hire-Industry.pdf.

9 Naomi Nix, "Meta to Begin Fresh Layoffs, Cutting Heavily among Business Staff," *Washington Post*, May 23, 2023, https://www.washingtonpost.com/technology/2023/05/23/meta-layoffs-misinformation-facebook-instagram/.

10 John Scott-Railton, Adam Hulcoop, Bahr Abdul Razzak, Bill Marczak, Siena Anstis, and Ron Deibert, *Dark Basin: Uncovering a Massive Hack-for-Hire Operation*, Research Report No. 128, Citizen Lab, University of Toronto, June 9, 2020, citizenlab.ca/2020/06/dark-basin-uncovering-a-massive-hack-for-hire-operation/.

11 Adam Hulcoop, John Scott-Railton, Peter Tanchak, Matt Brooks, and Ron Deibert, *Tainted Leaks: Disinformation and Phishing with a Russian Nexus*, Research Report No. 92, Citizen Lab, University of Toronto, May 25, 2017, citizenlab.ca/2017/05/tainted-leaks-disinformation-phish/.

12 Spencer Walrath, "Activists Now Suggest Exxon Is Responsible for . . . a Global Hacking Ring?," *EID Climate* (blog), June 10, 2020, https://eidclimate.org/activists-now-suggest-exxon-is-responsible-for-a-global-hacking-ring/; Emily Holden, "Hack-for-hire group targeted climate activists behind #ExxonKnew campaign," *Guardian*, June 11, 2020, https://www.theguardian.com/technology/2020/jun/11/exxon-hack-for-hire-climate-activists-campaign.

13 Jasper Jolly, "Covert Cameras and Alleged Hacking: How Bust Payments Company Wirecard 'Hired Spies and Lawyers to Silence Critics,'" *Guardian*, March 4, 2023, www.theguardian.com/business/2023/mar/04/covert-cameras-alleged-hacking-how-bust-payments-company-wirecard-hired-spies-lawyers-silence-critics; see also Zatarra Research & Investigations, viceroyresearch.org/wp-content/uploads/2020/07/final-main-report-zatarra-edited-3.pdf.

14 Dan McCrum, "Wirecard and Me: Dan McCrum on Exposing a Criminal Enterprise," *Financial Times*, September 3, 2020, https://www.ft.com/content/745e34a1-0ca7-432c-b062-950c20e41f03.

15 Kate Connolly, "Ex-Wirecard CEO Arrested on Suspicion of Falsifying Accounts," *Guardian*, June 23, 2020, www.theguardian.com/business/2020/jun/23/former-wirecard-ceo-markus-braun-arrested-in-germany; "Wirecard: Scandal-Hit Firm Files for Insolvency," BBC, June 25, 2020, https://www.bbc.com/news/business-53176003.

16 Olaf Storbeck, "German Spies Shunned Offer to Meet Wirecard Fugitive Jan Marsalek in Moscow," *Financial Times*, April 13, 2022, www.ft.com/content/5ba4eedc-992e-4e64-9bb1-9d81b379ea00.

17 Helen Warrell, Sam Jones, and Paul Murphy, "From Payments to Armaments: The Double Life of Wirecard's Jan Marsalek," *Financial Times*, July 10, 2020, www.ft.com/content/511ecf86-ab40-486c-8f76-b8ebda4cc669.

18 Paul Murphy, "Wirecard Critics Targeted in London Spy Operation," *Financial Times*, December 11, 2019, www.ft.com/content/d94c938e-1a84-11ea-97df -cc63de1d73f4.

19 Murphy, "Wirecard Critics Targeted in London."

20 Christo Grozev, "World's Most Wanted Man Jan Marsalek Located in Belarus; Data Points to Russian Intel Links," Bellingcat, July 18, 2020, https://www.bellingcat .com/news/uk-and-europe/2020/07/18/worlds-most-wanted-man-jan-marsalek -located-in-belarus-data-points-to-russian-intel-links/.

21 Sam Jones, "Wirecard Fugitive Helped Run Russian Spy Operations across Europe," *Financial Times*, April 5, 2024, https://www.ft.com/content/c3b50060-aa53 -40fd-a698-579e8e1ae67d; Jörg Diehl et al., "An Agent for Russia? The Double Life of the Former Wirecard Executive Jan Marsalek," *Der Spiegel*, March 5, 2024, https://www.spiegel.de/international/business/jan-marsalek-an-agent-for-russia -the-double-life-of-the-former-wirecard-executive-a-7e667c03-6690-41e6-92ad -583d94ba97e0.

22 Warrell, Jones, and Murphy, "From Payments to Armaments."

23 Ben Taub, "How the Biggest Fraud in German History Unravelled," *New Yorker*, February 27, 2023, https://www.newyorker.com/magazine/2023/03/06/how-the -biggest-fraud-in-german-history-unravelled.

24 Matthew Karnitschnig, "Putin's Hijacked Austria's Spy Service. Now He's Going after Its Government," *Politico*, May 24, 2024, https://www.politico.eu/article /vladimir-putin-austria-spy-service-bvt-government-intelligence-wirecard-jan -marsalek-freedom-party/.

25 Michael Copley and Jeff Brady, "Private Detective Who Led a Hacking Attack against Climate Activists Gets Prison Time," NPR, November 16, 2023, https://www .npr.org/2023/11/16/1213320496/azari-israeli-private-detective-hacking-climate -change-activists-exxonmobil.

26 "BellTrox Affair Scares Corporate Intelligence World," *Intelligence Online*, June 24, 2020, https://www.intelligenceonline.com/corporate-intelligence_corridors-of -power/2020/06/24/belltrox-affair-scares-corporate-intelligence-world,109240236 -gra.

27 US Attorney's Office, Southern District of New York, "Israeli Hacker-for-Hire Sentenced to 80 Months in Prison for Involvement in Massive Spearphishing Campaign," press release, November 16, 2023, https://www.justice.gov/usao -sdny/pr/israeli-hacker-hire-sentenced-80-months-prison-involvement-massive -spearphishing; Joe Miller, "Wirecard Hacker Sentenced to 80 Months in Prison," *Financial Times*, November 16, 2023, https://www.ft.com/content/5557859d-6eb8 -4ccd-a78f-ec252f4e64ac.

28 Sam Tobin, "Israeli Private Eye Arrested in London over Alleged Hacking for US Firm," Reuters, May 2, 2024, https://www.reuters.com/world/israeli-private-eye -arrested-uk-over-alleged-hacking-us-pr-firm-2024-05-02/.

29 Raphael Satter and Christopher Bing, "Israeli Private Eye Accused of Hacking Was Questioned about DC Public Affairs Firm, Sources Say," Reuters, May 24, 2024, https://www.reuters.com/world/israeli-private-eye-accused-hacking-was-questioned -about-dc-public-affairs-firm-2024-05-24/; Christopher M. Matthews, Bradley

Hope, and Jenny Strasburg, "U.S. Prosecutors Probe Global Hacking-for-Hire Operation," *Wall Street Journal*, June 4, 2024, https://www.wsj.com/business/u-s -prosecutors-probe-global-hacking-for-hire-operation-75ab73e7.

30 Shaun Waterman, "CIA Spying on Assange 'Illegally' Swept Up US Lawyers, Journalists: Lawsuit," *Newsweek*, August 15, 2022, https://www.newsweek.com/cia -spying-assange-illegally-swept-us-lawyers-journalists-lawsuit-1731570.

31 Waterman, "CIA Spying on Assange."

32 José María Irujo, "Spanish Company That Spied on Assange Allegedly Informed CIA about Meetings Held by Latin American Leaders," *El País*, July 18, 2023, https://english.elpais.com/international/2023-07-18/spanish-company-that-spied -on-assange-allegedly-informed-cia-about-meetings-held-by-latin-american -leaders.html; José María Irujo, "A Spanish Company and the CIA Found Guilty of Violating Rights of Julian Assange's Visitors," *El País*, December 22, 2023, https:// english.elpais.com/international/2023-12-22/a-spanish-company-and-the-cia -found-guilty-of-violating-rights-of-julian-assanges-visitors.html. Charges are still pending at the time of writing.

33 Leo Eiholzer and Andreas Schmid, "'Project Merciless': How Qatar Spied on the World of Football in Switzerland," SWI Swissinfo.ch, November 2, 2022, www .swissinfo.ch/eng/business/project-merciless-how-qatar-spied-on-the-world-of -football-in-switzerland/48022952.

34 Leo Eiholzer, "Qatar Bugged Secret Meeting between Swiss Attorney General and FIFA President Infantino," *Neue Zürcher Zeitung*, March 11, 2023, https://www .nzz.ch/english/qatar-wiretapped-federal-prosecutor-and-fifa-president-infantino -ld.1730044; Graham Dunbar, "Qatar Spied on Swiss Prosecutor, FIFA Boss Meeting," Associated Press, March 12, 2023, https://apnews.com/article/soccer-fifa -qatar-spying-cia-world-cup-eef4838300a9f014acdcee0c38020d9f.

35 Alan Suderman, "FBI Probing Ex-CIA Officer's Spying for World Cup Host Qatar," Associated Press, October 27, 2022, https://apnews.com/article/world-cup -technology-sports-soccer-religion-5af544d34cded38ff4093587d2efa0de.

36 Eiholzer and Schmid, "'Project Merciless.'"

37 David D. Kirkpatrick, "A Confession Exposes India's Secret Hacking Industry," *New Yorker*, June 1, 2023, https://www.newyorker.com/news/annals-of-crime/a -confession-exposes-indias-secret-hacking-industry.

38 Raphael Satter and Christopher Bing, "How Mercenary Hackers Sway Litiga- tion Battles," Reuters, June 30, 2022, https://www.reuters.com/investigates/special -report/usa-hackers-litigation/.

39 Christopher Bing and Raphael Satter, "How an Indian Startup Hacked the World," Reuters, November 16, 2023, https://www.reuters.com/investigates/special-report /usa-hackers-appin/.

40 Lachlan Cartwright, "Who Is Killing All These Stories about a Controversial Tech Mogul?," *Daily Beast*, December 18, 2023, https://www.thedailybeast.com/who-is -killing-all-these-stories-about-rajat-khare-controversial-tech-mogul.

41 Lachlan Cartwright, "#MeToo 'Media Assassins' Clare Locke Still Repping Russian Oligarchs," *Daily Beast*, March 15, 2022, https://www.thedailybeast.com/metoo -media-assassins-clare-locke-still-repping-russian-oligarchs.

42 Ronald Deibert, "Jail Time for Private Detective," Ronald Deibert, November 22, 2023, https://deibert.citizenlab.ca/2023/11/jail-time-for-private-detective/.

43 Ronen Bergman and Scott Shane, "The Case of the Bumbling Spy: A Watchdog Group Gets Him on Camera," *New York Times*, January 28, 2019, https://www.nytimes.com/2019/01/28/world/black-cube-nso-citizen-lab-intelligence.html; Raphael Satter, "Undercover Spy Exposed in NYC Was 1 of Many," Associated Press, February 11, 2019, https://apnews.com/general-news-9bdbbfe0c8a2407aac14a1e995659de4.

44 "Darryl Levitt's Court Filing," Associated Press, February 21, 2019, https://www.documentcloud.org/documents/5750598-Darryl-Levitt-s-Court-Filing.

45 Satter, "Undercover Spy Exposed in NYC."

46 Ronan Farrow, "The Black Cube Chronicles: The Private Investigators," *New Yorker*, October 7, 2019, https://www.newyorker.com/news/annals-of-espionage/the-black-cube-chronicles-the-private-investigators.

47 Ronan Farrow, "How Democracies Spy on Their Citizens," *New Yorker*, April 18, 2022, https://www.newyorker.com/magazine/2022/04/25/how-democracies-spy-on-their-citizens.

48 Stephanie Kirchgaessner and Harry Davies, "Private Equity Executive Sought to Undermine NSO Critics, Data Suggests," *Guardian*, April 28, 2022, https://www.theguardian.com/world/2022/apr/28/private-equity-executive-sought-to-undermine-nso-critics-data-suggests.

49 Bill Curry and Colin Freeze, "Ties to 'Harmful' Spyware Company Bring Criticism of Ottawa Adviser on Internet Regulation," *Globe and Mail*, May 10, 2022, https://www.theglobeandmail.com/politics/article-ottawa-internet-regulation-expert-nso-group-spyware/.

50 Kirchgaessner and Davies, "Private Equity Executive Sought to Undermine."

CHAPTER 7: "TRUST NO ONE"

1 "Hydroacoustic Monitoring," CTBTO Preparatory Commission, accessed March 6, 2024, https://www.ctbto.org/our-work/monitoring-technologies/hydroacoustic-monitoring; "Infrasound Monitoring," CTBTO Preparatory Commission, accessed March 6, 2024, https://www.ctbto.org/our-work/monitoring-technologies/infrasound-monitoring; "Radionuclide Monitoring," CTBTO Preparatory Commission, accessed March 6, 2024, https://www.ctbto.org/our-work/monitoring-technologies/radionuclide-monitoring.

2 Wawrzyniec Muszyński-Sulima, "Cold War in Space: Reconnaissance Satellites and US-Soviet Security Competition," *European Journal of American Studies* 18, no. 2 (Summer 2023): https://doi.org/10.4000/ejas.20427; David Zikusoka, "Spying from Space," *Foreign Affairs*, February 2, 2024, https://www.foreignaffairs.com/united-states/spying-space; Jeffrey T. Richelson, "Scientists in Black," *Scientific American*, February 1998, 48–55; Jeffrey T. Richelson and Danielle Gordon, "High Flyin' Spies," *Bulletin of the Atomic Scientists* 52, no. 5 (1996): 48–54; Ronald J. Deibert, "Unfettered Observation: The Politics of Earth Monitoring from Space," in *Space Policy in the Twenty-First Century*, ed. W. Henry Lambright (Baltimore, MD: Johns Hopkins University Press, 2003), 89–114.

3 Wilfred P. Deac, "The Navy's Spy Missions in Space," *Naval History*, April 2008, https://www.usni.org/magazines/naval-history-magazine/2008/april/navys-spy -missions-space.

4 Kelsey Herndon, Franz Meyer, Africa Flores, Emil Cherrington, and Leah Kucera, "What Is Synthetic Aperture Radar?," Earthdata, https://www.earthdata.nasa.gov /learn/backgrounders/what-is-sar.

5 "RADARSAT Program," Government of Canada, updated October 18, 2023, https://www.asc-csa.gc.ca/eng/satellites/service-desk/radarsat-program.asp.

6 Eliot Higgins, "How Open Source Evidence Was Upheld in a Human Rights Court," Bellingcat, March 28, 2023, https://www.bellingcat.com/resources/2023/03/28/how -open-source-evidence-was-upheld-in-a-human-rights-court/; Eliot Higgins, "The Open Source Hunt for Syria's Favourite Sarin Bomb," Bellingcat, April 21, 2020, https://www.bellingcat.com/news/2020/04/21/the-open-source-hunt-for-syrias -favourite-sarin-bomb/; Christo Grozev, "The Remote Control Killers behind Russia's Cruise Missile Strikes on Ukraine," Bellingcat, October 24, 2022, https:// www.bellingcat.com/news/uk-and-europe/2022/10/24/the-remote-control-killers -behind-russias-cruise-missile-strikes-on-ukraine/.

7 "The International Monitoring System," CTBTO Preparatory Commission, accessed March 8, 2024, https://www.ctbto.org/our-work/international-monitoring -system; "International Monitoring System Map," CTBTO Preparatory Commission, accessed March 8, 2024, https://www.ctbto.org/our-work/ims-map.

8 John Keess, "Strategic Parasitism, Professional Strategists and Policy Choices: The Influence of George Lindsey and Robert Sutherland on Canadian Denuclearisation, 1962–1972," *Canadian Military History* 29, no. 1 (2020): https://scholars.wlu.ca /cgi/viewcontent.cgi?article=2015&context=cmh.

9 Charles Tilly, "War Making and State Making as Organized Crime," in *Bringing the State Back In*, ed. Dietrich Rueschemeyer, Peter B. Evans, and Theda Skocpol (Cambridge: Cambridge University Press, 1985), 169–91, https://doi.org/10.1017 /CBO9780511628283.008.

10 James Cox, "Canada and the Five Eyes Intelligence Community," Strategic Studies Working Group Papers, Canadian Defence & Foreign Affairs Institute and Canadian International Council, December 2012, https://web.archive .org/web/20150910204519/http://www.cdfai.org.previewmysite.com/PDF /Canada%20and%20the%20Five%20Eyes%20Intelligence%20Community.pdf.

11 "*The X-Files*: Filming & Production," IMDb, accessed March 8, 2024, https://www .imdb.com/title/tt0106179/locations/.

CHAPTER 8: SURVEILLANCE SPECIALISTS

1 Jonathan Peterson, "Where in the World Is Kobi Alexander?," *Baltimore Sun*, August 26, 2006, https://www.baltimoresun.com/2006/08/26/where-in-the-world -is-kobi-alexander/.

2 Paul E. Ceruzzi, "The Chip and Its Impact, 1965–1975," in *A History of Modern Computing* (Cambridge, MA: MIT Press, 1998), 177–206; Chris Miller, *Chip War: The Fight for the World's Most Critical Technology* (New York: Scribner, 2022).

3 Ernest Holsendolph, "U.S. Settles Phone Suit, Drops I.B.M. Case; A.T.& T. to Split Up, Transforming Industry," *New York Times*, January 9, 1982, https://www.nytimes.com/1982/01/09/us/us-settles-phone-suit-drops-ibm-case-at-t-to-split-up-transforming-industry.html.

4 "A Brief History of NSF and the Internet," US National Science Foundation, August 13, 2003, https://www.nsf.gov/news/news_summ.jsp?cntn_id=103050.

5 "Telecommunications Act of 1996," Federal Communications Commission, June 20, 2013, https://www.fcc.gov/general/telecommunications-act-1996.

6 John Labate, "Companies to Watch," *Fortune*, May 17, 1993, https://money.cnn.com/magazines/fortune/fortune_archive/1993/05/17/77847/index.htm.

7 "Tapping into Fax and Modem Links," *Intelligence Online*, March 15, 1995, https://www.intelligenceonline.com/technology/1995/03/15/tapping-into-fax-and-modem-links,65292-art.

8 Labate, "Companies to Watch."

9 "Tapping into Fax and Modem Links."

10 Brian Hochman, "How the Drug War Convinced America to Wiretap the Digital Revolution," *Humanities*, Winter 2023, https://www.neh.gov/article/how-drug-war-convinced-america-wiretap-digital-revolution.

11 Dave Banisar, "CPSR Alert 2.05," *CPSR Alert*, November 12, 1993, https://cypherpunks.venona.com/date/1993/11/msg00462.html.

12 Susan Landau, "National Security on the Line," *Journal on Telecommunications and High Technology Law* 4, no. 2 (Spring 2006): 409–47.

13 Greg Walton, *China's Golden Shield: Corporations and the Development of Surveillance Technology in the People's Republic of China*, Rights & Democracy, International Centre for Human Rights and Democratic Development, 2001, https://publications.gc.ca/collections/Collection/E84-7-2001E.pdf.

14 "FAQ on the CALEA Expansion by the FCC," Electronic Frontier Foundation, https://www.eff.org/pages/calea-faq.

15 John Markoff, "F.B.I. Seeks Access to Mobile Phone Locations," *New York Times*, July 17, 1998, https://www.nytimes.com/1998/07/17/us/fbi-seeks-access-to-mobile-phone-locations.html.

16 Hochman, "How the Drug War Convinced America."

17 Christopher Ketcham, "An Israeli Trojan Horse," *CounterPunch*, September 27, 2008, https://www.counterpunch.org/2008/09/27/an-israeli-trojan-horse/.

18 Office of the Inspector General, *The Implementation of the Communications Assistance for Law Enforcement Act*, Audit Report 06-13, US Department of Justice, March 2006, https://oig.justice.gov/reports/FBI/a0613/findings.htm.

19 John Markoff, "Cellular Phone Groups to Sue Over Wiretapping Regulations," *New York Times*, April 24, 1998, https://www.nytimes.com/1998/04/24/business/cellular-phone-groups-to-sue-over-wiretapping-regulations.html; Office of the Inspector General, *The Implementation of the Communications Assistance for Law Enforcement Act by the Federal Bureau of Investigation*, Audit Report 08-20, US Department of Justice, March 2008, https://oig.justice.gov/reports/FBI/a0820/final.pdf; Susan Landau, "If We Build It (They Will Break In)," *Lawfare*, February 28, 2020, https://www.lawfaremedia.org/article/if-we-build-it-they-will-break.

20 "Tapping into Fax and Modem Links."

21 Verint Systems Inc., Form 10-K, US Securities and Exchange Commission, April 30, 2003, https://www.sec.gov/Archives/edgar/data/1166388/000115752303001569 /a4383530.txt.

22 Comverse Technology Inc., Form 10-K, US Securities and Exchange Commission, March 15, 1996, https://www.sec.gov/Archives/edgar/data/803014/0000950130-96 -001018.txt.

23 Simon Clark, "U.S. Software Firm Verint Is in Talks to Buy NSO for about $1 Billion," *Wall Street Journal*, May 28, 2018, https://www.wsj.com/articles/u-s -software-firm-verint-systems-is-in-talks-to-buy-nso-group-for-about-1-billion -1527491415.

24 "NICE Marks 20th Anniversary," Nice News, March 2006, https://web.archive.org /web/20071022204124/http://www.nice.com/news/newsletter/6_03s/anniversary .php; "Executive Profile: Ori Cohen," Businessweek, October 15, 2012, https:// web.archive.org/web/20121015214857/http://investing.businessweek.com/research /stocks/private/person.asp?personId=1635969&privcapId=29785875&previous CapId=22903&previousTitle=Sequoia%20Capital.

25 "Boeing to Acquire Narus," Tech Monitor, July 8, 2010, https://techmonitor.ai /technology/software/boeing-to-acquire-narus_080710.

26 James Bamford, *The Shadow Factory: The Ultra-Secret NSA from 9/11 to the Eavesdropping on America* (New York: Anchor Books, 2009).

27 Bamford, *Shadow Factory*.

28 Bamford, *Shadow Factory*.

29 Sari Horwitz, "Israeli Experts Teach Police on Terrorism," *Washington Post*, June 11, 2005, https://www.washingtonpost.com/archive/local/2005/06/12/israeli-experts-teach -police-on-terrorism/8cc7830c-df28-4ac1-8bfb-17bc0d3fda28/.

30 Bamford, *Shadow Factory*.

31 Labate, "Companies to Watch."

32 Bamford, *Shadow Factory*.

33 "Tower's Top Executives to Step Down," *EE Times*, March 4, 2003, https://www .eetimes.com/towers-top-executives-to-step-down/.

34 Richard Sanders, "Israeli Spy Companies: Verint and Narus," *Press for Conversion!*, Spring 2012, https://coat.ncf.ca/P4C/66/spy.pdf; Nicky Blackburn, "Israeli Voice Verification Keeps Track of Visa Holders to US," *Israel21c*, December 11, 2005, https://www .israel21c.org/israeli-voice-verification-keeps-track-of-visa-holders-to-us/.

35 Blackburn, "Israeli Voice Verification Keeps Track."

36 Russell A. Stone, Eliahu Elath, William L. Ochsenwald, and Harvey Sicherman, "Israel," *Encyclopedia Britannica*, updated August 2, 2024, https://www.britannica .com/place/Israel; Tom Segev, *A State at Any Cost: The Life of David Ben-Gurion* (New York: Farrar, Straus and Giroux, 2019).

37 Ephraim Kahana, "Reorganizing Israel's Intelligence Community," *International Journal of Intelligence and CounterIntelligence* 15, no. 3 (2002): 415–28, https://doi.org /10.1080/08850600290101686.

38 John Reed, "Unit 8200: Israel's Cyber Spy Agency," *Financial Times*, July 10, 2015, https://www.ft.com/content/69f150da-25b8-11e5-bd83-71cb60e8f08c.

39 Gerald Estrin, "The WEIZAC Years (1954–1963)," *Annals of the History of Computing* 13, no. 4 (October–December 1991): 317–39, https://doi.org/10.1109/MAHC.1991.10037.

40 Reed, "Unit 8200."

41 Gil Press, "6 Reasons Israel Became a Cybersecurity Powerhouse Leading the $82 Billion Industry," *Forbes*, July 18, 2017, https://www.forbes.com/sites/gilpress/2017/07/18/6-reasons-israel-became-a-cybersecurity-powerhouse-leading-the-82-billion-industry/.

42 Yair Evron, "French Arms Policy in the Middle East," *World Today* 26, no. 2 (February 1970): 82–90.

43 Itai Shapira, "The Yom Kippur Intelligence Failure after Fifty Years: What Lessons Can Be Learned?," *Intelligence and National Security* 38, no. 6 (2023): 978–1002, https://doi.org/10.1080/02684527.2023.2235795.

44 Eric Sof, "Sayeret Matkal: A Israel's Equivalent to the Delta Force," *Spec Ops Magazine*, May 15, 2013, https://special-ops.org/sayeret-matkal/.

45 Reed, "Unit 8200."

46 Dan Senor and Saul Singer, *Start-up Nation: The Story of Israel's Economic Miracle* (Toronto: McClelland & Stewart, 2011).

47 Press, "6 Reasons Israel Became a Cybersecurity Powerhouse."

48 Catherine de Fontenay and Erran Carmel, "Israel's Silicon Wadi: The Forces behind Cluster Formation," SIEPR Discussion Paper No. 00-40, Stanford Institute for Economic Policy Research, June 2001, https://drive.google.com/file/d/1QU-BxZBAjZq_64KztKY0m8QQG4IYYzBB/view.

49 "The Unit," *Forbes*, February 8, 2007, https://www.forbes.com/2007/02/07/israel-military-unit-ventures-biz-cx_gk_0208israel.html.

50 Amos Barshad, "Inside Israel's Lucrative—and Secretive—Cybersurveillance Industry," *Rest of World*, March 9, 2021, https://restofworld.org/2021/inside-israels-lucrative-and-secretive-cybersurveillance-talent-pipeline/.

51 Eitay Mack, "A Deep Dive into Shady Nexus between Israel Foreign Ministry and Private Firms," *Wire*, July 27, 2023, https://thewire.in/world/leaked-diplomatic-cables-reveal-shady-nexus-between-israel-foreign-ministry-and-private-firms; Eitay Mack, "How Israel Helped Prop Up Rwanda's Hutu Regime before the Genocide," *+972 Magazine*, April 29, 2019, https://www.972mag.com/rwanda-genocide-hutu-israel/.

52 Hagar Shezaf and Jonathan Jacobson, "Revealed: Israel's Cyber-Spy Industry Helps World Dictators Hunt Dissidents and Gays," *Haaretz*, October 20, 2018, https://www.haaretz.com/israel-news/2018-10-20/ty-article-magazine/.premium/israels-cyber-spy-industry-aids-dictators-hunt-dissidents-and-gays/0000017f-e9a9-dc91-a17f-fdadde240000.

53 Alexandra Konn, "Israel's Information Control Regime in the Occupied Palestinian Territories," Organization for World Peace, June 7, 2021, https://theowp.org/reports/israels-information-control-regime-in-the-occupied-palestinian-territories/.

54 Antony Loewenstein, *The Palestine Laboratory: How Israel Exports the Technology of Occupation around the World* (London: Verso Books, 2023).

55 Reed, "Unit 8200."

56 Loewenstein, *Palestine Laboratory.*

57 Loewenstein, *Palestine Laboratory.*

58 Julie Creswell, "At Comverse, Many Smart Business Moves and Maybe a Bad One," *New York Times,* August 21, 2006, https://www.nytimes.com/2006/08/21/technology /21options.html.

59 Kevin Dugan, "A Decade on the Lam, Ex-Comverse CEO to Return to US," *New York Post,* August 22, 2016, https://nypost.com/2016/08/22/a-decade-on-the-lam-ex -comverse-ceo-to-return-to-us/.

60 Dugan, "Decade on the Lam."

61 Dugan, "Decade on the Lam."

62 "Verint Delisted from NASDAQ," *Security Systems News,* March 1, 2007, https://www .securitysystemsnews.com/article/verint-delisted-nasdaq.

63 "Verint to Buy Comverse Technology," Reuters, August 13, 2012, https://www .reuters.com/article/idUSBRE87C10F/.

CHAPTER 9: CLOSE CALLS IN GUATEMALA CITY

1 Brett Forester, "'You're Not Alone': Guatemalan Anthropologist Offers Support for Unmarked Graves Searches," CBC News, March 5, 2023, https://www.cbc.ca/news /indigenous/fafg-peccerelli-guatemala-unmarked-graves-1.6765949.

2 "Guatemala," *New York Times,* July 15, 2004, https://www.nytimes.com/2004/07/15 /travel/guatemala.html.

3 "Guatemala Murder/Homicide Rate 1960–2024," Macrotrends, accessed March 20, 2024, https://www.macrotrends.net/global-metrics/countries/GTM/guatemala /murder-homicide-rate.

4 "Justice in Guatemala," Center for Justice and Accountability, accessed March 20, 2024, https://cja.org/where-we-work/guatemala/related-resources/general-rios-montt-trial -in-guatemala-2/justice-in-guatemala/.

5 "Uncovering the Truth: The Guatemalan Forensic Anthropology Foundation," Amnesty International, September 9, 2008, https://www.amnesty.org/en/documents /amr34/019/2008/en/.

6 Leslie H. Gelb, "Israelis Said to Step Up Role as Arms Suppliers to Latins," *New York Times,* December 17, 1982, https://www.nytimes.com/1982/12/17/world /israelis-said-to-step-up-role-as-arms-suppliers-to-latins.html.

7 Cheryl Rubenberg, "Israel and Guatemala," *Middle East Report,* May/June 1986, https://merip.org/1986/05/israel-and-guatemala/.

8 Rubenberg, "Israel and Guatemala."

9 Rubenberg, "Israel and Guatemala."

10 Rubenberg, "Israel and Guatemala."

11 *Guatemala: A Government Program of Political Murder,* Amnesty International, 1981, https://www.amnesty.org/en/wp-content/uploads/2021/06/amr340021981en.pdf.

12 Rubenberg, "Israel and Guatemala."

13 Rubenberg, "Israel and Guatemala."

14 Rubenberg, "Israel and Guatemala."

15 Edward Cody, "El Salvador, Israel Set Closer Ties," *Washington Post*, August 16, 1983, https://www.washingtonpost.com/archive/politics/1983/08/17/el-salvador-israel-set -closer-ties/f36aa9a5-2f69-488f-afd1-771dd1eb866b/.

16 Rubenberg, "Israel and Guatemala."

17 *Guatemala: Memory of Silence*, Commission for Historical Clarification, 1999, https://hrdag.org/wp-content/uploads/2013/01/CEHreport-english.pdf.

18 Bishara Bahbah with Linda Butler, "Israel and Latin America," in *Israel and Latin America: The Military Connection* (London: Palgrave Macmillan, 1986), 59–109, https://doi.org/10.1007/978-1-349-09193-5_3.

19 Jennifer Schirmer, "A Violence Called Democracy," *ReVista*, Fall 2003, https://revista .drclas.harvard.edu/a-violence-called-democracy/.

20 "Legitimacy on the Line: Human Rights and the 2003 Guatemalan Elections," Amnesty International, September 18, 2003, https://www.amnesty.org/en/documents /amr34/051/2003/en/.

21 "Legitimacy on the Line."

22 "Legitimacy on the Line."

23 "Espionaje ilegal del Gobierno: Aquí está la investigación de Nuestro Diario (Parte I)," *Nómada*, August 6, 2018, https://nomada.gt/pais/la-corrupcion-no-es-normal /espionaje-ilegal-del-gobierno-aqui-esta-la-investigacion-de-nuestro-diario-parte -i/; Lee Fang, "Former AK-47 Dealer Goes Cyber, Supplied Surveillance Tools to Honduras Government," *Intercept*, July 27, 2015, https://theintercept.com /2015/07/27/ak-47-arms-dealer-goes-cyber-supplied-surveillance-tools-honduras -government/; *Report of the General Secretariat of the Organization of American States on the Diversion of Nicaraguan Arms to the United Self Defense Forces of Colombia*, Organization of American States, January 6, 2003, https://www.oas.org/OASpage/NI -COarmas/NI-COEnglish3687.htm.

24 Fang, "Former AK-47 Dealer Goes Cyber."

CHAPTER 10: "SO, YOU ARE PAID BY THE AGA KHAN?"

1 Information Warfare Monitor, *Tracking GhostNet: Investigating a Cyber Espionage Network*, Munk School of Global Affairs, University of Toronto, March 29, 2009, https://citizenlab.ca/wp-content/uploads/2017/05/ghostnet.pdf; Information Warfare Monitor and Shadowserver Foundation, *Shadows in the Cloud: Investigating Cyber Espionage 2.0*, Munk School of Global Affairs, University of Toronto, April 6, 2010, https://citizenlab.ca/wp-content/uploads/2017/05/shadows-in-the-cloud.pdf.

2 John Markoff and David Barboza, "Researchers Trace Data Theft to Intruders in China," *New York Times*, April 5, 2010, https://www.nytimes.com/2010/04/06 /science/06cyber.html.

3 Thomas Vinciguerra, "The Revolution Will Be Colorized," *New York Times*, March 13, 2005, https://www.nytimes.com/2005/03/13/weekinreview/the-revolution-will -be-colorized.html.

4 Tim Eaton, "Internet Activism and the Egyptian Uprisings: Transforming Online Dissent into the Offline World," *Westminster Papers in Communication and Culture* 9, no. 2 (2013): 3–24, https://doi.org/10.16997/wpcc.163.

5 Larry Diamond, "Liberation Technology," *Journal of Democracy* 21, no. 3 (July 2010): 69–83, https://doi.org/10.1353/jod.0.0190.

6 "Are They Allowed to Do That? A Breakdown of Selected Government Surveillance Programs," Brennan Center for Justice, July 15, 2013, https://www.brennancenter .org/our-work/research-reports/are-they-allowed-do-breakdown-selected -government-surveillance-programs.

7 "National Security Letters: FAQ," Electronic Frontier Foundation, https://www.eff .org/issues/national-security-letters/faq.

8 T. C. Sottek and Janus Kopfstein, "Everything You Need to Know about PRISM," *Verge*, July 17, 2013, https://www.theverge.com/2013/7/17/4517480/nsa-spying -prism-surveillance-cheat-sheet.

9 Steven Loleski, "From Cold to Cyber Warriors: The Origins and Expansion of NSA's Tailored Access Operations (TAO) to Shadow Brokers," *Intelligence and National Security* 34, no. 1 (January 2, 2019): 112–28, https://doi.org/10.1080 /02684527.2018.1532627.

10 Mark Klein, interview by *Frontline*, season 25, episode 8, "Spying on the Home-front," aired May 15, 2007, on PBS, https://www.pbs.org/wgbh/pages/frontline /homefront/interviews/klein.html.

11 Glenn Greenwald, Ewen MacAskill, and Laura Poitras, "Edward Snowden: The Whistleblower behind the NSA Surveillance Revelations," *Guardian*, June 11, 2013, https://www.theguardian.com/world/2013/jun/09/edward-snowden-nsa-whistle blower-surveillance; Barton Gellman, *Dark Mirror: Edward Snowden and the American Surveillance State* (New York: Penguin Books, 2021).

12 Jedidiah R. Crandall, Masashi Crete-Nishihata, Jeffrey Knockel, Sarah McKune, Adam Senft, Diana Tseng, and Greg Wiseman, "Chat Program Censorship and Surveillance in China: Tracking TOM-Skype and Sina UC," *First Monday* 18, no. 7 (2013): https://doi.org/10.5210/fm.v18i7.4628; Nart Villeneuve, *Breaching Trust: An Analysis of Surveillance and Security Practices on China's TOM-Skype Platform*, Information Warfare Monitor and Citizen Lab, Munk School of Global Affairs, University of Toronto, October 1, 2008, https://www.nartv.org/mirror/breachingtrust.pdf.

13 See Ronald Deibert, John Palfrey, Rafal Rohozinski, and Jonathan L. Zittrain, eds., *Access Denied: The Practice and Policy of Global Internet Filtering* (Cambridge, MA: MIT Press, 2008), https://doi.org/10.7551/mitpress/7617.001.0001.

14 Jonathon Penney, Sarah McKune, Lex Gill, and Ronald J. Deibert, "Advancing Human-Rights-by-Design in the Dual-Use Technology Industry," *Journal of International Affairs* 71, no. 2 (2018): 103–10; Ronald Deibert, "What to Do about 'Dual Use' Digital Technologies?," Ronald Deibert, November 29, 2016, https://deibert .citizenlab.ca/2016/11/dual-use/; Siena Anstis, Niamh Leonard, and Jonathon W. Penney, "Moving from Secrecy to Transparency in the Offensive Cyber Capabilities Sector: The Case of Dual-Use Technologies Exports," *Computer Law & Security Review* 48 (April 2023): 105787, https://doi.org/10.1016/j.clsr.2022.105787.

15 Greg Walton, *China's Golden Shield: Corporations and the Development of Surveillance Technology in the People's Republic of China*, Rights & Democracy, International Centre for Human Rights and Democratic Development, 2001, https://publications.gc.ca /collections/Collection/E84-7-2001E.pdf.

16 Jim Yardley, "Two Concerns for Olympics: Air and Access," *New York Times*, July 9, 2008, https://www.nytimes.com/2008/07/09/sports/olympics/09beijing.html.

17 Ryan Singel, "Espionage against Pro-Tibet Groups, Others, Spurred Microsoft Patches," *Wired*, April 10, 2008, https://www.wired.com/2008/04/espionage-against-pro-tibet-groups-others-spurred-microsoft-patches/; Maarten Van Horenbeeck, "Overview of Cyber Attacks against Tibetan Communities," Internet Storm Center, SANS Technology Institute, March 24, 2008, https://isc.sans.edu/diary/Overview+of+cyber+attacks+against+Tibetan+communities/4177/.

18 John Markoff, "Tracking Cyberspies through the Web Wilderness," *New York Times*, May 11, 2009, https://www.nytimes.com/2009/05/12/science/12cyber.html.

19 Omar El Akkad, "Meet the Canadians Who Busted GhostNet," *Globe and Mail*, March 30, 2009, https://www.theglobeandmail.com/technology/meet-the-canadians-who-busted-ghostnet/article1214210/.

20 Information Warfare Monitor and Shadowserver Foundation, *Shadows in the Cloud*.

21 Markoff and Barboza, "Researchers Trace Data Theft."

22 "A New Approach to China," *Google Official Blog*, January 12, 2010, https://googleblog.blogspot.com/2010/01/new-approach-to-china.html.

23 Christopher Parsons, "CSE Summaries," *Technology, Thoughts & Trinkets* (blog), updated January 17, 2023, https://christopher-parsons.com/resources/the-sigint-summaries/cse-summaries/.

24 Brigitte Bureau, "Stephen Harper Involved in Company Looking to Arrange Sale of Surveillance Tech to UAE," CBC News, September 29, 2021, https://www.cbc.ca/news/politics/harper-united-arab-emirates-surveillance-technology-1.6192281.

25 TED Blog Video, "Shyam Sankar: Who Hacked the Dalai Lama's Email? TED BLOG EXCLUSIVE," September 6, 2012, video, 3:38, https://www.youtube.com/watch?v=zE6xvQeMqqE.

26 Ronen Bergman, "Weaving a Cyber Web," *Ynetnews*, January 11, 2019, https://www.ynetnews.com/articles/0,7340,L-5444998,00.html.

27 Bergman, "Weaving a Cyber Web."

28 Hagar Shezaf and Jonathan Jacobson, "Revealed: Israel's Cyber-Spy Industry Helps World Dictators Hunt Dissidents and Gays," *Haaretz*, October 20, 2018, https://www.haaretz.com/israel-news/2018-10-20/ty-article-magazine/.premium/israels-cyber-spy-industry-aids-dictators-hunt-dissidents-and-gays/0000017f-e9a9-dc91-a17f-fdadde240000.

29 Shezaf and Jacobson, "Revealed: Israel's Cyber-Spy Industry."

CHAPTER 11: *"MÁTALO! MÁTALO!"*

1 Jon Lee Anderson, "Mexican Journalists Lose Another Colleague to the Drug War," *New Yorker*, May 20, 2017, https://www.newyorker.com/news/news-desk/mexican-journalists-lose-another-colleague-to-the-drug-war; Ioan Grillo, "Inside the Brilliant Career and Tragic Death of Javier Valdez," *Esquire*, September 19, 2018, https://www.esquire.com/news-politics/a22996658/javier-valdez-luis-guzman-el-chapo-journalist/.

2 Center for Preventive Action, "Criminal Violence in Mexico," Global Conflict

Tracker, updated July 24, 2024, https://cfr.org/global-conflict-tracker/conflict/criminal-violence-mexico.

3 Anderson, "Mexican Journalists Lose Another Colleague."

4 Leónidas Alfaro Bedolla, "¿QUIÉN MATÓ A JAVIER VALDEZ? Capítulo No. 9: Una Infamia Imperdonable," *Espejo*, January 22, 2023, https://web.archive.org/web/20230202214916/https://revistaespejo.com/reflexiones/quien-mato-a-javier-valdez-capitulo-no-9-una-infamia-imperdonable/.

5 Catalina Gonella, "Journalists Protest, Mourn Killing of Mexican Reporter Javier Valdez Cárdenas," NBC News, May 16, 2017, https://www.nbcnews.com/news/latino/journalists-protest-mourn-killing-mexican-reporter-javier-valdez-c-rdenas-n760161; Phil Davison, "Javier Valdez Cardenas, Obituary: Crusading Journalist Who Covered Mexican Drug Trade," *Independent*, May 17, 2017, https://www.independent.co.uk/news/obituaries/javier-valdez-cardenas-a7740786.html.

6 John Scott-Railton, Bill Marczak, Siena Anstis, Bahr Abdul Razzak, Masashi Crete-Nishihata, and Ron Deibert, *Reckless VI: Mexican Journalists Investigating Cartels Targeted with NSO Spyware Following Assassination of Colleague*, Research Report No. 116, Citizen Lab, University of Toronto, November 27, 2018, https://citizenlab.ca/2018/11/mexican-journalists-investigating-cartels-targeted-nso-spyware-following-assassination-colleague/.

7 John Scott-Railton, Bill Marczak, Siena Anstis, Bahr Abdul Razzak, Masashi Crete-Nishihata, and Ron Deibert, *Reckless VII: Wife of Journalist Slain in Cartel-Linked Killing Targeted with NSO Group's Spyware*, Research Report No. 117, Citizen Lab, University of Toronto, March 20, 2019, https://citizenlab.ca/2019/03/nso-spyware-slain-journalists-wife/.

8 Ronen Bergman and Mark Mazzetti, "The Battle for the World's Most Powerful Cyberweapon," *New York Times*, January 28, 2022, https://www.nytimes.com/2022/01/28/magazine/nso-group-israel-spyware.html.

9 Edward Hunt, "The U.S. Has Spent Billions Trying to Fix Mexico's Drug War. It's Not Working," *Washington Post*, March 15, 2021, https://www.washingtonpost.com/politics/2021/03/15/us-has-spent-billions-trying-fix-mexicos-drug-war-its-not-working/; Jess Ford, *Mérida Initiative: The United States Has Provided Counternarcotics and Anticrime Support but Needs Better Performance Measures*, Government Accountability Office, July 2010, https://www.gao.gov/assets/gao-10-837.pdf; Clare Ribando Seelke and Ramon Miro, "Mexico's Immigration Control Efforts," Congressional Research Service, March 13, 2023, https://crsreports.congress.gov/product/pdf/IF/IF10215.

10 Cécile Schilis-Gallego, "Spying on Mexican Journalists: Investigating the Lucrative Market of Cyber-Surveillance," Forbidden Stories, December 7, 2020, https://forbiddenstories.org/spying-on-mexican-journalists-investigating-the-lucrative-market-of-cyber-surveillance/.

11 US Attorney's Office, Eastern District of New York, "Ex–Mexican Secretary of Public Security Genaro Garcia Luna Convicted of Engaging in a Continuing Criminal Enterprise and Taking Millions in Cash Bribes from the Sinaloa Cartel," press release, February 21, 2023, https://www.justice.gov/usao-edny/pr/ex-mexican-secretary-public-security-genaro-garcia-luna-convicted-engaging-continuing.

12 Keegan Hamilton, "El Chapo's Inside Man Was America's Closest Partner in Mexico," *Vice*, February 24, 2023, https://www.vice.com/en/article/3adxp9/genaro -garcia-luna-us-trial-drug-trafficking-conviction.

13 US Attorney's Office, Eastern District of New York, "Ex–Mexican Secretary of Public Security"; United Mexican States v. Genaro Garcia Luna et al., File # 135011567 (11th Cir. Sept. 21, 2021), https://insightcrime.org/wp-content/uploads/2021/09 /2021-09-21-UIF-Garcia-Luna-Florida.pdf; Peniley Ramírez, *Los millonarios de la guerra: el expediente inédito de García Luna y sus socios* (Mexico City: Grijalbo, 2020).

14 Zedryk Raziel and Elías Camhaji, "García Luna Sold Spy Technology to the Mexican Government during the Peña Nieto Administration," *El País*, May 8, 2023, https://english.elpais.com/international/2023-05-08/garcia-luna-sold-spy -technology-to-the-mexican-government-during-the-pena-nieto-administration .html; Maria Hinojosa and Peniley Ramírez, "Operation Miami," *USA v. García Luna*, podcast, 43:16, December 30, 2022, https://podcasts.apple.com/us/podcast /episode-4-operation-miami/id1657286545?i=1000591790925; Peniley Ramírez, "Denuncias contra exsecretario de seguridad de México muestran red de empresas fachada que movió más de 50 millones de dólares en 11 países," Univision, May 18, 2020, https://www.univision.com/noticias/america-latina/denuncias-contra-exsec retario-de-seguridad-de-mexico-muestran-red-de-empresas-fachada-que-movio -mas-de-50-millones-de-dolares-en-11-paises.

15 Raziel and Camhaji, "García Luna Sold Spy Technology."

16 Tim Golden, "U.S. Investigators Uncovered Alleged Corruption by Mexico's Former Security Minister Years before He Was Indicted," ProPublica, January 22, 2023, https://www.propublica.org/article/genaro-garcia-luna-bribery-trial-dea -mexico-cartel.

17 Richard Silverstein, "Mexican Government Cancels NSO Group Cyber-Surveillance Contract, Launches Corruption Investigation," *Tikun Olam* (blog), May 11, 2020, https://www.richardsilverstein.com/2020/05/11/mexican-government-cancels -nso-group-cyber-surveillance-contract/.

18 Oded Yaron, "The Secret of NSO's Success in Mexico," *Haaretz*, November 30, 2020, https://www.haaretz.com/israel-news/tech-news/2020-11-30/ty-article/.highlight /the-secret-of-nsos-success-in-mexico/0000017f-e0f5-d568-ad7f-f3ff5cff0000.

19 Stephanie Kirchgaessner, "Dominican Investigative Journalist Targeted with NSO Spyware, Report Says," *Guardian*, May 2, 2023, https://www.theguardian.com /world/2023/may/02/nuria-piera-spyware-target-nso-group.

20 Bergman and Mazzetti, "Battle for the World's Most Powerful Cyberweapon."

21 Richard Silverstein, "Former GOP National Finance Chair, Eliott Broidy, and Convicted Mexican Billionaire, Brokered First Foreign Sale of NSO Group Malware to Mexico," *Tikun Olam* (blog), February 25, 2020, https://www.richardsilverstein .com/2020/02/25/former-gop-bundler-eliot-broidy-and-convicted-mexican -billionaire-brokered-first-foreign-sale-of-nso-group-malware-to-mexico/.

22 Silverstein, "Former GOP National Finance Chair."

23 Yaron, "Secret of NSO's Success in Mexico."

24 Seth Hettena, "Scandal, Spyware, and 69 Pounds of Weed," *Daily Beast*, August 3, 2021, https://www.thedailybeast.com/scandal-spyware-and-69-pounds-of-weed.

25 Hettena, "Scandal, Spyware, and 69 Pounds of Weed."

26 Tomer Ganon and Hagar Ravet, "The Dodgy Framework and the Middlemen: How NSO Sold Its First Pegasus License," *CTech*, February 24, 2020, https://www .calcalistech.com/ctech/articles/0,7340,L-3796112,00.html.

27 Ganon and Ravet, "Dodgy Framework and the Middlemen."

28 "Israeli Eitanium Emerges from Woodwork Financed by Sector Heavyweights," *Intelligence Online*, November 18, 2021, https://www.intelligenceonline.com /surveillance—interception/2021/11/18/israeli-eitanium-emerges-from-woodwork -financed-by-sector-heavyweights,109705703-eve.

29 Ganon and Ravet, "Dodgy Framework and the Middlemen."

30 Thomas Brewster, "A Multimillionaire Surveillance Dealer Steps Out of the Shadows . . . and His $9 Million WhatsApp Hacking Van," *Forbes*, August 5, 2019, https://www.forbes.com/sites/thomasbrewster/2019/08/05/a-multimillionaire -surveillance-dealer-steps-out-of-the-shadows-and-his-9-million-whatsapp -hacking-van/.

31 Hettena, "Scandal, Spyware, and 69 Pounds of Weed."

32 Natalie Kitroeff and Ronen Bergman, "How Mexico Became the Biggest User of the World's Most Notorious Spy Tool," *New York Times*, April 18, 2023, https://www .nytimes.com/2023/04/18/world/americas/pegasus-spyware-mexico.html.

33 Katitza Rodriguez and Gabriela Manuli, "Mexicans Need Transparency on Secret Surveillance Contracts," Electronic Frontier Foundation, July 24, 2012, https://www.eff.org/deeplinks/2012/07/mexicans-need-transparency-secret -surveillance-contracts; Yaron, "Secret of NSO's Success in Mexico."

34 "Mexico: Army Used Pegasus to Spy on Human Rights Defender Raymundo Ramos," Article 19, March 7, 2023, https://www.article19.org/resources/mexico -army-used-pegasus-to-spy-on-human-rights-defender-raymundo-ramos/.

35 Oded Yaron, "NSO Spyware Used by Private Firm against Reporter, Top Mexican Official," *Haaretz*, November 11, 2021, https://www.haaretz.com/israel-news /tech-news/2021-11-11/ty-article/.premium/nso-spyware-used-by-private-firm -against-reporter-first-arrest-in-mexico/0000017f-f2c6-d487-abff-f3fe3b940000; Amitai Ziv, "Revealed: The Israelis Making Millions Selling Cyberweapons to Latin America," *Haaretz*, December 8, 2020, https://www.haaretz.com/israel-news /tech-news/2020-12-08/ty-article/.highlight/revealed-the-israelis-selling-cyber weapons-to-latin-america/0000017f-e130-d9aa-afff-f9784e320000.

36 Ganon and Ravet, "Dodgy Framework and the Middlemen."

37 Tomer Ganon and Hagar Ravet, "The Rayzone Group's Secret Cyber Intelligence Activities Revealed," *CTech*, December 29, 2020, https://www.calcalistech.com /ctech/articles/0,7340,L-3884553,00.html.

38 Omer Kabir, "Report Reveals Which Countries Are Using Circles Technologies' Invasive Spyware," *CTech*, December 1, 2020, https://www.calcalistech.com/ctech /articles/0,7340,L-3878410,00.html.

39 Rebecca Ballhaus and Julie Bykowicz, "Elliott Broidy Quits RNC Post after Report on Payment to Ex-Model," *Wall Street Journal*, April 13, 2018, https://www.wsj .com/articles/elliott-broidy-quits-rnc-post-after-report-on-payment-to-ex-model -1523645801; Kenneth P. Vogel, "Elliott Broidy Pleads Guilty in Foreign Lobbying

Case," *New York Times*, October 20, 2020, https://www.nytimes.com/2020/10/20
/us/politics/elliott-broidy-foreign-lobbying.html; Ryan Grim and Alex Emmons,
"Trump Fundraiser Offered Russian Gas Company Plan to Get Sanctions Lifted for
$26 Million," *Intercept*, April 20, 2018, https://theintercept.com/2018/04/20/elliott
-broidy-trump-russia-sanctions/.

40 David D. Kirkpatrick, "A Top Trump Fund-Raiser Says Qatar Hacked His Email,"
New York Times, March 5, 2018, https://www.nytimes.com/2018/03/05/world
/middleeast/qatar-trump-hack-email.html.

41 Ziv, "Revealed: The Israelis Making Millions."

42 Ziv, "Revealed: The Israelis Making Millions."

43 Yaron, "NSO Spyware Used by Private Firm"; "Mexico," Database of Israeli Military and Security Export, accessed April 22, 2024, https://www.dimse.info/mexico/;
"Secretaría de la Defensa Nacional de México," Distributed Denial of Secrets,
January 23, 2024, https://ddosecrets.com/article/secretaria-de-la-defensa-nacional
-de-mexico.

44 Arturo Angel, "Translated from Spanish: Videgaray, Cienfuegos and Duarte, behind
Payments to Pegasus for Espionage," Ana Noticias, July 22, 2021, https://ananoticias
.com/2021/07/22/translated-from-spanish-videgaray-cienfuegos-and-duarte
-behind-payments-to-pegasus-for-espionage/.

45 Yaron, "Secret of NSO's Success in Mexico."

46 Suhail Gharaibeh, "Israel, Cybersurveillance, and the Case of the Ayotzinapa 43,"
NACLA, September 14, 2022, https://nacla.org/israel-cybersurveillance-mexico
-case-ayotzinapa-43.

47 "Hacking Team," WikiLeaks, July 8, 2015, https://wikileaks.org/hackingteam
/emails/.

48 Elizabeth Gonzalez, "Explainer: Hacking Team's Reach in the Americas," AS
/COA, July 30, 2015, https://www.as-coa.org/articles/explainer-hacking-teams
-reach-americas.

49 Lorenzo Franceschi-Bicchierai, "Hacking Team's 'Illegal' Latin American Empire,"
Vice, April 18, 2016, https://www.vice.com/en/article/gv5v8q/hacking-team-illegal
-latin-american-empire.

50 Eric Banoun, "MEXICO PGR URGENT," email, November 29, 2014,
https://wikileaks.org/hackingteam/emails/emailid/5986, in "Hacking Team," Wiki-
Leaks, July 8, 2015.

51 "Mexico: $300 Million in Spyware Spending Included Kickbacks," Associated Press,
July 21, 2021, https://apnews.com/article/technology-middle-east-mexico-spyware
-ee103912620f5d7267f3369a95e5fe2d.

52 Raúl Olmos, "Subordinado de Murillo Karam, ligado a grupo empresarial que
vendió Pegasus a la PGR," Mexicanos Contra la Corrupción y la Impunidad,
February 20, 2017, https://contralacorrupcion.mx/pegasus-pgr/.

53 Lilach Baumer, "Lawsuit Asks to Restrict Sales of Israeli Spyware," *CTech*, September
2, 2018, https://www.calcalistech.com/ctech/articles/0,7340,L-3745470,00.html.

54 Amitai Ziv, "Raising Concerns over Press Freedom, Israel's NSO Reportedly Sold Ghana Surveillance Tech," *Haaretz*, July 3, 2019, https://www.haaretz
.com/israel-news/2019-07-03/ty-article/.premium/raising-concerns-over-press

-freedom-israels-nso-reportedly-sold-ghana-spyware/0000017f-e94b-df5f-a17f
-fbdfa9510000; Rolando Rodríguez B., "Abren sumario en caso Hacking Team,"
La Prensa, August 6, 2015, https://www.prensa.com/locales/Espiar-obsesion
-Martinelli_0_4271572998.html; "Rwandan Authorities Chose Thousands of
Activists, Journalists and Politicians to Target with NSO Spyware," Amnesty Inter-
national, July 19, 2021, https://www.amnesty.org/en/latest/press-release/2021/07
/rwandan-authorities-chose-thousands-of-activists-journalists-and-politicians
-to-target-with-nso-spyware/; Ellen Ioanes, "Israeli Spyware Was Used against
US Diplomats in Uganda," *Vox*, December 4, 2021, https://www.vox.com/2021
/12/4/22817236/nso-group-israeli-spyware-pegasus-hack-us-diplomats-uganda;
John Scott-Railton, Bill Marczak, Irene Poetranto, Bahr Abdul Razzak, Sutawan
Chanprasert, and Ron Deibert, *GeckoSpy: Pegasus Spyware Used against Thailand's
Pro-Democracy Movement*, Research Report No. 157, Citizen Lab, University of
Toronto, July 17, 2022, https://citizenlab.ca/2022/07/geckospy-pegasus-spyware
-used-against-thailands-pro-democracy-movement/; Ronen Bergman and Mark
Mazzetti, "Israeli Companies Aided Saudi Spying despite Khashoggi Killing," *New
York Times*, July 17, 2021, https://www.nytimes.com/2021/07/17/world/middleeast
/israel-saudi-khashoggi-hacking-nso.html; Chaim Levinson, "With Israel's Encouragement, NSO Sold Spyware to UAE and Other Gulf States," *Haaretz*, August 25,
2020, https://www.haaretz.com/middle-east-news/2020-08-25/ty-article/.premium
/with-israels-encouragement-nso-sold-spyware-to-uae-and-other-gulf-states
/0000017f-dbf3-d856-a37f-fff3a4ba0000.

55 Dolia Estevez, "Mexico's Proposed Tax on Soda, Junk Food Opposed by Billionaire
Beverage and Food Barons," *Forbes*, October 28, 2013, https://www.forbes.com/sites
/doliaestevez/2013/10/28/mexicos-proposed-tax-on-soda-junk-food-opposed-by
-billionaire-beverage-and-food-barons/.

56 Gharaibeh, "Israel, Cybersurveillance, and the Case."

57 Gharaibeh, "Israel, Cybersurveillance, and the Case."

58 Interdisciplinary Group of Independent Experts, "GIEI Ayotzinapa Report
Summary," National Security Archive, October 12, 2015, https://nsarchive.gwu.edu
/document/27608-1-giei-ayotzinapa-report-summary.

59 Gharaibeh, "Israel, Cybersurveillance, and the Case."

60 Juan Omar Fierro, "Niega PGR fragmentación de indagatoria del caso Iguala,"
El Universal, February 21, 2016, https://www.eluniversal.com.mx/articulo/nacion
/seguridad/2016/02/21/niega-pgr-fragmentacion-de-indagatoria-del-caso-iguala/.

61 John Scott-Railton, Bill Marczak, Bahr Abdul Razzak, Masashi Crete-Nishihata,
and Ron Deibert, *Reckless Exploit: Mexican Journalists, Lawyers, and a Child Targeted
with NSO Spyware*, Research Report No. 93, Citizen Lab, University of Toronto,
June 19, 2017, https://citizenlab.ca/2017/06/reckless-exploit-mexico-nso/.

62 Azam Ahmed, "Mexico Spyware Inquiry Bogs Down. Skeptics Aren't Surprised,"
New York Times, February 20, 2018, https://www.nytimes.com/2018/02/20/world
/americas/mexico-spyware-investigation.html.

63 Ronen Bergman and Oscar Lopez, "Former Official Wanted by Mexico Takes
Refuge in Israel," *New York Times*, July 15, 2021, https://www.nytimes.com/2021/07
/15/world/middleeast/israel-mexico-zeron-extradition.html.

64 Tomer Ganon, "The Wanted Mexican That Is Hiding Out at the Luxury Home of the Rayzone Group Entrepreneur," *CTech*, May 18, 2022, https://www.calcalistech .com/ctechnews/article/u1ahyselk.

65 NMás, "Conferencia matutina AMLO—Miércoles 6 de Noviembre 2019," November 6, 2019, video, 1:52:00, https://www.youtube.com/watch?v=BjzRY-nQT2w.

66 Nina Lakhani, "Fifty People Linked to Mexico's President among Potential Targets of NSO Clients," *Guardian*, July 19, 2021, https://www.theguardian.com/news /2021/jul/19/fifty-people-close-mexico-president-amlo-among-potential-targets -nso-clients.

67 Centro de Produccion CEPROPIE, "Conferencia de prensa matutina del martes 20 de julio, 2021," July 20, 2021, video, 2:03:55, https://www.youtube.com/watch?v= HOrjI2dMl4U.

68 Suzanne Smalley, "Pegasus Spyware Trial Implicating Former President Kicks Off in Mexico," *Record*, December 5, 2023, https://therecord.media/mexico-pegasus -spyware-trial-kicks-off; Mary Beth Sheridan, "Mexico Makes First Arrest in Pegasus Spying Scandal," *Washington Post*, November 9, 2021, https://www.washingtonpost .com/world/2021/11/09/mexico-pegasus-nso/.

69 Associated Press, "Israeli Spyware Firm Distances Itself from Mexico Suspect," *Ynetnews*, November 9, 2021, https://www.ynetnews.com/article/sytka1fwy.

70 "Mexico: Investigations into the Use of Pegasus Spyware Must Continue," Article 19, January 15, 2024, https://www.article19.org/resources/mexico-investigations -into-the-use-of-pegasus-spyware-must-continue/.

71 "Mexico: Investigations into the Use of Pegasus."

72 Daina Beth Solomon, "Mexican Opposition Lawmaker Says He Was Target of Pegasus Spyware," Reuters, October 18, 2022, https://www.reuters.com/world /americas/mexican-opposition-lawmaker-says-he-was-target-pegasus-spyware -2022-10-18/.

73 "CPJ Welcomes 2nd Conviction in Case of Slain Mexican Journalist Javier Valdez Cárdenas," Committee to Protect Journalists, June 9, 2021, https://cpj.org/2021/06 /cpj-welcomes-2nd-conviction-in-case-of-slain-mexican-journalist-javier-valdez -cardenas/.

74 Keegan Hamilton, "Who Ordered the Murder of a Legendary Mexican Journalist? El Chapo's Trial Only Adds to the Mystery," *Vice*, January 24, 2019, https://www .vice.com/en/article/43zd3g/el-chapos-former-right-hand-man-says-drug-lords -sons-were-behind-killing-of-legendary-journalist.

75 Keegan Hamilton, "Mexico Wants the US to Hand Over El Chapo's Godson for Killing of Legendary Journalist," *Vice*, September 19, 2022, https://www.vice.com /en/article/4ax4q9/damaso-lopez-journalist-killing-extradition.

76 Ahmed, "Mexico Spyware Inquiry Bogs Down"; Luis Fernando García, "Spyware in Mexico: An Interview with Luis Fernando García of R3D Mexico," interviewed by Deji Bryce Olukotun, Access Now, June 22, 2017, https://www.accessnow.org /spyware-mexico-interview-luis-fernando-garcia-r3d-mexico/.

77 "Secretaría de la Defensa Nacional de México," Distributed Denial of Secrets, January 23, 2024, https://ddosecrets.com/article/secretaria-de-la-defensa-nacional -de-mexico.

78   Dina Temple-Raston and Will Jarvis, "Internal Documents Show Mexican Army Used Spyware against Civilians, Set Up Secret Military Intelligence Unit," *Record*, March 7, 2023, https://therecord.media/mexican-army-spyware.

79   Natalie Kitroeff and Ronen Bergman, "Spying by Mexico's Armed Forces Brings Fears of a 'Military State,'" *New York Times*, March 7, 2023, https://www.nytimes .com/2023/03/07/world/americas/mexico-military-surveillance.html.

80   "Mexican President Slams Report Military Spied on Activist as 'Made Up,'" Reuters, March 10, 2023, https://www.reuters.com/world/americas/mexican-president-slams -report-military-spied-activist-made-up-2023-03-10/.

81   Mary Beth Sheridan, "Pegasus Spyware Reaches into Mexican President's Inner Circle," *Washington Post*, May 24, 2023, https://www.washingtonpost.com/world /2023/05/24/pegasus-spyware-ayotzinapa-mexico/.

CHAPTER 12: ANARCHY IN THE UNITED KINGDOM

1   Bill Marczak and John Scott-Railton, *Move Fast and Roll Your Own Crypto: A Quick Look at the Confidentiality of Zoom Meetings*, Research Report No. 126, Citizen Lab, University of Toronto, April 3, 2020, https://citizenlab.ca/2020/04/move-fast-roll -your-own-crypto-a-quick-look-at-the-confidentiality-of-zoom-meetings/.

2   US Federal Trade Commission, "FTC Requires Zoom to Enhance Its Security Practices as Part of Settlement," press release, November 9, 2020, https://www .ftc.gov/news-events/news/press-releases/2020/11/ftc-requires-zoom-enhance-its -security-practices-part-settlement.

3   Stephanie Kirchgaessner, "Jeff Bezos Hack: Amazon Boss's Phone 'Hacked by Saudi Crown Prince,'" *Guardian*, January 22, 2020, https://www.theguardian.com /technology/2020/jan/21/amazon-boss-jeff-bezoss-phone-hacked-by-saudi-crown -prince.

4   Kim Zetter and Joseph Cox, "Here Is the Technical Report Suggesting Saudi Arabia's Prince Hacked Jeff Bezos' Phone," *Vice*, January 22, 2020, https://www.vice .com/en/article/v74v34/saudi-arabia-hacked-jeff-bezos-phone-technical-report.

5   David Brown, "Cherie Blair Is Adviser to NSO, the Firm behind Pegasus Spyware," *Times* (UK), October 7, 2021, https://www.thetimes.co.uk/article/cherie-blair-is -adviser-to-nso-the-firm-behind-pegasus-spyware-rjdhhvr2s.

6   "Al Maktoum Judgments," Courts and Tribunals Judiciary, October 6, 2021, https://www.judiciary.uk/judgments/al-maktoum-judgments/.

7   Frank Gardner, "Dubai's Sheikh Mohammed Abducted Daughters and Threatened Wife—UK Court," BBC, March 5, 2020, https://www.bbc.com/news/world-middle -east-51756984; "Profile," HRH Princess Haya Bint Al Hussein, September 30, 2005, https://web.archive.org/web/20050930232238/http:/princesshaya.net/profile .shtm.

8   Katie Thomas, "Princess Shakes Up Equestrian World," *New York Times*, September 24, 2010, https://www.nytimes.com/2010/09/25/sports/25horses.html; Frank Gardner, "Princess Haya: Dubai Ruler Had Ex-Wife's Phone Hacked—UK Court," BBC, October 6, 2021, https://www.bbc.com/news/world-middle-east -58814978; Vivian Yee and David D. Kirkpatrick, "Princess Haya, Wife of Dubai's

Ruler, Seeks Refuge in London," *New York Times*, July 2, 2019, https://www.nytimes .com/2019/07/02/world/middleeast/princess-haya-sheikh-mohammed-bin.html.

9 Vanessa Grigoriadis, "'You're Essentially a Prisoner': Why Do Dubai's Princesses Keep Trying to Escape?," *Vanity Fair*, February 20, 2020, https://www.vanityfair .com/news/2019/11/why-do-dubais-princesses-keep-trying-to-escape.

10 Joshua Hammer, "The Runaway Princesses of Dubai," *Town & Country*, January 4, 2022, https://www.townandcountrymag.com/society/money-and-power/a29848986 /dubai-princess-disappearance-divorce/.

11 Bill Bostock, "UK Court Orders Sheikh Mohammed to Pay $734 Million Divorce Settlement to Princess Haya, Who Fled in 2019 after He Was Accused of Imprisoning His Daughter," *Business Insider*, December 21, 2021, https://www.business insider.com/princess-haya-wins-734m-settlement-divorce-sheikh-mohammed-flee -2021-12.

12 Mehul Srivastava and Jane Croft, "Dubai Ruler's 'Campaign of Fear and Intimidation' against Princess Haya," *Financial Times*, October 8, 2021, https://www.ft.com /content/752a36e9-6148-4d9c-87af-63d806a7d667.

13 Gardner, "Dubai's Sheikh Mohammed Abducted Daughters."

14 Sara Lieser, "British Court Confirms Validity of Threats to Princess Haya," *Chronicle of the Horse*, March 6, 2020, https://www.chronofhorse.com/article/british-court -confirms-validity-of-threats-to-princess-haya/.

15 David Pegg and Paul Lewis, "Dubai Suspected after Princess Haya Listed in Leaked Pegasus Project Data," *Guardian*, July 21, 2021, https://www.theguardian.com /world/2021/jul/21/dubai-suspected-after-princess-haya-listed-in-leaked-pegasus -project-data.

16 Pegg and Lewis, "Dubai Suspected after Princess Haya Listed."

17 Jess Glass, "Hacking and House-Hunting: High Court Issues Rulings against Sheikh Mohammed," *Evening Standard*, October 6, 2021, https://www.standard.co.uk/news /uk/princess-hacking-high-court-cherie-blair-court-of-appeal-b959185.html.

18 Paul Waldie, "How Toronto's Citizen Lab Uncovered the Hacking of Princess Haya," *Globe and Mail*, October 11, 2021, https://www.theglobeandmail.com/world /article-how-torontos-citizen-lab-uncovered-the-hacking-of-princess-haya/.

19 Heidi Blake, "The Fugitive Princesses of Dubai," *New Yorker*, May 1, 2023, https://www.newyorker.com/magazine/2023/05/08/the-fugitive-princesses-of -dubai; Daniela Elser, "'Never Seen Again': Dubai Princess a 'Prisoner' 20 Years after Failed Attempt to Flee," *News.com.au*, July 6, 2019, https://www.news.com.au /entertainment/celebrity-life/royals/never-seen-again-dubai-princess-a-prisoner -20-years-after-failed-attempt-to-flee/news-story/7d269e93cfa28b416f43e78f2 166c7b3.

20 Elser, "'Never Seen Again.'"

21 Blake, "Fugitive Princesses of Dubai."

22 Crofton Black, "Spy Companies Using Channel Islands to Track Phones around the World," Bureau of Investigative Journalism, December 16, 2020, https://www.thebureauinvestigates.com/stories/2020-12-16/spy-companies-using -channel-islands-to-track-phones-around-the-world.

23 "Rayzone's Interception Modus Operandi Exposed by Legal Cases," *Intelligence*

Online, January 21, 2021, https://www.intelligenceonline.com/surveillance—inter
ception/2021/01/21/rayzone-s-interception-modus-operandi-exposed-by-legal
-cases,109636393-art.

24 Tomer Ganon, "Israel Police Purchased New Surveillance Software without AG
Approval," *CTech*, May 29, 2023, https://www.calcalistech.com/ctechnews/article
/bkq6eef8h; Ryan Gallagher, "Your Ad Data Is Now Powering Government
Surveillance," *Bloomberg*, May 10, 2023, https://www.bloomberg.com/news/articles
/2023-05-11/surveillance-company-turns-ad-data-into-government-tracking-tool.

25 Black, "Spy Companies Using Channel Islands."

26 Black, "Spy Companies Using Channel Islands."

27 Kim Hjelmgaard and Kevin Johnson, "How the FBI Played a Role in
the Capture of Princess Latifa of Dubai," Yahoo News, July 12, 2021,
https://www.yahoo.com/news/fbi-played-role-capture-princess-090042592
.html. Originally published as "Princess Latifa of Dubai Caught at Sea—
and FBI Played Key Role," *USA Today*, July 7, 2021, https://www.usatoday.com/in
-depth/news/2021/07/07/princess-latifa-dubai-caught-sea-and-fbi-played-key-role
/7584218002/.

28 Hjelmgaard and Johnson, "How the FBI Played a Role."

29 Douglas Guilfoyle, "Maritime Law Enforcement Operations and Intelligence in
an Age of Maritime Security," *International Law Studies* 93 (2017), https://digital
-commons.usnwc.edu/ils/vol93/iss1/11.

30 Blake, "Fugitive Princesses of Dubai."

31 Hjelmgaard and Johnson, "How the FBI Played a Role."

32 Waldie, "How Toronto's Citizen Lab Uncovered the Hacking of Princess Haya."

33 Bob Chaundy, "Faces of the Week," BBC, March 23, 2007, http://news.bbc.co.uk
/1/hi/magazine/6483785.stm.

34 Timothy Smith, "WTF Tony Blair?," openDemocracy, November 22, 2014, https://
www.opendemocracy.net/en/opendemocracyuk/wtf-tony-blair/; Robert Mendick,
"£1.6m in the Bank for Cherie Blair's Law Firm, Thanks to Advising 'Dictatorships,'"
Telegraph, February 27, 2016, https://www.telegraph.co.uk/news/politics/tony-blair
/12176182/1.6m-in-the-bank-for-Cherie-Blairs-law-firm-thanks-to-advising
-dictatorships.html; Ian Black and Patrick Kingsley, "Tony Blair Accused of Conflict
of Interests in Middle East," *Guardian*, June 27, 2014, https://www.theguardian.com
/politics/2014/jun/27/tony-blair-conflict-interests-middle-east; Jim Pickard and
George Parker, "Tony Blair Shuts Down Advisory Firm That Made Him Millions,"
Financial Times, September 20, 2016, https://archive.ph/iDTve.

35 "Blair Advising Saudis under $12m Deal with His Institute: Report," *Middle East
Eye*, July 22, 2018, https://www.middleeasteye.net/news/blair-advising-saudis-under
-12m-deal-his-institute-report.

36 Randeep Ramesh, "Tony Blair Courted Chinese Leaders for Saudi Prince's Oil
Firm," *Guardian*, April 28, 2016, https://www.theguardian.com/politics/2016/apr
/28/tony-blair-chinese-leaders-saudi-princes-oil-firm-middle-east-envoy.

37 Luke Harding, "Hillary Clinton Emails: Cherie Blair Lobbied for Qatari Crown
Prince," *Guardian*, September 1, 2015, https://www.theguardian.com/politics/2015
/sep/01/hillary-clinton-emails-cherie-blair-lobbied-qatari-royal-family.

38 Oliver Bullough, *Butler to the World: How Britain Helps the World's Worst People Launder Money, Commit Crimes, and Get Away with Anything* (New York: St. Martin's Press, 2022).

39 Brown, "Cherie Blair Is Adviser to NSO."

40 Stephanie Kirchgaessner, "Ex–Obama Official Exits Israeli Spyware Firm amid Press Freedom Row," *Guardian*, February 4, 2020, https://www.theguardian.com /world/2020/feb/04/ex-obama-official-juliette-kayyem-quits-israeli-spyware-firm -amid-press-freedom-row.

41 Gardner, "Princess Haya."

42 Ronan Farrow, "How Democracies Spy on Their Citizens," *New Yorker*, April 18, 2022, https://www.newyorker.com/magazine/2022/04/25/how-democracies-spy -on-their-citizens; see also Ron Deibert, "UK Government Officials Infected with Pegasus," Citizen Lab, April 18, 2022, https://citizenlab.ca/2022/04/uk-government -officials-targeted-pegasus/; Stephanie Kirchgaessner, "No 10 Suspected of Being Target of NSO Spyware Attack—Boris Johnson 'Told,'" *Guardian*, April 18, 2022, https://www.theguardian.com/politics/2022/apr/18/no-10-suspected-of-being -target-of-nso-spyware-attack-boris-johnson.

43 Lizzie Dearden, "Saudi Human Rights Activist Attacked by Men 'Shouting about Crown Prince Mohammad bin Salman' in London," *Independent*, September 17, 2018, https://www.independent.co.uk/news/uk/crime/saudi-arabia-human-rights -activist-attacked-london-mbs-ghanem-al-dosari-show-a8538406.html.

44 Stephanie Kirchgaessner, "British Judge Rules Dissident Can Sue Saudi Arabia for Pegasus Hacking," *Guardian*, August 19, 2022, https://www.theguardian.com /world/2022/aug/19/british-judge-rules-dissident-ghanem-almasarir-can-sue -saudi-arabia-for-pegasus-hacking.

45 Dearden, "Saudi Human Rights Activist Attacked."

46 Dearden, "Saudi Human Rights Activist Attacked."

47 Stephanie Kirchgaessner, "New Evidence Suggests Spyware Used to Surveil Emirati Activist Alaa al-Siddiq," *Guardian*, September 24, 2021, https://www.theguardian .com/world/2021/sep/24/new-evidence-suggests-spyware-used-to-surveil-emirati -activist-alaa-al-siddiq.

48 Kirchgaessner, "New Evidence Suggests Spyware Used."

49 Kirchgaessner, "New Evidence Suggests Spyware Used."

50 Dominic Nicholls, "Death of 'At Risk' UAE Dissident Must Be Investigated, Police Urged," *Telegraph*, June 20, 2021, https://www.telegraph.co.uk/news/2021/06/20 /campaigners-call-probe-intoat-risk-uae-dissidents-death-rule/.

51 Nicholls, "Death of 'At Risk' UAE Dissident."

52 Kirchgaessner, "New Evidence Suggests Spyware Used."

53 Karrie Kehoe, "UK Moves to Clamp Down on Dirty Russian Money," International Consortium of Investigative Journalists, March 4, 2022, https://www.icij.org /investigations/fincen-files/uk-moves-to-clamp-down-on-dirty-russian-money.

54 David Conn, Harry Davies, and Sam Cutler, "Revealed: The Huge British Property Empire of Sheikh Mohammed," *Guardian*, April 14, 2021, https://www.theguardian

.com/world/2021/apr/14/revealed-the-huge-british-property-empire-of-sheikh
-mohammed.

55 Dan Roan, "What Does Princess Latifa Case Mean for British Sport?," BBC, February 18, 2021, https://www.bbc.com/news/uk-56119788.

56 "Legal Case Launched against Kingdom of Saudi Arabia for Alleged Use of Spyware to Target Dissident," Leigh Day, May 28, 2019, https://www.leighday.co.uk /news/news/2019-news/legal-case-launched-against-kingdom-of-saudi-arabia-for -alleged-use-of-spyware-to-target-dissident/.

57 Kirchgaessner, "British Judge Rules Dissident Can Sue."

58 Sally Weale, "Cambridge University Accused of Faustian Pact in Planned £400m Deal with UAE," *Guardian*, July 7, 2021, https://www.theguardian.com/education /2021/jul/07/cambridge-university-accused-of-faustian-pact-in-planned-400m -deal-with-uae; Richard Adams, Georgia Goble, and Nick Bartlett, "Cambridge University Halts £400m Deal with UAE over Pegasus Spyware Claims," *Guardian*, October 14, 2021, https://www.theguardian.com/education/2021/oct/14/cambridge -university-halts-400m-deal-with-uae-over-pegasus-spyware-claims.

59 "Al Maktoum Judgments."

60 Michael Holden, "Dubai Ruler's Ex-Wife Gets Custody of Children after 'Exorbitant' Domestic Abuse," Reuters, March 24, 2022, https://www.reuters.com/world /middle-east/dubai-rulers-ex-wife-gets-custody-children-after-exorbitant-domestic -abuse-2022-03-24/.

61 Manaal Fatimah, "Queen Elizabeth II's Funeral: Arab Royals Pay Their Respects Ahead of the Ceremony," *Harper's Bazaar Arabia*, September 19, 2022, https://www .harpersbazaararabia.com/culture/royal-watch/arab-royals-at-queen-elizabeth-ii -funeral; "UK Invites Saudi Crown Prince for Official Visit, in First since Khashoggi Killing," Middle East Monitor, July 16, 2023, https://www.middleeastmonitor .com/20230716-uk-invites-saudi-crown-prince-for-official-visit-in-first-since -khashoggi-killing/.

CHAPTER 13: "CAN YOU SIT ON YOUR PHONE?"

1 "COVID-19: Ontario Now under Provincewide 'Shutdown' to Control Spread of Virus," Global News, April 3, 2021, https://globalnews.ca/news/7736868/covid -ontario-provincewide-shutdown/.

2 Laurent Richard and Sandrine Rigaud, *Pegasus: How a Spy in Your Pocket Threatens the End of Privacy, Dignity, and Democracy* (New York: Henry Holt, 2023).

3 "Pegasus Project," Forbidden Stories, accessed May 6, 2024, https://forbiddenstories .org/case/the-pegasus-project/.

4 "The Pegasus Project," *Guardian*, accessed May 20, 2024, https://www.theguardian .com/news/series/pegasus-project; "Takeaways from the Pegasus Project," *Washington Post*, August 2, 2021, https://www.washingtonpost.com/investigations/2021 /07/18/takeaways-nso-pegasus-project/.

5 Bill Marczak, John Scott-Railton, Siena Anstis, and Ron Deibert, "Independent Peer Review of Amnesty International's Forensic Methods for Identifying Pegasus

Spyware," Citizen Lab, University of Toronto, July 18, 2021, https://citizenlab.ca /2021/07/amnesty-peer-review/; *Forensic Methodology Report: How to Catch NSO Group's Pegasus*, Amnesty International, July 18, 2021, https://www.amnesty.org/en /latest/research/2021/07/forensic-methodology-report-how-to-catch-nso-groups -pegasus/.

6 David Pegg and Sam Cutler, "What Is Pegasus Spyware and How Does It Hack Phones?," *Guardian*, July 18, 2021, https://www.theguardian.com/news/2021/jul/18 /what-is-pegasus-spyware-and-how-does-it-hack-phones.

7 Joseph Cox, "Here's the FBI's Internal Guide for Getting Data from AT&T, T-Mobile, Verizon," *Vice*, October 25, 2021, https://www.vice.com/en/article/m7vqkv /how-fbi-gets-phone-data-att-tmobile-verizon.

8 Brigitte Bureau, Catherine Cullen, and Kristen Everson, "Hackers Only Needed a Phone Number to Track This MP's Cellphone," CBC News, November 22, 2017, https://www.cbc.ca/news/politics/hackers-cellphone-security-1.4406338.

9 Stephanie Kirchgaessner, "NSO Offered US Mobile Security Firm 'Bags of Cash,' Whistleblower Claims," *Guardian*, February 1, 2022, https://www.theguardian .com/news/2022/feb/01/nso-offered-us-mobile-security-firm-bags-of-cash -whistleblower-claims.

10 Gary Miller and Christopher Parsons, *Finding You: The Network Effect of Telecommunications Vulnerabilities for Location Disclosure*, Research Report No. 171, Citizen Lab, University of Toronto, October 26, 2023, https://citizenlab.ca/2023/10/finding-you -teleco-vulnerabilities-for-location-disclosure/; Ronald J. Deibert and Gary Miller, "When You Roam, You're Not Alone," *Lawfare*, December 28, 2023, https://www .lawfaremedia.org/article/when-you-roam-you-re-not-alone.

11 Dana Priest, Craig Timberg, and Souad Mekhennet, "Private Israeli Spyware Used to Hack Cellphones of Journalists, Activists Worldwide," *Washington Post*, July 18, 2021, https://www.washingtonpost.com/investigations/interactive/2021/nso-spyware-peg asus-cellphones/.

12 Stephanie Kirchgaessner, Paul Lewis, David Pegg, Sam Cutler, Nina Lakhani, and Michael Safi, "Revealed: Leak Uncovers Global Abuse of Cyber-Surveillance Weapon," *Guardian*, July 18, 2021, https://www.theguardian.com/world/2021/jul /18/revealed-leak-uncovers-global-abuse-of-cyber-surveillance-weapon-nso-group -pegasus; Nina Lakhani, "Fifty People Linked to Mexico's President among Potential Targets of NSO Clients," *Guardian*, July 19, 2021, https://www.theguardian.com /news/2021/jul/19/fifty-people-close-mexico-president-amlo-among-potential -targets-nso-clients; Craig Timberg, Michael Birnbaum, Drew Harwell, and Dan Sabbagh, "On the List: Ten Prime Ministers, Three Presidents and a King," *Washington Post*, July 20, 2021, https://www.washingtonpost.com/world/2021/07 /20/heads-of-state-pegasus-spyware/; Diana Moukalled, "UAE: Israel's (Pegasus) Spyware in the Service of Autocracy," *Daraj*, July 18, 2021, https://daraj.media/en /76524/.

13 Kirchgaessner et al., "Revealed: Leak Uncovers Global Abuse."

14 Kirchgaessner et al., "Revealed: Leak Uncovers Global Abuse."

15 Stephanie Kirchgaessner, "Saudis behind NSO Spyware Attack on Jamal Khashoggi's Family, Leak Suggests," *Guardian*, July 18, 2021, https://www.theguardian.com

/world/2021/jul/18/nso-spyware-used-to-target-family-of-jamal-khashoggi-leaked
-data-shows-saudis-pegasus.

16 Dana Priest, "A UAE Agency Put Pegasus Spyware on Phone of Jamal Khashog-gi's Wife Months before His Murder, New Forensics Show," *Washington Post*, December 21, 2021, https://www.washingtonpost.com/nation/interactive/2021/hanan-elatr-phone-pegasus/.

17 Shaun Walker, "Viktor Orbán Using NSO Spyware in Assault on Media, Data Suggests," *Guardian*, July 18, 2021, https://www.theguardian.com/news/2021/jul/18/viktor-orban-using-nso-spyware-in-assault-on-media-data-suggests.

18 "Szabolcs Panyi," Forbidden Stories, accessed May 20, 2024, https://web.archive.org/web/20240225030323/https://forbiddenstories.org/journaliste/szabolcs-panyi/.

19 Szabolcs Panyi and András Pethö, "Hungarian Journalists and Critics of Orbán Were Targeted with Pegasus, a Powerful Israeli Cyberweapon," Direkt36, July 19, 2021, https://www.direkt36.hu/en/leleplezodott-egy-durva-izraeli-kemfegyver-az-orban-kormany-kritikusait-es-magyar-ujsagirokat-is-celba-vettek-vele/.

20 *Forensic Methodology Report: Pegasus Forensic Traces per Target*, Amnesty International, July 18, 2021, https://www.amnesty.org/en/latest/research/2021/07/forensic-methodology-report-appendix-d/.

21 Shaun Walker, "Classes Move to Vienna as Hungary Makes Rare Decision to Oust University," *Guardian*, November 16, 2019, https://www.theguardian.com/world/2019/nov/16/ceu-classes-move-to-vienna-orban-hungary-ousts-university.

22 Michael Birnbaum, Andras Petho, and Jean-Baptiste Chastand, "In Orban's Hungary, Spyware Was Used to Monitor Journalists and Others Who Might Challenge the Government," *Washington Post*, July 19, 2021, https://www.washingtonpost.com/world/2021/07/18/hungary-orban-spyware/.

23 Walker, "Viktor Orbán Using NSO Spyware."

24 Anuj Srivas and Kabir Agarwal, "Snoop List Has 40 Indian Journalists, Forensic Tests Confirm Presence of Pegasus Spyware on Some," *Wire*, July 18, 2021, https://thewire.in/media/pegasus-project-spyware-indian-journalists.

25 Ajoy Ashirwad Mahaprashasta, Sukayna Shantha, and Kabir Agarwal, "Days after Accusing CJI Gogoi of Sexual Harassment, Staffer Put on List of Potential Snoop Targets," *Wire*, July 19, 2021, https://thewire.in/rights/ranjan-gogoi-sexual-harassment-pegasus-spyware.

26 Michael Safi, "Key Modi Rival Rahul Gandhi among Potential Indian Targets of NSO Client," *Guardian*, July 19, 2021, https://www.theguardian.com/news/2021/jul/19/key-modi-rival-rahul-gandhi-among-indian-targets-of-nso-client.

27 Siddharth (@svaradarajan), "Not just another day at the office for @thewire_in after #PegasusProject Policeman arrived today with inane inquiries. 'Who's Vinod Dua?' 'Who's Swara Bhaskar?' 'Can I see your rent agreement?' 'Can I speak to Arfa?' Asked why he'd come: 'Routine check for Aug 15' Strange," X, July 23, 2021, https://x.com/svaradarajan/status/1418513671764865024.

28 Srivas and Agarwal, "Snoop List Has 40 Indian Journalists."

29 See, for example, Bill Marczak, Adam Hulcoop, Etienne Maynier, Bahr Abdul Razzak, Masashi Crete-Nishihata, John Scott-Railton, and Ron Deibert, *Missing Link: Tibetan Groups Targeted with 1-Click Mobile Exploits*, Research Report No. 123,

Citizen Lab, University of Toronto, September 24, 2019, https://citizenlab.ca/2019/09/poison-carp-tibetan-groups-targeted-with-1-click-mobile-exploits/.

30 Michael Safi, "Dalai Lama's Inner Circle Listed in Pegasus Project Data," *Guardian*, July 22, 2021, https://www.theguardian.com/news/2021/jul/22/dalai-lama-inner-circle-listed-pegasus-project-data.

31 David Pegg, Paul Lewis, Michael Safi, and Nina Lakhani, "*FT* Editor among 180 Journalists Identified by Clients of Spyware Firm," *Guardian*, July 20, 2021, https://www.theguardian.com/world/2021/jul/18/ft-editor-roula-khalaf-among-180-journalists-targeted-nso-spyware; Miranda Patrucic and Kelly Bloss, "Life in Azerbaijan's Digital Autocracy: 'They Want to Be in Control of Everything,'" OCCRP, July 18, 2021, https://www.occrp.org/en/the-pegasus-project/life-in-azerbaijans-digital-autocracy-they-want-to-be-in-control-of-everything.

32 "Spyware: Governments Can Hack into Your Phone while You Sleep," Amnesty International, September 26, 2023, https://amnesty.ca/human-rights-news/spyware-governments-can-hack-into-your-phone-while-you-sleep/.

33 Giorgi Lomsadze, "Azerbaijan Reporter Wins Sex Tape Case," Eurasianet, January 11, 2019, https://eurasianet.org/azerbaijan-reporter-wins-sex-tape-case.

34 Kim Willsher, "Pegasus Spyware Found on Journalists' Phones, French Intelligence Confirms," *Guardian*, August 2, 2021, https://www.theguardian.com/news/2021/aug/02/pegasus-spyware-found-on-journalists-phones-french-intelligence-confirms.

35 "French Prosecutors Open Probe into Alleged Use of Pegasus Malware to Spy on Journalists," France 24, July 20, 2021, https://www.france24.com/en/europe/20210720-french-prosecutors-open-probe-into-alleged-use-of-pegasus-malware-to-spy-on-journalists.

36 Lisa O'Carroll, "Draft EU Plans to Allow Spying on Journalists Are Dangerous, Warn Critics," *Guardian*, June 22, 2023, https://www.theguardian.com/world/2023/jun/22/draft-eu-plans-to-allow-spying-on-journalists-are-dangerous-warn-critics.

37 Nina Lakhani, "Revealed: Murdered Journalist's Number Selected by Mexican NSO Client," *Guardian*, July 18, 2021, https://www.theguardian.com/news/2021/jul/18/revealed-murdered-journalist-number-selected-mexico-nso-client-cecilio-pineda-birto.

38 Lakhani, "Fifty People Linked to Mexico's President"; Timberg et al., "On the List."

39 Lakhani, "Fifty People Linked to Mexico's President."

40 Natalie Kitroeff and Ronen Bergman, "Mexican President Said He Told Ally Not to Worry about Being Spied On," *New York Times*, May 23, 2023, https://www.nytimes.com/2023/05/23/world/americas/mexico-president-spying-pegasus.html; Daina Beth Solomon, "Pegasus Spyware Attacks in Mexico Continued under Lopez Obrador, Report Says," Reuters, October 2, 2022, https://www.reuters.com/world/americas/pegasus-spyware-attacks-mexico-continued-under-lopez-obrador-report-2022-10-03/.

41 Bill Marczak, John Scott-Railton, Sarah McKune, Bahr Abdul Razzak, and Ron Deibert, *Hide and Seek: Tracking NSO Group's Pegasus Spyware to Operations in 45 Countries*, Research Report No. 113, Citizen Lab, University of Toronto, September 18, 2018, https://citizenlab.ca/2018/09/hide-and-seek-tracking-nso

-groups-pegasus-spyware-to-operations-in-45-countries/; Joe Tidy, "'I Was a Victim of the WhatsApp Hack,'" BBC, October 31, 2019, https://www.bbc.com /news/technology-50249859.

42 Jennifer Hansler, Bethlehem Feleke, Mostafa Salem, and Jack Guy, "'Hotel Rwanda' Hero to Be Freed after 25-Year Terrorism Sentence Commuted," CNN, March 24, 2023, https://www.cnn.com/2023/03/24/africa/paul-rusesabagina-released-rwanda -intl/index.html.

43 Stephanie Kirchgaessner, "*Hotel Rwanda* Activist's Daughter Placed under Pegasus Surveillance," *Guardian*, July 19, 2021, https://www.theguardian.com/news/2021 /jul/19/hotel-rwanda-activist-daughter-pegasus-surveillance.

44 Michela Wrong, "Rwandans Have Long Been Used to Pegasus-Style Surveillance," *Guardian*, July 23, 2021, https://www.theguardian.com/commentisfree/2021/jul/23 /rwanda-pegasus-surveillance.

45 "Princess Latifa and Princess Haya Listed as Potential Targets by Clients of Spyware Company NSO Group," Amnesty International, July 21, 2021, https://www.amnesty .org/en/latest/press-release/2021/07/pegasus-project-nso-spyware-princess-latifa -princess-haya/.

46 Dan Sabbagh, "Data Leak Raises New Questions over Capture of Princess Latifa," *Guardian*, July 21, 2021, https://www.theguardian.com/world/2021/jul/21/data -leak-raises-new-questions-over-capture-of-princess-latifa.

47 Sabbagh, "Data Leak Raises New Questions."

48 Sabbagh, "Data Leak Raises New Questions."

49 Timberg et al., "On the List."

50 Pete Jones, Vyacheslav Abramov, and Miranda Patrucic, "World Leaders on Pegasus List Include France's President Macron, Morocco's King Mohammed, Kazakhstan's President," OCCRP, July 20, 2021, https://www.occrp.org/en/the-pegasus-project /world-leaders-on-pegasus-list-include-frances-president-macron-moroccos-king -mohammed-kazakhstans-president-tokayev.

51 Craig Timberg, John Hudson, and Kristof Clerix, "Key Question for Americans Overseas: Can Their Phones Be Hacked?," *Washington Post*, July 19, 2021, https://www.washingtonpost.com/national-security/2021/07/19/us-phone-num bers-nso/.

52 Kylie Atwood, Alex Marquardt, Jeremy Herb, and Zachary Cohen, "Biden's Iran Envoy Placed on Leave after Security Clearance Suspended amid Investigation into Possible Mishandling of Classified Material, Sources Say," CNN, June 29, 2023, https://www.cnn.com/2023/06/29/politics/rob-malley-leave-investigation -classified-material/index.html.

53 Steven Feldstein, "Biden Cracks Down on the Spyware Scourge," *Foreign Policy*, July 31, 2023, https://foreignpolicy.com/2023/07/31/spyware-nso-cytrox-intellexa -pegasus-predator-biden-sanctions-entities-list-israel-europe/.

54 "Enough Is Enough!," NSO Group, accessed May 10, 2024, https://www.nsogroup .com/Newses/enough-is-enough/.

55 Omer Kabir and Hagar Ravet, "NSO CEO Exclusively Responds to Allegations: 'The List of 50,000 Phone Numbers Has Nothing to Do with Us,'" *CTech*, July 20, 2021, https://www.calcalistech.com/ctech/articles/0,7340,L-3912882,00.html.

56 Stephanie Kirchgaessner, "Officials Who Are US Allies among Targets of NSO Malware, Says WhatsApp Chief," *Guardian*, July 24, 2021, https://www.theguardian .com/technology/2021/jul/24/officials-who-are-us-allies-among-targets-of-nso -malware-says-whatsapp-chief.

57 "About the Project," OCCRP, July 18, 2021, https://www.occrp.org/en/the-pegasus -project/about-the-project; "About the Pegasus Project," Forbidden Stories, July 18, 2021, https://forbiddenstories.org/about-the-pegasus-project/.

58 Stephanie Kirchgaessner and Sam Jones, "Phone of Top Catalan Politician 'Targeted by Government-Grade Spyware,'" *Guardian*, July 13, 2020, https://www .theguardian.com/world/2020/jul/13/phone-of-top-catalan-politician-targeted-by -government-grade-spyware.

CHAPTER 14: "A VERY SPECIAL GUEST"

1 Santa J. Ono, "UBC Statement on Release of Alumna Loujain al-Hathloul," UBC News, February 10, 2021, https://news.ubc.ca/2021/02/ubc-statement-on-release -of-alumna-loujain-al-hathloul/.

2 "Saudi Arabia: Release Women Human Rights Defenders Now!," Amnesty International, accessed May 20, 2024, https://www.amnesty.ca/what-we-do/womens -human-rights/saudi-arabia-release-women-human-rights-defenders-now/.

3 "Saudi Arabia: Women's Rights Advocates Arrested," Human Rights Watch, May 18, 2018, https://www.hrw.org/news/2018/05/18/saudi-arabia-womens-rights-advo cates-arrested.

4 Loujain Alhathloul, "Kidnapped Freedoms," Edinburgh International Book Festival, 2018, https://www.edbookfest.co.uk/look-and-listen/writing/freedom-papers/kid napped-freedoms.

5 "للحدود السعودية وهي تقودبنقسها! #أسوق_بنفسي #قيادة26 اكتوبر #هو_لها, حملة 26 أكتوبر لجين الهذلول في طريقها," November 29, 2014, video, 0:18, https://www.youtube.com /watch?v=m7r-p7FHxqo.

6 Robert Mackey, "Saudi Women Free after 73 Days in Jail for Driving," *New York Times*, February 12, 2015, https://www.nytimes.com/2015/02/13/world/middleeast /saudi-women-free-after-73-days-in-jail-for-driving.html.

7 Tracy McVeigh, "Fears for Female Saudi Activist as Detention for Driving a Car Is Extended," *Observer*, December 13, 2014, https://www.theguardian.com /world/2014/dec/14/fears-saudi-female-acitivist-detained-driving-ban-loujain-al -hathloul.

8 Jess Staufenberg, "Saudi Arabia Is 'Not Ready' for Women Drivers, Says Deputy Crown Prince," *Independent*, April 28, 2016, https://www.independent.co.uk /news/world/middle-east/saudi-arabia-is-not-ready-for-women-drivers-says -deputy-crown-prince-mohammed-bin-salman-a7004611.html.

9 Stephen Kalin and Summer Said, "Saudi Women's Rights Activist Sentenced to Nearly Six Years in Prison," *Wall Street Journal*, December 28, 2020, https://www.wsj.com/articles/saudi-womens-rights-activist-convicted-by -terrorism-court-11609168687.

10 "'I'll Kill You . . . but before That, I'll Rape You': Loujain Alhathloul's Arrest and

Torture for Advocating for the Right to Drive," DAWN, updated February 10, 2021, https://dawnmena.org/ill-kill-you-but-before-that-ill-rape-you-loujain-alhathlouls -torture-in-a-saudi-prison-2/.

11 UN Human Rights Council Working Group on Arbitrary Detention, "Opinions Adopted by the Working Group on Arbitrary Detention at Its 87th Session, 27 April–1 May 2020: Opinion No. 33/2020 Concerning Loujain Alhathloul (United Arab Emirates and Saudi Arabia)," June 25, 2020, https://digitallibrary.un.org /record/3933637.

12 "Female Activists Detained Ahead of Saudi Driving Ban Reversal," *National*, May 20, 2018, https://www.thenational.scot/news/16238142.female-activists-detained -ahead-saudi-driving-ban-reversal/.

13 Moustafa Bayoumi, "Mohammed bin Salman's Talk of Reform Is a Smokescreen," *Guardian*, March 22, 2018, https://www.theguardian.com/commentisfree/2018 /mar/22/mohammed-bin-salmans-talk-reform-smokescreen.

14 Bayoumi, "Mohammed bin Salman's Talk of Reform."

15 Megan K. Stack, "The West Is Kidding Itself about Women's Freedom in Saudi Arabia," *New York Times*, August 19, 2022, https://www.nytimes.com/2022/08/19 /opinion/saudi-arabia-women-rights.html.

16 "Tony Blair Consultancy Firm 'Working with Saudi Government,'" *New Arab*, July 22, 2018, https://www.newarab.com/news/tony-blair-consultancy-firm-working-saudi -government.

17 Alia al-Hathloul, "My Sister Is in a Saudi Prison. Will Mike Pompeo Stay Silent?," *New York Times*, January 13, 2019, https://www.nytimes.com/2019/01/13/opinion /saudi-women-rights-activist-prison-pompeo.html.

18 Al-Hathloul, "My Sister Is in a Saudi Prison."

19 Joel Schectman and Christopher Bing, "Insight: How a Saudi Woman's iPhone Revealed Hacking around the World," Reuters, February 17, 2022, https://www .reuters.com/technology/how-saudi-womans-iphone-revealed-hacking-around -world-2022-02-17/.

20 Joseph Hincks, "Saudi Activist Loujain al Hathloul Is Out of Jail. But Justice Remains a Distant Hope," *Time*, February 11, 2021, https://time.com/5938331 /loujain-hathloul-saudi-arabia/.

21 Joel Schectman and Christopher Bing, "Pegasus: How a Glitch on a Saudi Activist's Phone Provided a Blueprint of Cyber Espionage," *Wire*, February 18, 2022, https://thewire.in/world/pegasus-glitch-iphone-saudi-activist-loujain-al-hathloul -blueprint.

22 Michelle Ghoussoub, "The Saudis Offered Her Freedom if She Denied Being Tortured. She Tore Up the Deal," CBC News, August 14, 2019, https://www.cbc .ca/news/canada/british-columbia/the-saudis-offered-her-freedom-if-she-denied -being-tortured-she-tore-up-the-deal-1.5247679; Walid al-Hathloul, "Canada Must Defend Women's Rights at G20 Summit in Saudi Arabia," *National Post*, November 18, 2020, https://nationalpost.com/opinion/walid-al-hathloul-canada -must-defend-womens-rights-at-g20-summit-in-saudi-arabia.

23 Bill Marczak, John Scott-Railton, Bahr Abdul Razzak, Noura al-Jizawi, Siena Anstis, Kristin Berdan, and Ron Deibert, *ForcedEntry: NSO Group iMessage Zero-Click*

Exploit Captured in the Wild, Research Report No. 143, Citizen Lab, University of Toronto, September 13, 2021, https://citizenlab.ca/2021/09/forcedentry-nso-group -imessage-zero-click-exploit-captured-in-the-wild/.

24 Schectman and Bing, "Insight: How a Saudi Woman's iPhone."

25 Bill Marczak, John Scott-Railton, Noura al-Jizawi, Siena Anstis, and Ron Deibert, *The Great iPwn: Journalists Hacked with Suspected NSO Group iMessage "Zero-Click" Exploit*, Research Report No. 135, Citizen Lab, University of Toronto, December 20, 2020, https://citizenlab.ca/2020/12/the-great-ipwn-journalists-hacked-with-sus pected-nso-group-imessage-zero-click-exploit/.

26 Virus Bulletin, "Exploit Archaeology a Forensic History of in the Wild NSO Group Exploits Donncha Ó Cearbhaill Amnest," October 24, 2022, video, 29:59, https://www.youtube.com/watch?v=NvS67qiq8bw.

27 Schectman and Bing, "Insight: How a Saudi Woman's iPhone."

28 "About the Security Content of iOS 14.8 and iPadOS 14.8," Apple Support, November 6, 2023, https://support.apple.com/en-ca/103150.

29 Ian Beer and Samuel Groß, "A Deep Dive into an NSO Zero-Click iMessage Exploit: Remote Code Execution," Project Zero, December 15, 2021, https://googleprojectzero.blogspot.com/2021/12/a-deep-dive-into-nso-zero-click .html.

30 Apple Newsroom, "Apple Sues NSO Group to Curb the Abuse of State-Sponsored Spyware," press release, November 23, 2021, https://www.apple.com/newsroom /2021/11/apple-sues-nso-group-to-curb-the-abuse-of-state-sponsored-spyware/.

31 Apple Newsroom, "Apple Sues NSO Group."

32 Yona TR Golding, "Q&A: The Citizen Lab's John Scott-Railton on Tackling the Ongoing Threat of Pegasus," *Columbia Journalism Review*, February 21, 2024, https://www.cjr.org/the_media_today/qa_john_scott-railton_citizen_lab_pegasus .php.

33 John Scott-Railton, Bill Marczak, Paolo Nigro Herrero, Bahr Abdul Razzak, Noura al-Jizawi, Salvatore Solimano, and Ron Deibert, *Project Torogoz: Extensive Hacking of Media & Civil Society in El Salvador with Pegasus Spyware*, Research Report No. 148, Citizen Lab, University of Toronto, January 12, 2022, https://citizenlab.ca/2022 /01/project-torogoz-extensive-hacking-media-civil-society-el-salvador-pegasus -spyware/.

34 John Scott-Railton, Bill Marczak, Irene Poetranto, Bahr Abdul Razzak, Sutawan Chanprasert, and Ron Deibert, *GeckoSpy: Pegasus Spyware Used against Thailand's Pro-Democracy Movement*, Research Report No. 157, Citizen Lab, University of Toronto, July 17, 2022, https://citizenlab.ca/2022/07/geckospy-pegasus-spyware -used-against-thailands-pro-democracy-movement/.

35 Bill Marczak, John Scott-Railton, Bahr Abdul Razzak, and Ron Deibert, *Triple Threat: NSO Group's Pegasus Spyware Returns in 2022 with a Trio of iOS 15 and iOS 16 Zero-Click Exploit Chains*, Research Report No. 165, Citizen Lab, University of Toronto, April 18, 2023, https://citizenlab.ca/2023/04/nso-groups-pegasus-spyware-returns -in-2022/; John Scott-Railton, Bill Marczak, Bahr Abdul Razzak, Nicola Lawford, and Ron Deibert, "Armenia-Azerbaijan Conflict: Pegasus Infections—Technical Brief [1]," Citizen Lab, University of Toronto, May 25, 2023, https://citizenlab.ca

/2023/05/cr1-armenia-pegasus/; John Scott-Railton, Bill Marczak, Bahr Abdul Razzak, Siena Anstis, and Ron Deibert, "Spyware Targeting against Serbian Civil Society," Citizen Lab, University of Toronto, November 28, 2023, https://citizenlab .ca/2023/11/serbia-civil-society-spyware/.

36 Dustin Volz and Tim Higgins, "Apple Notified State Department Employees of Phone Hacking Linked to NSO Group Software," *Wall Street Journal*, December 3, 2021, https://www.wsj.com/articles/apple-notified-state-department-employees-of -phone-hacking-linked-to-nso-group-software-11638568687.

37 Office of Public Affairs, "Commerce Adds NSO Group and Other Foreign Companies to Entity List for Malicious Cyber Activities," press release, US Department of Commerce, November 3, 2021, https://www.commerce.gov/news/press-releases /2021/11/commerce-adds-nso-group-and-other-foreign-companies-entity-list.

38 Davide Scigliuzzo, "Israeli Spyware Firm NSO Seen at Risk of Default as Sales Drop," *Bloomberg*, November 22, 2021, https://www.bloomberg.com/news/articles /2021-11-22/israeli-spyware-firm-nso-seen-at-risk-of-default-as-sales-drop.

39 Schectman and Bing, "Insight: How a Saudi Woman's iPhone."

40 Alhathloul v. DarkMatter Grp., 3:21-cv-01787-IM (D. Or. Feb. 8, 2024).

41 "Ex–U.S. Intel Operatives Who Worked for UAE Barred from Arms Exports, State Dept Says," Reuters, August 26, 2022, https://www.reuters.com/world/state -dept-concludes-settlements-with-ex-us-intel-operatives-who-worked-uae-2022 -08-26/.

42 Electronic Frontier Foundation, "Saudi Human Rights Activist, Represented by EFF, Sues Spyware Maker DarkMatter for Violating U.S. Anti-Hacking and International Human Rights Laws," press release, December 9, 2021, https://www.eff .org/press/releases/saudi-human-rights-activist-represented-eff-sues-spyware -maker-darkmatter-violating.

CHAPTER 15: THE COOLEST DICTATOR IN THE WORLD

1 "Governance," NSO Group, accessed May 30, 2024, https://www.nsogroup.com /governance/.

2 Ronen Bergman and Mark Mazzetti, "Israeli Companies Aided Saudi Spying despite Khashoggi Killing," *New York Times*, July 17, 2021, https://www.nytimes .com/2021/07/17/world/middleeast/israel-saudi-khashoggi-hacking-nso.html; Dan Sabbagh, David Pegg, Paul Lewis, and Stephanie Kirchgaessner, "UAE Linked to Listing of Hundreds of UK Phones in Pegasus Project Leak," *Guardian*, July 21, 2021, https://www.theguardian.com/world/2021/jul/21/uae-linked-to-listing -of-hundreds-of-uk-phones-in-pegasus-project-leak; Natalie Kitroeff and Ronen Bergman, "How Mexico Became the Biggest User of the World's Most Notorious Spy Tool," *New York Times*, April 18, 2023, https://www.nytimes.com/2023/04/18 /world/americas/pegasus-spyware-mexico.html.

3 Mike Allison, "El Salvador's Brutal Civil War: What We Still Don't Know," Al Jazeera, March 1, 2012, https://www.aljazeera.com/opinions/2012/3/1/el-salvadors -brutal-civil-war-what-we-still-dont-know.

4 Allison, "El Salvador's Brutal Civil War."

5 Mat Youkee, "Nayib Bukele Calls Himself the 'World's Coolest Dictator'—but Is He Joking?," *Observer*, September 26, 2021, https://www.theguardian.com/world /2021/sep/26/naybib-bukele-el-salvador-president-coolest-dictator.

6 Sarah Kinosian, "Trolls, Propaganda and Fear Stoke Bukele's Media Machine in El Salvador," Reuters, November 29, 2022, https://www.reuters.com/investigates /special-report/el-salvador-politics-media/.

7 Youkee, "Nayib Bukele Calls Himself"; Kinosian, "Trolls, Propaganda and Fear."

8 Reuters, "Does Money Grow on Volcanoes? El Salvador Explores Bitcoin Mining," Yahoo News, June 9, 2021, https://ca.finance.yahoo.com/news/does-money-grow -volcanoes-el-213733783.html.

9 Nelson Rauda Zablah, "El Salvador's Bitcoin Paradise Is a Mirage," *New York Times*, July 2, 2022, https://www.nytimes.com/2022/07/02/opinion/bitcoin-el-salvador -bukele-crypto.html.

10 Kinosian, "Trolls, Propaganda and Fear."

11 Manuel Meléndez-Sánchez, "Latin America Erupts: Millennial Authoritarianism in El Salvador," *Journal of Democracy* 32, no. 3 (July 2021): 19–32, https://doi.org /10.1353/jod.2021.0031.

12 Megan Janetsky, "Amid Criticism over His War on Gangs, El Salvador's President Bukele Turns to Sports," *Independent*, July 7, 2023, https://www.independent.co.uk /news/world/americas/us-politics/nayib-bukele-ap-el-salvador-mohammed-bin -salman-sport-b2371041.html.

13 Jonathan Blitzer, "The Rise of Nayib Bukele, El Salvador's Authoritarian President," *New Yorker*, September 5, 2022, https://www.newyorker.com/magazine/2022/09/12 /the-rise-of-nayib-bukele-el-salvadors-authoritarian-president.

14 Blitzer, "Rise of Nayib Bukele."

15 Kinosian, "Trolls, Propaganda and Fear."

16 Blitzer, "Rise of Nayib Bukele."

17 Kinosian, "Trolls, Propaganda and Fear"; Blitzer, "Rise of Nayib Bukele."

18 Blitzer, "Rise of Nayib Bukele."

19 Blitzer, "Rise of Nayib Bukele."

20 Kinosian, "Trolls, Propaganda and Fear."

21 Jane Esberg, "All the President's Trolls: Real and Fake Twitter Fights in El Salvador," International Crisis Group, July 13, 2020, https://www.crisisgroup.org /latin-america-caribbean/central-america/el-salvador/all-presidents-trolls-real-and -fake-twitter-fights-el-salvador.

22 Kinosian, "Trolls, Propaganda and Fear."

23 Blitzer, "Rise of Nayib Bukele."

24 David Agren, "Nayib Bukele's Military Stunt Raises Alarming Memories in El Salvador," *Guardian*, February 16, 2020, https://www.theguardian.com/world/2020 /feb/16/el-salvador-nayib-bukele-military-alarming-memories.

25 Scott Neuman, "Troops Occupy El Salvador's Legislature to Back President's Crime Package," NPR, February 10, 2020, https://www.npr.org/2020/02/10/804407503 /troops-occupy-el-salvadors-legislature-to-back-president-s-crime-package.

26 Blitzer, "Rise of Nayib Bukele."

27 Blitzer, "Rise of Nayib Bukele."

28 Blitzer, "Rise of Nayib Bukele."

29 Blitzer, "Rise of Nayib Bukele"; Youkee, "Nayib Bukele Calls Himself."

30 Kinosian, "Trolls, Propaganda and Fear."

31 Kinosian, "Trolls, Propaganda and Fear."

32 "El Salvador," Reporters without Borders, accessed February 9, 2024, https://rsf.org/en/country/el-salvador.

33 "El Salvador."

34 Blitzer, "Rise of Nayib Bukele."

35 Zack Beauchamp, "Meet the MAGA Movement's New Favorite Autocrat," *Vox*, April 8, 2023, https://www.vox.com/2023/4/8/23653324/nayib-bukele-trump-american-right-crime.

36 Beauchamp, "Meet the MAGA Movement's New Favorite Autocrat"; Blitzer, "Rise of Nayib Bukele"; Kinosian, "Trolls, Propaganda and Fear."

37 Beauchamp, "Meet the MAGA Movement's New Favorite Autocrat."

38 Ronan Farrow, "A Hacked Newsroom Brings a Spyware Maker to U.S. Court," *New Yorker*, November 30, 2022, https://www.newyorker.com/news/news-desk/a-hacked-newsroom-brings-a-spyware-maker-to-us-court-pegasus.

39 Juan Pappier, "'We Can Arrest Anyone We Want': Widespread Human Rights Violations under El Salvador's 'State of Emergency,'" Human Rights Watch, December 7, 2022, https://www.hrw.org/report/2022/12/07/we-can-arrest-anyone-we-want/widespread-human-rights-violations-under-el.

40 Ellen Ioanes, "El Salvador's Massive New Prison and the Strongman behind It, Explained," *Vox*, March 5, 2023, https://www.vox.com/world-politics/2023/3/5/23621004/el-salvador-prison-bukele-ms13-barrio-18.

41 Associated Press, "US Accuses El Salvador of Secretly Negotiating Truce with Gang Leaders," *Guardian*, December 8, 2021, https://www.theguardian.com/world/2021/dec/08/el-salvador-us-gang-leaders-truce.

42 Carlos Martínez, Óscar Martínez, Sergio Arauz, and Efren Lemus, "Bukele Has Been Negotiating with MS-13 for a Reduction in Homicides and Electoral Support," *El Faro*, September 6, 2020, https://elfaro.net/en/202009/el_salvador/24785/Bukele-Has-Been-Negotiating-with-MS-13-for-a-Reduction-in-Homicides-and-Electoral-Support.htm; Carlos Martínez, "Collapsed Government Talks with MS-13 Sparked Record Homicides in El Salvador, Audios Reveal," *El Faro*, May 17, 2022, https://elfaro.net/en/202205/el_salvador/0000026177-collapsed-government-talks-with-ms-13-sparked-record-homicides-in-el-salvador-audios-reveal?u=st-full_text=all&tpl=11&utm_source=farotext&utm_medium=initdocu&utm_campaign=text-0000026177_collapsed-government-talks-with-ms-13-sparked-record-homicides-in-el-salvador-audios-reveal.

43 Carlos Martínez, "Collapsed Government Talks with MS-13."

44 Associated Press, "US Accuses El Salvador."

45 John Scott-Railton (@jsrailton), tweet thread, Thread Reader, February 25, 2024, https://threadreaderapp.com/thread/1629318031766884352.html.

46 Farrow, "Hacked Newsroom Brings a Spyware Maker."

47 Blitzer, "Rise of Nayib Bukele"; Farrow, "Hacked Newsroom Brings a Spyware Maker."

48 Blitzer, "Rise of Nayib Bukele."

49 John Scott-Railton, Bill Marczak, Paolo Nigro Herrero, Bahr Abdul Razzak, Noura al-Jizawi, Salvatore Solimano, and Ron Deibert, *Project Torogoz: Extensive Hacking of Media & Civil Society in El Salvador with Pegasus Spyware*, Research Report No. 148, Citizen Lab, University of Toronto, January 12, 2022, https://citizenlab.ca/2022 /01/project-torogoz-extensive-hacking-media-civil-society-el-salvador-pegasus -spyware/.

50 Carlos Martínez et al., "Bukele Has Been Negotiating with MS-13."

51 Scott-Railton et al., *Project Torogoz*, appendix A.

52 Farrow, "Hacked Newsroom Brings a Spyware Maker."

53 Farrow, "Hacked Newsroom Brings a Spyware Maker."

54 Farrow, "Hacked Newsroom Brings a Spyware Maker."

55 Farrow, "Hacked Newsroom Brings a Spyware Maker."

56 Farrow, "Hacked Newsroom Brings a Spyware Maker."

57 Nelson Rauda Zablah, "Pegasus Spyware Was Used to Hack Reporters' Phones. I'm Suing Its Creators," *Guardian*, December 5, 2022, https://www.theguardian.com /commentisfree/2022/dec/05/pegasus-spyware-journalists-phone-hacking-lawsuit.

58 Scott-Railton et al., *Project Torogoz*.

59 Sam Jones, "Pegasus Spyware Used in 'Jaw-Dropping' Phone Hacks on El Salvador Journalists," *Guardian*, January 13, 2022, https://www.theguardian.com/news/2022 /jan/13/pegasus-spyware-target-journalists-activists-el-salvador.

60 Maria Abi-Habib, "Journalists in El Salvador Targeted with Spyware Intended for Criminals," *New York Times*, January 12, 2022, https://www.nytimes.com/2022/01 /12/world/americas/el-salvador-journalists-spyware.html.

61 Jones, "Pegasus Spyware Used in 'Jaw-Dropping' Phone Hacks."

62 José de Córdoba and Santiago Pérez, "Pegasus Spyware Deployed against El Salvador Journalists and Activists," *Wall Street Journal*, January 12, 2022, https://www.wsj .com/articles/pegasus-spyware-deployed-against-around-35-el-salvador-journalists -11642040676.

63 Córdoba and Pérez, "Pegasus Spyware Deployed."

64 Natalie Kitroeff and Ronen Bergman, "Mexican President Said He Told Ally Not to Worry about Being Spied On," *New York Times*, May 23, 2023, https://www.nytimes .com/2023/05/23/world/americas/mexico-president-spying-pegasus.html.

65 Mary Beth Sheridan and Craig Timberg, "Report: 22 Journalists at Salvadoran News Site Hit with Pegasus Hack," *Washington Post*, January 12, 2022, https://www .washingtonpost.com/world/2022/01/12/salvador-pegasus-faro-nso/.

66 Jose Luis Benitez, "El Salvador's Pegasus Spyware Case Left Uninvestigated Ten Months Later," Global Voices, November 16, 2022, https://globalvoices.org/2022 /11/16/el-salvadors-pegasus-spyware-case-left-uninvestigated-ten-months-laterent -is-reluctant-to-investigate/.

67 Benitez, "El Salvador's Pegasus Spyware Case."

68 Xenia Oliva, "Fiscalía defiende al gobierno ante CIDH y afirma que no espía a periodistas con Pegasus," *GatoEncerrado*, March 17, 2022, https://gatoencerrado.news /2022/03/17/fiscalia-defiende-al-gobierno-ante-la-cidh-y-afirma-que-no-espia-a -periodistas-con-pegasus/.

69 Roman Gressier, "El Salvador Obtained Three New Spyware Tools in 2020 from Israeli Intermediary," *El Faro*, January 30, 2023, https://elfaro.net/en/202301/el_salvador/26688/El-Salvador-Obtained-Three-New-Spyware-Tools-in-2020-from-Israeli-Intermediary.htm; "Tracer," Wave Guard Technologies, accessed July 29, 2004, https://waveguardtechnologies.com/tracer/.

70 Gressier, "El Salvador Obtained Three New Spyware Tools."

71 Gressier, "El Salvador Obtained Three New Spyware Tools."

72 Gressier, "El Salvador Obtained Three New Spyware Tools."

73 Jorge Beltrán Luna, "Familiar de director del OIE, vinculado a empresa de espionaje en México," ElSalvador.com, January 14, 2022, https://historico.elsalvador.com/historico/918150/espionaje-oie-pegasus-periodistas.html.

74 Carolina de Assis, "Congreso de El Salvador 'legaliza espionagem digital' após escândalo Pegasus que afetou jornalistas," *LatAm Journalism Review*, February 9, 2022, https://latamjournalismreview.org/pt-br/articles/apos-escandalo-pegasus-el-salvador-legaliza-espionagem-digital-e-preocupa-jornalistas/.

75 Assis, "Congreso de El Salvador."

76 Gabriel Labrador and Óscar Martínez, "One Year under a Police State in El Salvador," *El Faro*, March 31, 2023, https://elfaro.net/en/202303/el_salvador/26793/one-year-under-a-police-state-in-el-salvador.

77 "El Salvador's Congress Votes to Allow Mass Trials in Gang Crackdown," Al Jazeera, July 26, 2023, https://www.aljazeera.com/news/2023/7/26/el-salvadors-congress-votes-to-allow-mass-trials-in-gang-crackdown.

78 "El Salvador's Congress Votes to Allow Mass Trials."

79 Will Grant, "El Salvador Gangs: Mass Arrests Bring Calm but at What Price?," BBC, May 18, 2023, https://www.bbc.com/news/world-latin-america-65596471.

80 Marcos Alemán, "El Salvador Extends State of Exception in Gang Crackdown," Associated Press, July 20, 2022, https://apnews.com/article/arrests-nayib-bukele-el-salvador-san-gangs-2a865def685627ecaf5a56de8247609e.

81 Luke Taylor, "El Salvador News Outlet Relocates to Costa Rica to Avoid Bukele's Crackdown," *Guardian*, April 19, 2023, https://www.theguardian.com/world/2023/apr/19/el-faro-el-salvador-moves-nayib-bukele.

82 Taylor, "El Salvador News Outlet Relocates."

83 Kinosian, "Trolls, Propaganda and Fear."

84 "El Salvador's Bukele Claims Landslide Election Win," Al Jazeera, February 4, 2024, https://www.aljazeera.com/news/2024/2/4/el-salvador-votes-with-nayib-bukele-poised-for-second-presidential-term.

85 "El Salvador President Pledges White-Collar Prison in 'War' on Corruption," Reuters, June 1, 2023, https://www.reuters.com/world/americas/el-salvador-president-pledges-white-collar-prison-war-corruption-2023-06-02/.

86 "El Salvador President Pledges White-Collar Prison."

87 "Honduras Extends, Expands State of Emergency for Second Time," Reuters, February 21, 2023, https://www.reuters.com/world/americas/honduras-extends-expands-state-emergency-second-time-2023-02-21/.

88 Sonia Pérez D., "Guatemala's Presidential Hopefuls Channel Heavy-Handed Tactics of El Salvador's Leader," Associated Press, June 5, 2023, https://apnews

.com/article/guatemala-president-election-security-bukele-6dff69e741871ffe17
ead623d451f221.

89 Will Grant and James Gregory, "Haiti: US to Boost Funding for Foreign Security Force as Violence Grips Country," BBC, March 11, 2024, https://www.bbc.com
/news/world-latin-america-68540753; See also https://x.com/nayibbukele/status
/1766698383132012674.

90 Julia Gavarrete, "15 Members of *El Faro* Sue NSO in US Federal Court for Pegasus
Hacks," *El Faro*, November 30, 2022, https://elfaro.net/en/202211/el_salvador
/26559/15-Members-of-El-Faro-Sue-NSO-in-US-Federal-Court-for-Pegasus
-Hacks.htm.

91 "El Salvador Journalists Sue Spyware Maker in US Court," Associated Press,
November 30, 2022, https://apnews.com/article/technology-business-canada-israel
-middle-east-1b16abed6e33242c72e2bd07a28cc075.

92 Nelson Rauda Zablah, "Pegasus Spyware Was Used to Hack Reporters' Phones. I'm
Suing Its Creators," *Guardian*, December 5, 2022, https://www.theguardian.com
/commentisfree/2022/dec/05/pegasus-spyware-journalists-phone-hacking-lawsuit.

93 Michael Gennaro, "Salvadoran Journalists' Suit against Israeli Spyware Supplier
Doesn't Belong in US, Judge Rules," Courthouse News Service, March 8, 2024,
https://www.courthousenews.com/salvadoran-journalists-suit-against-israeli
-spyware-supplier-not-in-us-jurisdiction-judge-rules/.

94 Gennaro, "Salvadoran Journalists' Suit."

95 "Dada v. NSO Group," Knight First Amendment Institute at Columbia University,
accessed May 31, 2024, http://knightcolumbia.org/cases/dada-v-nso-group.

CHAPTER 16: "FINALLY A EUROPEAN STATE"

1 John Scott-Railton, Elies Campo, Bill Marczak, Bahr Abdul Razzak, Siena Anstis,
Gözde Böcü, Salvatore Solimano, and Ron Deibert, *CatalanGate: Extensive Mercenary Spyware Operation against Catalans Using Pegasus and Candiru*, Research Report
No. 155, Citizen Lab, University of Toronto, April 18, 2022, https://citizenlab.ca
/2022/04/catalangate-extensive-mercenary-spyware-operation-against-catalans
-using-pegasus-candiru/.

2 Paul Kirby, "Spain Dismisses Spy Chief in Pegasus Phone Spyware Scandal," BBC,
May 10, 2022, https://www.bbc.com/news/world-europe-61391849.

3 Andrés Villena-Oliver, Bernabé Aldeguer, and Delio Lucena-Piquero, "Invisible
Rulers: The 'Latent Power Structure' in Two Spanish Governments (2004 and
2012)," *Government and Opposition* 59, no. 1 (2024): 130–145.

4 Ximena Villagrán, "El CNI pagó más de 200.000 euros a Hacking Team para espiar
móviles," *El Confidencial*, July 7, 2015, https://www.elconfidencial.com/tecnologia
/2015-07-06/cni-hackers-team-espionaje-contratos_916216/.

5 Stephanie Kirchgaessner and Sam Jones, "Phone of Top Catalan Politician
'Targeted by Government-Grade Spyware,'" *Guardian*, July 13, 2020, https://www
.theguardian.com/world/2020/jul/13/phone-of-top-catalan-politician-targeted-by
-government-grade-spyware.

6 "Torrent y Maragall fueron espiados por un programa exclusivo de los gobiernos," *El*

Periódico, July 14, 2020, https://www.elperiodico.com/es/politica/20200714/parlament
-roger-torrent-espia-movil-catalunya-8038888; Stephanie Kirchgaessner, Sam Jones,
and Jennifer Rankin, "Second Catalan Politician Says Phone Was Targeted by
Spyware," *Guardian*, July 14, 2020, https://www.theguardian.com/world/2020/jul/14
/second-catalan-politician-says-phone-was-targeted-by-spware; Kirchgaessner and
Jones, "Phone of Top Catalan Politician 'Targeted,'"; Sam Jones and Stephanie Kirchgaessner, "Who Has Been Using Spyware on Catalan Independence Campaigners?,"
Guardian, July 17, 2020, https://www.theguardian.com/world/2020/jul/17/who
-has-been-using-spyware-on-catalan-independence-campaigners; "Report Alleges
Targeting of Swiss-Based Catalan Separatist's Phone," SWI swissinfo.ch, July 14,
2020, https://www.swissinfo.ch/eng/politics/report-alleges-targeting-of-swiss-based
-catalan-separatist-s-phone/45902640; Raquel Castillo and John Miller, "Spanish
Supreme Court Orders Arrest of Former Catalan MP Anna Gabriel," Reuters,
February 21, 2018, https://www.reuters.com/article/idUSKCN1G515G/.

7 Vicente Rodriguez, "Catalonia," *Encyclopedia Britannica*, updated July 28, 2024,
https://www.britannica.com/place/Catalonia.

8 James Sturcke, "Catalan Conundrum," *Guardian*, June 7, 2006, https://www.the
guardian.com/world/2006/jun/07/spain.jamessturcke.

9 Spanish Constitution, Boletín Oficial del Estado, https://www.boe.es/buscar/pdf
/1978/BOE-A-1978-40001-consolidado.pdf.

10 Sam Jones and Stephen Burgen, "Catalan Referendum: Preliminary Results
Show 90% in Favour of Independence," *Guardian*, October 1, 2017, https://www
.theguardian.com/world/2017/oct/01/dozens-injured-as-riot-police-storm-catalan
-ref-polling-stations.

11 "Catalan referendum: 'Hundreds hurt' as police try to stop voters," BBC News,
October 1, 2017, https://www.bbc.com/news/world-europe-41461032.

12 Isa Soares, Vasco Cotovio, and Hilary Clarke, "Catalonia Referendum Result
Plunges Spain into Political Crisis," CNN, October 2, 2017, https://www.cnn.com
/2017/10/01/europe/catalonia-spain-independence-referendum-result/index.html.

13 "Spain: Police Used Excessive Force in Catalonia," Human Rights Watch, October
12, 2017, https://www.hrw.org/news/2017/10/12/spain-police-used-excessive-force
-catalonia; "Spain: Excessive Use of Force by National Police and Civil Guard
in Catalonia," Amnesty International, October 3, 2017, https://www.amnesty.org
/en/latest/news/2017/10/spain-excessive-use-of-force-by-national-police-and-civil
-guard-in-catalonia-2/.

14 "UN Human Rights Chief Urges Probe into Violence during Referendum in Catalonia," UN News, October 2, 2017, https://news.un.org/en/story/2017/10/567542.

15 "Catalonia Independence: Rajoy Dissolves Catalan Parliament," BBC, October 27,
2017, https://www.bbc.com/news/world-europe-41783289.

16 Sam Jones, "Catalan Leaders Facing Rebellion Charges Flee to Belgium," *Guardian*,
October 31, 2017, https://www.theguardian.com/world/2017/oct/30/spanish-pro
secutor-calls-for-rebellion-charges-against-catalan-leaders; Stephen Burgen, "Catalan
Politicians Charged a Year after Independence Vote," *Guardian*, November 2, 2018,
https://www.theguardian.com/world/2018/nov/02/catalan-politicians-charged-a-year
-after-independence-vote-referendum.

17 Stephen Burgen and Sam Jones, "New Generation, New Tactics: The Changing Face of Catalan Protests," *Guardian*, October 18, 2019, https://www.theguardian .com/world/2019/oct/18/new-generation-new-tactics-the-changing-face-of -catalan-protests.

18 Sam Jones, "Spanish Government Pardons Nine Jailed Catalan Leaders," *Guardian*, June 22, 2021, https://www.theguardian.com/world/2021/jun/22/spanish -government-pardons-nine-jailed-catalan-leaders.

19 Jones, "Spanish Government Pardons Nine."

20 Nicholas Casey and Raphael Minder, "In Bid to End Secession Dispute, Spain Tries Talking with Catalonia," *New York Times*, September 15, 2021, https://www.nytimes .com/2021/09/15/world/europe/catalonia-spain-sanchez-aragones.html.

21 "Aragonès Calls to 'Strengthen' Catalonia in Face of Spanish 'Authoritarianism,'" *Catalan News*, February 14, 2022, https://www.catalannews.com/politics/item /aragones-calls-to-strengthen-catalonia-in-face-of-spanish-authoritarianism.

22 Miguel González, "Los servicios secretos españoles tienen el programa que espió a Torrent," *El País*, July 15, 2020, https://elpais.com/espana/2020-07-15/los-servicios -de-informacion-tienen-programas-como-el-que-espio-a-torrent.html.

23 Lorenzo Franceschi-Bicchierai and Joseph Cox, "Source: Spain Is Customer of NSO Group," *Vice*, July 14, 2020, https://www.vice.com/en/article/pkyzxz/spain -nso-group-pegasus-catalonia.

24 Nicolas Tomás, "El CNI admite haber espiado a Aragonès y el entorno de Puig- demont con autorización," *El Nacional*, May 5, 2022, https://www.elnacional.cat/es /politica/cni-espiado-independentismo-aval-judicial_752346_102.html.

25 Jones, "Spanish Government Pardons."

26 Alexandra Borgeaud, "Market Share Held by Smartphone Operating Systems in Spain from 2017 to 2023, by Month," Statista, August 1, 2023, https://www.statista .com/statistics/260419/market-share-held-by-smartphone-operating-systems-in -spain/.

27 "Would You Click?," Citizen Lab, updated December 23, 2022, https://catalonia .citizenlab.ca/.

28 Ronan Farrow, "How Democracies Spy on Their Citizens," *New Yorker*, April 18, 2022, https://www.newyorker.com/magazine/2022/04/25/how-democracies-spy-on -their-citizens.

29 "Democracies Shouldn't Surrender to a Future of Limitless Surveillance," editorial, *Washington Post*, April 21, 2022, https://www.washingtonpost.com/opinions/2022 /04/21/democracies-should-write-rules-spyware-not-abuse-it/.

30 Sam Jones, "Catalan President Calls for Investigation as Spyware Targets Pro- Independence Leaders," *Guardian*, April 19, 2022, https://www.theguardian.com /world/2022/apr/19/catalan-president-calls-for-investigation-as-spyware-targets -pro-independence-leaders.

31 Jones, "Catalan President Calls for Investigation."

32 Nicolas Tomás, "ERC Calls for Support from Junts: 'Head-on Opposition Would Not Be Understood,'" *El Nacional*, October 10, 2022, https://www.elnacional.cat /en/politics/erc-calls-support-junts-opposition-not-understood-catalonia_897888 _102.html.

33 Fernando Heller, "'Catalan Gate' Puts Spanish Government Stability at Risk Ahead of Crucial Vote," *Euractiv*, April 27, 2022, https://www.euractiv.com/section/politics /short_news/catalan-gate-puts-spanish-government-stability-at-risk-ahead-of -crucial-vote/.

34 "Spanish Prime Minister's Mobile Phone Infected by Pegasus Spyware, Government Says," Reuters, May 2, 2022, https://www.reuters.com/world/europe/spanish -prime-ministers-telephone-infected-by-pegasus-spyware-2022-05-02/.

35 Nicolas Tomás, "Spanish Minister Robles, Defiant on CatalanGate Espionage: 'Go to the Courts,'" *El Nacional*, April 26, 2022, https://www.elnacional.cat/en/politics /spanish-minister-robles-defiant-catalangate_747783_102.html.

36 "Spanish Defense Minister, on Espionage: 'What Should a State Do When Someone Declares Independence?,'" *Catalan News*, April 27, 2022, https://www.catalannews .com/politics/item/spanish-defense-minister-on-espionage-what-should-a-state -do-when-someone-declares-independence.

37 Sam Jones, "Spanish Prime Minister's Phone 'Targeted with Pegasus Spyware,'" *Guardian*, May 2, 2022, https://www.theguardian.com/world/2022/may/02/spain -prime-minister-pedro-sanchez-phone-pegasus-spyware.

38 "Spyware in Spain Targeted the Prime Minister and His Enemies," *Economist*, May 7, 2022, https://www.economist.com/europe/spyware-in-spain-targeted-the-prime -minister-and-his-enemies/21809099; Mayte Piulachs, "Catalangate Could End Up in Hands of a Judge at Spain's National Audience," *El Nacional*, May 2, 2022, https://www.elnacional.cat/en/politics/catalangate-hands-judge-spain-national -audience_750840_102.html; J.M. Zuloaga, "Marlaska, el miembro del Gobierno al que han robado más datos de su teléfono," *La Razón*, May 11, 2022, https://www .larazon.es/espana/20220510/gwxedc4drzhali5bqi4vbhk7kq.html; Sophie in 't Veld, *Report of the Investigation of Alleged Contraventions and Maladministration in the Application of Union Law in Relation to the Use of Pegasus and Equivalent Surveillance Spyware*, Committee of Inquiry to Investigate the Use of Pegasus and Equivalent Surveillance Spyware, European Parliament, May 22, 2023, https://www.europarl.europa .eu/doceo/document/A-9-2023-0189_EN.pdf.

39 "Luis Planas Puchades, nuevo embajador en Marruecos," *El Mundo*, April 30, 2004, https://www.elmundo.es/elmundo/2004/04/30/espana/1083337276.html.

40 Sam Jones, "Catalans Demand Answers after Spanish Spy Chief Confirms Phone Hacking," *Guardian*, May 5, 2022, https://www.theguardian.com/world/2022/may /05/catalans-demand-answers-after-spanish-spy-chief-confirms-phone-hacking.

41 Jones, "Catalans Demand Answers"; Nicolas Tomás, "Spain's CNI Admits Spying on Aragonès and on Puigdemont's Circle, with Court Approval," *El Nacional*, May 5, 2022, https://www.elnacional.cat/en/politics/spain-cni-admits-spying-catalan-inde pendence-judge_752448_102.html.

42 Tomás, "Spain's CNI Admits Spying."

43 Adam Hulcoop, John Scott-Railton, Peter Tanchak, Matt Brooks, and Ron Deibert, *Tainted Leaks: Disinformation and Phishing with a Russian Nexus*, Research Report No. 92, Citizen Lab, University of Toronto, May 25, 2017, https://citizenlab.ca/2017/05 /tainted-leaks-disinformation-phish/.

44 "Pegasus Infection of Galina Timchenko, Exiled Russian Journalist and Publisher,"

Citizen Lab, September 13, 2023, https://citizenlab.ca/2023/09/pegasus-infection -of-galina-timchenko-exiled-russian-journalist-and-publisher/; John Scott-Railton, Bill Marczak, Bahr Abdul Razzak, Ksenia Ermoshina, Siena Anstis, and Ron Deibert, *By Whose Authority? Pegasus Targeting of Russian & Belarusian-Speaking Opposition Activists and Independent Media in Europe*, Research Report No. 176, Citizen Lab, University of Toronto, May 30, 2024, https://citizenlab.ca/2024/05/pegasus-russian -belarusian-speaking-opposition-media-europe/.

45 "Russia Labels Two Canadian Schools, Democracy NGO as 'Undesirable Organi- zations,'" Radio Free Europe/Radio Liberty, March 18, 2024, https://www.rferl.org /a/russia-labels-canadian-schools-ngo-undesirable/32867431.html.

46 Jeffrey Knockel, *Cross-Country Exposure: Analysis of the MY2022 Olympics App*, Research Report No. 149, Citizen Lab, University of Toronto, January 18, 2022, https://citizenlab.ca/2022/01/cross-country-exposure-analysis-my2022-olympics -app/.

47 Mona Wang, Pellaeon Lin, and Jeffrey Knockel, *Should We Chat? Privacy in the WeChat Ecosystem*, Research Report No. 167, Citizen Lab, University of Toronto, June 28, 2023, https://citizenlab.ca/2023/06/privacy-in-the-wechat-ecosystem-full -report/.

48 Bill Marczak and John Scott-Railton, *Move Fast and Roll Your Own Crypto: A Quick Look at the Confidentiality of Zoom Meetings*, Research Report No. 126, Citizen Lab, University of Toronto, April 3, 2020, https://citizenlab.ca/2020/04/move-fast-roll -your-own-crypto-a-quick-look-at-the-confidentiality-of-zoom-meetings/.

49 Sam Jones, "Spain's Spy Chief Sacked after Pegasus Spyware Revelations," *Guardian*, May 10, 2022, https://www.theguardian.com/world/2022/may/10/spains-spy-chief -paz-esteban-sacked-after-pegasus-spyware-revelations.

50 Jose Javier Olivas (@josejolivas), "This is a thread on the curious #catalangate and on the presumed espionage of separatist leaders in Catalonia. First a disclaimer: I do not intend to defend in any way the Spanish secret services, whose in my view either for action or omission have contributed to the scandal 1/," X, April 23, 2022, https://x.com/josejolivas/status/1517996367939084288.

51 Ariel Kahana, "'NSO Accusations Were Part of International Disinformation Campaign,'" *Israel Hayom*, September 2, 2022, https://www.israelhayom.com/2022 /09/02/the-accusations-against-nso-were-part-of-a-disinformation-campaign/.

52 Alfonso Valero, "Presentación / Introduction," Foro de Profesores, February 15, 2019, https://paginadelforodeprofesores.wordpress.com/.

53 Carlos Conde Solares, "Re: Independent Investigation Request on Citizen Lab's Report 'CatalanGate: Extensive Mercenary Spyware Operation against Catalans Using Pegasus and Candiru,'" email, July 5, 2022, https://paginadelforodeprofesores .wordpress.com/wp-content/uploads/2022/07/letter-to-university-of-toronto-by -foro-de-profesores-5-july-2022-re-catalangate-report.pdf.

54 Jose Javier Olivas Osuna, *The Pegasus Spyware Scandal: A Critical Review of Citizen Lab's "CatalanGate" Report*, March 2023, https://doi.org/10.13140/RG.2.2.17511.93603.

55 Stephanie Kirchgaessner and Sam Jones, "Pegasus Spyware Inquiry Targeted by Disinformation Campaign, Say Experts," *Guardian*, November 28, 2022, https://www.theguardian.com/world/2022/nov/28/pegasus-eu-parliament-spyware

-inquiry-targeted-disinformation-campaign; Antoaneta Roussi, "EU Spyware Inquiry Fails to Put Spain on List of Fact-Finding Trips," *Politico*, July 7, 2022, https://www.politico.eu/article/pedro-sanchez-spain-spyware-inquirys-visit-falls -flat-for-fear-of-embarrassment/.

56 Runa Sandvik, "Fact Check: Gregorio Martin's Presentation to the European Parliament," *Untidy* (blog), March 18, 2023, https://www.untidy.news/p/fact-check -gregorio-martins-presentation; Jonathan Scott, *Uncovering the Citizen Lab—An Analytical and Technical Review Disproving CatalanGate*, July 2022, https://static .ecestaticos.com/file/b9e/fff/e37/b9efffe37b7e3cf717aa7cd584db8fba.pdf.

57 Runa Sandvik, "Fact Check: José Javier Olivas-Osuna's Review of Citizen Lab's CatalanGate Report," *Untidy* (blog), March 16, 2023, https://www.untidy.news /p/fact-check-jose-javier-olivas-osunas.

58 Ronald Deibert, "About the Citizen Lab's CatalanGate Report," Ronald Deibert, May 14, 2022, https://deibert.citizenlab.ca/2022/05/about-the-citizen-labs-catalan gate-report/.

59 Jose Javier Olivas (@josejolivas), "Apple keeps on funding Citizens Lab via the Ford Foundation and #CitizenLab still conceals in their 'academic reports' that Apple (and who knows what other big techs) fund their research that blame others for security breaches 958/ @UofT @munkschool https://T.Co/s4QFoqPDAy," X, March 12, 2024, https://x.com/josejolivas/status/1767452378188431766.

60 Quico Sallés, "La Guàrdia Civil va espiar durant mesos l'investigador del Catalan-gate," *El Món*, January 18, 2024, https://elmon.cat/politica/tribunals/guardia-civil -espiar-mesos-investigador-catalangate-787559/.

61 "Windows Kernel Elevation of Privilege Vulnerability: CVE-2021-31979," Micro-soft Security Update Guide, July 13, 2021, https://msrc.microsoft.com/update -guide/vulnerability/CVE-2021-31979; "Windows Kernel Elevation of Privilege Vulnerability: CVE-2021-33771," Microsoft Security Update Guide, July 13, 2021, https://msrc.microsoft.com/update-guide/vulnerability/CVE-2021-33771.

62 Microsoft Threat Intelligence, "Protecting Customers from a Private-Sector Offen-sive Actor Using 0-Day Exploits and DevilsTongue Malware," Microsoft Secu-rity, July 15, 2021, https://www.microsoft.com/en-us/security/blog/2021/07/15 /protecting-customers-from-a-private-sector-offensive-actor-using-0-day-exploits -and-devilstongue-malware/.

63 "Consell de Degans i Deganes Emèrits i Emèritcs," Bar, accessed May 29, 2024, https://www.icab.cat/en/colegi/coneix-el-col-legi/organs-consultius/consell-de -degans-i-deganes-emerits-i-emerites/index.html; "Former Presidents," FBE, accessed May 29, 2024, https://www.fbe.org/about/former-presidents/.

64 Quino Petit and Miguel González, "Ronald Deibert, fundador de Citizen Lab: 'Los gobiernos usan Pegasus porque tienen apetito de espiar,'" *El País*, May 14, 2022, https://elpais.com/espana/2022-05-15/ronald-deibert-fundador-de-citizen-lab -los-gobiernos-usan-pegasus-porque-tienen-apetito-de-espiar.html; Sam Jones, "Use of Pegasus Spyware on Spain's Politicians Causing 'Crisis of Democracy,'" *Guardian*, May 15, 2022, https://www.theguardian.com/world/2022/may/15/use-of -pegasus-spyware-on-spains-politicians-causing-crisis-of-democracy.

65 "Investigation of the Use of Pegasus and Equivalent Surveillance Spyware," Euro-

pean Parliament, June 7, 2023, https://www.europarl.europa.eu/thinktank/en /document/EPRS_ATA(2023)747923.

66 Cornelia Ernst (@ErnstCornelia), "Truly unbelievable and an insult to all MPs: The secret service chief from #Spain reads a bit of blah blah off the page, then simply refuses to answer our 28 questions and leaves the @EP_PegaInquiry. Here is our transcript of today's hearing: https://cornelia-ernst.eu/2022/11/country-hearing -spain-29-november/ #CatalanGate," X, November 29, 2022, https://x.com /ErnstCornelia/status/1597558061828214785; Efi Koutsokosta, "All Questions and No Answers, as Spanish Spy Chief Stays Mute on Pegasus Hacking Scandal," Euronews, November 29, 2022, https://www.euronews.com/my-europe/2022/11 /29/all-questions-and-no-answers-as-spanish-spy-chief-stays-mute-on-pegasus -hacking-scandal.

67 Jones, "Use of Pegasus Spyware on Spain's Politicians."

68 Laura Hülsemann, "Spanish Court Halts Probe into Israeli Spyware Hacking of Pedro Sánchez's Phone," *Politico*, July 10, 2023, https://www.politico.eu/article /spain-shutters-investigation-into-pegasus-hacking-of-pedro-sanchez-phone/.

69 "Spain Reopens Israeli Spyware Probe, Sharing Information with France," Reuters, April 23, 2024, https://www.reuters.com/technology/cybersecurity/spain-reopens -israeli-spyware-probe-sharing-information-with-france-2024-04-23/.

70 Lorenzo Franceschi-Bicchierai and Carly Page, "Hackers Used Spyware Made in Spain to Target Users in the UAE, Google Says," *TechCrunch*, March 29, 2023, https://techcrunch.com/2023/03/29/hackers-variston-spyware-uae-google/.

71 "Barcelona Emerges as New Cyber-Offensive Hub in Europe," *Intelligence Online*, July 21, 2023, https://www.intelligenceonline.com/surveillance—interception/2023 /07/21/barcelona-emerges-as-new-cyber-offensive-hub-in-europe,110005885-gra.

CHAPTER 17: EUROPE FLOODED WITH WATERGATES

1 Elena Becatoros, "Greece: Intelligence Chief Resigns amid Spyware Allegations," Courthouse News Service, August 5, 2022, https://www.courthousenews.com /greece-intelligence-chief-resigns-amid-spyware-allegations/.

2 "Greek Spy Chief Resigns over Israeli Spyware Surveillance Claims," *New Arab*, August 7, 2022, https://www.newarab.com/news/greek-spy-chief-resigns-over-israeli -spyware-claims.

3 "History of EYP," Εθνική Υπηρεσία Πληροφοριών, accessed June 1, 2024, https://www.nis.gr/en/agency/historical-background.

4 Helena Smith, "Journalists Who Revealed Greek Wiretapping Scandal Appear in Court," *Guardian*, January 25, 2024, https://www.theguardian.com/world/2024/jan /25/journalists-who-revealed-greek-wiretapping-scandal-appear-in-court.

5 Bill Marczak, John Scott-Railton, Bahr Abdul Razzak, Noura al-Jizawi, Siena Anstis, Kristin Berdan, and Ron Deibert, *Pegasus vs. Predator: Dissident's Doubly-Infected iPhone Reveals Cytrox Mercenary Spyware*, Research Report No. 147, Citizen Lab, University of Toronto, December 16, 2021, https://citizenlab.ca/2021/12 /pegasus-vs-predator-dissidents-doubly-infected-iphone-reveals-cytrox-mercenary -spyware/.

6 Marczak et al., *Pegasus vs. Predator.*

7 Saska Cvetkoska, Ivana Nasteska, Bojan Stojanovski, Tasos Telloglou, Eliza Trianta-
fillou, and Miroslava Simonovska, "Israeli Company Developed Spyware in Skopje,
Local Officials Looked the Other Way," Investigative Reporting Lab Macedonia,
April 12, 2023, https://irl.mk/israeli-company-developed-spyware-in-skopje-local
-officials-looked-the-other-way/.

8 Patrick Howell O'Neill, "The Lucrative Government Spyware Industry Has a
New 'One-Stop-Shop' for Hacking Everything," *Gizmodo*, February 15, 2019,
https://gizmodo.com/the-lucrative-government-spyware-industry-has-a-new-one
-1832568791.

9 Marczak et al., *Pegasus vs. Predator.*

10 Thomas Brewster, "A Multimillionaire Surveillance Dealer Steps Out of the
Shadows . . . and His $9 Million WhatsApp Hacking Van," *Forbes*, August 5, 2019,
https://www.forbes.com/sites/thomasbrewster/2019/08/05/a-multimillionaire
-surveillance-dealer-steps-out-of-the-shadows-and-his-9-million-whatsapp
-hacking-van/.

11 Mark Mazzetti, Ronen Bergman, and Matina Stevis-Gridneff, "How the Global
Spyware Industry Spiraled Out of Control," *New York Times*, December 8, 2022,
https://www.nytimes.com/2022/12/08/us/politics/spyware-nso-pegasus-paragon
.html.

12 Tasos Telloglou et al., "Flight of the Predator," Lighthouse Reports, November 30,
2022, https://www.lighthousereports.com/investigation/flight-of-the-predator/.

13 Grace Woodruff, "What We Know about the Secretive Company behind the
Pegasus Spy Software," *Slate*, July 20, 2021, https://slate.com/technology/2021/07
/nso-group-pegasus-spyware.html.

14 Mazzetti, Bergman, and Stevis-Gridneff, "How the Global Spyware Industry
Spiraled."

15 David Agranovich and Mike Dvilyanski, "Taking Action against the Surveillance-
for-Hire Industry," Meta, December 16, 2021, https://about.fb.com/news/2021/12
/taking-action-against-surveillance-for-hire/.

16 Agranovich and Dvilyanski, "Taking Action."

17 Nektaria Stamouli, "Data, Spies and Indifference: How Mitsotakis Survived His
'Watergate,'" Balkan Insight, June 12, 2023, https://balkaninsight.com/2023/06/12
/data-spies-and-indifference-how-mitsotakis-survived-his-watergate/.

18 Tasos Telloglou and Eliza Triantafyllou, "Who Was Tracking the Mobile Phone of
Journalist Thanasis Koukakis?," *Inside Story*, April 11, 2022, https://insidestory.gr
/article/who-was-tracking-mobile-phone-journalist-thanasis-koukakis.

19 Telloglou and Triantafyllou, "Who Was Tracking the Mobile Phone?"

20 Telloglou and Triantafyllou, "Who Was Tracking the Mobile Phone?"

21 Omer Benjakob, "'Great Alarm': First Detected Use of Mysterious Israeli
Spyware on EU National," *Haaretz*, April 19, 2022, https://www.haaretz.com
/israel-news/tech-news/2022-04-19/ty-article/israeli-predator-spyware-found
-in-phone-of-top-greek-investigative-reporter/00000180-6565-dc5d-a1cd
-757f069c0000; Telloglou and Triantafyllou, "Who Was Tracking the Mobile
Phone?"

22 Benjakob, "'Great Alarm.'"

23 Thanasis Koukakis (@nasoskook), "Η κυβέρνηση τοποθετήθηκε στο δημοσίευμα του @insidestory_gr με τη βεβαιότητα πως η παρακολούθηση μου έγινε από ιδιώτη. Αναμένω το πόρισμα της ΑΔΑΕ που θα επιβεβαιώνει τον ισχυρισμό αυτό," X, April 11, 2022, https://twitter.com/nasoskook/status/1513459956581871616.

24 Koukakis (@nasoskook), "Η κυβέρνηση τοποθετήθηκε στο δημοσίευμα του."

25 Nikolas Leontopoulos and Thodoris Chondrogiannos, "Εχθρός του Κράτους: Αποδεικνύουμε ότι η κυβέρνηση Μητσοτάκη παρακολουθούσε τον δημοσιογράφο Θανάση Κουκάκη," Reporters United, April 15, 2022, https://www.reportersunited.gr/8646/eyp-koukakis/.

26 Leontopoulos and Chondrogiannos, "Εχθρός του Κράτους."

27 "Four Greek Investigative Journalists Say Intelligence Authorities Followed Them, Tracked Their Phones," Committee to Protect Journalists, November 4, 2022, https://cpj.org/2022/11/four-greek-investigative-journalists-say-intelligence-authorities-followed-them-tracked-their-phones/.

28 "Four Greek Investigative Journalists."

29 "Four Greek Investigative Journalists."

30 "Four Greek Investigative Journalists."

31 Spiros Sideris, "EU Commission Alarmed by New Spyware Case against Greek Socialist Leader," *Euractiv*, July 27, 2022, https://www.euractiv.com/section/politics/news/eu-commission-alarmed-by-new-spyware-case-against-greek-socialist-leader/.

32 Sideris, "EU Commission Alarmed by New Spyware."

33 Benjakob, "'Great Alarm.'"

34 Moira Lavelle, "Reporters Dig Up More Links between Greek Government and Spyware," Al Jazeera, November 17, 2022, https://www.aljazeera.com/news/2022/11/17/reporters-dig-up-more-links-between-greek-government-and-spyware; Helena Smith, "Greek PM denies knowing about tapping of opponent's phone," *Guardian*, August 8, 2022, https://www.theguardian.com/world/2022/aug/08/greek-pm-denies-knowing-about-tapping-of-opponents-phone.

35 "Greek Spy Chief Resigns."

36 Jason Horowitz and Niki Kitsantonis, "A Greek Scandal Reverberates as Eavesdropping Expands in Europe," *New York Times*, August 12, 2022, https://www.nytimes.com/2022/08/12/world/europe/greece-surveillance-europe-kyriakos-mitsotakis.html.

37 "Hungary 2023," Amnesty International, https://www.amnesty.org/en/location/europe-and-central-asia/western-central-and-south-eastern-europe/hungary/report-hungary/; Paul Kirby and Nick Thorpe, "Who Is Viktor Orban, Hungarian PM with 14-Year Grip on Power?," BBC, February 13, 2024, https://www.bbc.com/news/world-europe-67832416.

38 Szabó and Vissy v. Hungary, No. 37138/14 (ECtHR Jan. 12, 2016).

39 András Király, "Mi ez a kémszoftver, amit a hírszerzésünk és a titkosszolgálatunk is használ?," *444*, July 8, 2015, https://444.hu/2015/07/08/mi-ez-a-kemszoftver-amit-a-hirszerzesunk-es-a-titkosszolgalatunk-is-hasznal.

40 Marczak et al., *Pegasus vs. Predator.*

41 Marczak et al., *Pegasus vs. Predator.*

42 Shaun Walker, "Viktor Orbán Using NSO Spyware in Assault on Media, Data Suggests," *Guardian*, July 18, 2021, https://www.theguardian.com/news/2021/jul/18/viktor-orban-using-nso-spyware-in-assault-on-media-data-suggests.

43 "Hungary: The Government Must Provide a Meaningful Response to the Pegasus Scandal," Amnesty International, July 20, 2021, https://www.amnesty.org/en/latest/press-release/2021/07/hungary-the-government-must-provide-a-meaningful-response-to-the-pegasus-scandal/.

44 Szabolcs Panyi and András Pethö, "Hungarian Journalists and Critics of Orbán Were Targeted with Pegasus, a Powerful Israeli Cyberweapon," Direkt36, July 19, 2021, https://www.direkt36.hu/en/leleplezodott-egy-durva-izraeli-kemfegyver-az-orban-kormany-kritikusait-es-magyar-ujsagirokat-is-celba-vettek-vele/.

45 Walker, "Viktor Orbán Using NSO Spyware."

46 Walker, "Viktor Orbán Using NSO Spyware."

47 Stephanie Kirchgaessner, "Phones of Journalist Who Tracked Viktor Orban's Childhood Friend Infected with Spyware," *Guardian*, September 21, 2021, https://www.theguardian.com/news/2021/sep/21/hungary-journalist-daniel-nemeth-phones-infected-with-nso-pegasus-spyware.

48 Kirchgaessner, "Phones of Journalist."

49 Kassai Zsigmond, "Nyomozást rendelt el az ügyészség Pegasus-ügyben," *24.hu*, July 22, 2021, https://24.hu/belfold/2021/07/22/pegasus-kemprogram-ugyeszseg-nyomozat/.

50 "Hungarians Protest against Alleged Illegal Surveillance with Pegasus Spyware," Reuters, July 27, 2021, https://www.reuters.com/world/europe/hungarians-protest-against-alleged-illegal-surveillance-with-pegasus-spyware-2021-07-26/.

51 Justin Spike, "Hungary: Politicians Demand Inquiry into Alleged Spying," Associated Press, July 19, 2021, https://apnews.com/article/technology-europe-hungary-5d42379b6ee15a4f309f4ae022c0f536.

52 Committee on Civil Liberties, Justice and Home Affairs, mission report, November 26, 2021, https://www.europarl.europa.eu/meetdocs/2014_2019/plmrep/COMMITTEES/LIBE/DV/2021/11-29/MissionreportHungary_EN.pdf.

53 "Hungary Admits to Using Pegasus Spyware," DW, April 11, 2021, https://www.dw.com/en/hungary-admits-to-using-nso-groups-pegasus-spyware/a-59726217.

54 Walker, "Viktor Orbán Using NSO Spyware."

55 Szabolcs Panyi, "The Inside Story of How Pegasus Was Brought to Hungary," Direkt36, September 28, 2022, https://www.direkt36.hu/en/feltarulnak-a-pegasus-kemszoftver-beszerzesenek-rejtelyei/.

56 Marton Dunai, "Hungary's Orban Welcomes Netanyahu, Vows to Fight Anti-Semitism," Reuters, July 18, 2017, https://www.reuters.com/article/idUSKBN1A31G8/.

57 Vlad Makszimov, "Hungary Hires Ex-Pegasus Spyware Lobbyist," *Euractiv*, January 24, 2022, https://www.euractiv.com/section/politics/short_news/hungary-hires-ex-pegasus-spyware-lobbyist/.

58 "Viktor Orban's Intelligence Corps Keeps Watch in Brussels," *Intelligence Online*, February 6, 2023, https://www.intelligenceonline.com/government-intelligence/2023/02/06/viktor-orban-s-intelligence-corps-keeps-watch-in-brussels,109910285-art.

59 "Hungarian Intelligence Presses Ahead with Reforms in Midst of Upheavals," *Intelligence Online*, January 9, 2023, https://www.intelligenceonline.com/government -intelligence/2023/01/09/hungarian-intelligence-presses-ahead-with-reforms-in -midst-of-upheavals,109879509-art.

60 Tani Goldstein, "Israeli Firm to Sell Social Media–Tracking Software to Orban's Hungary," *Times of Israel*, September 28, 2022, https://www.timesofisrael.com /israeli-firm-to-sell-social-media-tracking-software-to-orbans-hungary/.

61 Stephanie Kirchgaessner, "More Polish Opposition Figures Found to Have Been Targeted by Pegasus Spyware," *Guardian*, February 17, 2022, https://www .theguardian.com/world/2022/feb/17/more-polish-opposition-figures-found-to -have-been-targeted-by-pegasus-spyware.

62 Federico Guerrini, "Pegasus Spyware Scandals Highlight Global Dangers as Activists Demand Action," *Forbes*, September 14, 2023, https://www.forbes.com/sites /federicoguerrini/2023/09/14/pegasus-spyware-scandals-highlight-global-dangers -as-activists-demand-action/.

63 Siena Anstis, "Litigation and Other Formal Complaints Related to Mercenary Spyware," Citizen Lab, University of Toronto, December 12, 2018, https://citizenlab .ca/2018/12/litigation-and-other-formal-complaints-concerning-targeted-digital -surveillance-and-the-digital-surveillance-industry/; Guerrini, "Pegasus Spyware Scandals Highlight Global Dangers."

64 Evon Huber, "Donald Tusk Claims 'Witch Hunt' in Warsaw Intelligence Probe," *Financial Times*, April 19, 2017, https://www.ft.com/content/3a8c83e0-2508-11e7 -a34a-538b4cb30025.

65 Guerrini, "Pegasus Spyware Scandals Highlight Global Dangers."

66 Vanessa Gera, "Two More Poles Identified as Victims of Hacking with Spyware," Associated Press, January 25, 2022, https://apnews.com/article/technology-europe -poland-hacking-spyware-4a410bda35df566632703e3578e5a99d.

67 Gera, "Two More Poles Identified."

68 "Citizen Lab: Andrzej Malinowski inwigilowany Pegasusem," TVN24, April 19, 2022, https://tvn24.pl/polska/pegasus-w-polsce-citizen-lab-andrzej-malinowski-in wigilowany-pegasusem-byly-prezes-pracodawcow-pr-komentuje-st5679884.

69 Tasos Telloglou and Eliza Triantafyllou, "Greek Ministry of Foreign Affairs Secret Investigation Reveals Spyware Export Licenses," *Inside Story*, May 7, 2023, https://insidestory.gr/article/greek-ministry-foreign-affairs-secret-investigation -reveals-predator-spyware-export-licenses.

70 "Who Is 'Hemedti,' General behind Sudan's Feared RSF Force?," Al Jazeera, April 16, 2023, https://www.aljazeera.com/news/2023/4/16/who-is-hemedti-the-puppeteer -behind-sudans-feared-rsf-fighters; Telloglou et al., "Flight of the Predator."

71 Telloglou et al., "Flight of the Predator."

72 "Freedom in the World 2024: Equatorial Guinea," Freedom House, https://freedom house.org/country/equatorial-guinea/freedom-world/2024.

73 "Report: Police Raid Israeli Spyware Company's Offices in Greece," *Haaretz*, December 14, 2022, https://www.haaretz.com/israel-news/security-aviation/2022 -12-14/ty-article/report-police-raid-israeli-spyware-companys-offices-in-greece /00000185-0f4b-d26d-a1b7-dfdfb9710000.

74 Lavelle, "Reporters Dig Up More Links"; Nikolas Leontopoulos and Thodoris Chondrogiannos, "Μεσοτοιχία το Μαξίμου με το Predator," Reporters United, August 4, 2022, https://www.reportersunited.gr/9529/mesotoichia-to-maximoy-me-to-predator/.

75 "Greece: SLAPP Award Winner Grigoris Dimitriadis Urged to Drop Defamation Lawsuits," European Centre for Press and Media Freedom, October 21, 2022, https://www.ecpmf.eu/greece-slapp-award-winner-grigoris-dimitriadis-urged-to-drop-defamation-lawsuits/.

76 Lavelle, "Reporters Dig Up More Links."

77 Alessio Giussani, "'Predatorgate,' Dozens of Greek Ministers and Journalists under Surveillance," Osservatorio Balcani e Caucaso Transeuropa, November 9, 2022, https://www.balcanicaucaso.org/eng/Areas/Greece/Predatorgate-dozens-of-Greek-ministers-and-journalists-under-surveillance-221605; "Predator," *Documento*, accessed May 29, 2024, https://www.documentonews.gr/tag/predator/.

78 Matina Stevis-Gridneff, "Meta Manager Was Hacked with Spyware and Wiretapped in Greece," *New York Times*, March 20, 2023, https://www.nytimes.com/2023/03/20/world/europe/greece-spyware-hacking-meta.html.

79 Stevis-Gridneff, "Meta Manager Was Hacked."

80 Stevis-Gridneff, "Meta Manager Was Hacked."

81 Stevis-Gridneff, "Meta Manager Was Hacked."

82 Eliza Triantafyllou and Tasos Telloglou, "Predatorgate: Τι έγραφαν τα SMS-παγίδα που έλαβαν επιχειρηματίες, υπουργοί και δημοσιογράφοι," *Inside Story*, July 27, 2023, https://insidestory.gr/article/predatorgate-ti-egrafan-ta-sms-pagida-poy-elavan-epiheirimaties-ypoyrgoi-kai-dimosiografoi.

83 Nektaria Stamouli, "Greek Spyware Inquiry Ends in Stalemate," *Politico*, October 11, 2022, https://www.politico.eu/article/greek-spyware-inquiry-ends-in-stalemate/.

84 Derek Gatopoulos, "Greece to Ban Spyware as Wiretap Scandal Grows," Associated Press, December 8, 2022, https://apnews.com/article/europe-greece-athens-government-14ea14a86dfecbf628395ff0674339a5.

85 Eleni Stamatoukou, "Greek Court Clears State Institutions of Involvement with Illegal Spyware," Balkan Insight, July 30, 2024, https://balkaninsight.com/2024/07/30/greek-court-clears-state-institutions-of-involvement-with-illegal-spyware/.

86 "About | PEGA | Committees | European Parliament," European Parliament, accessed June 1, 2024, https://web.archive.org/web/20240519141132/https://www.europarl.europa.eu/committees/en/pega/about.

87 European Parliament, "Spyware: MEPs Sound Alarm on Threat to Democracy and Demand Reforms," press release, May 8, 2023, https://www.europarl.europa.eu/news/en/press-room/20230505IPR84901/spyware-meps-sound-alarm-on-threat-to-democracy-and-demand-reforms.

88 European Parliament, "Spyware Inquiry: Statement of Committee Coordinators on Polish Authorities' Refusal to Cooperate," press release, September 15, 2022, https://www.europarl.europa.eu/news/en/press-room/20220915IPR40601/statement-of-pega-coordinators-on-polish-authorities-refusal-to-cooperate.

89 Vincent Manancourt and Shannon Van Sant, "EU Spyware Probe Has a Problem:

Spain," *Politico*, November 28, 2022, https://www.politico.eu/article/eu-spyware-probe-problem-spain-pedro-sanchez-margaritas-robles/.

90 Elisa Braun, Gian Volpicelli, and Eddie Wax, "The Qatargate Files: Hundreds of Leaked Documents Reveal Scale of EU Corruption Scandal," *Politico*, December 4, 2023, https://www.politico.eu/article/european-parliament-qatargate-corruption-scandal-leaked-documents-pier-antonio-panzeri-francesco-giorgi-eva-kaili/.

91 Braun, Volpicelli, and Wax, "Qatargate Files."

92 Nektaria Stamouli and Shannon Van Sant, "Probe Slams '4 or 5' EU Governments for Spyware Use," *Politico*, November 8, 2022, https://www.politico.eu/article/eu-spyware-probe-slams-government-leaders-as-perpetrators-of-abuse/.

93 Eugenia Lostri, "PEGA Committee Votes on Spyware Recommendations," *Lawfare*, May 17, 2023, https://www.lawfaremedia.org/article/pega-committee-votes-on-spyware-recommendations; "LIBE Committee's Opinion Fails to Include a Total Ban on the Use of Spyware in the European Media Freedom Act," EDRi, July 20, 2023, https://edri.org/our-work/eu-parliament-libe-committee-opinion-spyware-ban-european-media-freedom-act/.

94 Niki Kitsantonis, "With His Party Ahead in Elections, Greek Leader Claims 'Political Earthquake,'" *New York Times*, May 21, 2023, https://www.nytimes.com/2023/05/21/world/europe/greece-elections-new-democracy.html.

95 Julia Tar, "EU Looks the Other Way as Greek Spyware Mess Heralds More Trouble," *Euractiv*, July 28, 2023, https://www.euractiv.com/section/law-enforcement/news/eu-looks-the-other-way-as-greek-spyware-mess-heralds-more-trouble/.

96 Andrew Higgins, "Donald Tusk Chosen as Poland's Prime Minister after Rival Is Rejected," *New York Times*, December 11, 2023, https://www.nytimes.com/2023/12/11/world/europe/poland-donald-tusk-government.html.

97 "Premier zaskoczył podczas narady z prezydentem. Ujawnił dokument ws. Pegasusa," Polskie Radio 24, February 13, 2024, https://polskieradio24.pl/artykul/3334313,premier-zaskoczyl-podczas-narady-z-prezydentem-ujawnil-dokument-ws-pegasusa.

98 "Almost 600 People Targeted with Pegasus Spyware under Former Polish Government," Notes from Poland, April 16, 2024, https://notesfrompoland.com/2024/04/16/almost-600-people-targeted-with-pegasus-spyware-under-former-polish-government/.

99 Wojciech Kość, "Poland Launches Pegasus Spyware Probe," *Politico*, February 19, 2024, https://www.politico.eu/article/poland-pegasus-spyware-probe-law-and-justice-pis-jaroslaw-kaczynski/.

100 US Department of State, "The United States Adds Foreign Companies to Entity List for Malicious Cyber Activities," press release, July 18, 2023, https://www.state.gov/the-united-states-adds-foreign-companies-to-entity-list-for-malicious-cyber-activities-2/.

101 Elias Groll, "U.S. Sanctions Maker of Predator Spyware," CyberScoop, March 5, 2024, https://cyberscoop.com/predator-intellexa-cytrox-sanctions/; US Department of the Treasury, "Treasury Sanctions Members of the Intellexa Commercial Spyware Consortium," press release, May 5, 2024, https://home.treasury.gov/news/press-releases/jy2155.

102 Bill Marczak, John Scott-Railton, Daniel Roethlisberger, Bahr Abdul Razzak, Siena Anstis, and Ron Deibert, *Predator in the Wires: Ahmed Eltantawy Targeted with Predator Spyware after Announcing Presidential Ambitions*, Research Report No. 171, Citizen Lab, University of Toronto, September 22, 2023, https://citizenlab.ca/2023/09/predator-in-the-wires-ahmed-eltantawy-targeted-with-predator-spyware-after-announcing-presidential-ambitions/.

103 "About the Security Content of iOS 17.0.1 and iPadOS 17.0.1," Apple Support, November 15, 2023, https://support.apple.com/en-us/106369.

104 Office of the Spokesperson, "The United States Adds Sandvine to the Entity List for Enabling Human Rights Abuses," press release, US Department of State, February 28, 2024, https://www.state.gov/the-united-states-adds-sandvine-to-the-entity-list-for-enabling-human-rights-abuses/.

105 Eleni Stamatoukou, "US Sanctions Spyware Enablers at Centre of Greek Wiretapping Scandal," Balkan Insight, September 17, 2024, https://balkaninsight.com/2024/09/17/us-sanctions-enablers-of-spyware-at-centre-of-greek-wiretapping-scandal/.

CHAPTER 18: MS. KANIMBA GOES TO WASHINGTON

1 Stephanie Kirchgaessner, "*Hotel Rwanda* Activist's Daughter Placed under Pegasus Surveillance," *Guardian*, July 19, 2021, https://www.theguardian.com/news/2021/jul/19/hotel-rwanda-activist-daughter-pegasus-surveillance.

2 "History and Jurisdiction," House Permanent Select Committee on Intelligence, accessed June 1, 2024, https://intelligence.house.gov/about/history-and-jurisdiction.htm.

3 "Combatting the Threats to U.S. National Security from the Proliferation of Foreign Commercial Spyware," US House Permanent Select Committee on Intelligence, July 27, 2022, https://docs.house.gov/Committee/Calendar/ByEvent.aspx?EventID=115048.

4 "Combatting the Threats to U.S. National Security"; Miles Kenyon, "John Scott-Railton Delivers Testimony to House Permanent Select Committee on Intelligence," Citizen Lab, University of Toronto, July 27, 2022, https://citizenlab.ca/2022/07/john-scott-railton-delivers-testimony-to-house-permanent-select-committee-on-intelligence/.

5 "Combatting the Threats to U.S. National Security."

6 "Combatting the Threats to U.S. National Security."

7 Adam Durbin, "Paul Rusesabagina: *Hotel Rwanda* Hero and Government Critic Arrives in US," BBC, March 30, 2023, https://www.bbc.com/news/world-africa-65120307.

8 Petula Dvorak, "She Escaped the Genocide in Rwanda. Now, 27 Years Later, She Can't Escape Its Politics," *Washington Post*, February 25, 2021, https://www.washingtonpost.com/local/she-escaped-the-genocide-in-rwanda-now-27-years-later-she-cant-escape-its-politics/2021/02/25/bfb2ea26-7786-11eb-948d-19472e683521_story.html.

9 Arthur Asiimwe, "'Hotel Rwanda' Hero in Bitter Controversy," Reuters, August 9, 2007, https://www.reuters.com/article/idUSL04209686/.

10 "Paul Rusesabagina: From *Hotel Rwanda* Hero to Convicted Terrorist," BBC, September 20, 2021, https://www.bbc.com/news/world-africa-58604468.

11 "Combatting the Threats to U.S. National Security."

12 Durbin, "Paul Rusesabagina."

13 "'Hotel Rwanda' Hero Given 25-Year Sentence in 'Terrorism' Case," Al Jazeera, September 20, 2021, https://www.aljazeera.com/news/2021/9/20/rwanda-court -finds-hotel-rwanda-hero-guilty-in-terrorism-case.

14 "*Hotel Rwanda* Hero Paul Rusesabagina Freed from Prison," Al Jazeera, March 24, 2023, https://www.aljazeera.com/news/2023/3/24/hotel-rwanda-hero-paul-rusesa bagina-prison-sentence-commuted.

15 "'Hotel Rwanda' Proceedings Were a Show Trial," Clooney Foundation for Justice, September 20, 2021, https://cfj.org/news/hotel-rwanda-proceedings -were-a-show-trial/; "Rwanda's Rusesabagina Guilty Verdict Declared Unfair by ABA Center for Human Rights," American Bar Association, September 23, 2021, https://www.americanbar.org/news/abanews/aba-news-archives/2021/09/rwandan -trial-verdict/.

16 Bill Marczak, John Scott-Railton, Sarah McKune, Bahr Abdul Razzak, and Ron Deibert, *Hide and Seek: Tracking NSO Group's Pegasus Spyware to Operations in 45 Countries*, Research Report No. 113, Citizen Lab, University of Toronto, September 18, 2018, https://citizenlab.ca/2018/09/hide-and-seek-tracking-nso-groups-pegasus -spyware-to-operations-in-45-countries/.

17 Mehul Srivastava and Tom Wilson, "Inside the WhatsApp Hack: How an Israeli Technology Was Used to Spy," *Financial Times*, October 29, 2019, https://www.ft .com/content/d9127eae-f99d-11e9-98fd-4d6c20050229.

18 Michela Wrong, *Do Not Disturb: The Story of a Political Murder and an African Regime Gone Bad* (New York: PublicAffairs, 2021).

19 Michela Wrong, "Rwandans Have Long Been Used to Pegasus-Style Surveillance," *Guardian*, July 23, 2021, https://www.theguardian.com/commentisfree/2021/jul/23 /rwanda-pegasus-surveillance.

20 "Combatting the Threats to U.S. National Security."

21 "Combatting the Threats to U.S. National Security."

22 Stephanie Kirchgaessner and Diane Taylor, "Nephew of Jailed Hotel Rwanda Dissi- dent Hacked by NSO Spyware," *Guardian*, July 18, 2022, https://www.theguardian .com/world/2022/jul/18/nephew-of-jailed-hotel-rwanda-dissident-hacked-by-nso -spyware.

23 "Combatting the Threats to U.S. National Security."

24 "Combatting the Threats to U.S. National Security."

25 "Combatting the Threats to U.S. National Security."

26 Judy Trinh, "Welcomed by Canada for Defying a Dictator, Syrian Activist Now Considered a Security Risk," CTV News, June 23, 2023, https://www.ctvnews .ca/canada/welcomed-by-canada-for-defying-a-dictator-syrian-activist-now -considered-a-security-risk-1.6453244.

27 The Citizen Lab's forthcoming report on digital transnational repression is coau- thored by Noura Aljizawi, Siena Anstis, Marcus Michaelsen, Veronica Arroyo, Shaila Baran, Maria Bikbulatova, Gözde Böcü, Camila Franco, Arzu Geybulla, Muetter

Iliqud, Nicola Lawford, Émilie LaFlèche, Gabby Lim, Levi Meletti, Maryam Mirza, Zoe Panday, Claire Posno, Zoë Reichert, Berhan Taye, and Angela Yang, with Ron Deibert as Principal Investigator.

28 Dina Temple-Raston and Sean Powers, "Pegasus Is Listening: Q&A with Paul Rusesabagina's Daughter Carine Kanimba," *Record*, August 1, 2022, https://therecord .media/pegasus-is-listening-a-q-and-a-with-paul-rusesabaginas-daughter-carine -kanimba.

29 "Combatting the Threats to U.S. National Security."

30 Jonathan Scott, *Exonerating Rwanda: The Spyware Case of Carine Kanimba*, 2022, https://doi.org/10.13140/RG.2.2.18522.41922 (content removed by author, but archived link can be found here: https://web.archive.org/web/20230602055352 /https://www.researchgate.net/publication/366298195_Exonerating_Rwanda_The _Spyware_Case_of_Carine_Kanimba).

31 Jonathan Scott (@jonathandata1), "The forensics report was sent to me from Carine Kanimba. I provide all my comms with her, proof of false Pegasus infections, & I provide validation of my claims via @ZecOps an unaffiliated 3rd party who discovered these results before me. It's a smear campaign against Rwanda," Twitter, September 3, 2022, https://web.archive.org/web/20220903072623/https://twitter .com/jonathandata1/status/1565963934930292736.

32 Jonathan Scott, Registration Statement Pursuant to the Foreign Agents Registration Act of 1938, as Amended, US Department of Justice, December 27, 2023, https://efile.fara.gov/docs/7355-Registration-Statement-20231227-1.pdf.

33 Jonathan Scott, Exhibit A to Registration Statement Pursuant to the Foreign Agents Registration Act of 1938, as Amended, US Department of Justice, December 27, 2023, https://efile.fara.gov/docs/7355-Exhibit-AB-20231227-1.pdf; Jonathan Scott, Exhibit B to Registration Statement Pursuant to the Foreign Agents Registration Act of 1938, as Amended, US Department of Justice, December 27, 2023, https:// efile.fara.gov/docs/7355-Exhibit-AB-20231227-1.pdf.

34 Cthulhu (@Cthulhu_Answers), "So here we go. A thread exposing a major fuck up by Rwanda National Police in the recruiting of Jonathan Boyd Scott aka Jonathan Lee Villarreal and a curious Russian connection. A thread," X, January 7, 2024, https://x.com/Cthulhu_Answers/status/1744057582757806467.

35 Rwanda National Police, "RNP Has Not Hired Jonathan Scott," press release, January 6, 2024, https://police.gov.rw/media/press-releases/press-in-details/news /rnp-has-not-hired-jonathan-scott/.

36 Runa Sandvik, "Fact Check: Jonathan Scott's Report on Morocco," *Untidy* (blog), March 6, 2023, https://www.untidy.news/p/fact-check-jonathan-scotts-report.

37 Alberto Daniel Hill—CYBERMIDNIGHT CLUB, "Facts: The Carine Kanimba False Positive Spyware Case & CatalanGate," September 8, 2022, video, 1:57:10, https://www.youtube.com/watch?v=VD3XhWUI8Fs.

38 Jose Javier Olivas (@josejolivas), "However that (false positive) 'infection' still fed into an statement for an investigation for presumed illegal espionage by Rwandan government on Carine Kanimba. Formal statement here on 27 July 2021 (5 day after): https://docs.house.gov/meetings/IG/IG00/20220727/115048/HHRG-117 -IG00-Wstate-KanimbaC-20220727.pdf&ved=2ahUKEwiWgcyJ1vr5AhUdg

_0HHRduDRMQFnoECAoQAQ&usg=AOvVaw3GyIfwBO9TuMAWmKR_mDLZ . . . 453/," X, September 4, 2022, https://x.com/josejolivas/status/1566371514756243456; Jose Javier Olivas (@josejolivas), "Precisely the false indicator/process 'Diagnosticd' they had already acknowledged to be a false positive in July 2021, appears in the first place as indicator of compromise in the report Amnesty Tech wrote and was submitted with Carine Kanimba complaint. 454/," X, September 4, 2022, https://x.com/josejolivas/status/1566371536411533313; Jose Javier Olivas (@josejolivas), "It didn't matter to @citizenlab who in June 2022 wrote another formal statement (@UofT @munkschool) to support the claim of illegal surveillance on Carine Kanimba omitting the fact that in her case there was at least a false positive 🐢. This could have legal implications 458/," X, September 4, 2022, https://x.com/josejolivas/status/1566371591897989121.

39 Jose Javier Olivas (@josejolivas), "Runa acting as Runa. #metoo🐢🐢🐢," X, May 17, 2023, https://x.com/josejolivas/status/1658876851316457495.

40 Ariel Kahana, "'NSO Accusations Were Part of International Disinformation Campaign,'" *Israel Hayom*, September 2, 2022, https://www.israelhayom.com/2022/09/02/the-accusations-against-nso-were-part-of-a-disinformation-campaign/.

41 Ariel Kahana, "היו חלק ממסע דיסאינפורמציה מתוכנן וארוך טווח NSO ההאשמות נגד," *Israel Hayom*, September 1, 2022, https://www.israelhayom.co.il/news/geopolitics/article/13023319.

42 Runa Sandvik, "Fact Check: Irina Tsukerman's Article on Pegasusgate," *Untidy* (blog), July 5, 2023, https://www.untidy.news/p/irina-tsukermans-article-on-pegasusgate.

43 Jonathan Scott, "Expelled: The Cost of Speaking Truth," Medium, March 10, 2023, https://jonathandata1.medium.com/expelled-the-cost-of-speaking-truth-d458a1ad2611 (account discontinued).

44 Sandvik, "Fact Check: Irina Tsukerman's Article."

45 Łukasz, "Jonathan Scott Is Becoming the Alex Jones of Cybersecurity," Medium, October 11, 2022, https://medium.com/@maldr0id/jonathan-scott-is-becoming-the-alex-jones-of-cybersecurity-4f6f79857905.

46 Catalan Fake, "Irina Tsukerman.mp4," August 16, 2022, video, 34:08, https://vimeo.com/740170493.

47 Karine Pfenniger, "From Trump Supporters to a Human Rights Attorney: The Digital Influencers Who Harassed a Journalist," Forbidden Stories, February 16, 2023, https://forbiddenstories.org/story-killers-digital-influencers/.

48 "*Hotel Rwanda* Hero Paul Rusesabagina Freed."

49 Intelligence Authorization Act for Fiscal Year 2023, H.R. 8367, 117th Congress (2022), https://www.congress.gov/bill/117th-congress/house-bill/8367/text.

CHAPTER 19: FIGHT THE FUTURE

1 Jim Heintz and Dasha Litvinova, "Russia Outlaws Top Independent News Site in Latest Crackdown," Associated Press, January 26, 2023, https://apnews.com/article/politics-russia-government-moscow-business-law-enforcement-132f628bb3eeb1d038cfd3fe835f4af2.

2 "Pegasus Infection of Galina Timchenko, Exiled Russian Journalist and Publisher,"

Citizen Lab, University of Toronto, September 13, 2023, https://citizenlab.ca/2023/09/pegasus-infection-of-galina-timchenko-exiled-russian-journalist-and-publisher/.

3 Andrei Soldatov, "Why Is Russia Not Using Pegasus Spyware?," *Moscow Times*, July 21, 2021, https://www.themoscowtimes.com/2021/07/21/why-is-russia-not-using-pegasus-spyware-a74572.

4 Natalia Krapiva and Rand Hammoud, "Hacking *Meduza*: Pegasus Spyware Used to Target Putin's Critic," Access Now, September 13, 2023, https://www.accessnow.org/publication/hacking-meduza-pegasus-spyware-used-to-target-putins-critic/.

5 Andrew Roth, "Russian TV station in Latvia loses license over Ukraine war coverage," *Guardian*, December 6, 2022, https://www.theguardian.com/world/2022/dec/06/rain-russian-tv-station-in-latvia-loses-licence-over-ukraine-war-coverage.

6 Nicolas Camut, "We Should Monitor All Russians Living in the West, Czech Leader Says," *Politico*, June 15, 2023, https://www.politico.eu/article/petr-pavel-russia-czech-republic-surveillance/.

7 Krapiva and Hammoud, "Hacking *Meduza*."

8 "'May Your Nits Not Sleep in Peace!' Unidentified People Threatening iStories' Journalists for More than Half a Year," *iStories*, September 19, 2023, https://istories.media/en/stories/2023/09/19/istories-journalists-threatening/.

9 "What Happened in Israel? A Breakdown of How Hamas Attack Unfolded," Al Jazeera, October 7, 2023, https://www.aljazeera.com/news/2023/10/7/what-happened-in-israel-a-breakdown-of-how-the-hamas-attack-unfolded; Daniel Byman, Riley McCabe, Alexander Palmer, Catrina Doxsee, Mackenzie Holtz, and Delaney Duff, "Hamas's October 7 Attack: Visualizing the Data," Center for Strategic and International Studies, December 19, 2023, https://www.csis.org/analysis/hamass-october-7-attack-visualizing-data.

10 Byman et al., "Hamas's October 7 Attack."

11 "Israel Revises Down Toll from October 7 Attack to 'Around 1,200,'" Al Jazeera, November 10, 2023, https://www.aljazeera.com/news/2023/11/10/israel-revises-death-toll-from-october-7-hamas-attack-to-1200-people; Lauren Fryer, "Israel Revises Down Its Death Toll from the Oct. 7 Hamas Attacks to About 1,200," NPR, November 11, 2023, https://www.npr.org/2023/11/11/1212458974/israel-revises-death-toll-hamas-attacks-oct-7.

12 Cassandra Vinograd and Isabel Kershner, "Israel's Attackers Took about 240 Hostages. Here's What to Know about Them," *New York Times*, November 20, 2023, https://www.nytimes.com/article/israel-hostages-hamas-explained.html.

13 Sheera Frenkel and Steven Lee Myers, "Hamas Seeds Violent Videos on Sites with Little Moderation," *New York Times*, October 10, 2023, https://www.nytimes.com/2023/10/10/technology/hamas-violent-videos-online.html.

14 Justin Salhani, "Did Israel's Overreliance on Tech Cause October 7 Intelligence Failure?," Al Jazeera, December 9, 2023, https://www.aljazeera.com/features/2023/12/9/did-israels-overreliance-on-tech-cause-october-7-intelligence-failure.

15 Haleigh Bartos and John Chin, "What Went Wrong? Three Hypotheses on Israel's Massive Intelligence Failure," Modern War Institute, October 31, 2023, https://mwi.westpoint.edu/what-went-wrong-three-hypotheses-on-israels-massive-intelligence-failure/.

16   Peter Beaumont, "Israeli Intelligence Leak Details Extent of Warnings over Hamas Attack," *Guardian*, November 28, 2023, https://www.theguardian.com/world/2023/nov/28/israeli-military-had-warning-of-hamas-training-for-attack-reports-say.

17   Bartos and Chin, "What Went Wrong?"

18   Ronen Bergman, Mark Mazzetti, and Maria Abi-Habib, "How Years of Israeli Failures on Hamas Led to a Devastating Attack," *New York Times*, October 29, 2023, https://www.nytimes.com/2023/10/29/world/middleeast/israel-intelligence-hamas-attack.html; Mehul Srivastava, "Israeli Intelligence 'Dismissed' Detailed Warning of Hamas Raid," *Financial Times*, November 23, 2023, https://www.ft.com/content/277573ae-fbbc-4396-8faf-64b73ab8ed0a.

19   Brian Osgood and Adam Muro, "Israel War on Gaza Updates: Gaza Becoming 'Uninhabitable'—UN Official," Al Jazeera, January 5, 2024, https://www.aljazeera.com/news/liveblog/2024/1/5/israel-war-on-gaza-live-israel-attacks-bombard-khan-younis-rafah; "Maps: Tracking the Attacks in Israel and Gaza," *New York Times*, https://www.nytimes.com/interactive/2023/10/07/world/middleeast/israel-gaza-maps.html.

20   "Israel-Gaza War in Maps and Charts: Live Tracker," Al Jazeera, https://www.aljazeera.com/news/longform/2023/10/9/israel-hamas-war-in-maps-and-charts-live-tracker.

21   "Journalist Casualties in the Israel-Gaza War," Committee to Protect Journalists, August 2, 2024, https://cpj.org/2024/08/journalist-casualties-in-the-israel-gaza-conflict/.

22   "Israel Bombs al-Maghazi Refugee Camp, Killing Dozens, Gaza Officials Say," Al Jazeera, November 5, 2023, https://www.aljazeera.com/news/2023/11/5/israel-bombs-al-maghazi-refugee-camp-killing-dozens-gaza-officials-say; "How Israel Has Destroyed Gaza's Schools and Universities," Al Jazeera, January 24, 2024, https://www.aljazeera.com/news/2024/1/24/how-israel-has-destroyed-gazas-schools-and-universities; Alessandra Bajec, "Israel's War on Hospitals in Gaza," *New Arab*, https://www.newarab.com/analysis/israels-war-hospitals-gaza.

23   "Netanyahu Deletes 'Racist' Tweet on Palestinian 'Children of Darkness' after Hospital Massacre," *New Arab*, October 18, 2023, https://www.newarab.com/news/netanyahu-deletes-palestinian-children-darkness-tweet; Megan K. Stack, "I've Been under Bombardment. There Must Be a Cease-Fire in Gaza," *New York Times*, October 30, 2023, https://www.nytimes.com/2023/10/30/opinion/ceasefire-israel-gaza-bombardment.html.

24   Raffi Berg, "What Is South Africa's Genocide Case against Israel at the ICJ?," BBC, May 24, 2024, https://www.bbc.com/news/world-middle-east-67922346; "Has Israel Complied with ICJ Order in Gaza Genocide Case?," Al Jazeera, February 26, 2024, https://www.aljazeera.com/news/2024/2/26/has-israel-complied-with-icj-order-in-gaza-genocide-case.

25   Office of the Prosecutor, "Statement of ICC Prosecutor Karim A.A. Khan KC: Applications for Arrest Warrants in the Situation in the State of Palestine," International Criminal Court, May 20, 2024, https://www.icc-cpi.int/news/statement-icc-prosecutor-karim-aa-khan-kc-applications-arrest-warrants-situation-state.

26   Harry Davies, "Revealed: Israeli Spy Chief 'Threatened' ICC Prosecutor over War

Crimes Inquiry," *Guardian*, May 28, 2024, https://www.theguardian.com/world /article/2024/may/28/israeli-spy-chief-icc-prosecutor-war-crimes-inquiry.

27 "About Apple Threat Notifications and Protecting against Mercenary Spyware," Apple Support, April 10, 2024, https://support.apple.com/en-us/102174.

28 "Digital Security Helpline," Access Now, accessed June 1, 2024, https://www .accessnow.org/help/.

29 John Scott-Railton, Bill Marczak, Paolo Nigro Herrero, Bahr Abdul Razzak, Noura al-Jizawi, Salvatore Solimano, and Ron Deibert, *Project Torogoz: Extensive Hacking of Media & Civil Society in El Salvador with Pegasus Spyware*, Research Report No. 148, Citizen Lab, University of Toronto, January 12, 2022, https://citizenlab.ca/2022 /01/project-torogoz-extensive-hacking-media-civil-society-el-salvador-pegasus -spyware/; John Scott-Railton, Bill Marczak, Irene Poetranto, Bahr Abdul Razzak, Sutawan Chanprasert, and Ron Deibert, *GeckoSpy: Pegasus Spyware Used against Thailand's Pro-Democracy Movement*, Research Report No. 157, Citizen Lab, University of Toronto, July 17, 2022, https://citizenlab.ca/2022/07/geckospy-pegasus-spyware -used-against-thailands-pro-democracy-movement/.

30 "About Lockdown Mode," Apple Support, January 10, 2024, https://support.apple .com/en-us/105120.

31 "Apple Expands Industry-Leading Commitment to Protect Users from Highly Targeted Mercenary Spyware," Apple Newsroom, updated July 6, 2022, https://www.apple.com/newsroom/2022/07/apple-expands-commitment-to -protect-users-from-mercenary-spyware/.

32 "About the Dignity and Justice Fund," Ford Foundation, accessed June 1, 2024, https://www.fordfoundation.org/work/our-grants/about-the-dignity-and-justice -fund/.

33 "Apple Expands Industry-Leading Commitment."

34 David E. Sanger, Nicole Perlroth, Ana Swanson, and Ronen Bergman, "U.S. Blacklists Israeli Firm NSO Group over Spyware," *New York Times*, November 3, 2021, https://www.nytimes.com/2021/11/03/business/nso-group-spyware-blacklist.html.

35 Bill Marczak, John Scott-Railton, Astrid Perry, Noura al-Jizawi, Siena Anstis, Zoe Panday, Emma Lyon, Bahr Abdul Razzak, and Ron Deibert, *Sweet QuaDreams: A First Look at Spyware Vendor QuaDream's Exploits, Victims, and Customers*, Research Report No. 164, Citizen Lab, University of Toronto, April 11, 2023, https://citizenlab.ca /2023/04/spyware-vendor-quadream-exploits-victims-customers/.

36 Omer Kabir and Meir Orbach, "Offensive Cyber Company QuaDream Shutting Down amidst Spyware Accusations," *CTech*, April 16, 2023, https://www.calcalistech .com/ctechnews/article/hy78kiym2.

37 US Department of State, "The United States Adds Foreign Companies to Entity List for Malicious Cyber Activities," press release, July 18, 2023, https://www.state .gov/the-united-states-adds-foreign-companies-to-entity-list-for-malicious-cyber -activities-2/.

38 US Department of the Treasury, "Treasury Sanctions Members of the Intellexa Commercial Spyware Consortium," press release, March 5, 2024, https://home .treasury.gov/news/press-releases/jy2155.

39 White House, "Fact Sheet: President Biden Signs Executive Order to Prohibit U.S. Government Use of Commercial Spyware That Poses Risks to National Security," March 27, 2023, https://www.whitehouse.gov/briefing-room/statements-releases /2023/03/27/fact-sheet-president-biden-signs-executive-order-to-prohibit-u-s -government-use-of-commercial-spyware-that-poses-risks-to-national-security/.

40 Alex Boutilier, "Canada to Back Biden Administration's Limits on 'Mercenary' Spyware Tools," Global News, March 30, 2023, https://globalnews.ca/news /9589163/canada-biden-spyware-limits/.

41 White House, "Joint Statement on Efforts to Counter the Proliferation and Misuse of Commercial Spyware," March 18, 2024, https://www.whitehouse.gov/briefing -room/statements-releases/2024/03/18/joint-statement-on-efforts-to-counter-the -proliferation-and-misuse-of-commercial-spyware/.

42 Communications Security Establishment Canada, "Canada Joins International Security Partners in Release of Advisory, Guidance on Growing Cyber Security Threat to Civil Society," Government of Canada, May 14, 2024, https://www .canada.ca/en/communications-security/news/2024/05/canada-joins-international -security-partners-in-release-of-advisory-guidance-on-growing-cyber-security -threat-to-civil-society.html.

43 Shaun Walker, "Poland Launches Inquiry into Previous Government's Spyware Use," *Guardian*, April 1, 2024, https://www.theguardian.com/world/2024/apr/01 /poland-launches-inquiry-into-previous-governments-spyware-use; "Spain Closes Pegasus Investigation over 'Lack of Cooperation' from Israel," *Guardian*, July 10, 2023, https://www.theguardian.com/world/2023/jul/10/spain-closes-pegasus -investigation-over-lack-of-cooperation-from-israel.

44 Andrew Higgins, "Donald Tusk Chosen as Poland's Prime Minister after Rival Is Rejected," *New York Times*, December 11, 2023, https://www.nytimes.com/2023/12 /11/world/europe/poland-donald-tusk-government.html; "Spain's Socialists Reach Gov't Coalition Deal with Hard-Left Sumar Party," Al Jazeera, October 24, 2023, https://www.aljazeera.com/news/2023/10/24/spains-socialists-reach-govt-coalition -deal-with-hard-left-sumar-party.

45 Davide Scigliuzzo, "Blacklisted Pegasus Spyware Firm Shunned by Wall Street, Too," *Bloomberg*, November 12, 2021, https://www.bloomberg.com/news/articles /2021-11-12/spyware-firm-nso-group-drops-deeper-into-distress-after-ceo-exit.

46 Eliza Ronalds-Hannon and Davide Scigliuzzo, "Israel's Pegasus Spyware Maker Takes Drastic Measures to Survive Global Scandal," *Bloomberg*, November 4, 2022, https://www.bloomberg.com/news/articles/2022-11-04/israel-s-nso-takes-drastic -measures-to-survive-spyware-scandal.

47 Kaye Wiggins, "NSO Group Deemed 'Valueless' to Private Equity Backers," *Financial Times*, April 11, 2022, https://www.ft.com/content/24584247-0fd4-4826-bcac -f726ad17af58.

48 "Defense Ministry Said to Freeze Export Licenses for Israeli 'Cyberattack' Tech," *Times of Israel*, February 5, 2022, https://www.timesofisrael.com/defense-ministry -said-to-freeze-export-licenses-for-israeli-cyberattack-tech/.

49 Patrick Kingsley and Isabel Kershner, "Israel Protests: Israeli Lawmakers Debate Judicial Overhaul Late into Night," *New York Times*, July 23, 2023, https://www .nytimes.com/live/2023/07/23/world/israel-protests.

50 Yonette Joseph and Patrick Kingsley, "Netanyahu Will Return with Corruption Charges Unresolved. Here's Where the Case Stands," *New York Times*, November 3, 2022, https://www.nytimes.com/2022/11/03/world/middleeast/netanyahu-corruption -charges-israel.html.

51 Isabel Kershner and Patrick Kingsley, "What's Next for Israel's Judicial Overhaul?," *New York Times*, September 13, 2023, https://www.nytimes.com/article/israel -judicial-overhaul-vote.html.

52 Anna Gordon, "What Israelis Think of the War with Hamas," *Time*, November 10, 2023, https://time.com/6333781/israel-hamas-poll-palestine/; Tamar Hermann and Or Anabi, "Even on the Right, Israelis Want Elections Immediately After the War," Israel Democracy Institute, December 19, 2023, https://en.idi.org.il/articles/51872.

53 Emma Goldberg, "Some Israeli Journalists Express Fear about Conveying Dissenting Views," *New York Times*, October 21, 2023, https://www.nytimes.com/2023/10/21 /business/media/israel-journalists-hamas-war.html.

54 "Israeli Ministers Join Gathering Calling for Resettlement of Gaza," Al Jazeera, January 29, 2024, https://www.aljazeera.com/news/2024/1/29/israeli-ministers-join -gathering-calling-for-rebuilding-settlements-in-gaza.

55 Yuliya Chernova, "Ex-CEO of NSO Group Raises $33.6 Million for Israeli Cyber Startup," *Wall Street Journal*, November 21, 2023, https://www.wsj.com/articles/ex -ceo-of-nso-group-raises-33-6-million-for-israeli-cyber-startup-ae8e7399.

56 Chernova, "Ex-CEO of NSO Group."

57 Chernova, "Ex-CEO of NSO Group."

58 Vas Panagiotopoulos, "Notorious Spyware Maker NSO Group Is Quietly Plotting a Comeback," *Wired*, January 24, 2024, https://www.wired.com/story/nso-group -lobbying-israel-hamas-war/.

59 *Between a Hack and a Hard Place: How Pegasus Spyware Crushes Civic Space in Jordan*, Access Now, February 1, 2024, https://www.accessnow.org/publication/between-a -hack-and-a-hard-place-how-pegasus-spyware-crushes-civic-space-in-jordan/.

60 Knight First Amendment Institute, "El Faro Journalists, Knight Institute Urge Court to Deny Motion to Dismiss Case against Spyware Manufacturer," press release, May 19, 2023, http://knightcolumbia.org/content/el-faro-journalists -knight-institute-urge-court-to-deny-motion-to-dismiss-case-against-spyware -manufacturer; Suzanne Smalley, "Federal Judge Rejects NSO's Effort to Dismiss Apple's Pegasus Lawsuit," *Record*, January 24, 2024, https://therecord.media/judge -rejects-nso-effort-to-dismiss-apple-lawsuit; Joseph Menn, "Apple Seeks to Drop its Lawsuit Against Israeli Spyware Pioneer NSO," *Washington Post*, September 13, 2024, https://www.washingtonpost.com/technology/2024/09/13/apple-lawsuit-nso -pegasus-spyware/; Harry Davies and Stephanie Kirchgaessner, "Israel Tried to Frus- trate US Lawsuit Over Pegasus Spyware, Leak Suggests," *Guardian*, July 25, 2024, https://www.theguardian.com/news/article/2024/jul/25/israel-tried-to-frustrate -us-lawsuit-over-pegasus-spyware-leak-suggests.

61 WhatsApp Inc. v. NSO Group Technologies Limited, 4:19-cv-07123 (ND Cal. Jan. 18, 2024), ECF No. 265, https://www.courtlistener.com/docket/16395340/265 /5/whatsapp-inc-v-nso-group-technologies-limited/.

62 WhatsApp Inc. v. NSO Group Technologies Limited, 4:19-cv-07123 (ND Cal. Jan. 18, 2024), Foreign Non-Party the Citizen Lab's Proposed Opposition to Defen-

dants' Motion for Issuance of Letter Rogatory, March 28, 2024, https://storage
.courtlistener.com/recap/gov.uscourts.cand.350613/gov.uscourts.cand.350613
.294.2.pdf.

63   Maggie Haberman and Jonathan Swan, "Trump Had Good Fortune So Far with
His Four Cases. Then Came a Verdict," *New York Times*, May 30, 2024, https://www
.nytimes.com/2024/05/30/us/politics/trump-verdict-analysis.html; Lazaro Gamio,
Karen Yourish, Matthew Haag, Jonah E. Bromwich, Maggie Haberman, and K. K.
Rebecca Lai, "The Trump Manhattan Criminal Verdict, Count by Count," *New York
Times*, May 30, 2024, https://www.nytimes.com/interactive/2024/05/30/nyregion
/trump-hush-money-verdict.html.

64   Antoaneta Roussi, "How Europe Became the Wild West of Spyware," *Politico*,
October 25, 2023, https://www.politico.eu/article/how-europe-became-wild-west
-spyware/.

65   Lorenzo Franceschi-Bicchierai, "Spyware Startup Variston Is Losing Staff—Some
Say It's Closing," *TechCrunch*, February 15, 2024, https://techcrunch.com/2024/02
/15/variston-spyware-losing-staff-some-say-closing/.

66   Bryan Fogel, dir., *The Dissident*, 2020; San Francisco, CA: Vertical Entertainment;
Kanopy, 2021. Online video.

Acknowledgments

Writing *Chasing Shadows* was a bit of a trip down memory lane. As I searched through my archives, I was reminded how lucky I am to have been acquainted with so many talented people over the course of my professional career—far too many to acknowledge here.

There will always be a special place in my heart for my PhD supervisor, the late professor Mark Zacher, who believed in me, gave me numerous opportunities, and was the one who sagely pointed me in the right direction to find my calling. Since that fateful day when he suggested I study information technology, I've never looked back.

I am extremely grateful to everyone who has ever worked at or collaborated with the Citizen Lab, past and present. I've tried my best to recruit people who get our mission and share my passion and then give them the freedom and resources they need to get the job done. There's never been a dull day, and for that I thank everyone who's ever played a part in that special lab's work. I want to thank those whose work I was not able to profile in this book, but whose contributions have been invaluable to the Lab's recent success: Gabby Lim, Pellaeon Lin, Nicola Lawford, Veronica Arroyo, Gözde Böcü, Marcus Michaelson, Levi Meletti, Rebekah Brown, Jon Penney, Astrid Perry, Emile Dirks, Ksenia Ermoshina, Kate Robertson, Alberto Fittarelli, Mona Wang, Lokman Tsui, Lex Gill, Justin Lau, Mari Zhou, Snigdha Basu, and Alyson Bruce. Thank you all.

Over the last decade, I have spent the majority of my own research time working closely with the targeted threats team whose work is featured prominently in this book. Special thanks to John Scott-Railton, our team leader; Bill Marczak, our technical genius; and Bahr Abdul Razzak, Siena Anstis, Adam Senft, and numerous others who have contributed to seminal projects unearthing abuses around the mercenary spyware industry. I'm also grateful to the digital transnational repression team, especially Noura Aljizawi, Siena Anstis, and Marcus Michaelsen, and all the many research fellows, research assistants, graduate students, and interns who have participated in that project. I hope I have done justice to our collective endeavors.

Thanks to Celine Bauwens, the Citizen Lab's manager, and to the Munk School of Global Affairs & Public Policy, especially its founding director, Professor Janice Stein, and all the subsequent directors over the years. I am very grateful to the University of Toronto for its ongoing support for what is a very unconventional and highly sensitive academic pursuit. Many other universities would likely not have the backbone to stand up for something like the Citizen Lab, but the University of Toronto has never wavered.

Thank you to all the individuals and organizations that have collaborated with the Citizen Lab on its many investigations, especially our partners at Access Now, Amnesty International, OONI, R3D, SocialTic, Article 19, the Committee to Protect Journalists, Forbidden Stories, Lighthouse Reports, EFF, Human Rights Watch, and the Knight First Amendment Institute. We are all extremely grateful to the many journalists that contributed to Citizen Lab investigations, especially Stephanie Kirchgaessner, Raphael Satter, Chris Bing, Joel Schectman, Lorenzo Franceschi-Bicchierai, Joseph Cox, Nicole Perlroth, Joseph Menn, Colin Freeze, Alex Boutillier, Thomas Brewster, Suzanne Smalley, Dina Temple-Raston, Andy Greenberg, David Sanger, Omer Benjakob, Ellen Nakashima, Azam Ahmed, Mehul Srivastava, and Sam Jones.

Thank you to my friend Mike Downie for digitally restoring the documentary footage of our memorable journey to Guatemala.

We would not be able to do what we do without our funders. Thanks to the John D. and Catherine T. MacArthur Foundation, Ford Foundation, Open Society Foundations, Oak Foundation, IDRC, Rossy Foundation, Sigrid Rausing Trust, and others.

For comments on earlier drafts, I am especially grateful to Siena Anstis, Adam Senft, John Scott-Railton, Bill Marczak, Bahr Abdul

Razzak, Luis Fernando García, Mazen Mazri, Igor Ostrovskiy, Elies Campo, Jane Gowan, Edin Omanovic, Eitay Mack, Gary Miller, Dan Breznitz, Masashi Crete-Nishihata, Robert Guerra, Greg Walton, Nart Villeneuve, and Noura Aljizawi. Special thanks to all the subjects, victims, and survivors who have consented to participate in our research and who bravely shared their experiences with us. None of the positive outcomes described in this book would have been possible without them.

I am extremely grateful to Mohamed Ahmed, Vuyo Kwakweni, and Zoë Reichart for their excellent research and editorial assistance.

Thanks to my former editor, Janie Yoon, who originally commissioned this project and provided comments on my first draft. Thanks to everyone at Simon & Schuster for seeing this project through to its successful completion. I am especially grateful to Rosemary Shipton for her extremely valuable editing suggestions and ongoing encouragement. It was a pleasure having you on my team! Thanks also to Sara Kitchen, Nancy Tan, Sarah Wight, and Sarah Vostok. I am very grateful to my literary agent, Michael Levine, for his continued support and wise counsel.

Lastly, I would like to thank my dear family, especially my wife, Jane Gowan, and our four children, Emily, Rosalind, Ethan, and Michael. Your amazing talents are an inspiration, and your love and encouragement give me hope for the future.

Index